POCKET ADVENTURES
BOLIVIA

Vivien Lougheed

Assisted in research, writing and survival
by John Harris

HUNTER PUBLISHING, INC,
130 Campus Drive, Edison, NJ 08818
732-225-1900; 800-255-0343; fax 732-417-1744
www.hunterpublishing.com

Ulysses Travel Publications
4176 Saint-Denis, Montréal, Québec
Canada H2W 2M5
514-843-9882, ext. 2232; fax 514-843-9448

Windsor Books
The Boundary, Wheatley Road, Garsington
Oxford, OX44 9EJ England
01865-361122; fax 01865-361133

Printed in the United States

ISBN 1-58843-526-1

© 2006 Hunter Publishing, Inc.

This and other Hunter travel guides are also available as e-books
in a variety of digital formats through our online partners,
including Netlibrary.com and Amazon.com.

This guide focuses on recreational activities. As all such activities contain
elements of risk, the publisher, author, affiliated individuals and companies
disclaim responsibility for any injury, harm, or illness that may occur to
anyone through, or by use of, the information in this book. Every effort was
made to insure the accuracy of information in this book, but the publisher
and author do not assume, and hereby disclaim, liability for any loss or
damage caused by errors, omissions, misleading information or potential
travel problems caused by this guide, even if such errors or omissions
result from negligence, accident or any other cause.

Cover photo: Dancer, Gran Poder Festival, La Paz © Mary Altier
Index by Nancy Wolff & Mary Ellen McGrath

Maps by Kim André, © 2006 Hunter Publishing, Inc.

1 2 3 4

www.hunterpublishing.com

Hunter's full range of guides to all corners of the globe is featured on our exciting website. You'll find guidebooks to suit every type of traveler, no matter what their budget, lifestyle, or idea of fun.

Adventure Guides – There are now over 40 titles in this series, covering destinations from Costa Rica and the Yucatán to Tampa Bay & Florida's West Coast, Ecuador, Switzerland, Paris and the Alaska Highway. Complete with information on what to do, as well as where to stay and eat, *Adventure Guides* are made for the active traveler, with comprehensive coverage of the area's history, culture and wildlife, plus all the practical travel information you need. Details on the best places for hiking, biking, canoeing, horseback riding, trekking, skiing, watersports, and all other kinds of fun, are included.

Alive Guides – This ever-popular line of books takes a unique look at the best each destination offers: fine dining, jazz clubs, first-class hotels and resorts. In-margin icons direct the reader at a glance. Top-sellers include *St. Martin & St. Barts*, *The US Virgin Islands* and *Aruba, Bonaire & Curaçao*.

And Hunter has long been known for its **one-of-a-kind** travel books that focus on destinations and vacations rarely found in travel books. These include *The Best Dives of the Bahamas; Golf Resorts; Cruising Alaska; A Traveler's Guide to the Galapagos* and many more.

Full descriptions are given for each book at www.hunter-publishing.com, along with reviewers' comments and a cover image. You can also view pages and the table of contents. Books may be purchased on-line via our secure transaction facility.

Acknowledgments

My first thank you goes to my husband, John Harris, for his constant dedication to my traveling and my writing. Without him, none of this would be possible. I also thank Kim André for her co-operation and collaboration in the writing of this book.

Paige Pedersen is always with me on my journeys, sometimes in person and always in spirit. I thank Barry and Joy McKinnon for bringing their humor and Canadian accent to Bolivia when we were most in need of it.

So many people in Bolivia helped me. I especially want to remember Sonia Cruz and Oscar Crispe, Margarina and Rick de Rave, Peter de Raad and Varga Van't Hoff, Jerome and Lillian Luis, and Hanne Inners. Also, Louis Demers, Manuel Español, Alex Shand, Peter McFarran and Wendy, Tomer Weingram, Elva Alfaro, Hugo Barrios and Damiska, and, finally, Eunice.

Contents

◆ Maps

DEDICATION

This book is dedicated to Barry and Joy for bringing us Canadian humor when we most needed it.

Introduction

Bolivia is a land-locked country with a smorgasbord of landscapes. There are tropical jungles in the Amazon River Basin and bleak but beautiful deserts on the Altiplano. The Andes Mountains, with four of the world's highest peaks, offer some of the best hiking, climbing and caving in the world. Lake Titikaka and its surrounding area allows the amateur anthro-pologist/historian to explore the ruins of the ancient Inca and pre-Inca civilizations. The only thing missing in Bolivia are ocean beaches.

Hubert Herring, in *History of Latin America*, called Bolivia the Tibet of the Americas. I agree with him if comparing the cultural richness of the two countries, but Bolivia is much cleaner and has far less poverty than Tibet.

Since Bolivia is such a diverse country, each district offers different kinds of adventures. For example, in the Andes, hiking is a must, but in the Amazon River Basin travel by boat is the only way to go. Some places have exceptional archeological sites, while other areas are especially interesting to birders and photographers. I recommend that everyone enjoy at least one activity that involves learning about the weavings made by indigenous people. Reducing your activities to suit your time frame will be the most difficult part of planning your trip to Bolivia.

Sucre is Bolivia's capital, but La Paz, perched at 12,000 ft/3,632 m above sea level, is the largest city in the country and the seat of government. It sits in a natural bowl three miles/five km in diameter that was carved out of the mountains by a river thousands of years ago.

In La Paz, as in Santa Cruz (soon to be the country's largest city), accommodations and restaurants can be luxurious or simple. Museums are plentiful and the treasures are well displayed. Movies are usually Hollywood fare with Spanish subtitles; cultural shows, especially Andean bands, are abundant, but jazz bars can also be found. All towns and cities have Internet cafés.

The roads in Bolivia are slowly being upgraded to accommodate modern transportation needs. The La Paz, Copacabana, Oruru, Sajama roads are well paved. Roads to and from Tarija, a prosperous city, are nightmares, as is the Santa Cruz to Villamontes road. Travelers who are weak in the stomach or afraid of unprotected 1,000-foot/300-meter sheer drops off blind curves should fly, which is cheap and comfortable.

And of course there is the La Paz/Coroico road, the main route from the seat of government through the Yungas to the Amazon. Coroico is coffee country. The area also grows bananas and other exotic fruits, so movement of these items along this horrendous road is heavy work. Due to the number of trucks and buses that go over the ledge each year, the route has been named by the Inter-American Development Bank the most dangerous road in the world. Also known as the Road of Death, it has become a major attraction to Kamikaze mountain bikers. Or to people like me, who prefer to be in control of their own fates and book "gravity assisted" rides with a back-up van carrying the luggage.

Crime, although usually petty rather than violent in nature, does occur and tourists are often the target. However, of all the Latin American countries, Bolivia is considered the safest. I have never been accosted, although I have been approached by phony National Police. I told them to buzz off. They did.

Health care in Bolivia is varied. Some villages have no medical facilities at all, but Cochabamba has a sophisticated teaching center that attracts students from both Brazil and Argentina. When sick, the patient must purchase everything from meals to needles. Nothing is included with the doctor's fee other than the expertise of the doctor. Cities have up-to-date clinics and laboratories with personnel trained in North America or Europe.

For the adventure traveler, there are outfitters who offer trips to remote areas, though most of them do not have high-tech gear. I recommend you bring some of your own gear, especially if climbing. English is not common; survival Spanish is essential and, if you're going to remote areas, a few words in Quechua or Aymara would be of great help.

In summary, if you want to try something different than what you have at home and are willing to give some of yourself in return, you will have one of the most exciting experiences of your traveling life when you come to Bolivia.

History

◆ Historical Time Line

10,500 BC	Monte Verde in Chile is inhabited by migrants whose ancestors are believed to have come from Asia.
6500 BC	Evidence has been found indicating that people were living at Tierra del Fuego on the tip of South America.
3000 BC	Farming and fishing societies are established in Bolivia.
1200 BC	Weaving is developed to superior levels as compared to other areas of the Americas. Pottery is produced using intricate designs. Copper and silver is mined.
600 BC	A sun-worshipping, Andean empire is established at Tihuanaco (tee-wan-A-ko) along the shores of Lake Titikaka. These people may have been predecessors of the Inca.
1000-1200 AD	Tihuanaco society collapsed.

1532	Spanish arrive. Francisco Pizarro, a Spanish explorer (conqueror) betrays and kills Atahualpa, the ruling Inca king, and about 2,000 of his men.
1538	Spanish conquer Bolivia.
1545	Cerro Rico in Potosi is discovered.
1650	Potosi becomes the largest city in the Americas. It is larger than London, England.
1809	Pedro Domingo Murillo leads a revolt in Upper Peru (Bolivia) and by the end of the year is joined by those living in Cochabamba, Oruro and Potosi.
1824	Bolivar liberates Bolivia.
1825	Bolivia is named in honor of their liberator.
1826	Constitution is adopted in November.
1829	Andres Santa Cruz becomes president. He holds the position for more than 10 years.
1836-39	Bolivia and Peru unite, but are separated after war with Chile.
1879-1883	War of the Pacific, in which Bolivia lost its only ocean access to Chile.
1932	Chaco War with Paraguay over control of the Paraguay River that flows into the Atlantic Ocean.
1936	Socialist Colonel David Toro takes power and nationalizes American oil holdings.
1937	Colonel German Busch becomes leader and puts stringent controls on mining.
1940-1952	Struggles with left and right wing political parties result in discontent and many lives lost to strikers and their families.
1952-1964	MNR comes to power and passes agrarian reform laws. They also make education available for the poor, build affordable clinics, establish cooperatives so profits go to the producers, develop roads and build hydroelectric dams. They help finance sugar mills and cotton-growing projects.
1966	General Rene Barrientos Ortuno becomes president. He is remembered for killing and Che Guevara and planting him under the tarmac of an airstrip in southern Bolivia.
1971-1978	President Hugo Banzer Suarez manages to survive 13 coup attempts and then wins a democratic election.
1969-1981	Nineteen presidents, some backed by drug cartels, are inaugurated during this period.
1994	Constitution is revised.
2003	War of Taxation leaves 33 dead and hundreds injured. But, to date, there is no personal income tax in Bolivia.

NATIVE INTEREST: *If traveling near Sajama or Ulla Ulla na-tional parks, you will see pre-Columbian (AD 1200-1550) grave towers, called **chullpares**, belonging to the early Aymara cul-ture. These towers, made from stones, are about 10 ft/three m high and eight ft/2.5 m in diameter. Each tower contains the re-mains of a prominent person who lived in the nearby community. The resident corpse is called a "mallku" (MAY-koo).*

Government

Bolivia is a republic with the seat of government in La Paz and the Judi-ciary seat in Sucre. The first constitution was adopted on November 19, 1826 and was re-drawn and re-adopted numerous times. The newest con-stitution was drawn up on February 2, 1967 and revised in 1994.

The president, who is the Chief of State, is elected for five years and he is the head of the democratically elected party. **Congress** is then ap-pointed by the president. If a party does not get 50% of the vote, congress chooses and appoints the president. This is done by secret ballot and the candidates are the leaders of the three leading parties.

National Congress is made up of the Chamber of Senators and the Chamber of Deputies. The 27 senators (three from each department) and the 130 deputies are elected by popular vote or appointed for a period of five years. The 1996 amendment to the constitution now allows for 65 dep-uties to be voted in by popular demand and the rest nominated by party leaders. The National Congress convenes for 90 days every year.

At present, the four major parties in Bolivia are the **National Revolution-ary Movement** (MNR), the **Movement of Revolutionary Left** (MIR), the **Movement to Socialism** (MAS) and the **New Republic Force** (NFR).

There are nine departments in Bolivia and these are divided into 112 provinces. They are further divided into sections and then cantons. Each department has a prefect appointed by the president and a legislature elected by municipal councilors. Elections are held once every five years.

DEPARTMENT KNOW-HOW: *The nine departments of Bolivia are Beni, Chuquisaca, La Paz, Cochabamba, Oruro, Pando, Potosi, Santa Cruz and Tarija.*

Bolivia is ruled by Spanish law and is under Napoleonic code. It is compul-sory for everyone to vote at the age of 18 if married and age 21 if not mar-ried.

The National Congress appoints Supreme Court judges for 10-year ses-sions. Each department also has a district court that looks after minor in-fractions of the law. The Supreme Court has five justices for criminal law and five for civil.

The **military** consists of an army with about 25,000 men and 36 light tanks, a navy of 3,500 men (1,700 of these are in the marines) and an air force of 3,000 men, with 37 combat aircraft and 16 armed helicopters. The air force was first established in 1923 with 4,000 men.

There is conscription for men at the age of 19 and the men must serve for 12 months. The army looks after six regions in the country and the navy patrols Lake Titikaka and the Beni, Bolivia and Paraguay rivers. In the event of a war, over two million men are available for service.

The **police** consist of the National Guard and the Tourist Police. The Tourist Police employ many women.

Economy

◆ Debt

Bolivia is in a state of permanent debt. More is spent on servicing that debt than is spent on health care. Foreign investment is minimal. There was a surge of it when government corporations (i.e., railways, telephones, electricity) were privatized, but the end result was failure (most rail lines were closed). Also, Bolivia's history of labor militancy (MNR in 1952) still scares off corporations. Fundamentally, after the tin markets collapsed, there was nothing left in Bolivia that anyone wanted, although there are promising signs of oil and gas reserves in the Santa Cruz/Villamontes area. Most Bolivians are subsistence farmers. There is an "informal sector" of street vending and sweat shops producing imitation brand-name clothing. **Tourism**, while still minimal, is becoming a major source of moveable income.

During the 1980s, 70% of the population was living far below the poverty line. But thanks to a half-stable government, elimination of some of the corruption and a genuine effort to improve life for the people, that is changing. Today, with 2.6 million people in the labor force, there is an unemployment rate of about 7.6%. However, there is still a large number of underemployed people.

◆ Industry

Bolivia's **Gross Domestic Product** (GDP) is about $25 billion, or $977 per person. Statistics make it appear that the GDP has stayed the same over the years but in fact, due to the devaluation of the boliviano and increased inflation, the GDP is lower. Of the entire GDP, 16.5% comes from agriculture, 35.5% from industry and the rest comes from services.

Bolivia's agricultural industry produces soybeans, coffee, cocoa, cotton, corn, sugar cane, rice, potatoes and lumber, with soy being the largest export. In the Santa Cruz area the farmers are able to grow two crops of soybeans a year. Quinoa, a food of the Incas, is grown in the Altiplano. The government is trying to make this a viable export also.

Industry includes mining, smelting, petroleum production, tobacco, wood, food and beverage production, handicrafts and clothing. Bolivia also has natural gas, zinc, lead, tin, antimony, tungsten, silver and gold for export. The soy, natural gas, zinc, gold and wood bring in about $1.5 billion a year. However, the import costs for capital goods, raw materials, chemicals, petroleum and food are close to $2 billion.

Bolivia has also become a partner in a number of common market agreements. The first was a free trade treaty with Mexico and some countries farther south more than a decade ago. In the subsequent agreement signed in 1993, Bolivia became a member of the **Andean Community** that includes Peru, Equator, Colombia and Venezuela. The United States signed the **Trade Preference Act** with Bolivia that resulted in tariffs only on leather and clothes going into the States. There is also a separate agreement with Peru that permits duty-free transit of imports and exports through the Desaguadero border crossing so that Peru can have access to the Atlantic via Bolivian roads and rail systems.

Because of the large amount of natural gas Bolivia produces, about 30 million metric cubic meters (40.5 million cubic yards) a day, a pipeline going through Brazil to the Atlantic was built and another to Arica, Chile was added shortly after. These lines, used for exporting the gas, have helped improve the economy of the country.

Three out of the four leading **banks** in Bolivia ran into financial problems in 1995. They were restructured under new owners and are now stable. Today, Banco Sol has 30% of Bolivia's banking customers. One of the reasons that Bolivian banks do well is that most borrowers pay their bills. However, investors and depositors are not protected by any government insurance (the government is talking about implementing some type of insurance in the near future). Today, the national debt is about $5 billion and is owed to foreign governments and multilateral development banks.

Coca has been a billion dollar contributor to the economy in the past, but the government, with the encouragement of the United States, is trying to eradicate the export of the plant to places like Colombia where it is used for cocaine production. Only coca grown in the Yungas is used for domestic purposes, while any plants grown in the Chapare region are reportedly used for cocaine production. The DEA is active in Bolivia, digging up and defoliating crops and searching buses to prevent the movement of precursor chemicals. This causes unrest among coca-growing *campesinos*, or *cocaleros*, as they are called. Regularly, Bolivian highways are blocked by the *cocaleros*.

❖ YOU'RE HOW OLD?

The old age pension, or Bonosol, was introduced in 2003 and everyone over the age of 65 will receive 1,800 bolivianos (US $240) per year. The plan, originally set up in 1997, is privately managed and individually funded. The biggest hurdle now is how to establish the age of people who have never registered their birth.

Trade unions have been legal for over half a century. It was the 50,000 workers who held a strike in Bolivia to demand land reform and the nationalization of the mining companies that eventually resulted in changes being made. The demands were met in 1952 after a period of revolution.

Today it is legal to organize and bargain collectively. Laws supporting labor unions were last amended and ratified in 1973. Today, about 50% of the working force belong to the **Bolivian Labor Federation**, which is an affiliate of the World Federation of Trade Unions. Protests and brief wildcat strikes are common, but prolonged picketing doesn't seem to happen.

People & Culture

◆ Cultural Groups

The **Aymara** and **Quechua** indigenous groups make up more than 55% of the population. These people were here long before the Inca and many still practice the traditions of their ancestors. The Aymara and Quechua occupied the lands as far north as Colombia and as far south as southern Chile and Argentina. The **mestizo** or cholo, as he is called in Bolivia, is part European and part Indian. These people make up 35% of the Bolivian population. The rest is made up of **Europeans**, mostly Spanish from the early settlers, but also those who arrived in the last 150 years from places like Germany, Yugoslavia, Asia and North America. Many minority groups are also represented, including Chinese, East Indians, Japanese and Africans, whose ancestors were brought as slaves to work in the mines of Potosi.

Of the many tribes and groups who are in the minority, there are the Tacana, the Pano, the Arauco, the Chapacura, the Guarani and the Botocudo, who are all, in turn, made up of smaller tribes. Most of these groups live in the Amazon Basin.

Quechua proverb:
It is better to die while standing than to live on your knees.

> **❖ SPANISH NAMES 101**
>
> Spanish names have a first or common name and then two family names. The first family name is the main one and is from the father, while the second one is from the mother's line. When speaking of a person, the common name and the name of the father is mentioned. For example, with the name "Hugo Banzer Suarez," Hugo is the common name, Banzer is the father's name and the one most used. Suarez, the mother's name, is added to the other two when formality dictates it.

The Aymara and Quechua were farmers and sheep or llama herders and lived in the higher valleys of the Andean Mountains or the Altiplano that sits between two mountain spines, the Cordillera Real or Eastern Cordillera and the main spine of the Andes or Western Cordillera. The split of the main chain starts in Peru and re-forms again in the southern tip of America, and the altiplano sits in that mountain embrace. The two groups have distinct and separate languages. It is commonly suggested that the Aymara sound more guttural. The two seldom intermarried.

Catholicism was introduced to Bolivia by the conquering Spaniards. The Indians integrated the new religion with their own. This resulted in a belief that honored Pacha Mama (Mother Earth), along with Christ and the Virgin Mary. Most villages have patron saints who are regularly paid respect with celebrations that include drinking of *chicha* (corn beer) dancing and music. Dances are especially important in Aymara celebrations and vary from one place to the other. The devil is naturally important to miners who work in his turf and is known as Tio (Uncle).

❖ **MOTHER EARTH**

Pacha Mama, or Mother Earth, protects all living things, including plants, but when angered she is cruel and causes droughts, floods, pestilence, accidents and any other hardship she can think of. To keep her happy, people offer her coca leaves or a sprinkle of alcohol before they go on a trip, plant or harvest a field, drive a car or give birth to a child.

Both the Aymara and the Quechua spin and weave cloth from wool or llama and alpaca hair. These same types of weavings have been found in tombs or wrapped around mummies that date as far back as 3000 BC. The cloth and the clothes made from the weavings are warm and practical for the cold climate of the Altiplano.

Traditional Andean music is still played by shepherds tending their flocks. The instruments used include pan flutes of every conceivable size, drums and the chorango, a ukulele-styled instrument traditionally made from the shell of an armadillo.

The Indian women of today wear traditional dress. This includes a multi-layered skirt, an apron (sometimes), a shawl (often of exquisite design embroidered with pearls and beads) and a hat, usually a bowler (called a *bambin* in local lingua). The other most common outfit seen on women is a black woven dress with a wide skirt embroidered at the hem. The sleeves come just past the elbow and the neck is high. These dresses are accompanied by a weaving worn either hanging at the back from a woven belt or around the shoulders, kept in place with a pin. This outfit is also accompanied by a hat, usually a felt one that looks like a bowl (rather than a bowler). However, there are an increasing number of women replacing their expensive bowlers for baseball caps. All the women wear their hair in two braids that hang out below their hats and down their backs.

❖ **SAFE SHAWL**

Silver pins, called *topos*, are made in the shape of spoons and worn by Quechua ladies to fasten their shawls.

For the most part, Indian men of Bolivia wear Western-styled clothes. However, you will find a few with colorful, hand-woven ponchos and their heads crowned with a leather form-fitting hat.

Geography

◆ Land

Surrounded by land, Bolivia is bordered on the north by Peru and Brazil, on the east by more of Brazil, on the south by Paraguay and Argentina and on the west by Chile.

Although landlocked, Bolivia is one of the most geographically interesting countries in the world. It is home to the six highest mountain peaks in the Andes, all of which stand over 20,000 ft/6,000 m. It has part of the highest navigable lake in the world. It has the richest silver mine ever discovered and the largest salt lake on the planet. It also has the highest volcano on earth and the highest archeological site known to man. It has the Altiplano, the rich platform of land where most Bolivians live. And then it has part of the Amazon Basin, with mighty rivers like the Beni, the Madre de Dios and

NOT TO SCALE

© 2005 HUNTER PUBLISHING, INC

the Mamore flowing into the Madeira, the second greatest tributary of the Amazon. Finally, Bolivia has the sparse dry deserts of the Chaco, rich in oil and good for canola production on large corporate or Mennonite farms.

The northwestern ridge of the Andes is known as the **Apolobamba Range** and is a group of peaks that include such features as Bolivia's longest glacier. The glacier runs six miles/11 km down the southwest face of the region's highest peak, **Mt. Chaupi Orkh**. The Apolobamba Range forms the border between Bolivia and Peru. It is difficult to access and is rarely visited.

The southeastern ridge of the Andes, angling off the Western Cordillera north of Lake Titicaca, is the most prominent and accessible range. It is known as the **Cordillera Real**.

> ❖   **TOUGH TERRAIN**
>
> The Cordillera Real has one section that runs continuously at a height of over 20,000 ft/6,000 m for a distance of 100 miles/ 160 km. At their widest point these mountains form a formidable barrier about 120 miles/200 km long.

The third ridge is a tiny speck of mountains, a single vertebrae, just south and east of La Paz in the direction of Oruro that is called the **Quimsa Cruz Range**. Often visited, the range is a mere 25 miles/40 km long and nine miles/15 km wide. It has glaciated peaks in the south and granite spires in the north, with mining roads running close to both the glaciers and spires.

Between the two major spines of the Bolivian Andes, the Western Cordillera and the Cordillera Real, is a dry plain, the world's largest, called the **Altiplano**. Starting at Lake Titikaka, the Altiplano runs 490 miles/800 km to the south. Standing at 11,000 ft/3,660 m above the sea, the Altiplano has been cultivated to grow high-altitude crops like potatoes, barley and quinoa. Half of the nation's population lives in the Altiplano, the main theater of Bolivia's history.

> ❖   **EARLY MEDICINE**
>
> Archeologists have discovered that quinoa was cultivated as early as 5800-4500 BC in the Ayacucho Basin of Peru and the people traded with those living in places as far away as southern Chile. Quinoa has many essential amino acids, including lysine, as well as iron, calcium and vitamins A, B and E.

Sloping off the Cordillera Real, just north of La Paz and descending northwards toward the Amazon, is the **Yungas**, with its rich rainforest. In the Yungas, the steaming jungles of the Amazon send humidity toward the snow-capped mountains of the Cordillera Real. As soon as the moisture-laden air comes in contact with the brisk mountain air, it causes a thermal inversion and turns to rain. This happens about 300 days of each year. The plentiful rain encourages a variety of lush plants, such as coffee, sugar, coca and tobacco to grow in abundance.

The **Amazon jungle** is a different world altogether, with isolated pockets of people, lush vegetation and numerous rivers that eventually flow into the

Amazon River. During rainy season, the Amazon is a quagmire of non-absorbing earth where residents are often forced to travel the roads by canoe rather than motor vehicle.

Sloping off the Eastern Cordillera to the east are the **Colinas** (Foothills) that are less precipitous than the Yungas. These descend to the Gran Chaco, and include large temperate valleys like those holding the cities of Cochabamba, Samaipata and Tarija.

Finally, there is the **Gran Chaco** area in the southeast of the country near the Paraguayan border. Temperatures in this part of the country average 99°F/37°C. It is in places a dry, inhospitable land and, except for a few desert animals and the odd cactus or small bush, it is sparsely populated. In other parts of the Chaco it can be humid and infested with dengue and malaria-bearing mosquitos. The largest settlement in the Chaco is **Camiri**, which proudly holds the record for the nation's highest recorded temperature at 126°F/52°C (although Villamontes, a few hours to the south, claims the same). Because of the small human population, the Gran Chaco has some of the rarer animal species, such as the jaguar and peccary. The biggest draw to the Chaco was the discovery of oil and gas.

◆ Water

Water covers 58,000 square miles/150,000 square km, 14% of Bolivia's total territory. That, of course, is in dry season. In the highland basin is **Lake Titikaka**, which alone covers 2,500 square miles/6,600 square km. The **Desaguadero River**, the main waterway in the highlands, is 235 miles/380 km long and flows from Lake Titikaka to Lakes Popoo and Uru Uru.

Uyuni Salt Lake on the Altiplano covers 4,200 square miles/11,000 square km of land and is the largest salt mass in the world. The main tributary to the Uyuni Salt Lake is the **Rio Grande de Lipez**. The second-largest salt lake in the highlands is **Coipasa**, which is fed by the **Lauca** and **Saboya rivers**. Although there are many small lakes in the highlands, those most often visited are the **Colorado**, the **Verde** and the **Celeste**.

The **Pantanal**, east of Santa Cruz, is the largest wetland in the world and covers an area of 81,000 square miles/210,000 square km, much of it underwater during rainy season.

The **Amazon Basin** covers over eight million square km of land, 44% of South America's territory. It spreads across Bolivia, Brazil, Colombia, Ecuador, Guyana, Peru, Surinam and Venezuela. Bolivia has 280,000 square miles/722,000 square km of that basin. Except for the Acre River, all Bolivian rivers from the Amazon Basin flow into the **Madera**, which in turn flows into the Amazon. The Madera River is fed by the **Mamore**, the **Madre de Dios** and the Beni.

The **Itenez** (also called the Guapore) and the **Mamore rivers** collect most of the runoff from the Bolivian savannas and jungles of Santa Cruz, Beni and Cochabamba districts. The Beni River collects most of the runoff from the Andes and its tributaries are often used for whitewater kayaking or rafting.

In the southeast, **La Plata Basin** has many small rugged rivers that are tributaries to the **Paraguay** and **Pilcomayo rivers**. These two waterways flow into the **Rio de la Plata**, which runs through Paraguay and down to the Atlantic Ocean. This basin is the fifth largest in the world and has a rich ecosystem.

Climate

Temperature and precipitation are almost totally dependent on altitude. The higher one goes, the colder and drier it gets. Generally speaking, the rainy season is from January to March throughout the country, except in the Amazon and Yungas, where it runs from September to April. The cloud forests of the Yungas get about 200 inches/5,000 mm of rain annually, while the southwestern highlands receive four inches/100 mm.

The highlands and mountains can be dry and cold and the nights are always cold, often below freezing. During wet season, this region is damp and cool in the morning, hot and dry during the day, dry and cool in the evening and freezing again at night. In winter, nighttime temperature can drop to -13°F/-25°C with a wind chill temperature of -40°F/-40°C.

The cloud forests of the Yungas and Colinas sit between 3,290 and 11,500 ft (1,000 and 3,500 m) and are always hot and humid. During rainy season it rains every day, all day. In the tropical lowlands of the Amazon and La Plata Basin areas, it is hot and humid in dry season, with average temperatures of 80°F/27°C. However, in rainy season there are torrential downpours that cool the temperatures drastically.

The Gran Chaco area is always hot and dry.

◆ Temperatures

Elevation plays a big role in temperatures. The higher the elevation, the cooler it will be. For an example, La Paz stands at 3,625 meters/11,900 feet, and has an average mid-day temperature during the month of December of 18°C (64°F). In Cochabamba, the elevation is 2,550 meters/8,400 feet and the average mid-day temperature during the same month is 26°C (79°F). In the Amazon region where the elevation is only 500 meters, the average daily temperature is 30°C (86°F). It is also good to remember that cold winter temperatures are during June, July and August and the warmer summer temperatures are in November, December and January.

Plant Life

Bolivia's different environments produce a variety of plants. The **Altiplano** is a grassland known for its **puna**, a spiky grass eaten by cameloids. The **cloud forests** are located where the cold mountain air comes in contact with the moist warm air of the Amazon. The Amazon and parts of the Gran Chaco offer **jungle** with dry woods like the mahogany being an important species.

> ❖ **FANTASTIC FLORA FIGURES**
>
> Bolivia has over 2,500 species of lichen, 1,950 to 2,500 species of trees, 1,200 species of moss, and 1,500 species of ferns.

It is beyond the scope of this book to list all the plants you could see here. If your interests lie in exploring the country for its diverse fauna and flora, purchase a guide book and head out.

◆ In the Highlands

The **Queñua** tree is a twisted, knurled species that grows at elevations up to 17,000 ft/5,200 m. It has red peeling bark and tiny leaves. This rare tree can be seen on the slopes of Mount Sajama.

Puma grass grows as spiky clumps in uncultivated fields of the Altiplano. The plant can grow up to three feet/one meter in height and diameter. The seeds are found in the stems and the roots are tough and fibrous. Those using traditional methods for farming burn this plant in potato fields. It acts as a fertilizer.

The **totora reed** that grows on Lake Titikaka (and a few other places in Bolivia) belongs to the same family as the papyrus. It grows 10 ft/three m above the level of the water and is used in the construction of the traditional boats and houses and to feed cattle. It can be harvested for the first time after a year and three times a year after that.

Yareta trees grow in clusters at about 13,000 ft/4,000 m above sea level. Because of the high resin content in the leaves, they are used for fuel.

A cactus called the *jacha quiriu* (huge stake) in Spanish (I was unable to find the English or scientific names) grows up to 33 ft/10 m in height and is used to make furniture. The plant is also dried, carved and placed over doorways or along stairways to bring good luck.

Puya raimondi is a giant bromeliad belonging to the same family as the pineapple. The raimondi is considered one of the most ancient plant species on the planet and grows as a rosette with tough waxy leaves that cluster up to seven ft/two m in diameter. It takes 100 years to mature before it flowers. The flower is a huge spike that can be 33 ft/10 m high and is covered with about 20,000 flowers. The plant flowers once, for three months, and then it dies.

◆ In the Lowlands

There are over 2,000 species of trees and orchids in the lower areas of Bolivia. Of them all, the rubber tree and the mahogany are the best known.

Mahogany trees grow well over 80 ft/25 m, with foliage that offers a great amount of shade. The trunk has a red, scaly bark and there are four to eight leathery leaves on each branch. Tiny white flowers appear in clusters and bear a pear-shaped fruit that has noticeable grooves along its length. The fruit produces wing-shaped seeds.

Rubber trees are actually a wide variety of plants that produce a milky liquid in the roots, stem, branches, leaves or fruit. This liquid, called the latex, contains globules that can be treated to form what we call raw rubber.

Orchids are so very beautiful, although most are actually parasitic. There are about 25,000 species worldwide. Their evolution has resulted in thick leaves that hold moisture. Some of the flowers are highly perfumed, such as the vanilla orchid.

Bromeliads or **air plants** are similar in appearance to orchids. Bromeliads can grow at elevations as high as 8,200 ft/2,500 m and in any terrain from rainforest to desert. They are also like orchids in the way they gather nutrients and moisture in their leaves; their roots are only for anchoring, not for gathering food. The pineapple is the most commonly known bromeliad.

Coca production dates back to 3000 BC. The leaf, called *hoja sangrada* (sacred leaf) by the Inca, has been used not only to decrease the sensation of hunger and cold and the symptoms of altitude sickness, but also for ceremonial purposes. More recently, Coca-Cola used it originally for flavoring and the medical profession used it as a local anesthetic. Finally, the production of cocaine began and grew to an estimated US $150-$300 million in Bolivia alone.

Coca & The Drug War

Bolivia is the second-largest grower of coca after Peru and the second-largest producer of cocaine after Colombia. Most of that cocaine hits the streets of American cities.

The United States started its drug war and gave aid money so the farmers could grow replacement crops. The US then trained military men to recognize and eradicate the plant.

However, there is a positive side to the coca plant that some governments try to ignore. The Department of Agriculture at Harvard University analyzed coca for nutritional value and found that it was high in calories, protein, carbohydrate and fiber. It also contained calcium, phosphorus, iron and vitamins A, E and B. A few years later, an anthropologist at Indiana University studied the plant and suggested that coca, chewed after dinner, may help regulate glucose metabolism and enhance the digestion of carbohydrates at high altitudes. These two reports gave the Andean people something with which to fight the eradication programs.

After farmers blockaded roads and conflicts between *cocaleros* and police left 10 dead, the government compromised and permitted 74,000 hectares/30,000 acres in the Yungas to be used for coca production. The rest of the farmers, when their crops are eradicated, are given $2,000 each to grow alternative crops, such as coffee, corn, rice or quinoa.

As the drug problems in the United States increase, the US Drug Enforcement Agency becomes even more intent on eradication. Production was estimated to be down 33% in 2001 and 60% in the last five years (33% in the last year).

There is another philosophy about the eradication of the coca plant. Wade Davis in his book *One River*, feels that the American attempt at eliminating the plant has little to do with controlling the drug trade, but is rather a war on the culture of the Andean people. Today, there are many in Bolivia who agree with Davis.

For travelers, the drug war causes three problems. There are the roadblocks as *cocaleros* protest eradication, bus and baggage searches for "precursor chemicals" used in cocaine production and a general dislike of *gringos* due to heavy-handed actions of the DEA and army. This is especially evident in the Trinidad, Santa Cruz and Cochabamba areas.

Animal Life

Like the flora, animals vary according to the elevation. There are 322 species of mammals, 1,358 species of non-migratory birds, 257 species of reptiles, 166 of amphibians and 550 species of fish. With a little work, you can see most of the species you want to see. And when a tour agent says that you will see certain birds, plants, animals and insects, he is usually telling the truth. This is especially true in the Amazon area. I was promised pink dolphins, howler monkeys, capybaras, cobras, anacondas, caimans, turtles, egrets, eagles, tarantulas and so on. I saw all of them on a three-day boat tour out of Rurrenabaque on the Yacuma River.

◆ In the Highlands

The most common animals are the three cameloids – llamas, alpacas and vicuñas. **Llamas** live at altitudes up to 18,000 ft/5,500 m and are used as beasts of burden, for food and for wool. **Alpaca** are smaller than llamas and have smaller noses. Their wool is also finer and thicker. Alpaca like to live near streams and grassy plains. **Vicuña** are small and short with long necks. Between the Apolabama region and Sajama National Park, there are 8,000-9,000 of these animals.

Vezcachas are rabbit-like rodents that jump. They have long fuzzy tails and live in colonies among the rocks located near streams. Related to the chinchilla, these animals can usually be spotted at sunrise or sunset.

The **Andean bear** is a rare and endangered animal that lives near the tree line. It was once hunted for meat and fat. It was believed that this cured disease.

The **puma** is a night hunter and is rarely spotted. Also called the mountain lion, cougar or panther, it is a bit smaller than the jaguar. Its main source of food is the deer, an animal that is abundant in Bolivia. When hunting, the puma strikes with lightening speed and can jump 25 ft/7.5 m in one leap.

The **Andean fox** looks like a coyote in color and size. It hunts guinea pigs and mice and is often seen on the Altiplano.

The **armadillo**, an insect-eating mammal with a bony-plated shell, is now an endangered species. The armadillo has simple rootless teeth at the back of its mouth and is able to eat snakes, chickens, fruit and eggs. It also likes to munch on the odd scorpion.

> ### ❖ BLIND FROGGIE
>
> The *Telmatobious culeus* belongs to the Leptodactylidae frog
> family. It is endemic to Lake Titicaca and was first identified by
> Jaques Cousteau, the famous French oceanographer. The
> frog grows to 45 to 60 cm (17-24 inches) in length. It is a night
> hunter and is believed to be blind. It obtains its oxygen from
> water through extra "fingers" that are quite vascular. The high
> flow of water allows for optimum oxygen consumption so lungs
> on this species have not developed. Because it is good eating,
> the frog has been hunted almost to extinction.

Of the 120 birds that live in the Altiplano, the **condor**, with its 10-foot/three-
m wingspan, is the most impressive. It is black with a bald red head, white
neck and white on the tops of its wings. The condor can weigh up to 45 lbs/
20 kg. It is the national bird of Bolivia. The **caracara** is another large bird
common to the Altiplano. This scavenger is black and white with a yellow
beak.

Flamingos are abundant near lakes. Their color is dependent on algae,
which they consume. The more algae, the pinker the birds become.

The **rhea** lives as high as 11,500 ft/3,500 m and as low as 1,300 ft/400 m.
It resembles an ostrich, minus the tail feathers, and stands just under
seven ft/two m in height and weighs 45-60 lbs/20-25 kg. It eats insects,
plants and small animals. The males sit on eggs laid by several females.
The eggs take between 35 and 40 days to hatch and weigh just under two
pounds/one kg.

Hummingbirds can live up to 16,500 ft/5,000 m. Their body temperature drops from 102°F/39°C during the day to 27°F/15°C during the night
and the heart rate drops from 1,200 beats per minute to 40.

As for insects, spiders, butterflies and ants, Bolivia has enough to keep
entomologists happy for years.

◆ In the Lowlands

The **coati** is a tree-climbing mammal related to the raccoon. It has a long
snout (tipped white) and an even longer tail that is usually the same length
as its body. It keeps its striped tail high and, as it walks, the tail swings from
side to side. Coatis are social animals and the females often travel with
their young in groups of up to 20. A full-grown male stands about 10 inches/
25 cm at the shoulder and will grow to about 1.5 ft/.5 m long. An omnivore,
the coati hunts both in the day and at night and eats just about anything.

The **peccary** is a pig-like creature that has been around for 40 million
years (according to fossil finds). It weighs about 50 lbs/23 kg and travels in
herds of a few individuals to as many as 300. The peccary has two distinct
features. One is the smell it exudes from a musk gland on its back whenever it feels irritated. The second is its amazing nose, the tip of which is flat
and reinforced with a cartilaginous disk that can lift logs and dig underground for roots and insects. A true omnivore, the peccary will eat anything
from poisonous snakes to cactus. Peccaries have no fixed mating season.
The female usually gives birth to one or two young about the size of a full-

grown rabbit, and after only a couple of days the offspring take their place in the herd.

The **ant bear** or the great anteater is known for its lack of teeth. Instead of teeth, its elongated head has a small hole about the size of a pen. Its tongue, which can extend up to 19 inches/48 cm, whips out and snatches up termites and other insects. The ant bear's front toes and claws curl under so it seems to be walking on its knuckles. It stands about 24 inches/60 cm at the shoulder and is (including tail) about seven ft/two m long. The female gives birth to one baby that stays with her for an entire year. The infant is often seen riding on its mother's back. The anteater is inoffensive and usually runs (and swims) away from perceived danger.

Skunks are found anywhere from northern Canada all the way down to Patagonia. Related to the weasel, this striped, furry critter is well known for its defense mechanism – spraying a horrid perfume up to a distance of 11.5 ft/3.5 m. The skunk aims for the eyes of its enemy, and the liquid it produces causes temporary blindness. A night hunter, the skunk comes out of its den when the temperatures cool and it forages for insects, larvae, mice and fallen fruits. Skunks mate in spring and have litters of five or six young that are ready to look after themselves after about two months. Their life span is around 10 years.

The **tapir** or mountain cow is related to the horse and rhinoceros, but it is unique in the fact that it is the last surviving ungulate with an odd number of toes that bears its weight on the middle toe. This short-haired animal stands about 4 ft/1.2 m at the shoulder and weighs around 600 lbs/275 kg when fully grown. It has a trunk-like snout that grabs leaves from aquatic plants or forest foliage. An excellent swimmer, the tapir can stay underwater for long periods of time, especially when hiding from its worst enemies, the jaguar and puma. Don't get too close to a tapir's rear end. He pees straight out back at high velocity.

Howler monkeys make a horrid growling sound that will spook the hell out of you. And that is what it is meant to do. This leaf-eating primate has a long grasping tail and little facial hair, except on its chin. Its skin is black and its jawbone protrudes to accommodate the bladder-like resonating chamber found in the throat. It is this chamber that allows the monkey to make the frightening racket it does. Howlers live in troops of no more than 10 and have one dominant male leader. Once a troop is formed, all members eat, sleep and travel together. Howlers weigh up to 25 lbs/11 kg and mothers nurse their young for about 18 months.

The **spider monkey** has grasping hands that have no functional thumbs and a grasping tail that is hairless at the end. These five "hands" allow for great maneuverability. Spider monkeys travel in bands of 20 to 30 that will attack threatening invaders. They use fruits and branches as weapons, and have been known to urinate on enemies walking below.

The **capybara** is the world's largest rodent, weighing about 120 lbs/55 kg. You will find them wallowing in mud at the edge of Amazon rivers, wiggling their tiny ears while enjoying the sun. Young ones are often eaten by caimans, which live in the same areas.

Pink and grey freshwater **dolphins** are considered the most intelligent of the five dolphin species. The only predator this mammal has is man. The dolphin grows up to 10 ft/three m in length and weighs in at 200 lbs/90 kg. They have a gestation period of between nine and 12 months and sexual maturity is determined by size, rather than age. This dolphin has a hump on its back. Because of its special fusing at the neck, it can turn its head 180°.

Geckos eat insects, especially mosquitoes, and can be seen on throughout the Amazon.

There are close to 1,400 birds in Bolivia. You will not be disappointed if taking a birding tour. The most sought-after bird in the Amazon is the **blue-throated macaw**, which can be seen along the rivers out of Trinidad.

The most common fish are the **pacu**, **surubi**, **palometa** and **piraña**. There are also snakes, lizards, turtles, frogs and caimans along the rivers and in the jungles.

National Emblems

The **Kantuta** is the national flower and it has the same colors as the flag. The chalice-shaped flower has a red cup with a yellow stem that attaches to the green plant.

The **condor** is the country's national bird.

Bolivia probably hasn't gotten around to naming a national tree, but the **Breadfruit Tree** is on the coat of arms. The breadfruit is a member of the fig family and grows up to 60 ft/20 m. It produces an edible round melon that weighs up to 10 lbs/4 kg. The meat of the melon tastes similar to chocolate and is used mostly for flavoring.

The **llama** is the national animal and is proudly shown on the coat of arms. It is used as a beast of burden, for its dung-fuel, for meat and for wool.

◆ National Anthem

Bolivians, a favorable destiny
Has crowned our vows and longings;
This land is free,
Your servile state has ended.
The martial turmoil of yesterday
And the horrible clamor of war
Are followed today, in harmonious contrast,
By sweet hymns of peace and unity.
Chorus
We have kept the lofty name of our country
In glorious splendor,
And on its altars we once more swear
To die, rather than live as slaves.
This innocent and beautiful land,
Which owes its name to Bolivar,

Is the happy homeland where men
Enjoy the benefits of good fortune and peace.
For the sons of the great Bolivar
Have sworn, thousands upon thousand of times,
To die rather than see the country's
Majestic flag humiliated.
Chorus
Eternal praise to the brave warriors
Whose heroic valor and firmness
Conquered the glories that now
A happy Bolivia begins to enjoy!
Let their names, in marble and in bronze,
Transmit to remote ages
And in resounding song repeat the call:
Freedom! Freedom! Freedom!
Lyrics of the national anthem were written by Jose Ignacio de Sanjines

◆ National Flag

The flag of Bolivia has three horizontal stripes. The top is red and represents the blood shed during the battle for independence; the center is yellow and represents gold or prosperity for the nation; the bottom is green
and symbolizes the home of the people. In the center of the flag sits the
country's coat of arms with 10 stars depicting the nine states plus the lost
maritime district that was taken by Chile. The coat of arms covers 9/10ths
of the yellow stripe.

◆ Coat of Arms

The coat of arms that appears on the flag and all Bolivian coins has a llama
in the center. During one of the battles for independence, the Indians were
in a field waiting for the Spanish to arrive. The Spaniards arrived on horses
and charged, but stopped when they saw that there were no people, only
llamas, on the field. The Spaniards left. This saved the lives of the Bolivian
people who were hiding behind the llamas.

Bolivia's Top Destinations

I have many favorite things to do in Bolivia. The following are ones that I
feel you should make every effort to experience while traveling the
country.

1. UYUNI – Tour Uyuni Salt Lake and Lago Colorado (page 149).

2. COPACABANA – Hike Isle del Sol (page 112) on Lake Titikaka.

3. SAJAMA – Climb the highest mountain in Bolivia and then soak in the
hot springs close to the village (page 123).

4. TUPIZA – Take a horse tour around the badlands and canyons of the
area (page 187).

5. RURRENABAQUE – Take a river trip to spot capybaras and anacondas (page 290).

6. SANTA CRUZ – Eat, visit the Jesuit Missions and then eat some more (page 243).

7. SAMAIPATA – Tour El Fuerte, a pre-Inca ruin (page 210).

8. SORATA – Hike around/to Illampu (page 158).

9. YUNGAS – Travel the Road of Death by bicycle from El Cumbre to Coroico, located in the rainforest of the Yungas (page 69).

10. POTOSI – Visit the silver mine and mint (page 134).

11. SUCRE – Visit the dinosaur tracks in the cleanest colonial city in South America and then purchase chocolate that is reputed to be better than Swiss (page 173).

Travel Information

Facts at Your Fingertips

PRESIDENT: Gonzalo Sanchez de Lozada, elected after Jorge Fernando Quiroga Ramez took over from Banzer on August 8, 2001, when Banzer was diagnosed with terminal cancer.

VICE PRESIDENT: Carlos D. Mesa Gisbert. At time of appointment he was 37 years old and the youngest Vice President ever to take office.

OPPOSITION LEADER: Evo Morales is the most controversial and colorful politician, leader of the *campesinos* generally and, more specifically, the *cocaleros*. He is also the first Indian to be elected into the Bolivian parliament.

SIZE: 424,163 square miles/1,098,581 square km, with 20% desert, 40% rainforest, 25% pasture, 2% arable land and 2% water. The remaining 11% is mountainous.

POPULATION: 8,150,000 – 15% Spanish, 30% Quechua and 25% Aymara and 30% other.

CAPITAL: Sucre is the capital city, but the seat of government is in **La Paz**. La Paz stands at 11,924 ft/3,625 m above sea level.

DISTRICTS: The nine districts are Beni, Chuquisaca, Cochabamba, La Paz, Oruro, Pando, Potosi, Santa Cruz and Tarija.

INDEPENDENCE DAY: August 6.

LANGUAGE: Spanish is the predominant language spoken in the cities. **Quechua** or **Aymara** is spoken in the countryside and in small mountain villages.

> **AUTHOR TIP:** *A word glossary for the Indian languages is quite helpful if traveling independently into isolated areas. Although some Aymara and Quechua people speak Spanish, it is their second language and, if it is yours too, confusion is bound to occur. For a smattering of Aymara, visit www.aymara.org/english/ index.php; for some Quechua, go to gibbons.best.vwh.net/index. html.*

EDUCATION: Schooling is compulsory for children between ages seven and 11. Those with the funds and desire to continue may take three years of intermediate and four years of secondary education. Secondary education can be a general or a specialized education. High school graduates may continue at the University of Bolivia or enter one of the many private institutions. Cochabamba is renowned for its medical schools and has students from other countries specializing in the study of tropical diseases.

The literacy rate is 75% in Bolivia. Elementary students attend from 8 am to noon, secondary students from 12:30 to 6 pm and adults go after 6 pm.

LIFE EXPECTANCY: Males live to an average of 60 years and females live to 62. The infant mortality rate is 124.4 per 1,000 births. Nutritional deficiency affects 70% of the population. Sanitary conditions are poor, especially in rural areas. Only 23% of the population has drinkable water, 15.6% has electricity and 1% has a sewage system.

GDP: US $977 per person, per year. The unemployment rate is 7.6%. Bolivia is an agricultural society: 60% of the population are farmers – they produce 23% of the GDP. Only 15% of agricultural products are exported. Of the industrial production, 20% is silver and tin, 36% of which is exported.

NATURAL RESOURCES: Tin, natural gas, petroleum, zinc, tungsten, antimony, silver, iron, lead, gold and timber are the main resources. Forests cover 138 million acers/56 million hectares.

HUMAN RIGHTS: Human rights violations do occur, although there have been no political assassinations in recent years. Most abuses occur between the military or police and the *cocaleros* living and growing coca in the Chapare region. Incarceration can occur for months and even years before a suspect is brought to trial.

The **police force** does not have a good reputation. The government does not complete or force investigations into alleged abuses in the jails, so once the police become involved, there is almost no law. More than 30% of the people in prison have been waiting for trial longer than the sentence they would have received for the accused crime. **Gay rights** demonstrations always result in harassment of both protestors and bystanders.

Newspapers are not permitted to criticize the government or the Catholic church and all quotes must have a name attached. Violators are subject to two months in prison.

There is wide **discrimination** against women, indigenous people and Afro-Bolivians. Sixty-two percent of women experience domestic violence at least once in their lives; rape is under reported. Four out of five illiterate people are women.

An estimated 800,000 children between the ages of seven and 14 hold jobs to help support their families.

On the bright side, women of reproductive years receive free **medical care**, as do all children under the age of five. However, it is unlikely that this care is timely or consistent in any individual case. Cleft palates and club feet, for example, are seldom treated unless payment is made.

Prisons in Bolivia are harsh, overcrowded and often life-threatening for those without access to money. In San Pedro Prison in La Paz, there are between 8,000 and 12,000 prisoners in a space that was designed to hold only 5,000. To use a cell, prisoners must pay between $20 and $5,000. The small, less-expensive ones have no ventilation, no lighting and no beds. Some prisoners must sit up to sleep due to lack of space, and their diet causes serious anemia. Medical care is unavailable unless one has money. Children under the age of six are permitted to live with incarcerated parents. At present, there are 665 children in San Pedro Prison. Because many would end up living on the street, they continue living in the prison after age six.

There is wide corruption in the **judicial system** due to low wages and the class system. Everyone is given the right to assembly – and Bolivians use this right often.

PARKS: Bolivia's 37 parks cover 17% of the country's total land mass. Fifteen of the parks have full-time wardens. Parks are administered by the Servicio Nacional de Areas Protegidas (SERNAP) in La Paz. Most parks require an admission fee and usually foreigners pay more than locals. This fee is collected near the parks' entrances.

These are not protected parks in the American or European sense; the land can be used for farming, ranching, logging and hunting. Although there are park land rules, they are seldom enforced. There are not enough rangers to prevent poaching.

CURRENCY: The boliviano is the Bolivian currency. At time of writing, it was exchanging at B 7.50 to US $1. Each boliviano is made up of 100 centavos. The boliviano bills are printed in denominations of 10, 20, 50, 100 and 200. There is also a five boliviano bill, but that is being taken out of circulation. The inflation rate is presently at 10%, making the boliviano one of the most stable currencies in Latin America.

When to Go

◆ Seasonal Considerations

Anytime is the best time to go to Bolivia. The winter months run from June to September and present clear skies and cold crisp days in the higher elevations. Rainy season, from November to March, is warmer but travel on the mountain roads can be treacherous and impossible in the Amazon. Peak climbing season during the winter months may require a few days leeway in your itinerary because the good guides are heavily booked. Festivals cause crowding on buses and airlines, so avoid travel during those times. Prices are low all the time.

◆ National Holidays & Celebrations

Bolivia has many celebrations and, although many are specific to a region, most are held throughout the country. Below is a compilation of holidays that are held throughout the country. Additionally, each district has its own celebrations, which are reviewed in the regional chapters.

TRAVEL INFORMATION

❖   **JANUARY**

January 6. **Dias del Reyo** (Day of the King) usually takes place in the main plaza.

January 24. **Alasista** is a celebration also known as the Festival of Abundance. Ekheko, an Aymara/Inca God, is honored at this time.

❖   **FEBRUARY**

February 1, 2 and 3. A week-long celebration for the **Virgin of Candeleria**, when the virgin's identity is re-asserted.

Near the end of February, 40 days before Easter, is **Carnival** throughout Latin America. It is a week-long event. Water fights start about a month before Carnival and escalate until they culminate during Carnival. *Globos* (balloons) half-filled with water are sold in the streets and thrown at everyone.

The most traditional Carnival is held in Oruro, where the world-famous parade takes place along with the not-so-famous *globos*-throwing games.

❖   **MARCH**

March 23 is the **Dia del Mar**, which honors Eduardo Avaroa, a hero from the War of the Pacific. March 23 is when Bolivia lost its land by the sea to Chile and is the day Avaroa died.

Semana Santa is at Easter. The date changes each year, but it is always held at the end of March or beginning of April. Copacabana is one of the best places to be during Semana Santa.

❖   **MAY**

May 1 is **Labor Day**. All government offices are closed, and many Bolivians also close their shops and private businesses.

May 27, Dia de la Madre, or **Mother's Day**. In the wars of independence, after the men were killed in some places, the women fought and won. Mother's Day honors the women who participated.

❖   **JUNE**

June 5 and 6 is the birthday of **Manco Capac**, the first male Inca ever born, according to legend.

June 23 is the **Dia de San Juan Bautista**. This is when everyone builds a fire in front of their house to celebrate the longest night and coldest day of the year.

July 15-17 is the **Dia de la Revolution**. This celebration is in honor of Pedro Murillo, a freedom fighter who, during a demonstration led by opposing forces, was hanged in the main square in La Paz.

❖   **AUGUST**

August 5 and 6 is **Independence Day**.

❖ **NOVEMBER**

November 1 and 2 is Todo Santo or **All Saints Day**. This event is celebrated at the cemetery.

❖ **DECEMBER**

December 24 is **Christmas**. It is celebrated with family and children, who go from door to door playing music and receiving small gifts.

December 31 and January 1 is **New Year**, celebrated with parties and fireworks.

What to Take

◆ Required Documents

To enter Bolivia a **passport** valid for six months after your entry date is required. You will be given a tourist card valid for 30 to 90 days. Do not lose the card as it must be returned to Immigration when you exit the country.

Citizens from Western countries do not need a visa for short stays, and most are given an automatic 90-day stamp when they arrive at the border or airport. Sometimes, officials give only 30 days. If that's not long enough for you, it can be extended at **Immigration** in La Paz, Calle Camacho #1433, open from 9 to 12:30 pm and 3 to 6 pm. However, with the cost ($25 per month of extension) and the time spent in the Bolivian bureaucratic quagmire, it is easier to leave the country and return a day later. You will be issued a new tourist card with another 30 days on it.

It is the law that you must carry **identification** at all times.

> **SAFETY WARNING:** *Be warned that tricksters pretending to be the National Police may demand your identification (passport) and then ask you to follow them because of an inconsistency. They get you into a vehicle and then rob you. The best thing to do is carry a photocopy of your passport and one of your entry stamp/tourist card and use those as identification.*

Anyone overstaying their tourist card limit will be subject to a fine of a dollar a day at Immigration, or $5 a day at the airport. This is an inexpensive fine, but you may also miss your flight, which could be costly.

Dept. of Immigration, Calle Camacho #1433, La Paz, is open from 9 to 12:30 pm and 3 to 6 pm, Monday to Friday.

For general information about Bolivia, go to www.boliviaweb.com.

Embassies & Consulates

Embassies and consulates are well represented in La Paz. See the *Appendix* for a list. If your country has a consulate or embassy here, I suggest that you register with them.

◆ Packing List

Bolivia has a large indigenous population that is strong in Catholic faith and in adherence to tribal custom, so conservative dress is essential. Like the women of the country, I wear a skirt that is calf length and a blouse with sleeves that cover my arms at least to the elbow. On the other hand, the Ladinos (the white population) do wear North American-styled clothing and provocative dress is often seen in urban areas. Most businesswomen wear skirts or dresses. Except in the Amazon area, shorts are not common. The men of Bolivia usually wear jeans or slacks with long-sleeved shirts.

You will need a warm **sweater** or jacket for evenings, especially in the higher elevations.

An **umbrella** is good at any time of year.

In the jungles of Bolivia, a **cotton skirt** is far cooler than pants or shorts. Men should wear loosely woven cotton clothing. During rainy season, locals wear gumboots.

A **money belt** should always be a natural-fiber pouch worn around the midriff under your clothes. Inside the belt, keep documents in plastic bags to protect them from damage by sweat and rain. Belts like the kind used to hold up pants are available with zippered pockets sewn on the underside.

Tiny pockets can be sewn into your clothing – in the hem of your skirt or the cuff of your shirt. Sports bras worn by women that have the water bottle containers in the back are excellent for hiding money and cards. Pin or Velcro the bottle containers shut so the money or cards won't work their way out.

A **day pack** is harder to pickpocket or snatch than a bag.

It seems to me that a map is really hard to follow if you don't have a **compass**.

Earplugs are essential.

A **first aid kit** should include things like mole skin, Advil, bandage, anti-histamines, topical antibiotic cream, Band Aids, prescription medicines and malaria prophylactics.

A **hat** is essential.

Photocopies of passports and other documents should be kept somewhere other than with your passport. Memorize your passport number. Keep a record of the numbers on your traveler's checks and record where and when you cashed them. Keep important addresses and phone numbers in two places, just in case you lose one list.

Scan your passport (and any other information you find valuable) and e-mail the scan to your traveling e-mail address (i.e., Yahoo or Hotmail). This way, you always have a copy available.

Reading material is expensive and bus trips are often long. Bring lots of thick anthologies of short stories. Unless you're fluent in Spanish, always carry a **Spanish dictionary** and a list of conjugated verbs. A phrasebook is useful too.

A **sleeping bag** is advisable if you are planning trips into high areas. If going to the Altiplano, even with a tour group, the accommodations will be rustic and a warm bag could be essential. If hiking in the Andes, a bag is vital. Purchasing a bag in Bolivia is difficult.

Camping gear should be brought from home. Climbing gear, especially, must be brought with you. If you are able, bring old equipment (such as tent, sleeping bag, stove, pots, etc.) And donate it to outfitters at the end of your trip.

Electricity is 220 volts. If carrying appliances, purchase a converter in your own country. Although they are available in Bolivia, they are heavy. Often, it is easier to purchase appliances like immersion heaters in Bolivia. Those using computers should carry a good surge protector.

A **flashlight** is often essential. Batteries are readily available.

> ❖   **FIDO FRIENDLY**
>
> Traveling with a dog is possible in Bolivia. Dogs are permitted on public transportation and allowed into restaurants and hotels, provided they are under your control.

Health Concerns

Bring with you anything you may need in the way of prescriptions, glasses, orthopedics, dental care and batteries for hearing aids. Things like vitamins, bandages, antihistamines and topical creams are readily available in the cities and are not expensive. If you become sick, contact your consulate for recommended doctors and medical clinics. They can usually put you in touch with doctors who speak your language.

Medical treatment is cheap in Bolivia. Minor ailments are better treated in local clinics and paid for on the spot, rather than going through an insurance. If you plan on climbing or taking buses along dangerous routes, travel insurance is recommended.

For official government updates on outbreaks, advisories and more, visit the **Centers for Disease Control & Prevention** run by the US Health Department at www.cdc.gov.

◆ Doctors & Clinics

Some hotel doctors are very expensive, usually $40 per visit, plus the cost of medication. Choosing a clinic used by a trustworthy local is an alternative that runs less than $10 per call.

You may also contact the **IAMAT** (International Association for Medical Assistance to Travelers) clinics. The information reported in this section is taken from either IAMAT or World Health Organization publications. If you feel so inclined, please become a member of IAMAT and send them a donation. Some of the money they raise goes toward a scholarship program that assists doctors in developing countries to train in more developed parts of the world. For addresses in your country, visit www.iamat.org.

❖   **IAMAT CLINICS**
Iamat Center, Edificio Servimed, 5th floor
Calle Baptista, Cochabamba
☎ (591-4) 423-1504 or (591-4) 423-3884

Clinica San Pedro, Calle Aurelio Melean S-154
Has 10 coordinators, all with a specialty.
☎ (591-4) 423-1504

IPPA La Clinica - High Altitude Pathology Clinic
Ave. Savedra 2302, La Paz
☎ (591-2) 224-5394 or (591-2) 222-2617; zubieta@bolnet.
bo

Clinica Angel Foianini, Ave. Irala 468, Santa Cruz
☎ (591-3) 336-2211 or (591-3) 336-5577

◆ Common Ailments

The following website, run by the IPPA Clinic (above) has excellent information about dealing with **high altitude sickness**. If going directly to La
Paz from a low altitude, read the recommendations and do what is suggested to make your arrival and stay more comfortable. Go to www.
geocities.com/zubietaippa.

High altitude sickness, or *soroche*, can affect anyone, regardless of
physical condition or age.

Serious altitude sickness is always possible if you ascend above 10,000
ft/3,000 m quickly. The atmospheric pressure at Potosi, which is about
1,650 ft/500 m higher than La Paz, is half of that at sea level. It is often as-
sumed that if you were at high elevations on previous trips and felt no side
effects, you will have no problems on your next trip. This is not the case.
There is no rule that can predict your body's reaction to a substantial
elevation change.

Know the symptoms of *soroche*. If you suspect you may be affected, descend immediately to an elevation where the symptoms disappear.

❖   The first symptom is shortness of breath and a racing
    pulse even with small amounts of exertion. Tiredness
    and lack of appetite are common, as is a mild headache.
    Other primary symptoms are insomnia, irritability, dizzi-
    ness, muscle aches, nausea and water retention in the
    face, hands and feet.

❖   Secondary symptoms include a severe headache and/or
    a persistent cough. The headache is an indication that
    water is starting to accumulate on your brain. A cough
    may indicate that water is accumulating in the lungs.

❖   Tertiary symptoms include confusion, inability to sleep
    lying down and a loss of coordination that causes stag-
    gering. At this point going to a lower elevation, or getting
    to a hospital where oxygen therapy can be administered,
    is essential.

❖   The final stages of *soroche* are unconsciousness and
    then death.

When arriving at a high elevation, drink lots of water (four liters or one gal-
lon a day) and stay away from alcohol. The rule is to drink enough water so
that you pee clear. Keep stimulants like coffee at a minimum as they are

dehydrating. Do not take tranquilizers, sleeping pills or other medications that slow down the breathing rate as this is counterproductive to acclimatization. For the first few days, do little except take short slow walks and eat light foods. When you feel fine, start moving toward higher elevations or more strenuous activity.

Drugs may be taken to counteract altitude sickness. Acetazolamide can lessen symptoms by increasing the breathing rate. Dexamethasone can reduce major symptoms long enough for very ill people to be taken to a lower elevation and/or seek medical help.

If you are not able to acclimatize after about a week of slow walking and lots of water drinking, do not fret. Head for the lowlands of Bolivia and then return to the higher elevations slowly, spending a few days in a town or village about 1,000 ft/300 m higher than the previous one. Do day-trips to higher elevations, then go back down to sleep.

You should also be aware of the condition of your traveling companions. There is always a tendency to ignore symptoms and, once confusion and lack of coordination occurs, the sick person is no longer able to help him/her self. Someone must step in. Locals recommend coca tea for altitude sickness. Since I drink it all the time, I like to think it works, but I don't know for sure.

Hypothermia can occur even when the temperatures are not below freezing. If you become wet and are in the wind, especially at a high elevation, hypothermia is a possibility. The symptoms start with shivering, which grows more severe – at which point the person often refuses to admit he is cold. Once confusion and loss of muscular control (staggering) occurs, the person can no longer help himself and intervention is required. Warm the person by putting him/her into a sleeping bag, out of the wind and rain. Small sips of warm water or tea can be administered, but never alcohol. If the person becomes unconscious, a doctor is needed.

Fevers & Worse

Malaria, transmitted by mosquitoes that bite at dawn and dusk, is a possibility at elevations below 8,000 ft/2,500 m.

Bolivia has both chloroquine-responsive and chloroquine-resistant malaria. Anyone traveling near or through the Amazon Basin must use a chloroquine-resistant prophylactic. See your doctor or the IAMAT reports for the type of protection you will need. Do not use outdated information.

Mephlaquine is the recommended prophylactic against chloroquine-resistant malaria. One person in 15,000 may develop side effects (severe paranoia, panic attacks or eye irritations) from mephlaquine. Most people have little or no reaction to the drug.

In the event that you develop a fever while in Bolivia, for no explicable reason like a cold or flu, especially if you are in or have been in the jungle, you should treat the condition as if it is malaria. Some forms of malaria are lethal, so immediate attention is imperative.

In case of a fever, a person between 45 and 60 kgs (100 and 125 lbs) should take five mephlaquine tablets within 24 hours. Larger people should take one tablet for every 10 kgs (five lbs) of body weight over 60 kg (125 lbs). The tablets should be taken in three separate doses of two tablets,

TRAVEL INFORMATION

two tablets and, finally, one tablet, eight hours apart. If vomiting occurs within 30 minutes of ingestion, a half-dose should be taken.

If you experience ringing in the ears, reduce the dosage until the noise goes away. Get to a doctor or clinic as soon as possible. The possibility of malaria should be considered for up to three months after leaving an infected area.

Dengue fever is transmitted by a mosquito that bites during the day, rather than at dawn and dusk like the malaria-infested mosquitoes. Dengue fever causes severe headaches and severe pain to the joints and muscles. The aches are accompanied by a high fever. The disease lasts about a week. The most important thing you can do when infected with dengue is drink lots of water.

A first-time infection of dengue will not be the hemorrhagic kind, but a second bout increases the chances of hemorrhagic dengue and the chances of death are much greater. The most notable sign of hemorrhagic dengue is small red dots on your skin. This is caused from the capillaries underneath breaking and seeping blood. You will die without good medical care. In Bolivia, signs are posted whenever dengue is a threat.

To help protect against malaria-bearing mosquitos, spray or soak your clothes and sleeping gear (including net or tent) with Permethrin solution. Protection lasts for up to three washings. The recommended dose is 20 mls of Permethrin (13%) in two liters (one pint) of water. For tents and mosquito nets, spray the item with a solution of 10 mls in two liters of water. Permethrin can be purchased in any garden shop that sells pesticides.

During early morning or at dusk, when mosquitos are most active, keep exposed skin covered. Repellents laced with DEET are recommended.

Yellow fever is present in all the jungles of South America. Though inoculation is not required for entrance to Bolivia it may be required for re-entry to your own country. Inoculation, good for 10 years, is recommended if you want to avoid a lengthy stay in quarantine. Children must also have a certificate of inoculation, but it is not recommended to inoculate children who are less than one year of age.

Routine inoculations common in your home country should be up to date. Besides these, immune globulin is recommended against **viral hepatitis** and inoculation against **typhoid fever** is suggested.

If traveling to the Apolobama area or along the border between Peru and Bolivia north of Lake Titikaka, inoculation against **plague** should be considered. Talk this over with your doctor.

Typhus may be present in areas that have poor sanitation. Vaccine against typhus is no longer available. Use mothballs or Permethrin for protection against infected fleas and don't stay in dirty hotels. Tetracycline is the recommended antibiotic – it kills the disease completely.

Rabies is still a threat here. Of the 2,100 cases of dog bites on humans tested during 1997, over 1,400 were rabid and of those six people died. Incubation after the bite is anywhere from three to 12 weeks and death is usually seven days after clinical symptoms become evident. If you are bitten by an animal, go immediately to a good clinic where a prophylactic will be administered.

Bugs & Critters

Worms and **parasites** are a big problem. Keep your feet free of cuts and open sores so that worm larva or parasites cannot enter. Wear sandals or neoprene booties when showering and closed shoes or hiking boots when outdoors.

The **Tumbu fly** is an insect that transports its eggs into its host by way of the mosquito. If you have a red swelling that sort of looks like a mosquito bite and you look closely you may see a small hole in the swollen area. Keep the hole covered with petroleum jelly to prevent the fly from breathing. Without air, it dies.

◆ Water

Drink treated or bottled water. Eat at places where locals are eating. If they remain healthy, you should too. If the sanitation looks dubious, don't eat salad – have some boiled soup instead.

Tap water is considered safe to drink in the major centers like La Paz or Cochabamba. Water in small hamlets is a potential hazard. Bottled water is available, and affordable, throughout Bolivia in both cities and most villages.

The best way to treat water is to boil it for 10 minutes. However, remember that the boiling point of water in La Paz is 86°F/30°C and water must boil for at least 10 minutes to get rid of any disease-bearing organisms.

If traveling in the mountains or any other area where creek/lake water must be used, I suggest you use a chemical such as iodine for purification. There is also a tablet available that has silver (as opposed to iodine) as a base, which makes it far more palatable. Chlorine bleach can also be used as a purifier. It is the least effective of chemicals, but the most available and can be purchased anywhere in Bolivia.

Water filters take a long time to process the water and they do not filter out all organisms that could cause problems. They are also much heavier than chemicals.

Money Matters

Bolivia is inexpensive to visit. By comparison, the cost of visiting Peru is double that of Bolivia. For a comparable meal or hotel room in North America, you'll pay about four times what you can expect to pay here. Depending on your plans, daily expenses should be less than $25 for basic travel, food, accommodations and a beer or two. A frugal backpacker can travel on $10. If climbing or trekking in the out regions with a tour company offering an all-inclusive package, the cost will be $50 to $100 a day (climbing costs a bit more than trekking). Taking a jeep tour around the Salar or a boat trip down the Tuichi River will run $20 a day.

For the most part, Bolivians are honest, although I have met many hotel owners who try to squeeze more money out of foreigners, money changers who add hidden charges and tour operators who promise more than they can produce. Use the prices in this book as a guide only. Bartering may get a lower price, but if you are traveling during a festival in high season, prices will be higher. Be certain to clarify the fee for services. Even when taking a taxi, be certain that you and the driver agree on the cost for your ride before you get into the taxi. I always ask someone on the street or at the hotel what the fare should be. I found most taxi drivers honest.

All prices in this book are in US dollars. Because inflation is at 10% a year, it is unreasonable for me to use bolivianos. For each restaurant, hotel or tour agency, I give my personal impression, followed by a brief review. My impressions may have been influenced by who I saw and how they treated me. Once you have used the book for a while, you will have an idea as to what events and experiences interest me and what level of service impresses me. I like to bargain when it is clear that the seller expects it. I love the bargaining banter of the markets where high prices are sometimes tossed out to tourists just to see what happens. The ladies welcome the subsequent exchange as much as they would welcome a higher price. I bargain for hotel rooms, too. Restaurants have fixed prices.

◆ Banking/Exchange

There are numerous banks and money exchange houses, although some smaller towns (Copacabana) are sadly short of these services and other towns (like Riberalto and Guayaramerin) have none.

Some hotels in smaller places will exchange **traveler's checks**, but usually only if you are staying there. Banks don't usually exchange traveler's checks, but money exchange houses do (look for the Casa de Cambio signs). They are open from 9 am until 1 pm and then again from 4 to 6 pm. Neither banks nor money exchange houses are open on Sunday. There is often a cost that can go as high as 10% for exchanging traveler's checks and it is not possible to get a receipt that specifies the commission. This is because they know the commission is illegal. Some hotels, souvenir shops and tour agencies will take traveler's checks but, again, there is a cost. Ask before you make a deal.

You should always carry a few US dollars in cash in case you need fast money. The dollars can be exchanged for local currency anywhere, even in the smallest of villages.

American dollars or traveler's checks in American funds are the easiest to exchange. Euros, British pounds, German marks and Spanish pesetas are also readily accepted.

There are numerous **ATMs** in major cities and ENLACE machines are hooked into MasterCard, Cirrus, Maestro, Visa Electron, Plus and Visa systems. Bolivian banks that are hooked into ENLACE are Banco Nacional de Bolivia, Banco Santa Cruz and Banco Redito. Bisa ATMs also network with Plus. ENLACE, however, seems to be connected to the highest number of systems. The cost of exchanging money by an ATM is about $1.50 per transaction (rather than by percentage like traveler's checks) but some are as high as $3 per transaction. Most ATMs offer the option of being operated either in English or Spanish.

If your bank offers Internet banking, consider setting up access before you leave home. This means you can access your bank statements from any Internet café and see any charges made for ATM transactions. Most banks require that you register while in your home country.

Because the electricity is sporadic, occasionally the machine will cancel out in the middle of the transaction. If this happens, your card will be returned without explanation. Wait a minute and attempt the transaction again. Should your card be gobbled up and not returned, each ATM has an emergency number posted on the machine. English is often spoken at this number; if it is not, ask your hotel owner to help.

Major **credit cards** can be used to obtain cash from bank machines and they can be used in high-end hotels to pay for your room. Some places may charge an extra commission for using VISA/MasterCard/American Express. Report this to your VISA credit card office in your home city or call the international office at ☎ 800-336-3386, http://mastercard.com. The extra charge violates the contract agreement between the credit card companies and the merchant. American Express is not widely accepted in Bolivia at present.

> **SAFETY ALERT:** *When taking money from a machine, do so during business hours at a location inside a building. This reduces the risk of robbery or fraud by someone watching nearby. Street machines are seldom guarded.*

If a machine takes your card, regardless of which company you deal with, or if you have any other problems, go to the ATC-SRL office on Avenida Camacho, in the Santa Cruz Bank Building, 11th floor, ☎ 231-4410, to report the incident. (See *Communications* for dialing instructions.)

In the event that you run out of all financial resources and need money sent from home, try one of the many Western Union offices around the country (there are 18 in La Paz and 20 in Santa Cruz). There are 110,000 Western Union agencies in 185 countries in the world. They are reliable and much quicker than any bank, although they may charge a lot for the service. In Bolivia, ☎ 800-10-5057.

You may occasionally encounter moneychangers on the streets, especially in places close to borders. The changers offer a peso or two less than Casa de Cambios for cash and are a good option if official change places are closed or far away. The changers exchange only dollars or currencies from neighboring countries.

◆ Taxes & Tipping

There are no taxes on food or hotels, although some restaurants charge a 10% service charge. There is a **user fee** at bus stations and airports (for buses, it is 50¢; airports charge up to $2 for domestic flights and $25 for international flights).

Tipping is not the norm, although those accustomed to working in tourist haunts are starting to expect it. As anywhere, tipping should be at the discretion of the customer. Taxi drivers do not expect a tip, but if the service is good I tip (usually one boliviano, 13¢) and it is always appreciated. Hotel personnel should be rewarded if you stay in a place for a few days and if they cheerfully clean your room. These people make around $3 or $4 a week, so a small tip helps them out a lot. Baggage handlers at the airport usually get between $1 and $1.50, depending on the amount of baggage.

Dangers & Annoyances

Every country in the world has its robbers and petty thieves, whether you are in the polite society of Japan or the northern wilds of Canada. If you hang out in the slums of a large city where you are unknown, if you are staggering drunk in a back alley, if you trust a stranger to hold your cash while you run to the washroom, if you leave your pack or camera on the seat of your bus while you go for a *salteña*, you are going to have a sad tale to tell.

◆ Common-Sense Precautions

Be aware of your surroundings. If you think you are being followed, go into a store or knock on someone's door. Make certain that expensive items like your camera or Rolex watch are out of sight. Carry only a bit of cash in your pocket and a larger amount in your money belt. Leave the rest in the hotel safe. Using ATMs keeps the amount of cash on hand to a minimum. Hide your card well.

Be inside at night or take a **taxi** back to your room if you have been out late. Don't be **drunk** in public – it makes you an easy target. Don't get mixed up in the **dope** trade. The mandatory sentence for possession of cocaine is eight years.

Women should walk with confidence. If you appear frightened or lost, you are a target. Don't walk alone in non-populated places or along secluded trails.

In the event that you are grabbed or accosted in any way, create a scene. Holler, scream, kick and fight with all your might. However, if you are approached by someone with a weapon, let them have it all. Being dead or seriously maimed isn't worth any possession, including your virginity. Most **robberies** are not violent.

There are a few **pickpockets** in the larger urban centers. In Copacabana, where pickpocketing during festivals is notorious, the Bolivians swear that it is Peruvians who come to target unsuspecting tourists.

Another common place for pickpockets is along Calle Santa Cruz, just below San Francisco Square in La Paz. The street is crowded and the pickpockets like to separate tourists from one another and then go after their packs. Also look for quick-handed thieves at the bus station area around El Cementerio.

A common trick to get you off guard is to have someone pour something onto your clothes or pack and then offer to clean it off. While they are cleaning your clothes, they are also frisking your pockets and bag. Move away from any such scene.

◆ Emergency Assistance

Should you be robbed, report the incident to the **Tourist Police**, Plaza del Stadium, Olympia Building #1314, ☎ 222-5016. You should make a report to your consulate or embassy. This is important, as most embassies inform other travelers of the latest scams. The police will investigate irregularities in prices with tourist agencies, hotels, shows or car rentals and will fill out forms that will allow you to claim any loss on your insurance. The chance of retrieving your goods, however, is almost nil.

The tourist police wear green uniforms (the army wears camouflage green) and can be seen walking the streets. However, my experience is that any police person will give a foreigner assistance in the event of a problem. They are also good for directions.

TRAVEL INFORMATION

❖   THE LATEST SCAM

You are approached by another "tourist" and asked directions or just engaged in conversation. The "tourist" claims to be from a neighboring country, which explains his accent and appearance. A second man will come up, flash an official "National Police" card and ask to see passports. The first "tourist" will readily turn over his passport; the idea is that you will do the same. If you refuse, the "police man" will offer to take you to the police station where you will feel safe turning over your passport. He will call a taxi on his cell phone. Before he gets to that stage, tell them where to go under no uncertain terms (I use strong profanity) and walk away quickly. Get into the nearest shop or hotel. These people are often armed and are considered dangerous. Their aim is to mug you inside the car.

The police in Bolivia wear uniforms and do not use taxis. You will meet plain-clothes Immigration officials at airports, bus and train stations. They will ask to see passports, often while the police are rummaging through your bags.

Communications

◆ Telephones

Bolivia's country code is 591. To call Bolivia from the US, dial 011-591, then the local number. To call the US from Bolivia, dial 1, plus the area code, plus the number. To call Bolivia from Canada, dial 011-591, then the number. To call Canada from Bolivia, dial 1, plus the area code, then the local number. If you are calling Bolivia from Great Britain, dial 00-591 and then the number. If you are calling Great Britain from Bolivia, dial 1, 44 (the country code), then the telephone number.

When in the country, only the city number and regional number are required. City numbers must be dialed only if calling from another city. La Paz's city number is 2. Regional numbers have seven digits.

For information, dial 800-10-4040. There is no charge for this service.

You may make a call from your hotel, from the telephones on the street or from the **Entel** and **Cotel** offices. If calling from the hotel, you'll pay almost double. Public phone booths require a calling card that can be purchased in 10, 20, 50 or 100 boliviano ($1.50 to $15) denominations. You may also call from a phone on the street that is like a private phone and usually on the counter of a street vendor's stall. This telephone is for local calls only and costs one boliviano (13¢). Calls from these phones automatically cut off after two minutes, at which time you will have to pay another boliviano to reconnect.

Locals calls are free from the phone offices. For long distance calls, the phones are often connected to a computer and display the time and cost as you talk. If you do not know a telephone number that you wish to reach, you must connect to an international operator to get it. If you know the country number, the area code and the telephone number you are trying to reach, you can call direct. The cost of phoning North America is $1 per minute and Europe is about $1.50 per minute.

◆ Media

The Llama Express, Avenida Arce 2131, Edificio Illampu, 10th floor, ☎ 244-1307, is an English-language paper that comes out once a month and is loaded with useful information for tourists. It contains travel reports, travel advice, restaurant reviews and entertainment listings. This free paper came to life to replace the much more elaborate *Bolivian Times*, a good weekly paper that has been bought by one of the dailies and is no longer in print. *Bolivia Touring* is another English/Spanish newspaper directed at tourists. This one allows you to read in Spanish and check your understanding by re-reading the article in English. It comes out on the 5th of every month and is distributed in tourist haunts in La Paz, Cochabamba, Sucre and Potosi and in major centers in Chile and Peru. If you have questions or comments, reach them at ☎ 241-4319, boliviatouring@megalink. com.

There are five daily newspapers in La Paz. All are in Spanish and cost around 50¢ each.

Bolivia has 125 **radio** stations, most of which are privately owned. I found none in English. Except for local stations, **television** is usually delivered by cable. There are 48 TV stations and all are in Spanish. English cable TV is available in a few hotels.

◆ Real Mail & E-Mail

Internet cafés are as common as shoe shine boys. Those cities that do not have cable connection charge about $2 per hour for Internet service, which is often slow. However, you can use the computer at a lower rate if not on line. Those with cable connection charge less than 50¢ an hour and the service is fast. If you want to connect your laptop to a cable outlet, go to an Entel office, where the hook-up charge is $4.50 an hour.

Postal service is fairly reliable. The cost to send a postcard or lightweight letter to North America is 50¢ and double that to get it to a country in Europe. It's best to send parcels from larger cities. If sending something valuable, insure and/or register it. There are also courier services like FedEx, UPS and DHL that cost about $30 to North America and more to Europe.

To receive mail, have it sent to "lista de correos" (the poste restante) in any large city. The mail is held for three months and in order to collect it you must have your passport for ID. The mail should be addressed to you, and then "Post Restante, Correo Central, City, District," with "Bolivia" clearly written on the envelope.

Culture Shock

Public affection is not uncommon in Bolivia. Young lovers can often be seen kissing, holding hands or hugging on a park bench. Anything beyond that is usually kept private.

Homosexual relationships exist, but public displays of such affection are dangerous. Homosexuality is treated as a perversion. In 2002 a group of lesbian feminists were filming a TV series on sexuality in Bolivia. The police beat and kicked the actors and tear-gassed the spectators. Many people suspected of being gay have been murdered or harassed. The constitution states that everyone has the right to a private life, but this means little.

There are a few organizations in Bolivia that promote equality for lesbigays. **Dignidad** was formed in 1980 in Cochabamba and in 1994 the first gay-day celebration was held. In 1995 the **MGLP**, a gay rights organization, was formed, and then **Mujeres Creando** for women was established. But members of these groups are often harassed.

Special needs travelers will find it difficult to travel here. Sidewalks are barely safe for walking with hiking boots, never mind trying to maneuver a wheelchair. The roads are mostly cobblestone, so crossing intersections is difficult. Wheelchair accessibility in hotels and restaurants is nonexistent.

At crosswalks or corners, pedestrians get no respect, even if they are in wheelchairs or have canes. However, police will help people cross if they notice that help is needed.

There are no communication services available for the deaf. Vision-impaired people use white canes and ask the same question (such as, "Is the light red?") until someone stops to give assistance. However, traveling with a seeing or hearing companion could make the trip an exceptional experience.

Traveling with **children** is always a positive in Latin American countries and Bolivia is no exception. There are many playgrounds and children's museums and hotels and restaurants can also be found that are clean and comfortable enough for little folk. Airlines give children under 12 a discount of 50%, but if they occupy a seat on the bus they pay full fare. Places like Dumbo's offer children's portions for meals and have play rooms.

Seniors will have to take common-sense precautions. Crossing roads could be a problem, as the traffic seems to aim at pedestrians; stoplights and crosswalks mean nothing, even if police are present. Use taxis and, on longer trips, hire a jeep rather than use public buses. LAB and AeroSur offer discounts on flights for anyone over 60.

Begging is as common in Bolivia as it is in any area in North America. There are a number of ways to deal with this problem. You can purchase and carry food to give to people. You can allow yourself a daily budget and give no more than that amount. A friend of mine liked to have a beer at night, so he would purchase a beer at a *tienda* close to the hotel. The bot-

Going Metric

GENERAL MEASUREMENTS

To make your travels a little easier, we have provided the following chart
that shows metric equivalents for the measurements you are familiar with.

1 kilometer	=	.6124 miles
1 mile	=	1.6093 kilometers
1 foot	=	.304 meters
1 inch	=	2.54 centimeters
1 square mile	=	2.59 square kilometers
1 pound	=	.4536 kilograms
1 ounce	=	28.35 grams
1 imperial gallon	=	4.5459 liters
1 US gallon	=	3.7854 liters
1 quart	=	.94635 liters

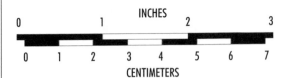

TEMPERATURES

For Farenheit: Multiply centigrade figure by 1.8 and add 32
For Centigrade: Subtract 32 from Farenheit figure and divide by 1.8.

Centigrade		Farenheit
40°	=	104°
35°	=	95°
30°	=	86°
25°	=	77°
20°	=	64°
15°	=	59°
10°	=	50°

tles required a deposit. When he returned the bottle, he left the deposit with the *tienda* attendant for her to give to whoever needed a handout, or he would give the bottles to a hungry-looking kid. Doggie-bags are common in most upscale cafés. I often had my leftovers put in these and gave them to a poor-looking family on the street.

Shoe shine boys in Bolivia wear face masks and have designated territories. The government gives them ID (the kids pay for it) and the police resolve turf disputes. Although the syndication of these kids is not perfect, it is making life for them much better.

Shopping

◆ Local Delights

Bolivia is known for its **Andean weavings**, pieces of material made from either llama, alpaca or sheep wool (vicuña wool is rarely used). The wool is hand-dyed and hand woven into designs that date back to times before Christ.

Indigenous people wear their weavings and make more to sell. There are co-ops to help the people in the outlying areas get a fair price for their work.

> ### ❖ WEAVING A YARN
>
> You will often see an Indian woman sitting with a spool in her hand, spinning wool or llama hair. This is the first stage of the spin. Next, two of these thin strands are combined to form a thicker strand. This is then dyed before the yarn is again spun. This process is unique to Bolivia. The third spinning is called the over spin, which produces a crepe twist, a yarn that is both strong and elastic.

Weaving designs indicate the social status of the weaver. The colors and positions of the stripes are usually artistic preference. Images of deities and mythical characters also appear on many pieces. Some of the more common figures are the llama, the condor and the puma.

If you want to purchase a weaving, distinguish between factory-made and hand-made pieces. Factory-made weavings are taking over the market and hand-made pieces are becoming harder to find.

> **LOCAL LOVE:** *In the highlands, men make belts for their wives or girlfriends on a lap-loom.*

Instruments, such as pan flutes, pipe flutes, charangos (ukulele-styled instruments) and drums, are found everywhere. One of my favorites is the musical rattle made of goat hooves. If you want to purchase good quality instruments, buy them from a reputable store in La Paz or Sucre. See recommendations under *Shopping* in these cities.

> **AUTHOR NOTE:** *Be aware that charangos made of armadillo shells cannot legally be taken into North America or most European countries. The armadillo is a protected species.*

◆ Antiques & Silver

Bolivia is inundated with new and old antiques. It is illegal to export any genuine antique without special permission. There is one shop in La Paz that sells good quality items not seen in the general market. Things like miner's lamps and saddle stirrups found in the market, although not classified as antiques, make interesting souvenirs.

Buying silver in Potosi is a must. There are many designs copied from colonial days, plus some new items like souvenir teaspoons and letter openers. The purer the silver, the softer it is. The price for a nice letter opener is about $5.

Food

Bolivian food is not distinctive, but the food is very good. There are llama steaks, *pico de la macho*, flan or *Para Ti* chocolates. I like to pick up fresh vegetables, homemade cheeses and crusty buns in the market and eat them in my room. I like the market cafés that specialize in specific meals or special soups, always hot and spicy. Street vendors serving their specialties like sausages or *salteñas* are worth a 10-minute wait. And restaurants like the Rincón Español in La Paz and Casa de Camba in Santa Cruz make French cuisine look almost second rate. There are also night clubs like Thelonius that make it worthwhile sitting up until midnight listening to first-rate jazz and digesting.

I also eat in the *tiendas* where the buses stop. Watch what you buy – see where the locals are flocking to and follow them. I suggest that you try things even if you don't have a clue as to what they are. For the most part, you will be pleasantly surprised.

❖ RESTAURANT PRICING	
$	under $5
$$	$5 to $10
$$$	$11 to $25
$$$$	$26 to $50
$$$$$	over $50

◆ Meals of the Day

Desayuno (dez-ay-OO-no) is the word for breakfast. Bolivians do breakfast in the street *tiendas*, with the big item being the *salteña* (see decription below). At the North American café-clones like Alexander and ice cream shops like Dumbos, you can get bacon and eggs or fruit with yogurt and granola.

> **WARNING: Bolivianos** *do not eat toast and when they make it for tourists, the results are always disappointing. They use some sort of wonder bread and toast it on one side. My husband smuggles panacitos into places like Alexander to eat with his bacon and eggs.*

Almuerzo (al-moo-ER-zo) is the main meal of the day, served from noon until two. Special restaurants make *almuerzo del día* for a reasonable price, usually just a couple of dollars. A typical *almuerzo del día* will consist of a lemonade or another type of drink made interesting with spices, a soup with noodles, meat, vegetables, French fries, and a dessert. Not all places serving *almuerzo del día* are the same. Sometimes black, red or blue potatoes are substituted for the fries. Sometimes the dessert is nothing more than a dish of gelatin. In smaller centers (away from La Paz), the *almuerzo* will be more traditional. In La Paz, the main course will be more like North American meals. There is almost always a sign outside the door of the restaurant advertising what is being served that day.

Cena (SAY-na) is supper and is usually a light meal served well after seven in the evening. Trying to get supper before seven is like trying to get a bus to depart on time.

◆ Foods – The Good, the Bad & the Tasteless

Panacitas are fresh crusty rolls that are excellent eaten with some fruit or cheese. The rolls are so tasty you need no butter.

Mate de coca is a mild tea made with coca leaves and enjoyed by everyone. It is believed to stave off altitude sickness.

Chicha is a beer brewed with aysuma and waltaco varieties of yellow corn (there are about 220 varieties of corn grown in Bolivia). *Chicha* is believed to be a drink of the gods. In small towns, *Chicha* bars have white flags flapping from poles outside houses.

> ### ❖ WELCOME TO THE FAMILY, LLAMA
>
> Upon arrival home after a long journey, lead llamas are given *chicha* that is placed in a special bowl called a *kerus*. These wooden bowls are always decorated with a llama, carved from wood and glued into the center of the bowl. Besides sharing the drinks of their owners, llamas are also considered family members and are often given family names.

Salteñas are a pastry stuffed with meat and vegetables (the filling varies). They originated in Salta, just across the border in Argentina. They are Bolivia's original fast food and everyone eats them all the time. Fall in line.

> ### ❖ COFFEE LINGO
>
> | | |
> |---|---|
> | Filtrado | drip (hard to find) |
> | Estilado | expresso |
> | Extracto | the syrup, café distilado |
> | Americano | strong coffee |
> | Expresso/cappicino | often from a powdered mix |

Laguas is a tasty corn soup.

Escabeche are pickled vegetables used as a side dish or sometimes stuffed inside a sandwich.

Chejchi is a speckled gray and white corn that is toasted and eaten with butter. This corn can be picked up from the street vendors.

LOCAL LINGO: *If eye contact is made by someone eating when you walk through a restaurant, proper conduct demands that you say Bien Provecho (bee-YAIN pro-BEY-cho) to them as you pass. The term is equivalent to bon appétit in French.*

Pique a la Macho is a spicy stew cooked with Bolivia's special sausage and served over French fries.

Choclo is a white, large-kernel corn that is boiled on the cob and, in season, sold everywhere.

Yucca is a root vegetable similar to potato. It has a stringy texture.

Potatoes need no explaining. However, the Andes has over 250 types of potatoes. They are served freeze-dried, fried, boiled, mashed, ground or raw. They can be white, red, yellow, black, blue or green and every shade between. The freeze-dried ones are the worst.

Surubi is a fresh-water catfish that is usually served grilled. It is excellent, as is the bonier **dorado**.

Llaucha paceña is a doughy cheese-bread sold at bus and train stations especially. This is an excellent snack that is sold in bags of a dozen for a couple of bolivianos.

Tamales are made from cornmeal stuffed in the center with spiced meat and/or vegetables, rolled into a banana leaf and baked.

Humitas are made with sweetened corn rolled into a banana leaf and steamed or baked.

Rellenos are a wheat flour pancake stuffed with cheese and deep fried.

Quinoa is a grain that grows at high elevations. It is high in protein and is often cooked in soups and stews. The plant comes in red, green or yellow and has clusters of grain along the upper portion of the stem.

Haba is short for *habichuela*, or bean in English.

Singani is distilled wine produced in the Tarija area. Singani is the base for the cocktail called *chuflay.*

Changa de pollo o de conejo is a soup made with chicken or rabbit, potato, peas, beans and green onions.

Sandwich de chola is a roast leg of pork sandwich.

Chicharron are pieces of fried pork sausage cooked with *chicha*.

Lechon is roast suckling pig.

Papas a la huancaina are potatoes with cheese, boiled eggs, tomatoes and olives, topped with a peanut sauce.

Selecting a Place to Stay

◆ Value & Pricing

When I describe places to stay, I make comments like, "The rooms have Inca beds." This sounds silly for those not familiar with Bolivia. However, an Inca bed is one that is hard as stone. Carpets are often dirty or moldy, so when I say a place has tile, that is good. The importance of a

❖ HOTEL PRICING	
$	$10 to $20
$$	$21 to $50
$$$	$51 to $75
$$$$	$76 to $100
$$$$$	over $100

closet in a room will be appreciated after staying in a few rooms that have no place to put things. The electrical showers are freaky for Westerners so, whenever possible, I make it known if a water tank is actually in use. Also note that just because the price is high, it does not mean the quality is as well. For example, in Oruro, generally the prices are high and the quality is low. Read the descriptions carefully before choosing to stay someplace, especially if arriving late at night when you are unable to look around.

Be aware that sewers are not able to flush out toilet paper, so in every bathroom there is a garbage can where used toilet paper must be deposited. If your room has not been cleaned for a day, your garbage has not either. If this happens, place your garbage can outside your door and use a plastic bag.

◆ Types of Accommodations

Bolivia has numerous names for accommodations, each indicating to some degree the quality of room you will get. Here's a quick rundown.

- ❖ *Alojamientos* are basic with an Inca bed, heavy blankets and not much more. They usually, but not always, have shared bathrooms with hot showers. Depending on quality, a room costs between one and two dollars per person.

- ❖ *Residenciales/Casas de Huespedes/*Hostels are usually much better in quality than *alojamientos*. You should get a clean room with the choice of a private or shared bathroom and hot showers. These places often offer laundry facilities and have restaurants or kitchens attached. The cost runs anywhere from $5-$25 per person.

- ❖ **Hotels** are usually a bit higher priced and offer anything from dirty and drab to luxurious. Prices vary accordingly but seldom did I find a hotel room costing more than $50 for two per night.

- ❖ **Motels**, for the most part, are heavily secured places that rent rooms by the hour. Guess what happens there.

- ❖ **Pensions** are for locals only and are boarding houses that do not rent rooms to the public.

Getting Here

◆ By Air

There are many options for getting in and out of Bolivia. Those with little time fly directly into and out of La Paz. There are no Canadian or American airlines with service to Bolivia. Bolivian airlines that fly internationally are **Lloyd Airlines Bolivia**, or LAB (☎ 800-337-0918 in US, 800-10-3001 in Bolivia, www.labairlines.com), **TACA** (☎ 800-525-8780, www.taca.com) and **TAM** (☎ 244-3487, www.tam.com.br).

Flying directly into La Paz is expensive and you run the risk of altitude sickness. It is much better to make your way up to this elevation slowly. If you do not have the time, a flight from Lima (Peru) or from Santiago (Chile) to La Paz is about $200. **Lan Chile** (☎ 800-735-5526, www.lanchile.com) and **Aerolineas Argentinas** (☎ 591-2-235-1711, www.aerolineas.com) also fly into La Paz. The other option is to fly into Santa Cruz via La Paz.

American Airlines, Pl. Venezuela #1440, Ed. Hermann, ☎ 235-3804 (local) or 800-433-7300, www.aa.com, now has daily flights from Miami direct to La Paz and Santa Cruz. The price, depending on the season, is about $600 for a return ticket. In my experience, American is an excellent company.

Although we give airline contact numbers throughout this book, it is not advisable to work directly with an airline in Bolivia. One should go to a travel agent if purchasing a ticket.

◆ By Car

Driving into Bolivia is not recommended, but some people still do it. The roads are bad and you must have a four-wheel-drive vehicle to handle them, as well as excellent Spanish skills to navigate the paper requirements. You must also have registration, insurance and a bill showing the value of the vehicle. Once in the country, every town has a control post and you must have papers permitting you to pass. If the papers are not in order, the bureaucratic quagmire starts. Also, the police, who are poorly paid, know you have money. Although many are honest, there are always some who will try every type of extortion possible to improve their incomes. It's worth noting that most ex-patriots who live in Bolivia do not drive because of the police hassles.

If you decide to drive, an International Driving Permit is required. If coming in with a motorcycle, it is best to cross during the early part of the day and not during the weekend. The paperwork takes a lot of time to process, partly because officials are not certain what to do with you.

Gasoline is available from international companies at all major centers. The national company is **YPFB** (Yacimientos Petroliferos Fiscales Bolivianos). In the back country and small villages, unleaded fuel may still be hard to come by.

◆ Other Options

Consider flying into Santiago, Chile or Lima, Peru and then busing it into Bolivia. This gives you time to acclimatize. Others who are traveling the latest Gringo Trail that starts in Rio de Janeiro, Brazil, cross the continent from east to west, going through Bolivia to either Chile or Peru. These people usually travel by bus and boat. From Rio, you can travel to the Brazilian Pantanal and come into Bolivia at Puerto Suarez.

Those with lots of time travel from Venezuela down to Brazil. Usually they bus to Manaus on the Amazon River and then catch a boat coming up the Madera. They eventually land in Guayaramerin.

You can also bus it up from Argentina or Paraguay.

◆ Border Crossings

Tourist cards can be obtained at all border crossings and at both the La Paz and the Santa Cruz international airports. Do not lose this card, or you will be fined. If you overstay your visa (the time on your tourist card), the (nego-

tiated) fine is $40, plus $10 in local currency. These fines take time to negotiate and process.

Crossing the Peruvian border at **Kasala** is no problem.

The **Desaguadero** crossing from Peru is often held up with transport
trucks. This is a duty-free zone for the transportation of Peruvian goods to
and from the Atlantic, so you may wish to avoid this crossing.

If coming or going to Brazil, the crossings are located at **Puerto Suarez**
out of Santa Cruz and **Guayaramerin** in the northern Amazon area.

There is one crossing into Argentina at **Villazon**, south of Tupiza and another at **Yacuiba**, south of Villamontes. This road goes down to Salta.

Crossing into Chile may be done just out of Sajama National Park at
Tambo Quemada or east of Laguna Colorada on the **Uyuni Salt Lake** trip.

Not many people cross from Bolivia into Paraguay. If you must, cross the
Gran Chaco by bus or boat it through the Pantanal. Buses leave from
Santa Cruz and travel down to Asuncion. Boats can be hired in Puerto
Suarez to go into Paraguay.

Bolivian border guards cannot extend visas; they can only issue new
ones. Some people are eligible for 30 days, while others receive 90 days.
This rule is stipulated by the government and changes constantly. At present, Canadians get 30 days, while Americans and Europeans get 90.

If you have questions or complaints about the border guards or the process, ☎ 0-800-3007, a toll-free number.

There are money-changers on both sides of all borders. Be aware that
there are counterfeit Peruvian one-sole pieces being passed by changers
at Kasala to tourists leaving Bolivia.

There are also basic bathroom facilities available at the borders. Drinks,
empanadas and a few trinkets are offered for sale by street vendors.

If traveling from Peru to Bolivia, do not buy a ticket from Puno to La Paz
as you will sit for a few hours in Copacabana waiting for your connection,
even though there are other buses going to La Paz.

◆ Outfitters Who Do All the Work

There are companies in Europe and North America who will arrange your
entire trip. They meet you at the airport, take you on your tour, negotiate all
accommodations, transportation and meals and, at the end of your stay,
deliver you back at the airport.

Kon-Tiki Tours & Travel, 940 Lincoln Road, Ste. 322, Miami Beach, FL
33139, ☎ 305-673-0092, 877-566-8454, www.kontiki.org, offer ecologically sound and culturally sensitive tours to Amboro National Park,
Serrania Volcano area, birding around Trinidad, Amazon rainforest, Chaco
woodlands and the Cerrado pampas. They are the only company who will
go to San Borja. They also run trips to Madidi National Park and offer
kayaking down the Mamore River. The all-inclusive tours run about $200 a
day, double occupancy.

Andean Summits, 710 Calle Prolongacion Armaza, Sopocachi area of
La Paz, ☎ 242-2106, www.andeansummits.com, is the best company for
climbing/hiking activities. In business since 1992, Andean offers climbs for
anyone from the curious with minimum skills to the intense climber who
wants maximum technical difficulty. Besides helping you bag a high peak,

Andean will take you rock climbing in places that are not usually explored by outsiders.

For trekkers, Andean covers routes that go to elevations over 16,500 ft/5,000 m with a gain of over 3,300 ft/1,000 m per day.

Andean Summits is affiliated with Gravity Assisted Mountain Biking, allowing you to customize your trip by adding a few days biking.

The guides have been trained and certified by groups like the German Alpine Club and The National Ski and Alpine School of Chamonix. All are members of the Bolivian Mountain Guides Association and some have had more than 25 years of experience in the mountains. There is one guide for every three or four people and one guide for every two people on technical climbs. The cooks, porters and muleteers are local people who are experienced and skilled at their jobs. The meals are exceptional.

Tours include round-trip transportation from La Paz, mules and porters, cooks, full board, specialized guides, common camping equipment (including two-person tents) and common climbing gear (including live ropes, ice screws, snow stakes and slings). Although they don't supply boots, crampons, ice axes and harnesses, these can be rented in La Paz.

Astronomical Tours, 149 NW 00 Highway Warrensburg, MO 64093, ☎ 888-734-0311, www.astronomicaltours.net or www.astronomicaltours.net/astrotours.htm, runs a specialized tour for star gazers and astrophotographers. Once a year they travel to a village on Lake Titikaka where they sleep most of the day and look at the heavens all night. The cost for a one-week, all-inclusive tour from Miami is less than $2,000 per person, including airfare. You may bring your own telescope, but luggage is limited to two bags of no more than 65 lbs/30 kg each, plus one carry-on of 45 lbs/20 kg. A certified doctor accompanies the trip in the event of altitude sickness among the star-gazers.

Explore Bolivia, 2510 N. 47th Street, Suite 204, Boulder, CO 80301, ☎ 303-545-5728, www.explorebolivia.com, has some excellent outdoor adventures. Their combination kayak/hike trip includes three days paddling around Lake Titikaka. The second leg of the trip includes a week-long hike through the Apolobamba region where the Kallawaya Medicine men live. This company looks after everything once you arrive in Bolivia. Their gear is North American quality and the food they provide is better than anything you would be able to prepare.

This company also offers a longer kayaking-only trip around the lake, as well as excursions specializing in climbing, birding, mountain biking and fishing that include terrain in the jungle and/or in the high Andes.

GAP Adventures, 19 Duncan Street, Toronto, Ontario, M5H 3H1, Canada, ☎ 800-465-5600, www.gap.ca, has a reasonably priced, 11-day tour called the Bolivian Discovery, that starts in La Paz and includes Sucre, Potosi, Uyuni and Tiahuanaco or Chacaltaya. The cost is $683 for 10 days and their tours take a maximum of 12 people, with an average of eight or nine in each group. They cater to people in 22 countries, so there's usually a mix of cultures.

GAP hires mostly Canadian leaders and has a bilingual guide who lives in Bolivia all year. They support locally owned businesses and work with NGOs such as Conservation International, International Eco-tourism Society and the Charles Darwin Foundation. GAP also offers trips to the isolated Pantanal area with the largest wetland complex in the world.

For the more adventuresome, GAP offers a longer 146 days of touring from Lima, Peru through Bolivia and down into Chile.

Wildland Tours, 3516 NE 155th Street, Seattle, WA, ☎ 800-345-4453, www.wildland.com, offers tours that are ecologically sensitive and physically challenging. One tour includes hiking across the Cordillera Real and over three passes at about 15,000 ft/4,600 m. It begins near Sorata and ends in the Apolobamba area. For acclimatization, they hike around Isla del Sol. For a grand finale, you spend your last night in La Paz at the luxurious Paris Hotel. The cost of this tour is about $150 per day.

Wildland also goes into Noel Kempff Mercado National Park in the eastern outback. This nine-day tour includes hiking and birding at a cost of around $250 per day.

Footprint Adventures, United Kingdom, ☎ 01522-804929, www.footprint-adventures.co.uk, has a combination kayak/hike trip that takes 15 days, starting with your arrival in La Paz. They paddle around Lake Titikaka for two days and then head on foot from Sorata through villages such as Kukoyo and Waraco, and then on to Checapa Valley and Alta Khota. They eventually end at Condoriri. Sorata, where the hike starts, is at 8,500 ft/2,600 m elevation and the route goes up as high as 16,500 ft/5,000 m. On the approach to Condoriri, you climb to 18,750 ft/5,700 m, where Juri Khota Lake is located. The per day cost of $100 includes kayaks, English-speaking guides, cooks, camping equipment and mules that will carry up to 45 lbs/20 kilos of luggage. Not included in this rate are your high altitude clothing, sleeping bags, insurance or headlamps.

❖ INFORMATION SOURCES

Government Tourist Offices, except for the occasional one that I mention in connection with certain cities, are not worth visiting. The workers have no material to share with tourists and less interest in giving information. Most seem to have been hired because they are related to someone important. It is best to get information from tour agencies. They have a vested interest in promoting their area and usually do so enthusiastically.

Getting Around

The standard of public transportation is not what most North Americans or Europeans are accustomed to. There are 25,100 miles/41,000 km of roads in Bolivia, 75% of which are dirt and gravel, in bad shape, and can be dangerous if they are in the mountains.

But conditions are improving. In 2002 the World Bank and the International Development Association lent money to be used for road improvements. One of the deciding factors for the loans was that there are about 1,000 fatalities a year due to road accidents.

Bolivia's rail system features 2,300 miles/3,700 km of narrow-guage track. During the last national transportation survey it was learned that the railway carries 535 million tons of freight and 2.4 million people per year. Passenger trains pass through major centers about twice a week, but it is the route between Oruro and Uyuni that is most often used by travelers.

◆ Air Travel

Both La Paz and Santa Cruz have international airports and there are 12 domestic airports with paved runways throughout the country. Unpaved runways like the one in Rurrenabaque, for example, during rainy season cause delays in flights due to wet landing strips. The capital cities in all districts have paved runways.

Lloyd Airlines Bolivia, LAB, (Av. Camacho # 1456-60, La Paz, ☎ 800-337-0918 in US, 800-10-3001 in Bolivia, www.labairlines.com) offers a $300, five-stop ticket that must be used in 30 days. Fares when flying without the five-stop ticket are also low. There is no discount for round-trip tickets. Lloyd gives a discount for married couples, but they must have the same last name on their passports or show a marriage certificate. Lloyd also gives a 20% discount for anyone over 60 years of age. For this you must show your passport.

AeroSur (Av. 16 de Julio # 616, La Paz, ☎ 231-3233 or 336-7400, www.aerosur.com) is Lloyd's competition. Their service is excellent, but their prices are higher. A flight from Sucre to Cochabamba is $42 and it takes 35 minutes. A flight from Tarija to Santa Cruz is $98 and takes 50 minutes. AeroSur offers many of the same flights and discounts as Lloyd and, in addition, they reach some outback places that Lloyd does not.

TAM, Transport Air Militar (Plaza Estudiante #11931, La Paz, (☎ 244-3487, www.tam.com.br) is the military airline that also takes civilians into the places they service. TAM and Amaszonas Air, for example, are the only airlines going into Rurrenabaque or San Borja. A TAM flight from La Paz to Rurrenabaque costs $46.50 each way. The only drawback with TAM is that you could get bumped from a flight if urgent military affairs dictate that a fat general needs your seat.

SAVE (Calle Federico Ziazo, La Paz, ☎ 212-1548) is a small company that flies between La Paz and Trinidad, between Trinidad and Cochabamba and between Santa Cruz and Puerto Suarez.

Amaszonas Air (Av Saavedra #1649, Miraflores, ☎ 333-8263) is a small airline that does most of the transporting of passengers in the Amazon Basin to places that have only small landing strips.

◆ Buses, Trucks & Taxis

Micros are small vehicles (usually Toyota vans) that carry up to 25 people city-wide and cost 30¢ per person. They go to any part of most cities.

Minibuses are actually vans that carry 12 passengers, cost 30¢ to 50¢ per person and go anywhere in the city. Some run directly from downtown to the airport. These are safe and high quality. When these buses go out of the city, they are called *trufis*.

Colectivos are taxis that carry four people legally and go anywhere in the downtown areas of larger cities. *Colectivos* cost about 45¢ per person. A ride, not the price, must be negotiated. You put your hand out, the driver stops, you yell where you want to go and he either lets you in because he is going in that direction or he leaves you standing because he isn't.

Taxis cost around 45¢ per person within city limits and they transport only your party. From the airport in La Paz a private taxi to downtown costs about $7. A minibus caught just outside the airport door costs 60¢. If you arrive after a long flight, I recommend you take a taxi to your hotel, especially if you do not know the city.

There are over 100 bus companies in La Paz alone. Long-distance buses called *flotas* usually have numbered seats for passengers who leave from the originating station.

All passengers boarding buses that are leaving from a bus terminal must pay a 25¢ tax before being permitted to board. Usually, the tax ticket, once you buy it, is pasted onto your bus ticket. However, occasionally when there is no tax booth a girl will stand at the door of the bus and collect the tax. She will give you a receipt.

Trufis are small buses that go between villages. They don't go much farther than 60 miles/100 km, at which point you can catch a second *trufi*.

Camiones are trucks that transport human cargo along with everything else from silver to beer. Occasionally, foreigners will be refused rides in the backs of trucks. If the trucks are full, the locals, who are the steady customers, come first.

You may catch a bus or truck either at the bus station or at the police post on the edge of town. If you go to the police post you give up almost all possibility of getting a seat. The only advantage is that you pay less.

◆ Driving

Driving your own vehicle or renting one is not recommended. See *Getting Here*, page 44, for more details. However, if you must rent a vehicle, I have listed a few places in the appropriate chapter.

Bicycles are difficult to use because of the high altitude and narrow roads. Cycling as a sport is different. I have included bicycle tours in regional chapters.

Motorbikes are available for rent in Sucre.

◆ Boating

There is one boat company that transports tourists between Puno, Peru and Copacabana on Lake Titikaka. See *Copacabana*, page 104, for that information.

Directory

GENERAL DIRECTORY

■ AIRLINES

Aerolinas Argentinas	☎ 235-1624	www.aerolineas.com.ar
Amaszonas Air	☎ 333-8263	
American Airlines	☎ 800-433-7300; 235-3804	www.aa.com
AeroSur	☎ 231-3233; 336-7400	www.aerosur.com
Lan Chile	☎ 800-735-5526 or 231-7108	www.lanchile.com
Lloyd Air Bolivia	☎ 800-337-0918 (US)	www.labairlines.com
	☎ 800-10-3001 (Bolivia)	
SAVE	☎ 212-1548	
TACA Airlines	☎ 800-535-8780	www.grupotaca.com
TAM	☎ 244-3487	www.tam.com.br

■ OUTFITTERS & TOUR OPERATORS

Andean Summits	☎ 242-2106	www.andeansummits.com
Astronomical Tours	☎ 888-734-0311	www.icstars.com
Explore Bolivia	☎ 303-545-5728	www.explorebolivia.com
Footprint Adventures	☎ 01522-804929	www.footprint-adventures.co.uk
GAP Adventures	☎ 800-465-5600	www.gap.ca
Kon-Tiki Tours	☎ 305-673-0092/877-566-8454	www.kontiki.org
Wildland Tours	☎ 800-345-4453	www.wildland.com

■ CAR RENTAL COMPANIES

Kolla Motors	☎ 241-9141	www.collamotors.com
Localiza	☎ 244-1011	
American Rent-a-car	☎ 7720-0367 (cell)	
AdMo-Tours	☎ 245-1660	www.adno-tours.com

■ EMERGENCIES

Tourist Police	☎ 222-5016	
US Center for Disease Control & Prevention		www.cdc.gov
Visa/Mastercard	☎ 800-336-3386	www.visa.com
		www.mastercard.com
Western Union	☎ 800-10-5057	www.westernunion.com

■ USEFUL WEBSITES

www.boliviabiz.com

www.bolivia.com (Spanish language)

www.bolivia-internet.com (Spanish language)

La Paz & Vicinity

Altitude: in town, 11,916 ft/3,632 m; at the airport, 13,392 ft/4,082 m.
Population: One million-plus

Introduction

La Paz is not a big city on the world scale, but it is certainly one of the more interesting ones. Built in a bowl created by the Choqueyapu River, the upper parts of the city stand 1,645 ft/ 500 m above the lower sections. Unlike any other city in the world, the richer neighborhoods are located at the lower levels. This is partly due to the fact that it is warmer and easier to breathe at the lower altitudes. Also, the pinnacles and spires of conglomerate rock and clay that have been sculptured by wind and water make a dramatic backdrop for those living below them. The higher up

the bowl one goes, the more unstable the land becomes and the more likely a landslide will occur.

The plazas, squares and Prado are well kept in La Paz and even in the depth of winter plants are tended to help make the city attractive. Street cleaners are out every day and local merchants regularly wash the area in front of their shops. On a clear day, Mount Illimani, a snow-covered monolith, can be seen as a sentry towering over the city.

❖ MURURALA MYTHOLOGY

Illimani has three main peaks. The northernmost peak is 21,500 ft/ 6,500 m high, the central and southernmost peaks are about 21,000 ft/6,200 m. Nearby is Mount Mururala, a snow-covered mountain with a flat top that stands below Illimani. Mythology claims that Mururala was at one time a tall and vain giant. But Illimani threw a stone and yelled, "Sarjami!," which means "be off with you" in Aymara. The giant's head rolled across the Altiplano and came to rest near two sisters. The head became the mountain now called Sajama, Bolivia's highest peak, and the sisters are the volcanoes, Parinacota and Pomerata.

The restaurants of La Paz offer both an exotic and ethnic smorgasbord for visitors. Hotels can be found tucked between artisan shops and street *tiendas* that are selling everything from mounted tarantulas (not considered endangered) to silver soup tureens. The nightlife is peppered with everything from Andean pan flute music to jazz bars featuring world-famous players to wild discos and secluded piano bars.

More than half of the one million people living in La Paz are of pure Andean descent and many of them are in the streets promoting the arts of their culture or selling the produce of their relatives. The markets around Plaza San Francisco and Plaza Murillo bristle with fresh produce, handmade artifacts and factory-produced junk. Every tour in the country can be booked through an agency in La Paz or the city can be visited solely for shopping or cultural events.

Getting Here & Around

◆ By Air

Lloyd Air Bolivia and AeroSur fly to most places in Bolivia. Destinations not covered by these two companies are serviced by TAM, SAVE and Amaszonas Air (see page 43 for contact details). Between them, these airlines provide numerous flights from La Paz. There are four flights a week to Cobija, 32 flights a week to Cochabamba, two flights a week to Guayaramerin, three flights a week to Puerto Suarez, two flights to Riberalta, 22 flights a week to Rurrenabaque, one daily to San Borja, 56 flights a week to Santa Cruz, 11 per week to Sucre, four a week to Tarija and three a week to Trinidad.

The airport is in El Alto, a place that is considered unsafe for tourists. A minibus (50¢) located just outside the airport doors goes on a freeway down a steep slope and along Avenida Santa Cruz, the city's main street. You must know where you want to get off, and then you must carry your baggage to the hotel. A taxi ($7 for up to four people) will take you all the way to your hotel. This is a fixed rate, with no room for negotiation.

TAM (☎ 244-3487, www.tam.com.br) has an airport beyond the international one at El Alto and it offers the only service to Rurrenabaque. A taxi to this airport from town is $5.50 for up to four people. The airport tax is 75¢ per person.

Often, TAM must cancel flights because their planes can't handle difficult weather conditions or wet landing fields so common in the jungle. Occasionally, they will land in Reyes, just a short bus ride from Rurrenabaque. If they offer you this alternative, it is a good one. If they cancel a flight and you can't make the next one, they will refund your money. The flights can be rocky. They do not pressurize the cabins and to protect your ears they supply cotton batten. Security is not intensive.

◆ By Bus

If arriving by bus you will arrive either at the main bus station on Avenida Guachalla #494 and the corner of Calle Sanchez Lima, ☎ 241-6545, or the Cementario, which runs along Heroes del Pacifico. It is a 45-minute walk from Cementario to San Francisco Plaza and less than half an hour from the main terminal to the plaza. Taking public buses with luggage is difficult and dangerous. A taxi will cost about 50¢ per person.

The main bus station has 39 bus lines that service the country. There is one bus a day to Arica, Chile, 24 to Cochabamba, one to Iquiqu and one to Llallagua, 35 to Oruro, four to Potosi, 20 to Santa Cruz, four to Sucre, five to Tarija, one to Tupiza, three to Yacuiba and one to Uyuni.

For the most part, you can show up whenever you are ready and wait for the next run. However, for trips with just one or two buses per day, it's best to purchase a ticket at least a day in advance.

◆ By Car & Motorcycle

Private vehicles with drivers can be hired to go anywhere. The cost ranges from $50 to $80 per day. I found **Huayna Tours** to be excellent (Calle Sagarnaga #398 at Illampu, ☎ 245-6717, berrios@mail.magalink.com). Their driver was cautious and courteous and the vehicle was in good shape. Jeeps are safer than buses for some routes.

Rentals

I don't recommend driving a car, but if you must, there are some reputable rental companies. Insurance is a must. Third-party liability coverage, although not compulsory, is highly advisable, despite the cost.

Localiza, Hotel Radisson, ☎ 244-1011, reserves@localizabolivia.com, has everything from a small Suzuki Swift to a Vagoneta Toyota Prado. Prices vary but a middle-of-the-list vehicle, such as a Vagoneta Suzuki Gran Vitara, rents for $68 a day with 92 miles/150 km at no charge and $420 per week with 643 miles/1,050 km at no charge. Localiza also has offices in Santa Cruz, Cochabamba and Tarija.

American Rent-a-Car, Avenida Camacho #1547, ☎ 7720-0367 (cell), has eight options of 4x4 vehicles. A Toyota jeep costs $70 a day with 122 miles/200 km at no extra charge. A Toyota Hilux truck is $60 a day or $400 a week, with up to 200 km/125 miles a day or 1,350 km/850 miles a week included in the price.

AdMo-Tours, Calle Illampu #815, ☎ 245-1660, www.adno-tours.com, rents motorcycles in Bolivia and Chile. You can get one with or without a guide. They have Honda XR 200R, Honda NT 400 Falcon, Honda XR 600R and 650R and Honda 750 Africa Twin. Without a guide they run $60 and $100 per day, $380 to $600 a week. With a guide the cost is $90 to $130 a day, $550 to $820 a week. For $100, they will handle all the paperwork and insurance needed to go to Peru or Chile. You must be 23 years old, have a valid and unlimited national motorcycle license and payment must be made by check or credit card. If reserving a motorcycle, you must pay four weeks prior to rental date. Cancellation fees are minimum $100 and no-shows are subject to full payment.

History

La Paz was originally a stop-off place for silver caravans going from Potosi to the coast. Mostly, the caravans stopped to dump passengers or llama skinners who got sick. Life in this outpost must have been pretty boring until some young officer decided to try his hand at gold panning and came up with a bundle. The city started to grow.

Peace was never a lasting thing in Bolivia, mostly because the Indians were treated so badly. The Spanish greed caused no end of hardship for locals and struggles for power continued among the Spanish. **Pedro de la Gasca**, the ruler of the area, beat the ruthless **Gonzalo Pizarro** at the battle of Saxahuana on April 9, 1548. In celebration, Gasco ordered **Alonzo de Mendoza**, who presided over the area now called Bolivia, to build a new city to honor this event.

On October 20, 1548, Alonzo deMendoza declared the city of Nuestra Señora de la Paz to be that place. Just over 100 years later there were over 500 Spaniards living in La Paz, on the river's west side, and twice as many indigenous people living on the opposite side of the river.

Within the first year, **Juan Gutierrez Paniagua** was hired as the city planner. His greatest achievement was the design of Plaza Murillo. The government buildings and the cathedral were placed on the square.

Services

◆ Useful Numbers

Ambulance, ☎ 118
Fire, ☎ 119
Police, ☎ 237-7385
Hospital, ☎ 222-9180

The **telephone office** is on Avenida Ayacucho #267, between Calle Camacho and Calle Mercado. It's open from 7:30 am until 10:30 pm daily. This is the main office; smaller offices are dotted around the city. Booths here are hooked up to a computer so you can see a digital display with your time and charge.

◆ Communications

The **post office** is on Avenida Mariscal Santa Cruz and Calle Oruro. It's open 8:30 am to 8 pm, Monday to Friday, and 9 am to 7 pm on Saturdays. Postage fees are about the same as in North America or Europe.

Photocopy shops are everywhere. A large business that has many machines will charge 25¢ for one 8x11 form, while a small company may charge as little as 15¢.

Internet Service. There are as many Internet cafés in Bolivia as there are shoe shine boys, so finding a machine is never difficult. If the service uses telephone lines, the average cost is $2 per hour; if there's a cable system, the cost is 50¢ an hour.

◆ Laundry

Laundry service is usually offered at hotels. There are also laundromats in town. The following are good and located near the tourist hotels. **La**

Famelia Laundry, Calle Tarija #340, ☎ 239-2943, 8 am-6 pm, charges by the kilo and does a good job. Unlike many laundry companies in town, this one opens on time and has things ready before your agreed time.

Lavenderia Maya, Calle Sagarnaga #339, ☎ 248-5639, charges by the kilo and will deliver your clothes to your hotel. They offer same-day service.

◆ Maps

Maps are available from the government office on Avenida Bautista Saavedra in Miraflorez, open 8:30 to noon and 2:30 pm to 4:30 pm. **Guzman** (☎ 273-3124, rguzman@acelerate.com) are the best Bolivian-made maps. A topographical map of Sajama, for example, costs $6. **Tu Musica**, Calle Sagarnaga #189, shop 17, ☎ 231-9162, has Berndston & Berndston maps, some trekking and climbing maps, road maps, Guzman maps and city maps.

◆ Medical Centers

UNIMED, Avenida Arce #2630, is a large association of general practitioners and specialists who charge $7 per visit. They patronize a laboratory across the street, Lab-tek, Avenida Arce and Campos, Edificio Illimani, #4, ☎ 243-1988. I think the lab needs some quality control training. If you need testing, have your doctor insist that the work be done when it is brought in. Blood tests run about $5 and stool examinations are $8.

Dr. Luis Jesus Garcia, Calle Chichas #1222, in lower Miraflores, ☎ 224-2974, is a general practitioner who has been trained in Europe. He is often recommended by the hotel administration. He will insist on coming to your hotel room and will charge $40 per visit, a steep fee for Bolivia. However, he speaks English well and gives fairly good service.

◆ Outdoor Adventure Clubs

If you are serious about climbing or skiing, you may contact either of the following clubs and go with locals. Contacting them gives you an "in" to places not mentioned in guidebooks and so not inundated with tour groups.

Club de Montañismo Halcones is actually based in Oruro at Casilla #179, cmh_oruro@yahoo.com (I could not obtain a phone number). Halcones translates into hawk or falcon, and this is a hang gliding club. A lot of their gliding is done around Lake Titikaka.

Andino Boliviano, Calle Mexico #1638, Casilla de Correos #1346, ☎ 232-4682. This organization registers solo hikers and climbers. During ski season, they will also go up to Chacaltaya to ski. They hire a van if the numbers warrant it. Foreigners are welcome.

Gravity Assisted, Avenida 16 de Julio #1490, ground floor of Edificio Avenida, ☎ 231-3849, www.gravitybolivia.com, gravity@unete.com, is for cyclists. If you would like information on places to cycle, to have your bike fixed, to purchase parts and to get information about weather, altitude or safety conditions or just to hang out with other cyclists, this is the place.

Hash House Harriers is for hashers (runners), www.lapazhash.com, ☎ 279-1524. A sister group in Santa Cruz offers a group run, followed by a dinner/party (see *Adventures on Foot*, page 248, for details).

Festivals

Make an effort to be in La Paz for one of their special festivals and you will be well rewarded. The people are friendly and you will be invited to join in the fun. Besides the big events listed here, most Saints' days are celebrated with traditional food and drink. Dates for these events can be obtained from the tourist office on the Plaza Estudiantes, at the south end of Avenida Santa Cruz.

◆ Alasita

Alasita ("buy from me" in Aymara) is held in honor of the god of fertility, happiness and prosperity. Known as Ekeko ("dwarf" in Aymara), he is a miniature doll, a stout smiling guy loaded with everything from money to musical instruments to food, from coca leaves to vehicles – anything that a living person may want. According to tradition, Ekeko, carrying the objects desired, should be purchased at noon on the 24th and blessed in a ceremony that uses alcohol, confetti, paper streamers and candy. He should then be blessed again with holy water. The hope is that the items your Ekeko carries are what you will be blessed with the following year.

> **❖ WHAT MORE COULD A MAN WANT?**
>
> Originally, Alasita was a celebration by the Aymara of the spring equinox and was in honor of the coming crops. The Spaniards changed the date of the celebration to the end of January for whatever reason. In retaliation, the Aymara made the festival into a mockery of the Spaniard's greed by creating Ekeko and loading him up with every conceivable item that could be purchased.

The event starts during the final week in January and lasts for two weeks. During this festivity, the city holds the largest handicraft fair in the country. It takes place in the grounds of the old zoo, across from the open-air theater. Ten thousand merchants play host to almost 100,000 visitors during this fair.

◆ Carnival

Carnival, held 40 days before Easter, is good here, although the best celebration is in Oruro. In La Paz, the event goes for four days with parades, drinking, eating, blessings and dancing.

The big thing during Carnival is to douse friend, foe and tourist with water. The most popular strategy is to fill a balloon with water and launch it at someone. Market ladies fill and sell buckets of *globos* all day long. Standing on a balcony with a bucket of water ready to dump is also common. During Carnival, rain gear is essential.

> ❖ **DEADLY GLOBOS**
>
> Some protestors are trying to have *globos* abolished because people have been injured and killed by them. During the 2003 Carnival, 11 people were killed in La Paz from the over exuberance of the festivities, although not all deaths were caused by the throwing of *globos*.

◆ Gran Poder

Gran Poder (Great Power), held in June, is almost as extravagant an event in La Paz as Carnival is in Oruro. First held in 1939 as a candlelight procession in the El Alto area and featuring a statue of Christ at the head of the line, it has grown to include all La Paz residents. Although it is no longer a candlelight event, Gran Poder is celebrated with a parade, costumes, dances and fiesta-type activities.

The parades go through the downtown area of La Paz, ending on Calle Camacho.

The date of this fiesta changes yearly (though it always takes place on a weekend) so you must check with the tourist office or your hotel owner.

◆ Smaller Events

September 28 is **World Tourism Day**, where promotional booths are set up along the Prado. There are also events like cooking competitions. Tickets to tourist events are raffled off.

October 20 is the day La Paz was **founded**. It's more fun to join the parties and parades.

The **Festival of Todos Santos** takes place on November 1 and 2. Locals bring special cakes, breads and candies to the cemetery and offer them to their ancestors. This event often features a band.

Sightseeing

◆ City Sights

City Tours are offered by a number of companies and I recommend them for first-time visitors. They usually run for a couple of hours in the morning and again in the afternoon, with a break in the middle of the day. The cost is around $10 for the day. English is usually spoken or piped through an audio system that you hear with earphones.

Vesty Pakos Zoo, just past Valle de la Luna, is the world's highest zoo. It houses 63 species that include snakes, birds, llamas, lions and even a jaguar. The zoo sits at 10,740 ft/3,265 m in an attractive landscape. The zoo is open from 10 am to 6 pm daily, and costs 50 cents to enter. To get there, take a bus from Plaza Estudiantes to Zoologia.

◆ Historical Churches

Most churches are open all day and visitors are welcome as long as they don't disturb services. There is no charge for this, unlike Peru where one must pay to visit historical churches.

San Francisco, on the plaza of the same name, was the inspiration of Francisco de Los Angeles. Construction was completed in 1549. The original building was of mud brick, but it crumbled under a heavy snow fall. The replacement was built between 1743 and 1753 of stone from the quarry in Viacha.

At the top end of the plaza is a stone carving known as *Pucara*, where meetings (usually political) are held and hundreds of people gather. The carving represents the melding of all Bolivian cultures.

Santo Domingo on Calle Ingavi Yanacocha was completed in 1760 and, like San Francisco, is a mestizo-baroque design. **San Pedro Church** on Plaza Sucre, built in 1790, has a façade that shows the end of the baroque period and the beginning of the neoclassic style.

For examples of neo-gothic architecture, visit the **San Calixton** church on Calle Pichincha near Avenida Jaen. It was built in 1882. **La Recoleta,** on Avenida America between Calle Pando and Plaza Alonzo de Mendoza, was finished in 1894 and is also an example of neo-gothic architecture.

The **Nuestra Señora de La Paz Cathedral** on Plaza Murillo was started in 1831 and completed in 1925. The cathedral is an imposing structure known mostly for its stained glass windows. Set on a hill, its entrance on Calle Potosi is 39 ft/12 m lower than the main entrance on the square.

◆ Architecture

Templete Semisubterraneo is across from the stadium at the end of Avenida Bolívar. This is a reproduction of the temple at Tihuanaco. At one time the main statue was the original, but that was moved to the Archeological Museum and replaced with a reproduction.

The **Presidential Palace** on Plaza Murillo is also called Palacio Quemado (Burnt Palace) because of the many fires the building has endured in the past. Most were set in rebellion against the presiding government. The Spanish, in 1810, hanged Don Pedro Murillo for treason in the square now bearing his name. Then, in 1946, a mob of angry women, mostly widows, grabbed President Gualberto Villarroel and hanged him from a lamppost in the same square. He was held responsible for the deaths of their husbands. There is a statue of Villarroel in the square commemorating his life, rather than his death.

Adventures

◆ Adventures in Culture

If you want a panoramic, colorful, and unique view of Bolivian history, culture, and artifacts, a visit to this group of four museums is a necessary and well-spent morning or afternoon. To reach the **Calle Jaen Museums**, walk

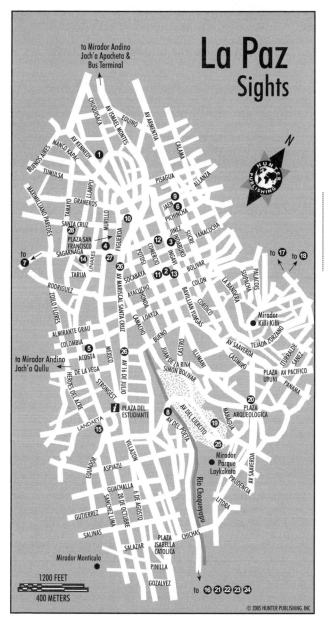

to Mirador Andino
Jach'a Apacheta &
Bus Terminal

La Paz
Sights

CHUQUISACA
AV KENNEDY
EQUINO
AV ISMAEL MONTES
AV ARMENTIA
CALAMA
MANCO KAPAC
BUENOS AIRES
TUMULSA
PISAGUA
ALIANZA
MAXIMILLIANO PAREDES
ILLIMANI
TAMAYO
GRANEROS
JAEN
PICHINCHA
YANACOCHA
SANTA CRUZ
OTTIUM
FIGUEROA
JINEZ
INDABURO
SUCRE
SAGARNAGA
LINARES
POTOSI
COMERCIO
INGAVI
BOLIVAR
TARIJA
AV MARISCAL SANTA CRUZ
SOCABAYA
AYACUCHO
COLON
RODRIGUEZ
BAVILIAN YUNGAS
COROICO
ZOILO FLORES
PANDILLA
LOAYZA
CAMACHO
PALACIOS
SUPACHA
LA BANDERA
ALMIRANTE GRAU
COLOMBIA
ACOSTA
MEXICO
AV 16 DE JULIO
BUENO
JUAN DE LA RIVA
CASTRO
ILLIMANI
AV SAAVEDRA
TEJADA ZORZANO
ITURRALDE
SANEZ
DE LA VEGA
SIMON BOLIVAR
CASIMIRO
AV PACIFICO
PANAMA
HEROES DEL ACRE
STRONGEST
PLAZA DEL
ESTUDIANTE
AV DEL EJERCITO
MANAGUA
PLAZA
ARQUEOLOGICA
LANDAETA
VILLAZON
AV DEL POETA
AV SAAVEDRA
ECUADOR
ASPIAZU
Mirador
Parque
Laykakota
PRUDENCIA
GUACHALLA
6 DE AGOSTO
20 DE OCTUBRE
SANCHEZ LIMA
Río Choqueyapu
GUTIERREZ
SALINAS
SALAZAR
CHICHAS
LITORA
Mirador Monticulo
PLAZA
ISABELLA
CATOLICA
PINILLA
GOZALVEZ

to ①⑦   to ①⑧

Mirador
Killi Killi

PLAZA
UYUNI

to Mirador Andino
Jach'a Qullu

to ⑯ ㉑ ㉒ ㉓ ㉔

N

HUNTER PUBLISHING

1200 FEET

400 METERS

© 2005 HUNTER PUBLISHING, INC

up Calle Jaen to Avenue Sucre to the Museo Costumbrista. Purchase your $2 ticket here; it's good for all four museums – Museo Costumbrista, Museo del Litoral, Casa de Don Pedro Domingo Murillo, and Museo Metals Preciosos Pre-Columbinos. The museums are open Tuesday to Friday, 9:30 am to noon and 12:30 to 2:30 pm, and on weekends, 10 am to 12:30 pm. On Saturday there is no admission fee.

Museo Costumbrista, Calle Jaen and Calle Sucre, ☎ 237-8478, shows La Paz and Bolivia in an array of pictorial representations of historic events, landscape paintings, photos, sculpture and ceramic doll displays.

Museo de Litoral, Calle Jaen #798 (no phone), showcases Spanish army uniforms, military scenes in watercolor, displays of swords, pistols, rifles, antique historical maps and life-size mannequins chronicling the war with Chile in 1884 when Bolivia lost its sea connection to the rest of the world. If you go to Copacabana on Lake Titikaka, you will see the remnants of the Bolivian navy: a few sailors, a few boats and, as one sailor humorously boasts, a large fleet of Bolivian submarines.

Museo de Metales Preciosos Pre-Columbinos (Gold Museum) at Calle Jaén #777, ☎ 237-1470, is a comprehensive precious metal museum showing pre-Columbian gold, silver and copper work.

Casa de Don Pedro Domingo Murillo, Calle Jaen #790, ☎ 237-5273, is a museum that holds a collection of colonial furniture, textiles, glass ware and household bric a brac – typical possessions of the colonial classes.

Museo de Instrumentos Musicales, Calle Jaen #711, ☎ 233-1077, holds a vast array of unimaginable instruments. The pan flute and its distinct sound symbolize the music of Bolivia, and here you will see the instrument's multiple types and sizes; one set of flutes (aerophonos) is taller than a man. The hundreds of guitars on display range from standard shapes, to one odd invention with five necks that circle the sound box. The drums are wonderful, wonky and out of round, with llama hide heads complete with hair. This incredible range of unique instruments, from the ancient to the conventional and contemporary, is of interest for its surprise, range and novelty. Admission is 75¢, a bargain.

The above museum profiles were written by Barry McKinnon from Canada.

National Art Museum, Calle Comercio, on the corner of Socabaya near Murillo Square, ☎ 237-1177, is open Tuesday to Friday, 9 am-12:30 pm and 3-7 pm, Saturday and Sunday, 10 am-1 pm. Admission is 50¢. The museum is located in a colonial structure built in 1775 by an official, Don Tadeo Diez de Medina. The arched walls surrounding the patio form hallways that are decorated with wood benches and large old vases.

It was inaugurated as a museum in 1964, and the religious art is dominated by paintings of Potosi's Mellchor Perez Holguin (1660-1735). Born in Cochabamba, Holguin moved to Potosi early in life and spent all his time in his adopted city. His paintings are of the Hispanic-American baroque style and his first works are in the Banco Central in La Paz.

The second school of art represented is in the Rollao style from the Lake Titikaka area. The greatest artist from that school was Leonardo Florez, a mestizo who worked around 1680. His painting, the *Adoration of Shepherds*, was reproduced on one of Bolivia's postage stamps.

Cecilio Guzman de Rojas and Arturo Borda, whose works are also featured in the museum, are credited with changing art in Bolivia. Guzman, born in Potosi, is known for his indigenous style, while Borda's subjects were always about the city of his birth, La Paz. Another artist represented here is Marina Nuñez del Prado, who has international acclaim and a museum of her own in the city.

The museum sells books in English or Spanish about Bolivian art.

Museum of Ethnic Art and Folklore, Calle Ingavi #916, on the corner of Jenaro Sanjines, ☎ 235-8859. Displays change monthly. The rest of the museum, located in a house built in the late 1700s, contains weavings and dolls. The weavings are from different regions and are laid out in drawers below an antique weaving from the same area. You'll see many variations of each style. I couldn't see enough. There's no entrance fee. If you go to just one museum, make it this one.

Museum of Natural History, Calle 26, Cota Cota, ☎ 279-5364, is open Monday to Friday, 8:30 am-12:30 pm and 2:30-6 pm. It contains specimens of plants, animals, rocks and fossils from all around the country.

Casa of Marina Nuñez del Prado, Avenida Equador #2034, ☎ 232-4906, displays sculptures by this famous Bolivian artist, teacher and sculptor. Born in La Paz in 1910, Nuñez studied art at the National school of Fine Arts and taught sculpture at the university. In 1930 she won the Best Execution of the Year award and her reputation was established. In 1936, she won a gold in Buenos Aires as the best foreign artist; in 1938 she won another gold at an international exhibition in Berlin; in 1946 she won an award in New York. All in all, Nuñez has won 20 international awards and had a public square named after her. Nuñez was married to Jorge Falon, a well-known Peruvian writer. She died on September 9, 1995. Her house in La Paz became the museum. It's open Monday to Friday, 9 am-1 pm.

The Children's Museum, also called Kusillo Museum, is on Mirador Laykakota on Avenida del Ejercito, ☎ 244-4311. It's open daily, 10:30 am-6:30 pm, and costs 75¢ for kids and $1 for adults. This interactive museum allows children to experience hands-on activities related to the culture of Bolivia. Peter McFarren and his wife Wendy are involved in this project. They had consultants from numerous Western countries help with the museum's building. Some of the financial assistance came from the Dutch government.

Next to the Children's Museum will be the **Museum of Bolivian Arts and Culture**, also an inspiration of Peter and Wendy McFarren. This museum will be built with the help of the Smithsonian Institution. It will feature pre- and post-Colonial art, including feather art, textiles, masks and instruments. Also on display will be the excellent photos of indigenous people taken by Peter McFarren. (This museum is scheduled to open in the near future.)

A **cable car**, El Fenicular, is located at the Kusillo Plaza below the Kusillo Cultural Complex that includes the plaza, artists shops (not yet open) and the museums. You can take the cable car either up or down for 15¢ or you may buy a ticket to the entire complex for $1. This cable car, which opened its tracks in October, 2003, sits at 3,600 m/11,800 ft, making it the highest in the world, superseding the one in Switzerland by 144 m/472 ft. The cars are powered by electricity and will hold up to 20 people or 1,500 kg/680 lbs. They travel at a rate 1.2 m/4 ft per second.

The Coca Museum, Calle Linares #906, open Monday to Friday, 10 am-noon and 2-7 pm, charges foreigners $1 and locals 25¢ to enter. As you go in, you'll be handed a pamphlet (English language) describing the history of coca. The displays inside cover the uses and abuses of the coca plant and how these came into being.

The **Textile Museum**, Calle Linares #906, open daily, 10 am-7 pm (closed noon-2 pm), charges a $1 entry fee. The museum is not strictly a textile museum as it has Inca artifacts and hats, as well as Spanish military decorations. There is also a collection of artifacts from Tihuanaco.

Museo Nacional de Arqueologia (Archeological Museum), Calle Tiwanacu #93 on the corner of Federico Zuarzo, Monday to Saturday, 9 am-noon and 3-7 pm, Sundays, 10 am-1 pm. Entrance fee, $1. This museum is set in a building that has been designed to look like the pre-Columbian temple found at Tihuanacu. The carving of Pacha Mama (Mother Earth) stands 24 ft/7.5 m high and weighs 17 tons.

Museo Tambo Quirquincha, Calle Evaristo Valle, ☎ 239-0969, is open 9:30 am to 12:30 pm and from 3 pm to 7 pm during the week and then from 10 am to 12:30 pm on weekends. This is a permanent exhibition that has early photos of La Paz. There are art works from the colonial and republican periods plus masks, sculptures and oil paintings. There is also a permanent collection of contemporary plastic art.

Museo de la Revolution National, Plaza Villaroel, is open 9:30 am-12:30 pm and 3 pm-7 pm during the week, and 10 am-12:30 pm on weekends. It costs 15¢ to enter and view the murals painted by famous artists who lived during the revolution of 1952.

Museo de Arte Sacro, Calle Socabaya #432, is open 9:30 am-12:30 pm and 3 pm-7 pm during the week, and 10 am-12:30 pm on weekends. Admission is 45¢. The museum contains religious art from the 16th and 17th centuries. There is a permanent exhibition of paintings, plus sacred ornaments, silver and furniture used by bishops of La Paz.

◆ Adventures on Foot

Around Town

El Prado is the main street in town. Walking El Prado with its throngs of people is a must. There are the large colonial houses and five-star hotels to admire. Starting at the more affluent end in the south, near the higher-priced hotels, it is called Avenida 16 de Julio. The street changes to Avenida Mariscal Santa Cruz that has, near the north end, the famous San Francisco Church and plaza built in 1549. Continuing north, the name of the street changes to Avenida Montes. Branching off El Prado at the San

Francisco Church is Avenida Sagarnaga, also known as "tourist street," lined with shops and vendors selling everything from llama fetuses to weavings and popcorn.

The **Witches Market**, on Calle Linares between Sagarnaga and Graneros, has objects, like llama fetuses, needed by locals who practice traditional ceremonies. There are herbs and spices, wines and amulets.

Above the Witches Market is **Mercado Negro** that covers hundreds of blocks going toward El Cementario. Each section covers a specific thing – electrical parts are in one area, while women's shoes and skirts are in another. The flower section is beautiful.

Hiking

MIRADORS: There are numerous miradors, or lookout points, in La Paz from which to see the city. **Mirador Monticulo** is on Calle Salazar, five blocks up from Plaza Isabel la Catolica that sits on Avenida Arce. Monticulo is also half a block from Plaza España, up a road that takes vehicles. At the bottom of the hill is the Contemporary Art Museum.

Mirador Templo Andino Jach'a Apacheta is on a hill above El Alto. Take a bus to Villa Victoria and have the driver point out the direction of the hill. This is the highest point in the city and was a lookout point for people living in the area for centuries. Due to robberies, it is advised to visit here in a group.

Mirador Killi Killi is in Agua de la Vida at the end of Avenida La Bandera. To get there, take a minibus from Avenida La Bandera and Calle Colon (Colon runs one block downhill from the palace on Plaza Murillo) to the top. This is an easy place to reach and, if walking, you can be on the hill in about 45 minutes.

Mirador Andino Jacha'Qullu is a tiny hill and park in the suburb of Nuevo Potosi in the west end of town, off Calle 3 de Mayo. To walk here is tricky, as the route has many curves and turns. Take a taxi instead. The advantage of coming here is that it offers a different view. The hill is an important ceremonial center of the Andean culture.

Mirador Parque Laykakota on Cerro Laykakota is in the Santa Barbara zone and is known as Witch Hill. The park offers a good view of the city.

CHIARKOTA LAKE: Lago Chiarkota can be visited as a day trip from La Paz. The bus going past Refugio Huayna Potosi will let you off at the hamlet just before. From there, walk the road past Lake Tuni to the dam. A track goes toward Condoriri (up) and climbs from 13,000 ft/4,000 m at the dam to 18,000 ft/5,400 m at the lake. A few signs show the way. It takes three to four hours to walk to Lake Chiarkota and another two or three to get back down. You can hire a local guide for $25 per person, per day.

VALLEY OF THE MOON: Valle de la Luna is six miles/10 km from the center of La Paz and can be reached by joining a tour or by taking micro bus #11 or minibus #231 or 273 to Mallasilla. These buses can be caught at Plaza Belzu on Avenida Mexico in San Pedro. Tell the driver where you want to go and he will point the way as you disembark. Because of the terrain, wear good shoes/boots and carry water. City tours that stop here are offered by many companies in La Paz.

The hillside features a maze of clay canyons and pinnacles that have been sculpted by wind and rain. Narrow trails through the landscape take about an hour to walk.

As you continue up the road you will come to **Parque National Mallasa** with its bird observatory and, across the road, the zoo area. The road passes under natural stone bridges and past Chulpani's Red Hill. There is no mistaking which hill this is. From Mallasa one can see across the river to the highest golf course in the world (see below).

DEVIL'S TOOTH: Muela del Diablo is a huge volcanic plug sticking out of the landscape to a height of 13,000 ft/3,950 m. The area is a popular picnic destination and can be reached by taking minibus #288 or #207 to El Pedregal from Plaza Belzu on Avenida Mexico in San Pedro. Several trails go to the right; follow the one that obviously leads to the village. From there, go to the left for .3 miles (about half a kilometer), to the foot of the rock.

VALLEY OF THE SPIRITS: Canyon de Palca, or Valle de Animas, is a deep canyon that was carved by the Rio Palca centuries ago. To get there, take a bus going to Huni from Plaza Belzu on Avenida Mexico in San Pedro. Or take a bus to Ovejuyo and then a second *trufi* toward Huni. Your hike will end in Palca and getting back to Huni and finally La Paz will require either good timing for buses, a taxi or a hired jeep with driver who will wait for you. Check with your bus driver as to when the last bus leaves Palca. Once in Huni, follow the main road through the village and into the valley. Mt. Illimani is constantly in view. Continue for 1½-two hours until you see the river (without much water) on your right. Follow it toward the canyon, filled with huge pinnacles and wind-carved conglomerates. The trail continues along the bottom of the canyon to a natural obelisk. Just past the obelisk is a rock that has the appearance of a human hiding in a cave. The rock is called the hermit of the canyon. Continue along the canyon to its end and climb to your left up to the village of Palca. This is a long day-hike. Be certain to carry water, wear good shoes and have a snack.

CHACALTAYA: Skiing on the world's highest ski hill, Chacaltaya, just 23 miles/37 km from the city, is a must for ski buffs who are in the area from February through to April. Hikers, of course, should go up any time. Chacaltaya, which means cold in Aymara, is 17,800 ft/5,400 m high and the ski run starts just below the summit and goes 2,300 ft/700 m down the steep tongue of a glacier.

❖ GOODBYE GLACIERS

With present weather conditions, the glacier is melting at a rate of 20-33 ft/six-10 m per year, so it won't be too long before the hill is out of commission for skiing. A French team from the Institut de Recherche pour le Developpement is studying the condition of three glaciers here, including Chacaltaya. The Zongo Glacier near Huayna Potosi loses three ft/one m of depth and 33 ft/10 m of length every year. The run-off from these glaciers is the basic water supply for La Paz.

To get there during ski season, **Club Boliviano**, Calle Mexico #1638, Casilla de Correso #1346, ☎ 232-4682, will take a bus up on weekends if numbers warrant the trip. Alternately, you must hire a vehicle through a tour agency for the two-hour trip to the parking lot.

On foot, it is a half-hour to the chalet above the parking lot and another hour to pass the first false summit before finally reaching the top. From there you can see Lake Titikaka, Illimani, Maururata and Huayna Potosi. The air density here is only half of what it is at sea level.

Entrance fee to the ski hill is $1.50 per person.

During high rains, the road up the mountain becomes impassable. Chacaltaya is a cycling destination for those who want a fast brake-gripping rush down from the summit. See page 70 for details.

Club Andinos, ☎ 231-2875, a mountain hut near Chacaltaya, has both private rooms and dorms, although there are no private bathrooms. You should have a warm sleeping bag if staying on the mountain overnight. You may also purchase meals at the hut during ski season. If you eat at the lodge, a sandwich or a piece of cake will cost about $1.50 and pop is $1.

CHORO TRAIL: The Choro Trail runs from El Cumbre to Coroico and follows a pre-Inca trail that takes three to four days to cover. You can take this trip back from Coroico on a horse (see *Coroico*, page 166, for details). There are outfitters who will include this section of the trail but they start in Tuni and the hike would include going from a pass near Mount Condoriri instead of El Cumbre. It is not advisable to walk from Coroico to El Cumbre because the trail is so steep.

You will need a tent, sleeping mats, food for three days (at least), water tablets, shorts and rain gear. You must have good boots and pack, a compass (although the only direction is down), first aid kit and a walking stick. Plan to go either with a tour group or hire a guide. A guide knows the way, knows where to sleep and get water, and can talk to locals who may be curious about you or opposed to your passing.

The trail starts at 15,789 ft/4,800 m and you drop to 4,934 ft/1,500 m within three days of walking. The descent is brutal and your shins will ache with fatigue. Rain is always a problem in this area.

To get to trailhead, take any bus from Villa Fatima going toward Coroico and get off at the pass (El Cumbre) beside a little lake. Even easier is to take a taxi, which can take four people.

The trail begins just beyond the statue of Christ on the hill across from the lake. The descent follows a well-defined trail paved with stones long before the Spanish arrived. This is the toughest section of the hike as it is steep and usually wet. The first night you should stop at Challapampa, sometimes called Achapalla Pampa. It will take approximately six hours to get there. Locals will expect to be paid for providing a campsite.

The Altiplano vegetation is left the following day and the lush rainforests become obvious. Once across the Choro River there is a long, dry walk to the Rio Jacu-Manini, nine miles/15 km from Challapampa. However, the descent is not as steep as the previous day's. The next stop is Sandillani, where a camping area is available. In Sandillani there is a place to stay. The heat will start to take its toll now, as Sandillani is at 6,579 ft/2,000 m above sea level.

From Sandillani a cobbled trail leads to Villa Esmeralda where the road to Chairo passes through coffee fields, fruit orchards and vegetable gardens. There is a place to eat, purchase supplies and generally freshen up in Chairo. It is another 10 miles/17 km to Yolosa, just below Coroico. This is a long way to walk after your arduous descent into the Yungas. However, hitching from Chairo is not a disgrace. Once at Yolosa, you can catch a bus or truck going up to Coroico another five miles/eight km into the Yungas, where you will undoubtedly spend a few days recuperating.

CHACALTAYA TO ZONGO PASS: This one-day hike takes you through barren but beautiful landscapes over to Huayna Potosi. From there you can either return to Chacaltaya or have a hired vehicle drive over to the Refugio at Huayna Potosi and pick you up. This hike should be done only by those who have acclimatized. From the pass, on a clear day you can see Lake Titikaka, Illimani and Sajama, the highest mountain in Bolivia.

 Chacaltaya has numerous walks. If you're interested, check out *Trekking in Bolivia* by Yossi Brain, Andrew North and Isobel Stoddart, published by The Mountaineers, Seattle, WA (1997).

TAKESI TRAIL: This trail goes from the San Francisco Mine just out of La Paz (below Chacaltaya) to the village of Yanacachi, a colonial town with the oldest church in the Yungas. This is the Inca Trail of Bolivia and is popular with both locals and tourists. Almost the entire trail, about 18 miles/30 km, is stone laid by those living in the area before the Inca arrived.

The trail starts with a three-hour grunt up to Apacheta Pass at 15,000 ft/ 4,650 m, the highest point on the trek. From there you leave the Altiplano and start down toward the Yungas, following the canyon. Within two or three hours you will be at Takesi Village, elevation 12,000 ft/3,600 m. There are numerous camp spots beside the Takesi River another hour or so past the village.

The second day you follow the paved Inca Road that has the remains of some sewer systems built at the same time as the road. By lunch you should be at Cacapi and into the rainforest. The elevation here is 8,550 ft/ 2,600 m. The rest of the day involves an undulating walk to the Chojlla Mine, just 650 ft/200 m lower than Cacapi. From there it is two hours to Yanacachi and the end of the hike. Or, you may continue for five or six hours to Mocori and the luxurious Tamampaya Hotel.

YUNGA CRUZ TRAIL: The Yunga Cruz Trail goes from Chuñavi to Chulumani, the capital city of the South Yungas. This is the least popular and most difficult of the three trails going down into the Yungas from La Paz.

To get to Chuñavi, hire a jeep. There are buses, but service is infrequent and conditions crowded. They reportedly leave from Villa Fatima daily at 9 am and the trip takes six or seven hours. Once at the village, there are numerous hiking routes.

 For detailed information, purchase *Trekking in Bolivia* by Yossi Brain, Andrew North and Isabel Stoddart, or hire a guide from a tour company.

Climbing

For those into climbing, the **Andes** of Bolivia offer three peaks over 20,000 ft/6,000 m that are not extremely technical. The tour companies that assist in climbing adventures are all highly skilled and able to offer world-class trips.

Most companies prefer that you bring your own gear (harness and helmet) while they provide the group gear (like ropes and biners). Acclimatization is essential so plan on being in La Paz for a few days before going up. Companies like **Andean Summits** (☎ 242-2106, www.andeansummits. com) offer packages that include acclimatizing. For more detailed information, contact one of the tour agencies.

 Read Yossi Brain's book, *Bolivia, A Climbing Guide*, published by The Mountaineers, Seattle, WA.

Huayna Potosi is the mountain most often climbed by foreigners and one of the world's most visited "six-thousanders." There are two approaches to this mountain, the east and the west face. The east face starts at the dam, just past Refugio. Base camp, called Campamento Argentino, is at 18,000 ft/5,500 m and is reached just two hours after your arrival at the Huayna Potosi Glacier. There are three alternatives for the approach to the peak. The first and most popular follows the ridge, the second, longer route goes to the bergschrund before ascending the ridge. Those doing the west face will climb the largest face in Bolivia. It's 3,300 ft/1,000 m high, with pitches around 50° and some as steep as 70°. This route is more for the strong, with lots of stamina, rather than the technically skilled.

Snow and ice conditions determine your times and sometimes your route. This mountain should not be climbed during rainy season due to the possibility of avalanches. Your guides will advise you as to the best routes to take depending on the conditions.

CONDORIRI: Condoriri climbs start with base camp at 15,300 ft/4,700 m above sea level beside Lake Chiarkhota.

From the base camp you can climb a total of 13 peaks that are over 16,500 ft/5,000 m and each peak has a number of routes. If you have a month, you could, in peak season, climb a new route every day. This group of mountains is difficult to reach, so either a private jeep or a tour company must be hired.

PAQUENA ALPAMAYO: This is the most popular peak reached from Lake Chiarkota base camp. Apparently, when you are sitting in base camp, the mountain looks more daunting than it is.

ILLIMANI: This is the highest mountain in the Cordillera Real, standing at 21,000 ft/6,400 m. Illimani is actually a group of seven peaks.

Pico Sur is the highest peak on Illimani. Its normal route is also its easiest and most often climbed. **Pico Norte** and **Central** can be added to make the rarely attempted five-peak traverse. This is the most impressive mountaineering expedition possible in Bolivia. These traverses all require at least three nights at an altitude of over 20,000 ft/6,000 m.

Hikers can walk up to the base camp at 16,500 ft/5,000 m, while climbers go one better, to Nido de Condores, the Condor's Nest, at 18,100 ft/5,500 m. The views up here are second to none.

The **Quimsa Cruz** group of mountains has at least 80 peaks, many unnamed, that can be climbed. The peaks run between 16,000 and 19,000 ft (4,900 and 5,800 m) in height. Because these mountains aren't as high, they are often ignored by climbing elitists. This is both a pity and a blessing. It is a blessing because it leaves the mountains for those wanting to find new routes, and it's a pity because the elitists miss some of Bolivia's most spectacular rock.

The northern side, often referred to as **Bolivia's Chamonix**, has a number of spires that beckon those preferring rock to ice (the south side, of course, is covered in ice). The other nice thing about this area is that it is accessible by bus or truck and there are usually campsites close to the peaks.

Golf

Mallasilla Golf and Country Club, Calle Casilla #4306, ☎ 274-5124, www.boliviagolf.com, opened in 1912 and is the world's highest golf course. It has a 6,900-yard, 18 hole course sitting at 11,000 ft/3,300 m. The par 72 course attracts visitors from around the world mainly because of its elevation. Its par-3, 12th hole, known as the Lunar Hole, requires a shot of at least 130 yards to clear the 50-foot drop over the moon-like landscape. Because of the elevation and light air, judging the distance is difficult.

Running

Hash House Harriers is a club of runners who have a fun run about once a month. This is undoubtedly the highest hash in the world. Runs are usually held on a Saturday, 11 am-3 pm. After a run, hashers often have a downdown (they down a few beers) and a pot luck dinner. Here's how a hash run works. There is a fixed route that the runners must follow. However, they don't know what the route is or what the markers are. They start running (someone tells them the direction to head) and as they figure out the markers and are able to follow them, they holler "on-on" and everyone follows. This is done at a jogging pace. When the run is finally over, everyone congregates for a few hours of socializing. In La Paz, contact Gary "Tin-Balls" Neale, ☎ 279-1524, www.lapazhash.com.

◆ Adventures on Water

Hotel Gloria at Urmiri, ☎ 239-1489, www.gloria-tours-bolivia.com, is just two hours (51 miles/83 km) from La Paz and has a natural spa and hot springs. The water runs consistently at 72°C down the side of the mountain into three pools. Other than resting, walking from Cumbre Pilar down to the resort (about 1½ hours), eating and drinking, there is nothing to do except pamper yourself. The hotel is part of the Gloria chain and offers some rooms with private pools. There is also a massage parlor, sauna, a pool with a waterfall and a restaurant that serves vegetarian food along with the standard fare. A single room runs $18, a double is $37 and a triple is $55. Meals cost $2.50 for breakfast and $6 for lunch or supper.

The spa specializes in treatments for skin problems, excess weight, gout and arthritis. The staff also works with people who have suffered physical trauma or injury, giving physiotherapy and assisting with exercises in the hot springs.

You may visit the resort and hot springs on a day tour from La Paz. Contact Hotel Gloria in La Paz and book a round trip in their van. They need a minimum of six people to make the run ($7 per person, round trip). The cost of using the hot springs and spa depends on the services you use.

◆ Adventures on Wheels

ROAD OF DEATH: The cycle from El Cumbre near La Paz to Coroico in the Yungas, along the Road of Death, is a popular seven-hour, hand-numbing, downhill thrill. I say hand-numbing because this is a brake-gripper; you drop almost 10,000 ft/3,000 m in just under 60 miles/100 km.

North American-made bikes can be rented in La Paz and the best company to work with is **Gravity Assisted Tours** (☎ 231-3849, www.gravitybolivia.com). Their bikes are top quality and well maintained.

With all companies, a guide and support vehicle comes with the price, as do helmets, bright-colored vests and gloves. Repair, rather than maintenance, is the rule, so be aware that the bike you get may not be super-safe.

Some of the cliffs along the road drop 2,300 vertical feet (700 meters) and there have been many deaths. Most have involved buses, but bikers have died because of faulty equipment. Tour agents are notorious for telling you everything you want to hear just to get your business. Once you are on your way, you sometimes find that they have not delivered what they promised.

However, the ride of death was excellent. The cold mountain air from the pass soon hits the warm moisture wafting up from the Amazon. The vegetation goes from bleak Altiplano grasses to rich jungle forests. The glaciers disappear and streams get larger.

Once we hit gravel, a short distance from El Cumbre, it became tougher because we had to dodge potholes, pull over while vehicles passed and pass under waterfalls or swerve around small landslides. The road in spots is no more than a 12-foot-wide (four-meter) ledge. Vehicles (including bikes) going down are less maneuverable than those coming up. Uphill travelers must give the right-of-way by pulling over.

❖ **LABOR OF LOVE**

As you cycle toward Coroico, you will meet one young man who directs traffic. He is in a dangerous spot where drivers can't see what is coming and he uses a plastic paddle, red on one side, green on the other, to signal traffic and catch the coins tossed at him for his services. He is there because he lost his entire family when the bus they were riding went over the cliff as it was backing up to allow passage of an oncoming vehicle.

After you finish cycling, you end up at Yolosa, a junction where the Road of Death continues to the Amazon and another route goes up to Coroico. Your back-up vehicle will take you to Coroico. Those who want to continue to Caravani and Rurrenabaque may do so by public transportation.

CHACALTAYA: This ski hill (see above, page 66) is another cycling spot, with several descent routes back to La Paz. The ride from the peak of Chacaltaya is very steep along scree and boulders, following a few lesser peaks before it starts to drop along walking trails and mining roads and ending in the Zongo Valley. This trip is only for the experienced mountain biker and can be done only when the road conditions going to the ski hill allow it.

ZONGO VALLEY: The Zongo Valley Cycle starts on the pass just past Huayna Potosi's Refugio and the spot where climbers access the Huayna Glacier. It follows the Zongo River down into the Yungas, descending rapidly from 15,000 ft to 5,000 ft (4,600 m to 1,500 m) in less than 21 miles/ 35 km. It can be split into two days. The first day runs from Huayna Potosi to Zongo Village, where you can camp. The following day, you will be driven up to Chacaltaya and, from there, cycle into La Paz.

WAL`LATA PASS TO SORATA:** You can cycle into Sorata from Wal`lata Pass on the road between Sorata and Achacachi. This is an excellent ride taking only four hours to drop 4,300 ft/1,300 m. Some make the claim that it is better than the Road of Death. The ride is shorter, the views are more dramatic and there is only one place where the road hangs on the edge of a sheer cliff. **New Milenium (☎ 245-1660, nmas@caoba.entelnet.bo) is one company that takes cyclists along this route. The cost for the cycle there, an overnight in Sorata and the shuttle back is just $100.

◆ Adventures on Horseback

Horseback riding is offered by **Sky Bolivia** (see *Tour Operators*, page 72) and can be enjoyed along a four-hour route to the Rio Abajo, which is 40 minutes by car from La Paz. The same company also offers a six-hour tour starting at Mallaso, passing Muebla del Diabla, Valencia and ends at Wuay Wuasi. This follows the Choqueyapu River in part. You may also go from Valencia to Illimani and back, passing Tawapalca and Cohoni on the way. For this overnight trip you would need a sleeping bag.

◆ Adventures of the Brain

ABC Spanish School, Calle Lenares #980 Apt. 202, ☎ 772-62657 (cell), www.studyspanish-lapaz-bolivia.tk, is owned and operated by William Ortez, who has been teaching Spanish for 10 years. He offers both beginner and intermediate levels, with flexible hours. One advantage of being in this school is that the classes are often small, which gives more one-to-one time. Visit the website, take the on-line test and go directly into the skill level you need.

The costs, which include all materials needed for study, are as follows: 21 hours, three hours per day, $115; 28 hours, four hours per day, $155; 30 hours, three hours per day, $160; 40 hours, four hours per day, $215; 45 hours, three hours per day, $235; 60 hours, four hours per day, $315; 60 hours, three hours per day, $300; 80 hours, four hours per day, $400.

William can also arrange for accommodations with a family in the center of the city, with breakfast included, for a total immersion experience.

Accommodation prices are as follows (lunch or dinner are $2 extra): One week, $50; two weeks, $100; three weeks, $140; four weeks, $185.

Reservations for classes and/or accommodations can be made in advance.

The **SpeakEasy Institute**, Avenida Arce #2047, ☎ 244-1779, www. speakeasyinstitute.com, speakeasyinstitute@yahoo.com, offers courses in Spanish, Quechua and Portuguese for everyone from the beginner to the advanced student. The institute uses native Spanish speaking teachers and specializes in courses for professionals and "quickie" courses for survival. SpeakEasy is part of the i-to-i international school that teaches people how to teach English as a second language. It's an efficient system.

Courses run from one week to eight weeks and you have the option of staying with a family.

Courses involve four hours of instruction daily. If a room with a host family is chosen, the fee includes room, two meals, laundry, trips to interesting places around the country and airport pickup. The costs of these courses, home-stay included, are $260 a week, $480 for two weeks, $700 for three. For courses without home stay, costs are $220 for one week, $400 for two and $620 for three.

The institute is involved with the publication of *Llama Express*, the English-language newspaper loaded with helpful and up-to-date information for tourists. If you need assistance on other matters, everyone at the institute speaks English well and is willing to answer questions.

LA PAZ & VICINITY

❖ NEEDY CHILDREN

The institute helps needy children, of which there are many in La Paz. If you are leaving the country and have clothes that you do not want to take home, please have them cleaned and delivered to the institute. Alix Shand, the coordinator, will see that they get onto needy bodies.

◆ Tour Operators

Anyone climbing should go to **www.mountainguides.com**, which has an excellent equipment list.

Gravity Assisted Mountain Biking, Avenida 16 de Julio #1490, ground floor of Edificio Avenida, ☎ 231-3849, www.gravitybolivia.com, has made a reputation as the best company for downhill bike trips. They have US-made Kona race bikes with Hayes disc-brakes and Shimano v-brakes. All bikes have either front or full suspension. Gravity maintains their bikes, rather than just repairing them. Their guides are English speaking, first-aid qualified and addicted to riding. The company offers 16 one-day rides and 10 multi-day adventures.

I like this company because safety is such an issue and because they are so much fun.

American Tours, Avenida 16 de Julio #1490, Edificio Avenida, main floor, ☎ 237-4204, www.america-ecotours.com, is across the hall from Gravity and the two compete for first-class quality. The company has teamed with Andean Summits, offering high-quality climbing and hiking trips. Andean Summits has one of the best reputations in South America.

The cost of hiking with this company depends on the number of participants. To climb Huayna Potosi and Charquini costs one person almost $500. If four people go, the cost drops to $236 per person. For trekking the Choro Trail, one person pays $467, but four participants pay $159 each. The most expensive (and exciting) trek on offer goes into the Apolobamba area (Pelichuco to Charazani). The fare for one person (taking a private jeep) is $1,535; if four people go (using public transportation), they pay just $331 each for the entire week. Trips include a guide, a cook, all meals and, if climbing, common climbing equipment like biners, ice screws, ropes and snow stakes. Porters and animals carry only common equipment during treks, so be prepared to carry your own gear. Food goes on the animals.

Andean Summits, 710 Calle Prolongacion Armaza, Sopocachi area of La Paz, ☎ 242-2106, www.andeansummits.com, works with a few agencies in Bolivia like American Tours and Gravity Assisted. See *Outfitters Who Do All the Work*, page 45.

Sky Bolivia, Calle Sagarnaga #367, ☎ 231-3254, www.skybolivia.com, offers horse trips near La Paz. Trips can last four hours, six hours or overnight. They also have a trip down the River Guanay to Rurrenabaque, one of the newer adventure trips in Bolivia.

Alba Tours, Calle Sagarnaga #139, ☎ 231-3052, offers a 3½-hour city tour with an English-speaking guide for $20. It also has trips to the Valley of the Moon and then to the Templete Semisubterraneo, in front of the stadium. From the stadium, the tour goes to Mirador Killi Killi for views of the city and then to Muela del Diablo or the Devil's Tooth. It passes through colonial streets to Plaza Murillo, where you visit the National Art Museum and the traditional Ethnographic Museum. The tour ends at the witches' market. Biking to Coroico is also offered.

This company has a minivan that goes to Copacabana, Puno, Arequipa, Tihuanaco, Chacaltya, Coroico, Rurenabaque, Uyuni or Cusco. If you feel uncomfortable taking local buses, this is a good alternative. The difference in cost is minimal.

Toñito Tours, Calle Sagarnaga #189, office 9, ☎ 233-6250, www. bolivianexpeditions.com, specializes in trips around Uyuni and the salt lakes. All-inclusive, four-day tours cost $110. Note that "all-inclusive" *excludes* transportation to or from Uyuni. Toñito is a family-run company that also offers custom one- to five-day tours by private car.

Vicuña Tours, Calle Sagarnaga #366, ☎ 231-0708, www.victoursbol. com, offers numerous excursions. The city tour costs $21 per person; Tihuanaco is $15; a walk around Chacaltya will cost $15; and two days and one night at Lake Titikaka costs $68.

High Camp Bolivia, Sagarnaga #189, office 101, ☎ 231-7497, high-campbolivia@hotmail.com, specializes in hiking and climbing in the Andes and has an excellent reputation. Owner Gonzalo Jaimes is a member of the Guiding Association of Bolivia and a rock and ice instructor. The company has decent equipment available for rent, including Italian (Ferrino) tents, the new-styled plastic mountain boots for climbing, Inca foams, Vau De tents, some good clothes, bags (North Face), ropes, harnesses, stoves (butane) and lamps. This company will also do custom trips; contact them for specifics.

This company, which works with Andean Summits, requests about a week to prepare summit trips to some of the higher peaks. Fees include guides, meals and transportation. Their prices are as follows, with a minimum of two people: Chaguini, one day, $140; Huana Potosi, two or three days, $350; Illimani, four days, $450; Condoriri, four days, $850; Sajama, four days, $725; Illampu to Ancohuma, seven days, $1,230.

Inca Land Tours, Calle Sagarnaga #213, ☎ 231-3589, www.inca-landtours.com, specialize in the Amazon, although they also offer tours to other places (all you need to do is ask). They have two camps out of Rurrenabaque – one in the jungle and the other in the *pampas*. These all-inclusive trips cost $25 per dy with a minimum stay of three days.

Also offered is the jungle trip that goes up the Beni and then the Tuichi River. Remember that hikes into the jungle are more for bird and plant lovers, as most jungle residents are not seen during the day.

Accommodations for both trips are in dorms that hold 10 people. Each bed has a mosquito net. There is also a dorm that has partial wood walls and a foundation. The cost for this accommodation is $35 per day (during low season, the prices drop by $5). The local guides speak their own language and Spanish, not English. However, you can hire an English-speaking translator for $5 per day.

Inca Land Tours is struggling with eco-tourism. Some clients want animals caught so they can be touched, but scientific research has shown that wild animals are traumatized by this. Note that cobras and anacondas cannot be seen unless they are caught. Feeding wild animals is also discouraged because the animals are inclined to stop foraging for themselves. If you wish to help preserve Bolivian wilderness, put pressure on fellow travelers to comply with the latest ecological practices. This will force companies like Inca Land Tours to offer only "no-touch" tours.

LA PAZ & VICINITY

Buho's Tours, Calle Sagarnaga #242, ☎ 247-1577, buhostours@ entelnet.bo, has three classes of bicycles for rent to use on the Road of Death trip to Coroico. A hi-tech US-made bike rents for $45; Italian bikes cost $39; and Chilean ones are $35. All the bikes at Buho's have spring suspension, but the Chilean ones have only front disc brakes operated at the handle bar. You can also rent bikes and a guide to cycle the Zongo Valley ($35/day), Valley of the Moon or Devil's Tooth ($28/day).

Trek Bolivia, Calle Sagarnaga #392, ☎ 231-7106, www.trekbolivia.8k. com, specializes in trekking. They have French-, German-, Japanese- and English-speaking guides. However, all trips are cheaper with a Spanish guide. The six-day hike they offer in the Apolobamaba area between Pelechuco and Curva costs $280, with a minimum of two people. It starts in Curva and goes up to Pelechuco. A three-day hike from Condorini to Chacape is $180 per person, with a minimum of two people. The first night is spent at Lake Cheracota; the second day is spent crossing a 16,440-foot/5,000-m pass and ending at Liveñosa Lake; the third day you come out. Gear and transportation is extra. This company offers other treks and, through their website, helps coordinate groups and thus keeps costs down.

New Horizon, Calle Sagarnaga #388, ☎ 231-6274, has three types of bikes that can be used for the Road of Death cycle trip. The best rents for $45, 2nd class is $35, and the cheapest is $30. The guide is a bike mechanic, but extra bikes are also carried just in case a problem arises that can't be fixed. This is one of the rare companies that practices maintenance. The crew is Peruvian, so specialized trips run to Machu Picchu, though not by bike.

Huayna Tours, Calle Sagarnaga #398 at Illampu, ☎ 245-6717, is run by Dr. Hugo Berrios and his wife Damiska. Anyone who climbs in Bolivia will come upon Dr. Hugo somewhere. Although they offer all the tours offered by other companies, their specialty is climbing. They will take climbers to any peak in Bolivia, but Hugo's specialty is Huayna Potosi. He knows every rock and grass blade on that mountain.

Hugo has a lodge at the base of Huayna Potosi that is a true refuge (called the Refugio) after the grueling trip to the summit of the mountain. The lodge is at 15,600 ft/4,800 m and the summit of Huayna Potosi is 20,000 ft/6,000 m. A bus goes to the Refugio every day so non-climbers can also enjoy this rustic place perched on the mountain.

Before going up any high peak in Bolivia, you can take **lessons** at Hugo's climbing school. All equipment is supplied, including plastic boots, ropes, tents, helmets and pitons, etc. They also provide experienced guides/porters.

The two-day Huayna Potosi climb costs $100. Any additional days cost $20 more per day. The six-day Apolobamba hike from Pelechuco to Charazani can be done for $250 per person (there must be more than two people in your group).

Should you need a private jeep (because you don't want to travel the roads by bus) this is the best place to rent one with a driver. The vehicles are in excellent shape, the driver is skilled and the price is the best in town.

> ### ❖ ACCLIMATIZATION AWARENESS
>
> Acclimatization is often difficult for those between 14 and 19 years of age because brain and lung tissue has not yet fully developed so adaptation to this drastic change is slower.

Tocando el Cielo, ☎ 279-1440, has a double-decker bus running city tours. The cost is $15 per person for a three- to four-hour tour that is offered in the mornings and the afternoons. Your ticket is good for two days, so you can do half one day, and half the next. The circuit has two sections – the first is to the south end of the city plus the Valley of the Moon, and the second includes the city center and Mirador Killi Killi.

To catch the bus, be at Plaza Isabel la Catolica just before 8:30 or 10:30 am for the morning tours and 2 or 4 pm for the afternoon tours. You can purchase your ticket on the bus.

Magri Turismo Ltd, Calle Capitan Ravelo #2101, ☎ 244-2727, www. bolivianet.com/magri/, specializes in custom tours for groups. If you want to do only specific things and have a time frame that is tight, this may be the way to go. The company also offers trips to Sucre, the Jesuit Mission Churches, Potosi or the Salar of Uyuni. On Isla del Sol they have an ecolodge (La Estancia) that is highly recommended. For lodge details, see page 113.

New Milenium Adventure Sports, Calle Illampu #815, ☎ 245-1660, nmas@caoba.entelnet.bo, offers two excellent trips. One is a 14-day hike down Rio Yariapu in Madidi National Park to Rio Tuhichi, where you float on a *callapo* (traditional raft made by the Tacana) to Rurrenabaque and then do another tour on the *pampas* looking for anaconda and boas. Depending on the number of persons, the trip can be as much as $1,350 per person or as low as $789. The other trip is a one-week excursion in the Apolobamba area that starts in Pelechuco and ends just below Viscachani Pass. The cost is $850 per person with only two people. Of course, the price goes down when more people are included. New Milenium takes cyclists on the great glide into Sorata.

International Mountain Guides, Ashford, WA 98304, www.mountainguides.com, offers a great trip that includes a package of climbs up Huayna Potosi, Illimani and Sajama for $3,000. This price does not include booze or your journey to and from La Paz.

Places to Stay

There are many hotels in La Paz and the only place I do not recommend staying is in El Alto. Most of the *aljamientos* up there are whore houses (if you want a whore it is safer to pick one up at Plaza Estudiantes) and I did not check out any of the hotels in that area. For the roughest, but not necessarily the cheapest, hotels I looked at the ones in the Mercado Negro area.

> ### ❖ HOTEL PRICING
>
> | | |
> |---|---|
> | $ | $10 to $20 |
> | $$ | $21 to $50 |
> | $$$ | $51 to $75 |
> | $$$$ | $76 to $100 |
> | $$$$$ | over $100 |

LA PAZ & VICINITY

1. Calle Sagarnaga: Naira Hotel & Café, Lak Smi Vegetarian Restaurant, Happy Days Hotel, Alem Hotel
2. Calle Illampu: Dynastia Hotel, Rosario Hotel & Restaurant
3. Calle Linares (north): Pepe's Coffee Bar, Layq'a Café
4. Calle Linares (south): Les Pot Pourris de Gourmets, Angelo Colonial Restaurant

PLACES TO STAY

5. Continental Hotel
6. Milton Hotel
7. Radisson Hotel
8. Hotel Gloria
9. Rey Palace Hotel
10. Ritz
11. Hotel Paris
12. Sagarnaga Hotel
13. Hotel Scala
14. Pachamama Residencial, Condessa & Arcabusaro
15. Hostal Señorial
16. Hotel Garcilazo
17. Hotel Sucre, Max Inn Hotel
18. Hostal Republica
19. Angelo Colonial Hostal
20. Hotel España

PLACES TO EAT

21. Chifa Amy
22. Café Cuidad
23. Café Colon
24. Wall Street
25. Alexander Coffee Shop
26. Confieteria Club de La Paz
27. Café Berlin
28. Café la Terraza
29. Surucachi Restaurant/Dumbos
30. La Casa del Corregidor, Cevichon
31. Rincon Español, Shian Restaurant
32. Beatrice Italian Restaurant
33. Wasamama Restaurant
34. Don Vittorio
35. Dumas Café
36. Seoul Restaurant
37. El Gaucho

NIGHTLIFE

38. Mongos
39. Coyote
40. Diesel National, Thelonius, Bizzaro

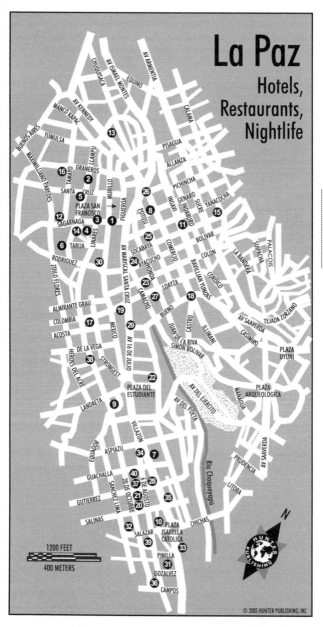

La Paz
Hotels, Restaurants, Nightlife

1200 FEET
400 METERS

© 2005 HUNTER PUBLISHING, INC

The better-class hotels are in the southern end of the city. Most tourists with a moderate budget stay in the Sagarnaga area. Reservations are not usually needed. If one hotel is full, the one down the street will have a room. If you are going to keep returning to La Paz and have a favorite place to stay, certainly make a reservation. When I did this, I was never asked for a deposit.

◆ Inca Campesino Class

Hotel Scala, *Calle Union #425 between Calle Chiquisaca and Avenida America, $, no phone.* Clean and off the main thoroughfare, this hotel is quiet, comfortable and has personable staff. Private bathrooms and hot-water showers are available, but there is no restaurant. This is a family-run business and the owners will take very good care of you.

Pachamama Residencial, *Pasaje Juan XXIII #32 between Illampu and Sagarnaga,* ☎ *212-0645, $,* has large rooms with large windows. Each room has a TV and a closet. Some feature hardwood floors. Only one room (that is a bit drab) has a private bathroom. However, there are just three rooms on each floor and one bathroom, so you don't share with many. The owners are friendly and the location quiet and central. You can safely leave things here while you travel around the country. The Pachamama is a real deal for those on a budget.

Hostal Señorial, *Calle Yanacocha #540,* ☎ *240-6042, $$, one block from Plaza Murillo.* Bedrooms have high doors, wood floors, TVs, closets, crooked mirrors and dim lighting. The unisex communal baths have two or three toilets and the same number of showers. A kitchen with plates, pots and a gas stove is available to guests.

Residencial Colonial, *Avenida Tarija #210 on the corner of Murillo, (no phone) $$.* The hotel's 14 small rooms are carpeted and have skylights to make them bright. Towels and soap are supplied and the beds are soft. A fully supplied kitchen is available for guests to use. The Colonial is clean and located in an attractive old building. It has rooms with and without private bathrooms. There are communal bathrooms on each floor.

Hotel Garcilazo, *Isaac Tamayo #560 on the corner of Garcilazo de la Vega,* ☎ *245-3075, $$,* is an enclosed building in the Mercado Negro area. Its rooms are overpriced – $6.75 for a room with bath but only a cold-water shower. For a hot shower you must go across the hall to the communal bath. Bedrooms are big and fairly clean. There is cable TV.

Hotel Dynastia, *Calle Illampu #684 near the corner of Graneros,* ☎ *245-1076, $$.* Rooms are large and clean, with a communal bathroom on each floor and hot water for showers. Those with private bath also have TVs. With six stories and no elevator, be prepared to hike to the top floor, where it is quiet (the climbing is good for acclimatization). There is a restaurant in the hotel, but it is seldom open for business. I found that since this hotel has appeared in other guide books, the staff has become indifferent to offering good service.

Hotel Happy Days, *Calle Sagarnaga #229,* ☎ *231-4759, happydays@ metalink.com, $$.* Located in the center of the tourist shopping area, Happy Days is run by a woman who will not put up with any hanky-panky, so it is fairly safe for a single girl. The carpets are dirty and the beds hard. I think it is overpriced.

Hotel Sucre, *Calle Colombia #340 on the Plaza San Pedro*, ☎ 249-2038, *$$*. The 24 rooms are set around a common courtyard that has flowers in the center. The floors are polished hardwood and the rooms have high colonial-style doors. There is a bed, cupboard, table and chair in each room, plus a window that opens onto the courtyard. Although some of the corners are chipped, the place is clean and the staff makes one feel welcome.

Hostal Republica, *Calle Comercio #1455 and Avenida Bueno*, ☎ 220-2742, *marynela@ceibo.entelnet.bo*, *$$*, is set in a colonial house that once belonged to one of the many presidents of Bolivia. Rooms are clean, the garden and courtyard are appealing and the staff members go out of their way to make you comfortable. Besides being a pleasant place to stay the hotel has a money exchange service, laundry, Internet, safe-deposit box, luggage deposit and parking. They also offer transportation to the airport.

Hotel Alem, *Calle Sagarnaga #334*, ☎ 236-7400, *$$*. The Alem is clean, friendly and inviting. It has rooms with and without private bathrooms. The rate includes a continental breakfast.

Milton Hotel, *Calle Illampu #1124, corner of Calle Calderon*, ☎ 236-8003, *www.khainata.com/hotelmilton.com/*, *$$*, has glittering hardwood floors at its entrance. Its 50 rooms are located on five floors and a terrace at the top offers a view over the city. Large rooms have private baths, cable TV, nice curtains, closets and counters. Some have chairs. A few rooms are a bit tattered. You may leave luggage and there is a place to leave valuables too. The rate goes up with each floor, and a single person must pay the same price as two people. Prices also go up during peak season. A continental breakfast is included in the price. Breakfast, if not staying at the hotel, costs less than a dollar per person. This includes juice, coffee, bread and eggs. Laundry service is available and there is a tour agency. The staff is pleasant.

Hotel Continental, *Avenida Illampu #826 on Plaza V. Juariste Eguino*, ☎ 245-1176, *$*, is a clean hotel/hostel with spacious rooms that come with or without private bathrooms. It's a member the International Hostelling Association.

◆ Inca Merchant Class

Arcabucero Hostal Inn, *Calle Viluyo #307, between Calle Velasco and Linares*, ☎ 231-3473, *$$$*. The Arcabucero is in a cheery colonial building with clear glass over the central courtyard that now holds a small bar and restaurant. The restaurant serves mainly breakfasts. Bedrooms are clean, with carpets, a phone, a small desk and dresser. Each room has a window that either overlooks the courtyard or the street. Antiques in the sitting areas and original art pieces around the building make it interesting and homey. The owner, a Bolivian, speaks perfect English. The 10 rooms are cleaned daily and the front door is kept locked – as a guest, you must ring the bell to enter.

Angelo Colonial Hostal, *Mariscal Santa Cruz #1058*, ☎ 212-5667, *hostalangelocolonial@yahoo.com*, *$$$*. This clean and friendly place is on the main drag and features antiques throughout and original art on the walls. The bedrooms, with glass doors and wooden shutters, circle a courtyard that has been closed off to hold an Internet café. It is the only place in town with a printer (the cost is about 5¢ per page).

Sagarnaga Hotel, *Calle Sagarnaga #326*, ☎ 235-0252, *$$$*, has rooms with and without private bathrooms. The price includes a continental breakfast. Located close to San Francisco Church, it is popular with the backpackers. I felt the staff was a bit aloof, but the place looked clean.

Condeza Hotel, *Pasaje Juan XXIII #190, Illampu and Sagarnaga*, ☎ 231-1193, *$$$*, has single, double and triple rooms. Continental breakfast is included and some English is spoken. There are seven floors and an elevator. Each average-size room has wood floors, closets, telephone, TV and a tiled bathroom.

◆ Inca Royalty

Residencial Rosario, *Calle Illampu 704*, ☎ 236-9542, *$$$$*. Rooms with a private bath cost 40% more than those without. Accommodations cluster around a courtyard that is comfortable and appealing. The rates include a good buffet breakfast served at the on-site restaurant. A tour agency in the hotel caters to climbers and a sauna caters to sore muscles. The owners have a second establishment in Copacabana and they will readily transfer you from one place to the other. This is a clean, safe and convenient place to stay.

Hotel España, *Avenida 6 de Agosto #2074*, ☎ 244-2643, *www.hotel-espana.com*, *$$$$*, is on the main street heading toward the better part of town. The large rooms (single, double or triple) have private baths, telephones and a TV. Rates include a continental breakfast and Internet access. There is a restaurant, laundry, beauty shop and garage.

Gran Hotel Paris, *Plaza Murillo*, ☎ 220-3030, *www.granparishotel.com*, *$$$$$*, was built in 1911 and its elegance has grown with age. It has everything from single rooms to suites that overlook the plaza. The rates include an American buffet breakfast. Each large room, tastefully decorated, has a full bath, with everything included – shampoo, hair dryer, bath beads, fluffy towels, soap and toilet paper. Set in a colonial mansion, the hotel has high ceilings and wide hallways. Each floor has a sitting area and the rooms have fireplaces, personal safes, a rich wood writing desk and bed lamps. Accessories, like curtains and carpets, are coordinated, and all rooms have small balconies. The suite has a sitting room and a sleeping room. The doors to the rooms are operated with electronic entrance cards. Artwork on the walls is mostly petit point and the chairs are tapestry. An entertainment hall often has professional performances with tickets costing around $10.

Max Inn Hotel, *Avenida Sucre #1494 on Plaza Mariscal Sucre*, ☎ 249-2247, *portalesip@kolla.net*, *$$$$$*. The Max has a large foyer and nice halls. The rooms are of moderate size, with bright lights, carpets, mini bars, cable TV and fans. Bathrooms feature hair dryers and small tub/showers. There is also a garage. Breakfast is included. I wasn't all that impressed with the staff, nor were they with me. They seemed suspicious when I wanted to look around.

Naira Hostal, *Sagarnaga #161 across from Plaza San Francisco,* ☎ *231-1214, Hnaira@ceibo.entelnet.bo, $$$$$.* Located in the center of the tourist area, across from San Francisco Church, the Naira is a convenient place to stay. The large, clean rooms are built around a central courtyard. Although the place is well kept and the showers are clean, I found a few paint chips along the baseboards. Hot water is supplied from a tank. There is laundry service and a safe for valuables. A restaurant, coffee/bakery shop and an Internet café are on site. Avoid the travel agency downstairs.

Hotel Gloria, *Calle Potosi #909,* ☎ *240-7070, www.hotelgloriabolivia. com, $$$$$,* is part of Bolivia's rendition of a chain hotel. The one in La Paz has a fairly well-kept lobby, but the rooms have seen better days. All 90 rooms have private baths, central heating and cable TV. Rates include breakfast and transportation to and from the airport. Parking is available and the hotel is located in a convenient area just up from the Prado and very close to Alexander Coffee (go there for breakfast, rather than eating at the Gloria). Other amenities include a money exchange service, Internet access, safe deposit boxes and laundry service. The staff is friendly and helpful. Some spoke English.

El Rey Palace Hotel, *Avenida 20 de Octubre #1947,* ☎ *241-8541, www. hotel-rey-palace-bolivia.com, hotelrey@caoba.entelnet.bo, $$$$$,* comes complete with doorman and elevator music in the halls. Each room has a king-sized bed (some have two) a radio, phone, cable TV, air conditioning, a safe, hair dryer, bidet, Jacuzzi bath, shampoo, soap and telephones in the bathroom and the bedroom. A mini-bar is stocked with good wine. The high-quality wood closets, colonial furniture and plush carpets are an added draw. Buffet breakfast is included in the price. The hotel also has a business center and Internet access at no extra cost. Single rooms are just a bit smaller than doubles. A discount is offered to those staying more than one night and you may have a room for just the day at the discounted price of $30. Weekend prices are much lower than during the week. There's a restaurant and a quiet piano bar. The staff speak English and some speak French Canadian.

Radisson, *Avenida Arce 2177,* ☎ *244-1111 (toll-free US 800-333-3333), www.radisson.com/lapazbo, $$$$$.* All 239 rooms in this giant chain hotel have private bathrooms. There is everything on site that any five-star hotel has anywhere in the world, from coffee shops to magazine stores to hairdressers to swimming pools. Dual pricing is practiced here; locals pay less.

Hotel Ritz, *Plaza Isabel la Catolica #2478,* ☎ *243-3131, www.hotel-ritz-bolivia.com, $$$$$,* has suites to suit all tastes. Located in the better part of town near the Bridge of the Americas, this hotel has British-styled décor (complete with John Peel paintings) and British-style reserve. The suites are large and well decorated and the price includes an excellent buffet breakfast. The starting rate is $121 and it goes up to $177 for two people. However, due to different plans and promotions available, they offer up to 47% discounts (weekends are one of the best times to get a deal).

Hacienda Villa-del-Sol, ☎ *274-0008, www.villa-del-sol.com, $$$$$* is an award-winning, five-star hotel that has one- , two- or three-bedroom suites. Located near the golf course, it looks like a North American walled city. The award it won was for the best constructed hotel in La Paz. Each suite has 60 channels on the cable TV, a bar, balcony, telephones, Internet connection, safes and a wood-burning fireplace.

Places to Eat

Gastronomic fairs are common and should be taken in if you are in town at the right times. The first one, held in June, features pork. Participating restaurants (usually associated with big hotels) offer a selection of their best pork dishes. The second gastronomic fair is in July, where

❖ RESTAURANT PRICING	
$	under $5
$$	$5 to $10
$$$	$11 to $25
$$$$	$26 to $50
$$$$$	over $50

freeze-dried potatoes (*chairo*) and *plato paceño* (dishes commonly made by the people of La Paz) are the specialty. The third fair takes place in August and features foods specific to different departments in the country. The last festival is on October 20th, La Paz Day, when all foods specific to La Paz are featured. Although you still pay for the food, the fairs provide you with an opportunity to taste dishes not commonly found on restaurant menus.

◆ Coffee, Desserts & Breakfast

Alexander Coffee Shops have five locations in La Paz and one in Santa Cruz. The ones in La Paz are on Calle Potosi #1091, ☎ 240-6482; on Avenida 16 de Julio #1832, ☎ 231-2790; on Plaza Avoroa, Avenida 20 de Octubre #2463, ☎ 243-1006. This last location is also a bar that's popular in the evenings with both locals and tourists. The fourth one is in Zona Sur is on Calle Montenegro and Avenida La Cheviña, ☎ 277-0465. You'll also find an Alexander kiosk at the airport, ☎ 281-0240, that opens by 7 am. Alexander serves filter coffee and great cappuccinos for 75¢ a single and $1 for a double. Newspapers are available for reading and there's an upstairs overlooking the street at the Potosi location. The chain serves one of the best breakfasts in town, as long as you order the items individually. The toast that goes with the breakfast is terrible. Get a croissant instead, or smuggle in a crusty bun from the market. The carrot cake is excellent, as is the strawberry cheesecake. This is not a place to miss. Open 8 am to 11 pm, Monday to Friday, and 9 am to 11 pm on weekends.

Confieteria Club de La Paz, *Calle Camacho and Mariscal Santa Cruz* ☎ 212-6265, has décor from the 1930s with wood walls part way up and photos of the city before World War II. This was once a meeting place for the famous Klaus Barbie, alias Klaus Altman while he was in La Paz. Barbie was a Nazi war criminal who worked as a consultant to the government leaders from the 1960s to the 1980s. He was also close to Stroessner (Paraguay) and Pinochet (Chile). His specialty was unlawful arrest, torture and murder. Today, there are no known consultants sitting in the pleasant restaurant that serves cappuccinos with thick sweet cream and pastries that are just as rich. This was also a favorite haunt of Bolivian poets Hector Borda and August Cespedes.

Torino Hotel/Café, *Calle Socabaya #457*, serves cappuccino and great pastries – like lemon pie and scones – that are famous. It offers a lunch buffet for less then $2. This includes a salad bar, soup, main dish (vegetarian meals included) and desserts. The *almuerzo* (main meal) is available from Monday to Friday, noon to 3 pm. This is a good deal for the hungry. Internet access is available. This is a popular restaurant for meeting other travelers. However, the surly waiter is still there three years after we first fought with him. The coffee is not nearly as good as at Alexander's, and the breakfast can be matched by any *tienda* on the street.

Café La Terraza, *Avenida 6 de Agosto #2296*, ☎ 764-3313, *Avenida Montenegro Bloque B #5 in San Miguel*, ☎ 799-5695, or *Avenida 16 de Julio along the Prado*, is a chain popular with Bolivian yuppies. Their chocolate cake is good and the coffee is okay. The service was slow.

Profumo di Caffe, *Plaza San Francisco #502*, ☎ 231-3824, is open daily from 8:30 am to 8 pm and has excellent pastry to go with a midday cappuccino or expresso. The coffee is as good as the pastry.

Residencial Rosario, *Calle Illampu #704*, ☎ 236-9542, offers a buffet breakfast with fruit, yogurt, dollar-size pancakes, Wunderbread (that you can toast) and granola for $2.50. The egg sandwich I had was inedible, but many foreigners choose to start their day here.

◆ **Snacks & Lunches**

Paseo Café Colon, *Avenida Camacho #1372 and Loayza*, ☎ 214-8992, has nice décor that includes photos from the early 1900s. The food, however, is sparse and ordinary and the coffee too strong. A New York sandwich consisting of bacon, lettuce, tomato, cheese and a smattering of French fries on the side cost $2. However, CNN television in Spanish was clear.

Wall Street Café, *Avenida Camacho 1363*, serves good burgers and falafels and draws a middle-class Bolivian clientele. The atmosphere is pleasant and the service excellent, but prices are a bit high. The café opens at eight every morning except Sunday.

Romano's, *Calle Santa Cruz #260, inside the Galeria Alexis, #5 (no phone)*, specializes in Italian foods and pastas, although they do make some international dishes. The place is tiny, but friendly and open seven days a week. If you have a meal here, you get 50% off your Internet costs. They had three computers when I was there.

Naira Restaurant, *Calle Sagarnaga #161, at the very lower level of the building*, has long wooden benches set along wooden tables. Entertainment is available late, after 10, for a cover charge of $5. The food is good but portions are small. However, the upstairs coffee shop and Internet café are excellent. Any and all of the baked goods are recommended.

Restaurant Surucachi, *Avenida 16 de Julio #1598 along the Prado*, ☎ 231-2135, has been around almost as long as La Paz itself. The restaurant is in an elegant old building that has many rooms on two floors. Meals are huge and reasonably priced. (Chicken soup at $3 sounds like a rip-off, but you get half a chicken plus a hard-boiled egg, rice, vegetables and potatoes all served in a soup tureen.) The *almuerzo* is probably one of the best in Bolivia and the main course changes daily. Surucachi is open every day, 9 am to 10:30 pm. The service is as good as the food and the place is patronized exclusively by Bolivian professionals and me.

Pizzeria Napoli *on Murillo Square #1131,* ☎ *220-4090,* has single slices of pizza laden with cheese for just over a dollar. Or try a triple-decker ice cream served on a waffle cone for just under a dollar. A family-sized pizza to go costs $6. Although the place is tiny, it is clean and the service is pleasant.

Dumbos, *across from Surucachi on Avenida Santa Cruz,* is the local hang-out for ice cream served as creative food art, for pastries laden with delicious things we are not supposed to eat and even for substantial food like fries and hamburgers. This is an "in" place for the young, up-and-coming Boliviano. As usual, the coffee is only so-so.

Lak Smi Vegetarian Restaurant, *Calle Sagarnaga #213,* ☎ *221-3048,* offers a great Indian-style *almuerzo* for $1.25. They serve many of their meals on a *talli* tray that contains six or eight containers with spiced foods, yogurt and rice. Specialties are things like puri, massala, chapattis and samosas (which, I feel, leave a bit to be desired).

Pepe's Coffee Bar, *Calle Jimenez #894 off Avenida Linares,* ☎ *245-0788,* is a tiny place that serves good meals. I had a toasted veggie sandwich for $2 and the banana milkshake I ordered was so thick I could hardly suck it through the straw. Take your pick from cappuccino, espresso and other non-alcoholic goodies. Pepe's was exceptionally clean and it's one of the few places in La Paz that offers take-out coffee.

Burger King, *Avenida Ballivian #312 and Calle Calacoto,* ☎ *279-6867, Calle Socabaya and Avenida Mercado,* ☎ *240-8593, or at the International Airport,* ☎ *282-5255,* has not been run out of town by local restaurants yet (MacDonald's has already left). If you want a touch of home, a clean bathroom, air conditioning and a burger for $3, then Burger King is the place.

Armonia Vegetarian Restaurant, *Avenida Ecuador #2286,* ☎ *241-2858,* offers an excellent buffet *almuerzo* from noon to 2:30 pm daily. It is one of the few vegetarian restaurants in Bolivia. I found that people here still find the concept of vegetarianism – like the desire for hot showers and freshly-roasted, filter coffee – a touch weird.

Cevichon, *Calle Murillo #1165,* ☎ *231-1889,* has the best and most varied menu of ceviche in Bolivia. The dining room is small, with décor a secondary concern. The first concern is the food and they carry every type of ceviche imaginable. The ceviche *piscado* (fish), enjoyed with a beer, is an excellent meal. A large plate of ceviche and a beer is under $3.

Pollo Pinocho, *Avenida Arce #2132, Illampu Building,* ☎ *244-1979,* despite its name, is not Italian, but Korean. Its spicy soup is worth stopping in for. Open 9:30 am to 10 pm.

◆ Fine Dining

Restaurant Angelo Colonial, *Calle Linares #922,* ☎ *236-0199,* is a classy place decorated with antiques and candles, often in candelabras. The food is good, too, but the service is slow. They serve only small beers and the cost is $1.25 per bottle (a large one elsewhere is usually $1). A moderate-size dish of delicious chicken with mushroom gravy was $4.50. The Angelo also has an Internet café, post office, a telephone office and a seldom-open tourist information office. Reservations should be made if arriving after 7:30 pm.

Les Pot Pourri des Gourmets, *Calle Linares #906*, ☎ *154-0082*, is in the same building as the coca and textile museums. The restaurant is a great find. For $2 they serve a choice of four meals that include soup, entrée and dessert. The menu allows for either a full or half-portion. A large bowl of garlic soup for a dollar is a good deal. Other dishes offered by this unique restaurant are *locro oreño*, squash cooked in pastry with a sprinkling of cheese on top. This dish is from the Santa Cruz area. *Pukacopa* is a pastry filled with cheese and onion and in Oruro, where it originated, it is eaten with or as dessert. The lemon pie is the best in town. Pot Pourri is open 7:30 am to 10:30 pm but, because Bolivians don't generally eat a big breakfast, service in the morning can be slow.

La Casa del Corregidor (House of the Magistrate), *Calle Murillo #1040*, ☎ *236-3633*, near the lawyers' area of town, is an upper-class joint that requires reservations in high season. Entrées run from $3.50 to $4.50 and the meal of the day is $6.50. Try the excellent onion soup, made with a smattering of oregano and wine. The shish kebab I had satisfied my protein requirement for a week. Plates are artistically presented and the waiters are attentive. The dining room has beamed ceilings, large chandeliers and a fireplace. The background music is just that – in the background. Live entertainment is presented every night except Sunday. La Casa is a treat.

Layq'a Café, *Calle Linares #897*, ☎ *246-0903*, has large beers and a salad bar that costs $3.50 for as many refills as you wish. But it's the huge meal of llama steak cooked with onions and tomatoes, for $6.50, that is their best offering. Don't come to Layq'a's for for breakfast – it took almost an hour to get a small cup of luke-warm coffee that cost $1.

Reineke Fuchs, *Calle Jauregui #2241*, ☎ *244-2979, or Avenida Montenegro and Calle 18, San Miguel*, ☎ *277-2103, www.reinekefuchs. com*. A visit to one of these upscale restaurants is a must. I had pasta stuffed with spinach, drizzled with béchamel sauce and sprinkled with parmesan. It was the best-tasting pasta dish I've had anywhere in the world. The price was $4. They carry the largest variety of German beer in the country and claim to have 28 varieties available almost all the time. The waiters are attentive and friendly. Open Monday to Saturday at 6 pm.

Gran Hotel Paris, *Plaza Murillo and Bolívar*, ☎ *220-3030*, built in 1911, is situated on the main square in town. Its elegant restaurant offers an *almuerzo* Monday through Thursday and a suckling pig baked in a brick oven on Friday. The cost for lunch of the day is about $6 per person.

El Gaucho Restaurant, *20 de Octubre #5696 and Central, no phone*, is an upscale Argentinean steakhouse. It has an impressive wine selection to complement the steaks cooked to perfection. Music – often Argentinean folk songs – is played at a reasonable volume and the service (waiters wear black tie and jackets) is commendable. The salad bar offers mostly sliced fresh veggies (not really salads) and the Argentinean wine we had was dry and excellent.

Chifa Emy, *Avenida 20 de Octubre #927, on Plaza Avaroa,* ☎ 244-0551, is attractive, clean and inviting. An extensive menu offers more than 170 dishes, most costing between $3 and $5. Servings are huge and the food is excellent. It's open Monday to Sunday, 11 am-3 pm and 6-11 pm (on Friday and Saturday it stays open until 1 am, and on Sunday it closes at 10 pm).

Ritz Hotel, *Plaza Isabel la Catolica #2478,* ☎ 243-3131, *www.hotel.ritz. bolivia.com,* has an excellent buffet breakfast on weekdays in the Oak Room. It is a bit expensive ($4 per person), but worth the price. Selections include fresh fruit, yogurt, buns, pastries, eggs, pancakes, sausages, bacon, cereals, coffee, fruit juice and toast. On the same premises is **Duke's Restaurant**, which specializes in Argentinean beef, Italian pasta and the house dish, Tablita Ritz. The *tablita* consists of an oak plank that carries a fillet of beef, chicken and/or sausage served with potatoes and covered with a choice of two sauces.

Restaurant Rincón Español, *Calle Hermanos Manchego #2550, between Pedro Salazar and Avenida Arce,* ☎ 243-5306, is by far the best restaurant in La Paz. It has just 12 tables, so reservations are essential. The specialty is seafood, but everything, including steak and salad bar, is excellent (the steak can be cut with a fork). The seafood stew had clams, shrimp, octopus, fish (and a few things I wasn't sure about) done in a tomato sauce and served in a hot pot. As I looked around, I noticed that many locals had ordered the same dish. The atmosphere is romantic, the service is top notch and I highly recommend at least one meal here. There is a small bar you can sit at if you have to wait for a table. Open at 7 pm. Reserve ahead.

Beatrice Italian Restaurant, *Calle Sanchez Lima, #2158,* ☎ 241-7198, is a tiny, intimate and tastefully decorated restaurant. The menu lists seven types of pasta dishes with a choice of nine different sauces. The main course is served with fresh, hot garlic bread and the dessert menu is tempting. At under $5 per meal, it's well worth a visit.

Wasamama Restaurant, *Avenida Arce and Pinilla #2557,* ☎ 243-4911, is behind Jalapeños and is the best (maybe the only) Japanese restaurant in town. Of course, their specialty is sushi and they make all kinds. But the sushi that made them famous is the trout.

Don Vittorio, *Avenida 6 de Agosto,* ☎ 244-0758, cooks the best pizza in town. Service is fast, the price is right and the food abundant. The restaurant is small, so you may have to sit at an outside table, on the street.

Dumas Café and Bar, *Avenida Arce #2390 on the corner of Belisario Salinas,* ☎ 244-2089, has such good gourmet food that it has been recommended in the *Gourmet's Guide* and *El Pais* from Spain. It serves fish from the mountains and Lake Titikaka, plus seafood and meats. The *pejerrey*, a fish from the lake, is the best dish. Dishes have either a French or a Spanish flare. Open daily, 9:30 am to 11 pm.

Maphrao-on Tai Restaurant, *Calle Claudio Aliaga #1182,* ☎ 279-3070, offers hot and spicy Thai foods that are excellent. It's open Tuesday to Saturday, noon-3 pm and 7 pm to midnight, Sunday and Monday, noon-3 pm.

Seoul Restaurant, *Calle Campos 232, between Avenida 6 de Agosto and Avenida Arce,* ☎ 243-1361, serves typical Korean foods that are good to taste and milder in flavor than most Chinese dishes. Open Monday to Saturday, noon-10 pm.

The Roman Palace, *Calle Santa Cruz #266A*, ☎ *775-72102 (cell),* is a pizzaria that has ravioli, spaghetti, fettuccine and calzone. They have other things too, but these are their best meals. Prices are reasonable. Open 9 am to 11 pm, seven days a week.

Shian Restaurant, *Calle Hermanos Manchego #2586, no phone,* is set in a classy two-storey building in the plush area of town. Seafood is their specialty. Open Monday to Friday, 11:45 am-2:30 pm and 6:45-11 pm, and on Sunday until 3 pm.

Nightlife

L ike any international city, La Paz has everything from a symphony or-chestra to a jazz bar with international musicians. Most shows featuring musicians playing traditional music, called *peñas*, are in the tourist area. Head to the south end of town for the more international entertainment. If you understand Spanish, live theater is a must. If not, movie theaters offer American movies in English with Spanish sub-titles. La Paz is not a danger-ous city, but I do recommend taking a taxi home after spending a night on the town.

◆ Live Music, Bars, Pubs & Discos

Thelonious Jazz Bar, *Avenida 20 de Octobre*, ☎ *242-4405*, is a tiny place that opens Tuesday to Saturday at 7 pm, although things rarely get going before 10 pm. There's a cover charge of $5 and drinks are not cheap, but the music is excellent. Thelonious is the kind of jazz club you would find in New York: a long rectangular bar, seating space for about 100, round ta-bles with candles, and walls covered with photos of jazz musicians.

Huari Peña Restaurant, *Calle Sagarnaga #339*, ☎ *231-6225*, is a pub that has live traditional music specifically for the tourist. It's a good show that you can enjoy with Andean food. The cover charge is $6 and the show starts at 8 pm, seven days a week.

Peña Bolivia, *Sagarnaga #189*, ☎ *231-6827*, is competition to Huari Peña and, for a dollar less cover charge, is much better. The hall is bigger and the food – things like llama kebab, lamb cooked in wine and spiced chicken – is good. The show starts daily at 8:30 pm.

Los Escudos Peña Restaurant, *Avenida Mariscal Santa Cruz #1201, on the corner of the Plaza of the Obelisco in the Club de La Paz*, ☎ *231-2133,* has grand shows of international quality. The cover charge of $5 in-cludes your first drink and the meal of the day can be ordered for $10.

The Diesel National, *20 de Octubre #2271*, is a funky place patronized by the young traveling crowd who want to dance and drink until dawn. Even if you don't want to party all night, you will find that the décor is an interest-ing attraction. Open Monday to Saturday at 7:30 pm.

Coyote Bar, *Avenida 20 de Octubre #2288*, ☎ *277-2856,* is a small but popular place to hang out, drink and meet the Bolivian version of the yup-pie.

Bizzarro Alternative Club, *Gualchalla and 20 de Octubre,* has two lounges – the Electric Floor and the Electronic Lounge. They open at 7 pm and have a Girl's Night on Friday where the girls get drinks at half price. Friday and Saturday nights feature Bizzaro DJ shows and performances.

Mongo's Rock Bottom Bar, *Calle Hermanos Manchego #2444,* offers international foods and lots of loud music for dancing. Once the miners' bar, it has been taken over by young professionals, foreign tourists and expats. The food is good and there are discounted prices for drinks during happy hour. Open weekdays at noon and on weekends at 6 pm.

La Casa del Tapado, *Calle Batallon Colorados,* is open Monday to Saturday from 3 pm until late. This is the new artists' hang-out that has over 200 pieces of original art donated by 130 Bolivian artists. Some are from the Fundacion RISCO and others are students from the Academia Nacional de Bellas Artes and UMSA. The three-room house has an auditorium, a bar in the motif of a mine, and a café with live music. The theater has presentations from the El Pequeño Teatro in La Paz and by the Cine al Margen. Come here to support the arts.

Scaramush Bar, *Calle Fernando Guachalla #521,* ☎ *242-1440,* is a cozy downstairs bar with lots of wood and polish. Live music, often jazz, is presented on Thursday and Friday nights. Open Monday to Saturday, 6:30 pm to midnight.

◆ Soccer Games

Football, or soccer, is an addiction here and even the youngest kids can be seen kicking a ball. If they don't have a ball, they make one out of a stone wrapped in a sock. At present, the three top teams are the **Bolívars**, the **Oriente Petrolero** and the **Strongest**. If you are a fan, watch the *Llama Express* for game times or check at the tourist office on Plaza Estudiantes.

Shopping

There are so many shops from which to choose it seems unfair to list only some here. You can purchase good-quality weavings from street vendors and you can get some shoddy stuff in shops with good displays. My advice is if you see something you like, and can afford it, buy it. Regardless of how much you pay in Bolivia, the price at home will be about 10 times as much. In La Paz, you may find better prices at shops that are a little away from Calle Sagarnaga, the main tourist spot. I also encourage you to purchase something from one of the co-ops throughout the country in support of their work with the local people. Shops open around 9 am and close for siesta during the afternoon. They re-open around 4 pm and stay open until 9pm. There are a few shops that stay open during siesta.

◆ Local Crafts

El Dorado Collection, *Calle Linares #892,* ☎ *246-0269 or 245-2646,* is open from 9:30 am to 7:30 pm. They specialize in fine silver products and Alpaca sweaters. The sweaters are of high quality and unique designs.

Artesanias Wara, *Calle Sagarnaga #131*, ☎ *231-6674*, carries Jalq'a weavings, including the prized belts. Those made from alpaca are so tightly woven that they appear to be painted. Prices are high, of course. The store also carries ceramics and leather goods that have weavings worked into them.

Artesania Curmi, *Calle Linares #958*, ☎ *241-5024*, sells Bolivian textiles and a good collection of bags. I didn't find much to buy as stock was low, but if you do buy something, they will ship the goods home for you.

Wiphala, *Calle Linares #906*, ☎ *237-1805*, has good prices on unique hats from all areas of the country.

Artesanias Quechua, *Calle Sagarnaga #340*, ☎ 231-8218, has masks, wood products, games and children's clothing. They offer a good price on the ceramic chess sets that have one team as Inca dressed in traditional dress with llamas (instead of horses) and funeral towers (instead of castles). They play against the conquistadors.

Inti Illimani, *Calle Linares #890*, ☎ *281-6832*, has excellent wool and alpaca carpets at reasonable prices. The carpets are large, with unique designs. A 6.5 x 10-foot/2 x 3-m carpet costs about $40 if made from wool, and $70 if made from alpaca.

Co-ops

Inca Pallay, *Calle Linares*, is a co-op center selling quality indigenous products at a fair price (for the crafts makers). The co-op opened the Textile Museum in Sucre as well as some museums in smaller centers. They have shops in Santa Cruz, Sucre and La Paz and support workshops for those living in the rural communities to help them make quality products. At present, the co-op has over 1,200 weavers, both men and women, working in 26 workshops throughout the country.

◆ Packs, Maps & Books

Kaypi Artesanias, *Calle Sagarnaga #189, shop 18,* has North Face backpacks and day packs, as well as Lowe Alpine packs. A large pack goes for about $120 and a small one is $50. Always remember that if the deal sounds too good to be true, it probably is. Some packs made in Bolivia carry "borrowed" labels.

Tu Musica, *Calle Sagarnaga #189, shop 17,* ☎ *231-9162,* has Berndston & Berndston maps, some trekking and climbing maps, road maps and city maps. They also carry better class Andean music CDs. Tu Musica also has posters, books (some of which are in English or German) and videos of Bolivia. The owner speaks fluent English.

Maps can also be purchased directly from Viviane and Ricardo Guzman, ☎ 273-3124 or 7725-1197 (cell), who have the best detailed maps of the country. Ricardo's father was the cartographer.

◆ Antiques

Javier Nuñez de Arco Antique Shop, *Avenida 16 de Julio #1615*, ☎ *211-6661,* is a fairly large shop with real antiques (as opposed to those sold on the street that are often just five weeks old). Nuñez de Arco, a famous Bolivian photographer, has a collection of photos that were originally Arthur Pasnansky's. Pasnansky was a photographer who in the 1940s convinced the archeological society that Tihuanaco was older than they thought at the time. He also wrote the book, *Tiwanaco; the Cradle of American Man*, a copy of which Nuñez de Arco holds. If for no other reason, go into the shop and purchase a collection of photos that have been reproduced as postcards – not to send, but to keep as souvenirs. They show Bolivia as it was 60 to 70 years ago. You are not permitted to take antiques out of the country.

Day Trip

◆ Tihuanaco Archeological Site

Tihuanaco ruins, the most impressive in Bolivia, are located near a small village of the same name just 43 miles/70 km along a paved road from La Paz. You can stay overnight at either the hotel or one of the smaller *alojamientos* in the village. The site itself takes a few hours to cover and for the two museums add another hour or two, depending on the depth of your interest.

About 21 miles/35 km from La Paz, on the way to the ruins, is the village of **Laja**, where the original La Paz was supposed to be constructed. Once the builder, Alonso de Mendoza, realized how cold the Altiplano was, he moved the city to its present site. The church here was the first built on the Altiplano. It was reconstructed in the late 1600s, at which time the mestizo baroque design was added.

Getting to the ruins from La Paz is easy. Go to El Cementario and take one of the *trufis* that leaves every half-hour for the village of Tihuanaco. If you are interested in Laja, get off the bus and visit that village before catching the next bus going to Tihuanaco. The bus may be full when it arrives at Laja so be prepared to stand. It takes about 1½ hours to reach Tihuanaco from La Paz and another 15 minutes to walk from the village square back to the ruins. Returning from Tihuanaco, you can either go to the square and wait for a bus or flag one down along the road that passes the ruins. The last bus leaves for La Paz at 7 pm.

History

The civilization that once used the Tihuanaco ruins as their ceremonial center started building the city around 600 BC and the decline, believed to have been caused by drought, didn't occur until AD 900. The site, during its peak, covered 1,040 acres/420 hectares and the surrounding lands occupied by those with allegiance to the city covered 231,660 square miles/ 600,000 square km.

Some archeologists believe that Tihuanaco had as many as 115,000 people in the city itself and another 250,000 people working and residing in the surrounding countryside. The country people farmed grains, herded llamas and built one of the longest paved roads in pre-Columbian history.

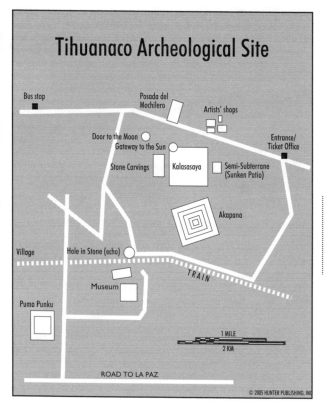

Tihuanaco Archeological Site

Bus stop

Posada del Mochilero

Artists' shops

Door to the Moon
Gateway to the Sun

Entrance/
Ticket Office

Stone Carvings   Kalasasaya   Semi-Subterrane
(Sunken Patio)

Akapana

Village

Hole in Stone (echo)

TRAIN

Museum

Puma Punku

1 MILE
2 KM

ROAD TO LA PAZ

© 2005 HUNTER PUBLISHING, INC

They also traveled and traded as far away as the coast of Peru. From findings there, it has been deduced that the Tihuanaco people were more advanced in pottery, astronomy and math than the Inca ever were.

It is also believed that Tihuanaco once sat on the shores of Lake Titikaka, but, due to drought, the lake receded, leaving the city almost 10 miles/16 km from the water. It was because of this drought that the entire civilization had to move.

Exploring the Ruins

The ceremonial center of the city is believed to have been constructed in the 5th century BC. At the city's peak, an outer wall had friezes that were either partially covered in gold or painted bright colors. People of this time were dressed in finely woven clothes, with jewelry and precious metal pins and carefully combed hair. Appearance was important; numerous mirrors have been found at the site. The heads of Tihuanaco residents were rather pointed. Boards were placed on the heads of infants (one at the back and one at the forehead) so the soft bone grew back from the nose. The boards remained on a child's head until around five years of age. This custom was identified through the examination of skulls found in the area.

Visitors to the city had to cross the moat and call to the guards through a hole in the stone. The sound reverberated to a listener inside the gate who would then give the visitor permission to enter. Though the moat is gone, you can still whisper through the hole and have your companion hear you on the opposite side of the courtyard.

To enter the sunken court of **Kalasasaya** you must go down a wide stairway made from a single block of stone. The sandstone used here came from a quarry six miles/10 km away, but the andesite used in other parts of the city came from about 60 miles/100 km away. Some of the stones weigh as much as 150 tons.

The heads that decorate the temple beside Kalasasaya are believed to be the trophy heads of sacrificed enemies. The sunken patio is called the Semi-Subterraneo and was first described in 1903 by Franciscan missionaries, but it wasn't until 1932 that it was excavated by Dr. Wendell Bennett. Three other temples surrounded Kalasasaya, but little remains of them today.

The huge monolith, excavated by Bennett at Tihuanaco, was moved to the city's archeological museum. It stood 24 ft/7.3 m high and was given the name "Bennett Monolith."

Along one side of the main ruins are small mounds that have a lot of stones missing. You may find some of them in the church on the plaza in the town of Tihuanaco and some on the railway bridge nearby.

> ❖ **CAN I CHANGE YOUR MIND?**
>
> The royalty of Tihuanaco used willka, red hallucinogenic seeds that were imported from the deserts along the coast and were then ground and snorted during religious ceremonies. They also used mescaline to alter their minds. The most extreme hallucinogenic used was the ayahuasca vine. This was administered as an enema.

Another archeologist, Dr. A. Posnansky, studied the site for 50 years. He believes that the people living here were a religious cult who worshipped the god of the sky and of thunder, Viracocha, whose image is represented in the bas-relief in the Gateway to the Sun. Beside him are warriors wearing masks and messengers wearing masks with condors on them.

The **Gateway to the Sun** is cut from a single block of stone that is 9.8 ft/three m high and three m wide and weighs about 10 tons. Through this gate is the carving of a regal figure, dressed in royal robes, carrying two scepters topped with condor heads. During the spring and fall equinox, the sun shines through the gate onto the figure. Today, during the spring equinox, Aymara priests come here to make offerings to their gods and watch through the gate as the sun rises. This is the Aymara New Year and once the sun has risen the priests and others join in celebration with music, dancing, rituals, food, coca and *chicha*.

The mound to the south of the Kalasasaya temple is the **Pyramid of Akapana**. It has seven levels, all of which were at one time faced with stones, some carved. The pyramid is believed to have been built in the image of the surrounding mountains and was used for ritual offerings. Only some stones remain intact, but the view from the top is worth the climb. The pyramid stands 92 ft/18 m high and each side is 375 ft/114 m long.

If you continue to circumnavigate the ruins you will come to a much smaller gate called the **Door of the Moon** (Puerta de la Luna), also made of stone. A tiny **museum** is open 9 am-6 pm daily. It is well organized, with areas dedicated to ceramics, textiles, gold and silver carvings, carved stones found in the area and seashells taken from the lake.

Places to Stay

La Posada del Mochilero, ☎ 289-8544, $$$, is across from the exit gate of the ruins on Camino Antiguo. An attached restaurant has *almuerzos* at reasonable prices.

There are some basic places to stay on the plaza and a few places to eat. The restaurants beside the museum are expensive.

Shopping

Artisan stalls are set around the square and museum. There isn't as much here as in La Paz, but if you are altruistic and want to support the local economy, purchase something.

Directory

LA PAZ – GENERAL DIRECTORY		
■ **OUTDOOR ADVENTURE CLUBS**		
Andino Boliviano	☎ 232-4682	
Club de Montanismo Halcones	no phone	based in Oruro
Gravity Assisted	☎ 231-3849	www.gravitybolivia.com
Hash House Harriers	☎ 279-1524	www.lapazhash.com
Mallasilla Golf & Country Club	☎ 274-5124	www.boliviagolf.com
■ **LANGUAGE SCHOOLS**		
ABC Spanish School	☎ 772-62657	www.studyspanish-lapaz-bolivia.tk
SpeakEasy Institute	☎ 244-1779	www.speakeasyinstitute.com

■ TOUR OPERATORS & OUTFITTERS

Alba Tours . . . . ☎ 231-3052

American Tours. . . . . ☎ 237-4204. www.american-ecotours.com

Andean Summits. . . . . ☎ 242-2106 . . www.andeansummits.com

Buho's Tours . . . . ☎ 247-1577

Explore Bolivia . . . . ☎ 303-545-5728 . . . www.explorebolivia.com

Footprint Adventures . . . . . ☎ 01522-804929 www.footprint-adventures.co.uk

Gravity Assisted Mountain Biking. . ☎ 231-3849 . . . www.gravitybolivia.com

High Camp Bolivia . . . . ☎ 231-7497

Huayana Tours . . . . ☎ 245-6717

Inca Land Tours. . . . . ☎ 231-3589 . . . www.incalandtours.com

International Mountain Guides ☎ 360-569-2609 . . www.mountainguides.com

Magri Turismo Ltd . . . . ☎ 244-2727 . . ww.bolivianet.com/magri

New Horizon . . . . ☎ 231-6274

New Milenium Adventure Sports. . ☎ 245-1660

Sky Bolivia . . . . ☎ 231-3254 . . . . . www.skybolivia.com

Toñito Tours . . . . ☎ 233-6250 www.bolivianexpeditions.com

Tocando el Cielo . . . . ☎ 279-1440

Trek Bolivia. . . . . ☎ 231-7106 . . . www.trekbolivia.8k.com

Vicuña Tours . . . . ☎ 231-0708 . . . . . www.victoursbol.com

The Altiplano

Copacabana/Lake Titikaka

Altitude: 12,533 ft/3,810 m
Population: 7,500

Copacabana, tucked into a sandy bay on Lake Titikaka, is often bypassed by those going to or coming from Peru. This is a pity. Not only is the area aesthetically exceptional, but the hiking is as challenging as it is interesting, with pre-Inca and Inca ruins to enjoy. On weekends, Lake Titikaka is host to every kind of water vehicle possible (except the obnoxious Jet Ski, and I am sure those will come in time). According to the *Guinness Book of World Records*, the highest kayak/skin dive in the world was done in this lake. But if watersports – *cold* watersports – are not your thing, you can always walk the beach looking for the Telmatobius frog. It is easy to spot because it is about a foot long.

The area is also a wetland with enormous amounts of aquatic vegetation and numerous bird species, like the cormorant and the heron.

> **AYMARA LINGO:** *Copacabana comes from two words. "Kgupac" means beautiful blue; "Kgawana" means "that you can see."*

Isla del Sol and Isla de la Luna have been pilgrimage sites since the days of the Chirpa, who preceded the Tihuanacan culture by almost a thousand years. There is convenient transportation from Copacabana to Isla del Sol and Isla de la Luna, the holiest islands, according to Tihuanacan and Inca legend. Today, religious pilgrimages arrive in Copacabana rather than on the islands but still it is the lake more than the beautiful cathedral that seems to be the draw for most foreigners.

There are ruins worth seeing both in town and on the islands. Accommodations and restaurants in Copacabana are excellent and the people are friendly. The only drawback is that money-changing services are poor. If you come from Peru, this can present a problem.

> ❖ **TAXES PLEASE**
>
> A 25¢ tax is imposed on all visitors coming into Copacabana. It is collected on the highway as you approach the town. This is a legal municipal tax ordinance that falls under section CXIII, item 142, of Bolivian law. It nets the municipality a lot of money, especially during special events, and helps pay for keeping the area aesthetically attractive. The tax is paid by everyone, including Bolivians who do not live in the town.

◆ Getting Here & Around

A bus from Copacabana to El Cementerio bus area in La Paz costs $2, plus 25¢ to cross the Straight of Tiquina. Buses are available on Calle 16 de Julio along Plaza Sucre. They leave every two hours between 7 am and 7 pm and take three to four hours to reach La Paz.

If you're going to Sorata, get off the bus at Huarina just after the ferry crossing and catch a *trufi* going north to Achicachi and then another going on to Sorata. You can also take a *colectivo* to La Paz. The time is about the same as a bus, but the comfort and cost is less.

Taxis go from Copacabana to the border town of Kasani and charge $1 per person. These go when full and there are lots of them.

◆ History

Lake Titikaka and its islands have been an important place for thousands of years as the ruins from past civilizations indicate.

> ❖ **BEND ME, SHAPE ME ANYWAY YOU WANT ME**
>
> Local legend has it that Lake Titikaka has three parts. The part belonging to Peru is shaped like a puma, the center is shaped like a condor and the area below the Straights of Taquina is like a man praying.

Once the Spanish took over in Peru, Copacabana became a safe place because there was no reason for the Spanish to invade. It was too far from civilized society and there was no gold in the area. Instead, the area was left to early religious zealots. **Christianity** was brought to the region in 1530, and the first church was erected by 1552. Locals converted to **Catholicism** and then struggles for power started and involved various sects of Catholicism.

◆ Services

The **Entel telephone office** is on Calle Murillo (just down from the Emperador) and up from the cathedral.

The **post office** is on Plaza 2 de Febrero just down from the tourist office.

The **Police** are next to the post office on Plaza 2 de Febrero and on the opposite side of the square from the cathedral.

The **hospital** is on the edge of town going toward Horca del Inca (signs indicate the direction). The phone number is ☎ 118.

The **bank** on Avenida 6 de Agosto, close to Plaza Sucre, charges a 2% commission for travelers' checks. However, being a bank, they are closed on weekends, holidays and by 6 pm every day. There is usually a line here.

A money-changer at Tienda Avenida 6 de Agosto on the corner of Calle 6 de Agosto and 15 de Julio, across from Plaza Sucre, sells many items and advertises the changing of travelers' checks. He is a cheat who plays on tourists not knowing the currency or the language very well.

American Express on Calle 6 de Agosto charges no commission. They are not open on Sundays and holidays, and often open quite late in the mornings.

The **tourist office** is on the Plaza 2 de Febrero just past the police station. They have some information, but seem reluctant to share it with travelers.

◆ Festivals of Copacabana

Samana Santa is the festival that has the most interesting ceremonies as pilgrims walk all the way from La Paz to Copacabana for the celebrations. Copacabana is special for Samana Santa and for the celebration around the Virgin of Candeleria. For more information about festivals, see page 23.

Alasista is held on January 24th to celebrate fertility, happiness and prosperity. Ekeko is the honored god.

The **Virgin of Candeleria** is celebrated February 2nd-4th. This is the most important event in the town because of the Virgin's reputation for performing miracles.

Carnival is at the beginning of Lent (40 days before Easter) and is celebrated throughout Latin America. See page 23.

Dia del Mar (Day of the Sea), March 23rd, is when the death of Eduardo Avaroa is remembered. The navy's fleet sits in Copacabana, so celebrations here are a bit more elaborate than in other places.

Semana Santa is at Easter. Pilgrims walk from La Paz to Copacabana. See page 23 for more information.

◆ Sightseeing

The **Copacabana Cathedral** was first, in the 16th century, a mud and brick structure. But after the Virgin of Candelaria started performing miracles, she needed a better home. The present building, with tiles on the Moorish-styled domes, was completed, according to some authorities, in 1820. However, according to five sources that I tried, the building was started as early as 1589 and completed as late as 1820. I suspect construction began around 1610 and was completed within 50 years, with re-construction and add-ons until 1820 or so.

The wooden entrance doors, carved by locals, are immense and worth looking at. The interior is not huge, but the altar and front are ornate and decorated in gold. The attached museum is open only on Sundays from 8:30 am until early afternoon.

THE ALTIPLANO

Copacabana is famous for its Virgin on the altar in the church. The statue stands 33 inches/84 cm high and is made of maguey wood. Her hands, arms and face are ceramic. In her left arm she carries an indigenous boy-child and in her right a gold candle. There is also a gold cane hanging from her left arm. Both the child and the Virgin have gold and silver crowns decorated with precious stones. The aura around the Virgin's head contains the sun, moon and 12 stars. She is adorned with jewelry – necklace, bracelets, rings and earrings – all heavily decked with semi-precious and precious stones. The belt she wears around her waist was given to her by Augustinian followers. The ruby imbedded in the belt is two inches in diameter. Imbedded in her foot is the Bolivian flag.

There are more stories of miracles performed by the Virgin and I am certain there will be more miracles to come. Because of her reputation, in 1925, the Virgin was crowned the Bolivian Queen and Copacabana became the most important pilgrimage site in the country.

To the side of the cathedral is the entrance to the Candelabria, a dark, stone-walled room where people come to ask for miracles. The walls in the first section of the room (that gets light from the street) are covered in words of hope like "walk, money, Volvo, food." Some scratchings are long, while others are one-word requests. At the far end of the room are candles that you can light before speaking directly to the Virgin.

◆ Adventures on Foot

BANDARINAS DE INCA: Hike to Bandarinas de Inca on Cerro Copacate, where there are rock paintings, some ruins, a marriage rock and an old hacienda. The rock paintings have been vandalized, but university students are restoring them. If taking a bus/taxi to the trailhead, this is a half-day excursion, but if walking all the way from town and stopping at the Inca tunnel, allow a full day.

To get there by vehicle, take any bus/taxi going to Kasani, the border village just five miles/eight km from Copacabana. Get off at the Km 42 sign. There is a school and an abandoned airport at the stop. Walk east up the gravel road. When you come to the first adobe hut just in from the road, look at the mountain to the north. The gully with the vegetation in it is your destination. Beside the house is a sign indicating your route (it was not yet installed when I was there). In the house lives Gregorio Ramos Kantuta who is knowledgeable about pre-Inca culture. He will guide you to the baths, the rock paintings and the temple for no charge, but a donation would be appreciated. Ramos has a generous heart and he is proud of the area's history.

After getting off the bus, take the first trail on your right, off the gravel road, and follow it up. At the end of this trail, go left. Follow the trail (it swings left) until you come to the remains of an adobe hacienda on your right.

You can go inside and snoop around. The estate was owned by a Spaniard who mistreated and enslaved local Indians until they rebelled. Seeing that they were too strong for him to fight or control, the man abandoned his estate and moved back to Spain. Who he was or when this occurred is unknown. The story probably goes back only as far as the land reforms of

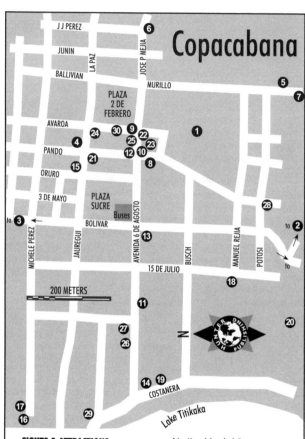

Copacabana

SIGHTS & ATTRACTIONS
1. Cathedral
2. Horca del Inca
3. Stations of the Cross (Calvario)

PLACES TO STAY
4. Porteñita Residencial
5. Hotel Emperador
6. Hostal La Luna
7. La Casa Viva
8. Hospedaje Florez
9. Hostal 6 de Agosto
10. Hostal Alison
11. Wara Hostal
12. Hotel Playa Azul
13. Colonial del Lago & Restaurant
14. Las Brisas del Titikaka & Restaurant
15. Kantutus
16. Hostal Cupula & Restaurant
17. Hotel Utama
18. Hotel Gloria & Sol y Luna Café
19. Hotel Chasqui de Oro
20. Hotel Rosario del Lago

PLACES TO EAT
21. Restaurant Sujma Wasi
22. Sol de los Andes Café
23. Kala Uta
24. Pizzeria Italia
25. Snack 6 de Agosto
26. Manka Uta Restaurant
27. Nimbos

NIGHTLIFE
28. Nikos Karaoke
29. Pub Mercurio de Almas
30. Tatu Correta

© 2005 HUNTER PUBLISHING, INC

THE ALTIPLANO

1952, and the man may have had most of his land taken from him by the government and distributed to the locals.

Continue past the hacienda along the trail and turn left at the end of that trail. Within 20 feet the rock paintings come into view. They are ochre in color and depict the Inca flag.

From the paintings, turn right off the trail and continue past the paintings up the mountain where you will find some ruins of bathing pools and footings for temple walls. It is believed that rich Inca came here to worship and to bathe. You can see how the water may have flowed from one shallow tub down to the next. Probably rocks and mud were used to block the flow of the water and fill the pools.

To go to the wedding rock, return to the rock paintings and continue around the mountain. Stay high, but always on a trail. When you are on the back side of the hill you will see two bright, rust-colored arches. This is where some Inca would come years ago to perform their marriage ceremony. Do not walk farther into the valley where homes can be seen. The people living there do not want visitors. A few years ago there was a dispute as to where the highway should go and these people didn't get what they wanted, so they are a bit hostile to outsiders. Return as you came.

INCA TUNNEL: The Inca Tunnel apparently goes through the mountain, under Lake Titikaka and opens up again at the ruins of Pilcocaina. Although the tunnel is impressive, the walk there is the best feature of the hike. You will pass terraced fields being worked by the owners. There are also a couple of old stone houses that are interesting to look at. The walk from Copacabana should take no more than half a day, unless you combine it with the walk to the Bandarinas de Inca. Exploring both would take a full day.

To get there, walk up Calle Murillo, on the east side of the cathedral, as far as Calle Felix Rosa. At the corner, jog a bit to the right and then the left to continue uphill. You pass a kind of landfill to your left and a wall to your right. Follow that trail all the way around the side of the mountain. It is walled for some of the way. When you are on the south side, continue into a fairly large eucalyptus grove until you come to an abandoned house made of squared stone. This is a ruin from Inca or maybe even Tihuanaco times. There is a second house above it, also abandoned. Just past the bigger house is an opening in the mountain with water trickling out. Peer inside. A flashlight would be useful. The floor and walls have been paved with rocks. Some believe that the tunnel goes all the way to Isla del Sol and was constructed by the Inca. Others believe that the tunnel is from colonial times and was made for mining purposes.

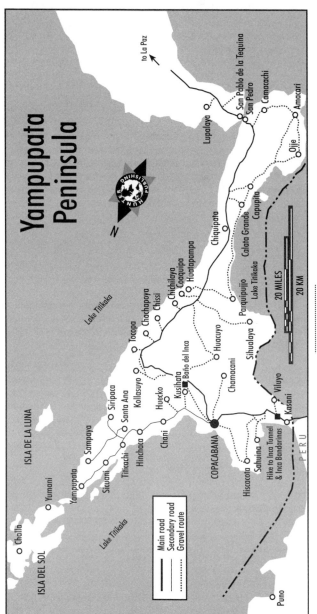

Yampupata Peninsula

to La Paz

THE ALTIPLANO

Main road
Secondary road
Gravel route

20 MILES
20 KM

> ❖ **INCA LEGEND**
>
> Inca legend, as told to me by an Aymara family, Sonia Cruz Condori and her husband, Oscar Quispe Yavi, who live in Copacabana, is that a man entered the cave after the Inca abandoned it. When he was part-way in, there was an earthquake and the man was hit on the head with a rock. He became crazy and never regained his sanity. This was warning for others not to enter the cave. Apparently, the tunnel has been sealed off at the other end. Also, some of the pools in the cave are deep.

YAMPUPATA PENINSULA: Yampupata is the village at the end of the peninsula that is just northeast of Copocaban town site. The peninsula reaches into Lake Titikaka and almost meets Isla del Sol. Many people like to visit the island by renting a reed boat at Yampupata and paddling across. This takes about 40 minutes if there is no wind. Taking a motorboat – available at the end of the peninsula for $2 per person – takes about 15 minutes. A rowboat costs $1.50 an hour. If you want someone to do the paddling/rowing for you, the cost is higher.

Consider staying at Hostal Yampu (see below) in the village of Sicuani (nine miles/15 km from Copacabana). This would allow more time to explore the peninsula. Sicuani is close to the trail leading to the stone village of Zampaya. The owner of the hostel, Jose Quispe, is friendly and knowledgeable.

To get there, take public transportation from Copacabana to the end of the peninsula and walk the 12 miles/20 km back along an almost flat road. If you walk there, getting back may be a problem as most vehicles do not travel that road after dark. A private taxi from Copacabana will cost $10 for up to four people. A truck leaves for Yampupata from Calles Junin and Copacabana every Monday, Tuesday and Saturday between 11 am and noon (when full). Buses leave on the alternate days and cost 75¢ per person. You can also hire a boat to go to the peninsula for $3.50 per person. Contact **Faustino Hillatarco** at the clock on the main square across from the cathedral in the mornings and he will take you over. To walk here from town, go along Calle Junin and down the hill, past the soccer field.

It's 2½ miles/four km from Copacabana to **Kusihata** where a small museum contains an Inca skull found near the baths. It is five miles/eight km to **Chani**, where there are nice views, and six miles/10 km to Henchaka and the Grotto of the Lourdes. The grotto is a small cave in the side of the mountain. It can be seen from the road. **Titicachi** is at the eight-mile/13 km point. As you walk, you will notice the stone and clay houses are clean and in good repair and the fields are tended. Trout farms dot the lake and people are generally well heeled.

Sicuani (sic-WAN-ee) is nine miles/15 km from Copacabana. Hostal Yampu is basic and costs $1.50 per person. The owners are presently building a reed hut for showers and will build a reed museum in the future. They also build and rent reed boats to take onto the lake. The cost at either place is $1.50 per hour. Jampu offers meals at reasonable prices. Lunch, for example, is about $1 and includes rice, salad, meat/fish (usually trout) and potatoes.

Sampaya can be reached by following a trail up the mountain from Sicuani. It's a beautiful stone village (good for photography) with no amenities except a few *tiendas* selling snacks and drinks. Ask José in Sicuani where the path that leads to Sampaya is located.

The final three miles/five km will take you to the village of **Yampupata** where you can tent on the beach for 75¢ per person. There is an outhouse available but no other amenities. If passing through, the cost of using the outhouse is one boliviano (15¢). A boat association here controls the cost of boat rentals. It also keeps operators going out sequentially so that everyone gets a turn to earn some income. A boat to the Isla de la Luna costs $10 for up to 10 people. For a really quiet night, stay at the basic hostel on Isla de la Luna for $1.50 per person. A *tienda* in town sells pop and biscuits.

TRONO DEL INCA: The hike to Trono del Inca starts by walking up Calle Potosi to its end. Turn right and then left again onto the road to La Paz. You will see seven stone carvings on your left that are believed to be seats of the sun. The niches in the stones are believed to have held numerous figures covered in gold. The seats were once used for council meetings of the leaders. It was once believed that the large stones represented smaller versions of the mountains and contained the souls of people now dead. Continue walking another 660 ft/200 m and you will find a huge stone with a seat carved into it. This is the Trono del Inca, or the Inca Throne. Aymara priests come here during the winter solstice in June to celebrate the Aymara New Year. The fee to enter three sites – this one, the Baño del Inca and Horca del Inca – is $1.25.

INCA BATHS: Baño del Inca, or Kusihata, can be reached by walking toward Yampupata out Avenida Junin, past the football field. A carved stone barrel is filled by a natural spring. It is believed that visiting Inca kings stopped here to bathe. Considering the temperature of the lake water, it is no surprise. A museum near the baths contains some archeological objects found near town.

❖ TINY TALENT

An artist from Copacabana by the name of Juan Gutierrez became famous for painting miniatures. Because he didn't have all the finer tools of a painter, he used bird feathers and rabbit hair to make paintbrushes and he used the back of his hand as a palette. In 1925 he received a gold medal from the Centennial of the Republic Committee for a picture of Sucre and Bolívar in two lockets. Then in 1942 he received 500 bolivianos (a large sum at the time) for painting the portrait of Salamanca surrounded by eight departmental shields and the Virgin of Copacabana in a pendant that was only 1.5 inches/four cm in diameter.

HORCA DEL INCA: Horca del Inca is also called Intiwatana. It's on top of the hill at the opposite end of the bay from the Stations of the Cross (Calvario). To get there, walk along Avenida 16 de Julio and, before you

THE ALTIPLANO

leave town, work your way up the trails to the hilltop. Intiwatana was an astronomical observatory for the Inca and/or pre-Inca. In 1978, Oswaldo Rivera from the National Institute of Archeology of Bolivia studied the site and arrived at this conclusion. Before his discovery, it was believed to have been a place of punishment. However, Rivera found that during the first hours of the morning at the summer solstice, the sun illuminates the entire monument. During the winter, a single sunbeam lights only the center of the crossbeam on the lentil. There are parts of walls visible that were used to separate the sacred areas from the public ones.

On top, the most noteworthy object is a natural stone doorway with a stone lentil. There is $1.25 ticket cost for visiting the three sites – Horca del Inca, Inca Baths and Torono del Inca. There are ticket sellers at all three sites.

STATIONS OF THE CROSS: Calvario, or the Stations of the Cross, can be reached by heading uphill along 16 de Julio until you reach a small church. Continue toward the lake, again uphill. The top is splendid and often used by the Kallawaya for ceremonies that blend Catholic and pre-Christian beliefs into a ritual. Like Intiwatana, Calvario should be climbed at least once while in Copacabana. The two hills can be climbed in one day.

◆ Adventures on Water

There are seven companies along the beach who rent equipment for about the same prices. Choose the one with the best life jackets. Some were pretty solid when I looked at them.

Association Union Marinas, ☎ 862-2078, near the dock at the end of Calle 6 de Agosto, rents water vessels for use on the lake. Pedal boats for four people cost $3 for a half-hour, $4 for one hour and $10 for the day. A rowboat for two people is $2 for a half-hour and $3 for one hour. A two-man plastic kayak costs $1.25 for a half-hour and $2 for an hour. Be aware when taking a vessel out onto the lake that winds can make it difficult to get back to shore. You can also get up to 10 people together and rent a motorboat to go to Isla del Sol and back for $25. A half-day trip goes to the south end of Isla del Sol and to Isla de la Luna.

Some agencies offer a few days kayaking/camping around the lake. See *Tour Operators*, below.

You can also take a boat to Yampupata and then follow an Inca Trail to Sampaya. See **Faustino Hillatarco**, on the main plaza in front of the cathedral, for transportation. For a description of the Yampupata Peninsula, see *Adventures on Foot*.

◆ Tour Operators

Titikaka Tours, Avenida 6 de Agosto #2, the last kiosk nearest the dock, ☎ 862-2060, www.titikakabolivia.com. Tickets can be purchased at almost any hotel or tour office in town. The cost to go to both the islands for a full day on a big boat is $7 per person and $2 for half a day. If walking on Isla del Sol, the full-day cost drops to $3 per person (because you don't use the boat to reach Isla de la Luna). A full-day trip leaves Copacabana at 8:15 am and goes to Callapampa at the north end of Isla del Sol, where you have two hours to visit the Gold Museum, Footprints of the Sun, the Sacred Rock and the Chenkana Ruins. For a description of the sites, see Lake Titikaka section, page 111.

For those hiking to the south end of the island, after visiting the above sites you continue on the trail along the island's spine to Yumani, where the boat will be waiting. While crossing the lake, the first mate of the boat gives a great speech about how much trouble tourists are, especially when they miss the boat. He explains that, in fact, it is not his problem but yours if you miss the boat. So, don't miss the boat.

Near the dock at the south end of the island is the Mil Gradas (Thousand Stairs) where the Fountain of Inca is located.

The half-day tour runs from 8:15 am to 12:15 pm and the afternoon tour runs from 1:30 to 6 pm. The half-day tour goes to the south end of Isla del Sol and to Isla de la Luna.

> **SAFETY ALERT:** *An overloaded ferry was crossing the lake at night and a bus slipped off the boat. Those who were sleeping on the bus died. Occasionally boats catch fire but this too is very rare. Generally speaking, boat travel on the lake is accident-free.*

Grace Tours, Avenida 6 de Agosto and Calle 16 de Julio, ☎ 862-2160, offers full- and half-day island tours. A full-day trip costs $3 per person. The boats are fairly decent. This company prefers to take customers by boat to both islands (as opposed to you taking the boat to the north end of Isla del Sol and walking to the south end).

Alba Tours, Avenida 6 de Agosto #450, ☎ 230-6499, offers first-class transportation to Peru and Chile. Their newest day tour goes around Isla del Sol starting and ending in La Paz. The trip leaves La Paz for Tihuanaco and Copacabana where they do a short paddle to the village of Sicuani on the peninsula. The next day they paddle to Isla del Sol and camp overnight. The following day they return to Sicuani where they board a van and leave for the Apolobamba region. This company also offers a kayak-only tour.

Explore Bolivia, 2510 N 47th Street, Suite 207, Boulder, CO 80301, ☎ 877-708-8810 or 303-545-5728, www.explorebolivia.com, offers a two-day kayaking trip around the lake that is combined with a hiking trip in the Apolobamba region.

Prices, depending on the numbers, are between $1,600 and $2,200 for the combination two-week tour and between $625 and $825 for a five-day paddle around the lake. All equipment and food is included. Explore Bolivia has knowledgeable guides and good equipment.

US-based **Nature Quest**, ☎ 800-369-3033, www.naturequesttours. com, offers a six-day kayaking trip around the lake. They go from Copacabana to Sicuani on the peninsula and then over to Isla del Sol and Isla de la Luna. From there they head to the Straights of Taquina and the north shore of the lake, where few tourists travel.

UK-based **Footprint Adventures**, www.footprint-adventures.co.uk, has a combination kayak/hike trip that takes 15 days, starting in La Paz. They paddle around the lake for two days and then head on foot from Sorata to Kukoyo, Nengruni, Chearoco, Waraco and on to Checapa Valley and Alta Khota, ending at Condoriri.

THE ALTIPLANO

◆ Places to Stay

Copacabana has many places to stay and the only time getting a room could be a problem is during Samana Santa. Be aware that electricity can go off at any time as electrical storms in this area can be fierce. Most of the hotels have candles for emergencies, but you should always carry a flashlight.

❖ HOTEL PRICING	
$	$10 to $20
$$	$21 to $50
$$$	$51 to $75
$$$$	$76 to $100
$$$$$	over $100

Inca Campesino Class

Porteñita Residencial, *Calle Gonzalo Jauregui and Panda*, ☎ 862-2006, *$*. Rooms have clean floors and private bathrooms with hot water from an electrical hookup unit, but the beds are bowed and some rooms have no windows. A few rooms without baths are less expensive. A clean patio is decorated with plants. There are 23 rooms with 85 beds in all. Laundry is 75¢ per kilo and there is a garage.

Hotel Emperador, *Calle Murillo #235*, ☎ 862-2083, *$*, has been made popular because of the person who runs it, Sonia Cruz, who keeps her hotel spotless. Rooms, a few of which have private bath, are located around a central patio. There are common showers with water that is electrically heated – for some reason, the hot water works best in the lower-level showers. Towels and toilet paper are included in the price. There is a luggage deposit and breakfast can be served to your room if booked ahead.

Hostal La Luna, *Avenida Jose P Mejia and Oruro, no phone, $*, has eight basic rooms with private bath and wood floors. The building overlooks the Inca hill and the hostel is quiet. Laundry is 75¢ per kilo. There's a small eating area and breakfast Americano with eggs costs just over a dollar. A simple bun with coffee is 75¢.

La Casa Viva, *Calle Murillo and Felix Rosa, $*. Sonia Cruz made the Hostal Emporador what it is and now she has her own tastefully designed place across from the Emperador. The entrance is nicely decorated with a dining area off to the side and a sitting area where guests can visit. The Casa's three floors have 15 rooms – 10 with private bath – with wood floors that are complemented by boldly colored walls and huge windows. The halls are wide and the doors are high, made especially for Westerners. Bathrooms feature tile and showers with hot water. A roof-top terrace has an undercover area in case it rains. Sonia supplies towels and toilet paper. This is one of the best deals in town.

Hospedaje Florez, *Avenida 6 de Agosto*, ☎ 862-2117, *$*, is just 1½ blocks from the main square. Some of the 13 basic rooms have single beds (that are actually three-quarter size). Electric water heaters are used in the showers. The family who owns the hotel is friendly. There is a roof-top terrace that has tables and chairs and a good view of the lake. Meals can be ordered from the restaurant and eaten on the terrace. Security is good; there is someone at the desk 24 hours a day. Laundry, done by hand, not by machine, is 75¢ a kilo.

Hostal 6 de Agosto, *Avenida 6 de Agosto*, ☎ 862-2292, *$*, has basic carpeted rooms with large, private, tiled baths. Most rooms have small writing desks and one even has a skylight of sorts (the covering is yellow fiberglass). The restaurant is small, but the service is excellent and the food is good.

Hostal and Restaurant Alison, *Avenida 6 de Agosto*, *$*, is a new hotel so they don't yet have a phone (phone lines are inherited, so it could take years before they get one). The hostal has a safe deposit, laundry service, and restaurant. Rooms are clean and have hardwood floors. They are well off the street and therefore are quiet. Run by Corina Alijo, an Aymara lady, the hostel's restaurant has Aymara influences that are countered by her husband's Playboy pin-ups. The clay oven, rather than being used for cooking, has an electric heater inside. You can exchange money here.

Wara Hostal, *Avenida 6 de Agosto*, ☎ 862-2346, *$*, below the Colonial, is popular with the younger crowd. It is clean, bright and close to the lake, but the beds are not all that comfy. There is a choice of private or communal bathroom (there is only one for all the guests who don't have one in their room). Laundry service is available. A restaurant on-site (but not associated with the hotel) serves an excellent breakfast for $1.50. However, the owner was a real grump, barking in English at me and in Spanish at his help.

Inca Merchant Class

Hotel Playa Azul, *Avenida 6 de Agosto*, ☎ 862-2283, *playaazul@latinmail.com*, *$$*. This colonial hotel has rooms set around a central patio. Although it's more than 50 years old, the building has been well maintained and is beautiful inside and out. Rooms are clean and come with tile bathrooms, reading lights over the beds, carpets and closets. Local art is interspersed around the building, making it bright and cheery. Playa Azul offers an all-inclusive rate and people who opt for this get a larger room.

Colonial del Lago, *corner of Avenida 6 de Agosto and 16 de Julio*, ☎ 862-2270, *titikakabolivia@yahoo.com*, *$$*, is a colonial-styled building that has been well maintained. All rooms are clean and have large windows, closets, tables and a view of the lake. Some bathrooms have been artistically designed to utilize all available space. There are 38 rooms, 25 with private bathrooms. Complimentary breakfast features eggs, toast and jam served in the garden. The owners offer a $1 discount to their guests for the boat ride to Isla del Sol and Luna.

Kantutas, *Avenita Jaureque and Bolívar*, ☎ 862-2093, *$$*, is a tastefully designed hotel across from Plaza Sucre. It is named after the national flower of Bolivia and is almost as beautiful, featuring red brick and white plaster. There are 22 rooms with hot showers, private baths and TVs. The hotel is exceptionally clean, has excellent décor and a private restaurant. There is also a roof-top terrace offering views of the city and the lake.

Hostal Cupula, *Calle Michel Parez #1-3*, ☎ 862-2029, *www.hotelcupula.com*, *$$$*, is up the hill just below the Stations of the Cross. There are 17 rooms of every variation: single, double, with or without bath, with or without view. The price starts at $10 for a single without bath and goes up to $32 for the honeymoon suite. Hot showers are available all day

and a fully supplied guest kitchen is kept as clean as the rest of the hotel. Hammocks are peppered around the well-kept grounds that are laden with flowers. There is a library and a book exchange with many German books. Hot water bottles will be supplied if you need one. An excellent vegetarian restaurant open to all is open every day, 7:30 am to 3 pm (except Tuesday) and 6 to 9:30 pm. For example, pancakes with apple and chocolate go for $2, a good salad costs $1.50, and a trout dinner is $4.

Hotel Utama, *Calle Michael Perez, just before the Cupula,* ☎ *862-2013, $$$.* Utama means "home" in Aymara and the Aymara owners try to make their guests feel as though they have entered the family home. The colonial-styled building has unique décor and rooms set around a central courtyard that will soon have a stone fountain. Beside it will be a table with fruit and tea for guests (you are in an Aymara home). All rooms have private bathrooms, tiled and clean. The large rooms have just been repainted and redecorated and feature hardwood floors and bold colors on the walls, with sitting areas that have comfortable lounge chairs and scatter rugs.

Breakfast, included in the price, is the best in town, featuring eggs, fresh juice, coffee, pancakes, cereal, fruit and coffee served by a friendly waiter wearing a white jacket and tie. Mineral water is supplied in the rooms at no charge. There is also a museum with artifacts from Aymara *campesino* life. The small shop contains locally made items for sale at reasonable prices.

Inca Royalty

Hotel Gloria, *16 de Julio,* ☎ *864-0707, www.gloria-tours-bolivia.com, $$$$,* is part of a chain with hotels in Copacabana, Coroico, Urmiri and La Paz. This location caters mostly to tours. Rooms overlook the lake and are clean and spacious, though other areas (like the games room, balcony and halls) could use some sprucing up. There are large windows in the rooms and decorative tile in the bathrooms, but the hall carpets are grotty. There is cable TV in each room and mineral water is supplied daily. A continental breakfast is included. Lunch ($4) includes salad, soup, main meal, dessert and tea. Suppers are à la carte, with trout being the most popular dish.

Hotel Chasqui de Oro, *Avenida Costanera #55,* ☎ *862-2343, $$$$$.* This new hotel on the beach is decorated in colonial Spanish design and is run by a quiet, unassuming man. The spacious rooms have wood floors and tiled bathrooms. The hot water comes from a tank and is not available between 1 and 5 pm. Rooms have writing desks, closets, mirrors and satellite TV, and the better ones have huge bathrooms with both tubs and showers. Even the single rooms are exquisite. Patios and balconies dot every corner of the building and there's a restaurant on the premises. This is a first-class establishment. Rates: $30 double; $20 single. Breakfast is included.

Hotel Rosario del Lago, *Rigoberto Paredes and Costañera,* ☎ *862-2002, caoba.entelnet.bo, $$$$$,* is run by the same people who own the Rosario in La Paz. This upscale hotel offers solar heat, good service and clean, well-kept rooms. Rates: from $15 single to $50 double, per person.

◆ Places to Eat

Restaurant Sujma Wasi, *Avenida Gonzolo Jauregui #127*, ☎ *862-2091*, has an indoor seating area and a patio that gets the warm afternoon sun. The tablecloths are woven Andean-style and the décor is inviting. A popular breakfast consists of quinoa flour pancakes with

homemade jam, bananas, nuts, raisins or honey and fresh fruit juice. I also recommend the granola with fruit and yogurt. A large serving of Sujma Wasi salad has lettuce and onion plus Roquefort cheese, nuts, apples, olives and parsley. These dishes cost about $2 each. A large bowl of homemade soup is about $1. A huge plate of *pique de macho*, a local dish of stewed meat, sausage, tomato, pepper, onion, cheese, boiled eggs, olives and parsley, costs just over $3. Bolivian wine is available at $1.25 a glass or $7-8 a bottle and a large beer is $1.25. They offer special Andean drinks – like *chuflay*, *yungeño* and *singani* sours – for $2.25 each.

Alfanet, *Avenida 6 de Agosto, next to the Colonial Hotel*, is an Internet café that serves coffee and cake while you do your e-mail. It has comfortable working desks with PCs for 75¢ for 15 minutes; $1.25 for 30 minutes; $1.75 for 45 minutes; and $2 for an hour. The time is computed and recorded on a small box at the bottom of the screen. Remember to sign off so the calculated time stops. There are two pool tables in the next room, English-language videos for rent and nice art on the walls. Alfanet is owned by the couple who own the Café Sol y Luna.

Colonial Restaurant, *corner of Avenida 6 de Agosto and 16 de Julio*, ☎ *862-2270, titikabolivia@yahoo.com,* is open 7:30 am to 10:30 pm. There's an indoor dining room, or you can eat out in the garden. The trout dish is a dollar less than most upscale places around town and it's delicious, cooked with lots of garlic, an herb claimed by many mountain people to help with altitude sickness. For $3 you can have the trout with rice, fries and salad. In the morning they serve large pancakes with chocolate and fruit for $1.

Sol de los Andes Café and Internet, *Avenida 6 de Agosto,* is upstairs and has six machines with lots of working space and bright light. The machines are fast and fairly new.

Café Sol y Luna, *in the same building as Hotel Gloria, Calle16 de Julio (no phone), solyluna@post.com,* is a really good place to hang out in the evenings when your requests for music taken from a printed list will be played. There is a two-for-one book exchange and the owner Rick Derave speaks English, Dutch and a host of other languages. His Argentinean wife, Margarina, makes a cappuccino that is second to none in Bolivia. The cost is 75¢ for a small and $1 for a large; a glass of Bolivian wine costs the same. Open hours are 6 pm until whenever. This place is popular with foreigners.

Kala Uta, *Avenida 6 de Agosto #115*, ☎ *862-2862,* is a popular vegetarian restaurant. Their *almuerzo* (less than $2) comes highly recommended

THE ALTIPLANO

by a number of people who really like to eat. A la carte dishes usually include nuts, quinoa, whole grains and/or yogurt.

La Cupula, *Calle Michel Parez #1-3*, ☎ 862-2029, is another vegetarian eatery with excellent food – the lasagna is especially good. The restaurant overlooks the lake and has tables outside on a balcony. There is often music, and the atmosphere lends itself to leisurely meals.

Restaurant Brisas, *Avenida 6 de Agosto and Calle Costanera*, ☎ 862-2033, also overlooks the lake. A sunset drink and dinner is recommended. The house specialty is *trucha criolla*, a spicy trout dish with tomatoes, for about $3. Portions are large.

Pizzeria Italia, *Avenida Jauregui #140 beside Residencial Solar*, ☎ 862-2009, is the best place for pizza in town. Pizzas come with thin crusts and thick toppings. This restaurant has branches in Sorata and Rurrenabaque, too.

Snack 6 de Agosto, *Avenida 6 de Agosto*, ☎ 862-2114 or 862-2430, specializes in vegetarian food and has both indoor and patio seating. The service is good and the people are friendly. The fries were crisp and fresh (not from a frozen package). *Café distilado* is about 30¢, and an omelet with salad, potatoes and rice runs about $3. The portion is enough for breakfast, but not for dinner. Pancakes, depending on what you have with them, cost up to a dollar. Choose from chocolate, fruit, ham, cheese, banana and /or yogurt.

Manka Uta Restaurant, *Avenida 6 de Agosto*, ☎ 862-4941, is close to the lake and has live music every evening starting at 8 pm. The restaurant has small tables with candles held in locally produced candleholders and with chairs covered in sheepskins. The ambiance is great, and so are the waiters. The restaurant opens at 7:30 am for breakfast and will make a box lunch to go. Pizza or spaghetti cost $3 and a beer is just over a dollar. The bar is heated at night – at this elevation, heat is often important. If the music isn't to your liking, try next door at Nimbos.

Nimbos, *at Avenida 6 de Agosto on the corner of Zapana #684*, opens from 7:30 am to 11 pm and often has local bands. The restaurant décor is attractive and cosy. If the electricity goes out, the candles placed on each table will light the room, the propane stove will cook your food, and the 1980s music that plays when there's no band will go off. For $2 you can have a complete meal – an appetizer, soup, main dish and dessert. This is an excellent place to eat. Come early as it is popular, but be sure to have change or small bills.

◆ Nightlife

Nikos Karaoke, just off Avenida 6 de Agosto and one street below the cathedral, is the "in" place for disco. The floor is painted cement and the dance section is lined in tinfoil, which makes the place a bit tacky. There is a good mike for anyone wanting to sing. The lounge area has 25-30 chairs and the bar is well stocked. When I asked for phone and address information the owner told me to buzz off, so I did.

Pub Mercurio de Almas is on Avenida Costanera along the beach just below the navy base. This is a pleasant stop with good music and good drinks. Happy hour runs from 8 pm to midnight, but the place stays open later. Mercurio often has live music. Meals are available.

Tatu Correta, Avenida 6 de Agosto and Oruro, is an intimate bar that will and does stay open until 3 am as long as the customers are having a good time (and spending money, of course). The prize of the house is the Tatu Correta milkshake made with milk, eggs, chocolate and cognac. It's often light on the milk and heavy on the cognac.

Sol y Luna, Calle 16 de Julio, solyluna@post.com, is a popular place for foreigners to hang out, listen to the music, have a few drinks and chat up other travelers.

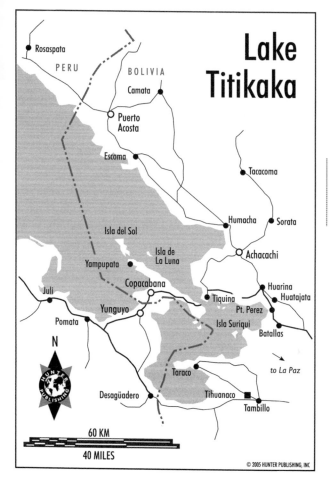

Lake Titikaka

PERU · BOLIVIA

Rosaspata
Camata
Puerto Acosta
Escoma
Tacacoma
Humacha · Sorata
Isla del Sol
Isla de La Luna
Yampupata
Achacachi
Juli
Copacabana
Huarina
Yunguyo
Tiquina
Huatajata
Pt. Perez
Pomata
Isla Suriqui
Batallas
N
to La Paz
Taraco
Desaguadero
Tihuanaco
Tambillo
60 KM
40 MILES

THE ALTIPLANO

© 2005 HUNTER PUBLISHING, INC

◆ Shopping

There are numerous little shops in Copacabana selling all the usual things from weavings to knitted socks. The dolls sold in the stalls around the church are a very good deal, much cheaper than any in La Paz.

Street vendors selling jewelry that is laid out on a piece of weaving or cloth are not, for the most part, Bolivians. They are traveling salespersons and their route runs from Ecuador to Argentina. Their goods are handmade and sell for fairly reasonable prices.

Bazar Agar, Avenida La Paz and Junin, has cameras, video tapes and all manner of batteries, including lithium batteries. They also have non-expired film such as Advantx or Elite Chrome (ASA 200) for $6, Agfa or Konica slide film, 36 exposures, 100 ASA, for $2. They carry only a limited supply of Fuji film.

◆ Trips on Lake Titikaka

Isla del Sol is the main island that is accessible from Copacabana and is the primary attraction of the area. The Chincana ruins are near the island's north end. To the south are the Pilcocaina ruins. Isla del Sol also has numerous minor ruins long forgotten.

There are many ways to visit the island. If you go by boat and walk from the north to the south, you will miss Isla de la Luna because crossing over to it after walking Isla del Sol would take too long. You could, of course, go on a different day. If you want to go to all the ruins on the two islands, you can go by boat but miss the island hike. Some people choose to overnight here in order to see and do it all. There are numerous places to stay. Most are fairly simple and inexpensive.

> **AUTHOR TIP:** *You should bring extra snacks you may want as the cost of these things on the island is far higher than the mainland. Meals, too, cost a bit more.*

Hiking Isla del Sol

The seven-mile/11-km trail takes three to four hours to complete. It is a groomed pathway that makes for easy walking. The highest hill you'll encounter is 13,000 ft/4,000 m. There are actually two trails from which to choose. One climbs high almost right away and stays on the ridge, while the other starts near the shore and undulates along the island's entire length. The most popular route is the upper one. The lower one takes almost twice as long and is definitely twice as difficult. Boat schedules are based on people doing the upper trail.

Always dress appropriately.

- ❖ Wear a hat as the sun coming through the thin atmosphere is strong and will burn you. There is no shade and the cool air at this altitude fools you into thinking you're safe.
- ❖ Wear good walking shoes as the distance is fairly long.

❖ It is also best if you bring a lunch so you can stop at a
good view point and enjoy the scenery while eating.
There are a couple of *tiendas* along the way selling pop,
crackers and candy.

The Mil Escoladas or Mil Gradas and Inca Fountain, the staircase and
baths that are almost invisible against the rocks and under the trees is
where your hike will end. The boat doesn't stop here until the return trip
later in the day. Instead, it stops farther up the island, at Cha'llapampa, the
village at the north end.

Rules from the Empire of the Sun
Ama Suwa, Ama Quella and Ama Llulla.
(Don't steal, don't lie, don't be lazy.)

Once off the boat, some Spanish/Aymara-speaking guides take visitors up
to the ruins, explaining in Spanish the legends surrounding the sites. Their
explanations are excellent, but if you don't understand Spanish, continue
on your own.

Head up the hill toward the **Gold Museum** (75¢) and then the ruins. The
price of the museum includes the entry fee to the ruins.

The museum displays artifacts, some of them gold pieces, found at the
city of Marka Pampa that was once on the edge of the island but is now 26
ft/eight m under water just off the north shore. The city was excavated in
1992 and the finds put into the museum.

The museum's most precious displays are the gold pieces found inside
carved stone boxes. There's a medallion, a cup, a puma and a figure of a
woman. The stone boxes are so well made that the gold never became wet
during all those years under water.

After the museum, the trail passes through a stone doorway with an impressive stone lintel on top. From there, follow the trail up the hill, past a
school and around and above a couple of bays.

Just as the trail starts to go down, veer to the right into the first yard and
the Piedra Sagrada (**Sacred Rock**), an upright piece with some carving on
it. Across from the rock but within the same yard is a low table that is believed to have been the sacrificial table where a living creature's heart
(sometimes human) was cut out and left for the gods.

Return to the main trail and continue to the back of the island where there
is first a ticket booth and then a huge round stone table with stone stools
around it. This is the **Ceremonial Table**, which some believe was also a
sacrificial table. The Inca brought humans, gold, silver, shells and animals
there to appease and thank the gods for whatever reason, be it drought,
floods, sickness or prosperity. The Aymara guides will encourage you to
rub your hand on the table in order to extract some energy from it. This way
you will be able to complete the hike to the south end before the boat
leaves.

The **Chincana ruins** are just beyond the table. The word "Chincana"
means a place to get lost. When looking at the ruins you will find many hiding places and rooms with false doors. If the ruins don't interest you, continue along the trail to your left at the ticket booth.

The ruins are believed to have been residences of people working for
aristocrats who came to the island on vacation.

THE ALTIPLANO

Those not hiking the island return to the boat from the ruins. Those continuing to the south end go up the trail that veers to the right just after the sacred table.

There are *tiendas* at around the 3.6-mile/six-km point that have tables and chairs. You'll go by spots where you can take photos of girls with llamas, men weaving, women with kids, and kids selling stones.

You are now at the apex of the island, more than half-way to Mil Gradas and the village of Yumani, where the boat will be waiting.

Places to Stay

Descending the steep part toward the dock and Mil Gradas (Thousand Steps) you will see many places to stay. Most are basic and clean, but if you want a bit more luxury, at the top of the island before coming down is **Puerta del Sol**, $. It has 15 rooms in a two-storey, mustard-yellow (symbolizing sun) building and charges $3 per person (with private bath and carpeted floors).

Near the Mil Gradas and the Inca Fountain is the **Inti Marka Hostal**, $, which rents basic rooms without a private bath for $1.50. It costs $1 extra for a hot shower. The rooms are clean, with cement floors, and there is an equally clean restaurant that serves full dinners for $2. **La Casa de la Yumani**, ☎ 7-193-4427, $$$, is run by an Argentinean known as Ricardo. His place is tiny – just four rooms, but all with private bath. It's clean and tastefully decorated. Rooms cost $20 for a couple. This is definitely the most upscale place on the island. Ricardo can help you hire a boat to travel around the island by water. To get to his place in the upper section of the town, ask in the village. Everyone knows where Ricardo's place is.

La Estancia is an eco-lodge run by Magri Turismo Ltd, in La Paz. The cost to stay here is $59 for a single, $88 for a double and $122 for a triple. This price includes breakfast and either lunch or dinner. This lodge is working with NGOs to help promote sustainable tourism and has restored the pre-Inca terraces on the property that are believed to be over 500 years old. The cabins are of adobe brick with thatch roofs in keeping with traditional aesthetics. However, inside they are modern and comfortable, with wood floors, tables and chairs, large windows and solar-powered electricity.

> ### ❖ CAN YOU SWIM?
>
> If someone falls into Lake Titikakca, it is traditional to leave them there as an offering to Pacha Mama. Remember this when you are on the boat.

Boating the Islands

If not hiking, you will see everything (including the Chincana ruins) before returning to the boat, although your time will be limited. From Cha'llapampa, the boat goes to Isla de la Luna across the way. Much smaller, the island is just 1.8 miles/three km long and barely one wide. During the reign of the Inca, the island represented the moon, female counterpart of the sun. It also had a nunnery that held the Virgins of the Sun. These women, chosen for their beauty, made *chicha* and wove cloth to be used in the religious ceremonies. The island was called Coati which, according to some linguists, means the place for elected women.

From the 1930s to the 1960s, the island was used to hold political prisoners. There was little left of the nunnery or the main palace at that time, but the prisoners were forced to reconstruct the 35-room building. From the ruins, it was learned that the palace was built in typical Aymara fashion, suggesting that the area was used before the Inca came. However, it was also learned that the doors were made in Inca style. This suggests that the site was used by both cultures, one reconstructing the remains of the previous one. Today, fewer than 50 people live here.

Achacachi

Altitude 12,533 ft/3,810 m
Population: 7,900

Achacachi is an Aymara market village and the crossroads for those going to Sorata or the Apolobamba, where Pelechuco, Curva and Charazani are located. Others go from Achacachi along the north shore of Lake Titikaka and end at Puerto Acosta on the border with Peru. Although villagers in the area have a reputation for being a bit more radical than most, the town is friendly and welcoming if you need to stay the night. In times of strife, this village is best known for the effective road blocks it is able to put up and maintain for long periods of time.

◆ Getting Here

Buses travel from La Paz to Achacachi daily starting at 5 am. You can also get onto a bus, *trufi* or shared taxi at Huarina. Those going to the Apolobamba or Sorata often hire a jeep in La Paz and stop in Achacachi for breakfast/lunch or a quick look around.

Buses go to Sorata from La Paz. They leave every two hours starting at 6 am; the last bus leaves mid-afternoon. Buses leaving Sorata start around 5 am and continue until mid-afternoon. Two companies service this route: Larecaja and Unificado Sorata.

Buses go to Pelechuco in the Apolobamba only on Wednesdays. A jeep costs $250 from La Paz and will carry six people and gear with ease.

◆ Places to Stay & Eat

Alojamiento Maya, *Calle Sucre #17*, ☎ *7154-7667 (cell)*, $, is run by Juan Verastique. Rooms are small and simple, but certainly clean enough and all have shared bathrooms. There is a slightly more upscale place across the street, but it doesn't have the ambiance of the Maya.

The Maya also has a restaurant where set meals are served. Other meals can be purchased at the restaurants around the square. Only set meals are available.

THE ALTIPLANO

Apolobamba Region

The only reason travelers go into this area is to hike/climb or raft. **Pelechuco**, at 11,842 ft/3,600 m, has a village medical post and one basic place to stay. While here, you can rub shoulders with the Kallawaya, the naturopaths of the Andes, who were traveling doctors long before the Inca came looking for cures. Today, Charazani, Amarete, Chari, Pelechuco and Curva are the most important centers for the Kallawaya culture.

Madidi National Park covers a total of 4.5 million acres with a variety of ecosystems unparalleled for their abundant wildlife. Vicuñas are seen grazing and Andean foxes will cross your trail while you are hiking. The estimated bird list is reported to be well over 1,000 species.

The village of **Pelechuco** is not modernized, although there is a hotel on the main square where you can sleep and eat. It has no showers or running water and electricity is available only a few hours a day. The owner will serve dinner and breakfast – the same meal for everyone. Although some purchases can be made in the village, most food needed for hiking or climbing should be brought with you. The medical post is usually open.

Curva has no hotels or restaurants, but finding a spot to pitch a tent is easy. Ask around. Generally, people are friendly. The village has some small shops and a school of medicine for Kallawaya, although it does not operate all the time because the doctors are traveling and taking their young protégés with them. Buses leave Curva twice a week. If that doesn't suit your plans, walk to Charazani and make your base there.

Charazani has one hotel, the **Inti-Haus** (no phone), located on the main street. It's operated by Claudio, a retired journalist who also seems to be the unofficial town mayor. A few smaller *alojamientos* can be found on the square. Charazani does not have electricity or running water, but the hot springs are just a 10-minute walk down the road. Across the street from the Inti-Haus, Doña Sophie serves meals. She will make only one type of meal per day and you must order four hours in advance. She often serves different groups at different times, as she has only one table, so she may hurry you along. "Quiete y come!" (shut up and eat) was her constant message to us. Her food, like her humor, is excellent.

◆ Getting Here

To get to Pelechuco you must hire a jeep or catch the once-a-week bus from La Paz. Depending on road conditions, the trip can take up to 24 hours. A jeep will cost $250-$400 (Huayna Tours had the cheapest I could find and their driver is exceptional) and it can carry up to six people with gear. The journey takes less than 12 hours by jeep. On the return, the driver may take on locals from Pelechuco heading south. You can also try getting to Pelechuco by truck, but that trip could take a week in itself.

The bus from La Paz leaves the cemetery bus area on Wednesday mornings at 8 am and it can take anywhere from 14 to 24 hours to reach Pelechuco. The cost is $7. The bus is crowded and those with climbing/hiking gear may find it difficult. Buses return to La Paz on Friday or Saturday, depending on the festival situation and the number of people going out.

A bus goes to and from Charazani once a day. The bus going to La Paz leaves around 7 pm and often takes about 15 hours to get to the city. You must catch it at the square and purchase tickets ahead of time. The buses go only at night and you will share the aisles with everything that can possibly be sold in a market, plus kids. The bus takes its time, but when you catch glimpses of the hair-pin turns and unguarded vertical drops along the road's edge, you will appreciate the driver's caution.

◆ Services

There is no electricity or water. For a shower, you should head to the hot springs. This is an isolated Andean hamlet that was here before Inca days because of the hot springs.

◆ Adventures on Foot

Hiking

ISKANWAYA RUINS: The Iskanwaya Ruins date back 800 years to the Mollo Culture. To reach them you can hike from Pelechuco for four days. Or you can stay in Aucapata and hike out to the ruins, but that's only for the dedicated archeologist or serious trekkers. Most people take a jeep to Ulla Ulla on the road between Charazani and Pelechuco and then cross a pass and descend into Aucapata (7,566 ft/2,300 m). From there, you can walk up to the ruins that sit on the edge of a cliff overlooking a river.

At one time the ruins had 75 buildings made of slate, mortar and mud. The people living here were skilled in gold carving and ceramic pottery. They also developed large aqueducts and holding ponds for agricultural purposes.

PELECHUCO TO CHARAZANI: The hike from Pelechuco to Charazani is considered difficult because it crosses one 16,440-foot/5,000-m pass and requires descending steep shale slopes. Trekkers also have to sleep at high elevations. But the trail goes into secluded valleys, often along pre-Inca roads that pass through terraced fields of peas, wheat, corn and beans. You will see shepherds playing pan flutes while tending their animals. You will pass through Kallawaya territory and, if they are feeling generous, you will go with no trouble. Dress appropriately and do not photograph the locals.

Should you choose to do this six-day hike from Pelechuco to Charazani or to Curva, you will see some spectacular country, lots of llamas and vicuñas, and will experience the thrill of being the only traveler for hundreds of miles. The trail passes through the Mapiri National Park and the Ulla Ulla National Reserve that was declared a biosphere reserve by UNESCO for its plants. This area also has the most condors in all the Andes.

> ### ❖   HIKING BACKWARDS
>
> Although some books describe the hike from Charazani, I suggest starting in Pelechuco and ending at Cherazani because of the transportation situation. It is easier to hire a jeep or catch the bus to Pelechuco, than it is to sit in Pelechuco waiting for transportation after completing a six- or seven-day hike. You have better bartering power when going in. If you are waiting to go out, the drivers know you will pay much more just to be gone. Also, Charazani has developed hot springs that will be appreciated after the hike.

Because of the high altitude and the types of camp stoves and fuel available for rent in Bolivia, choose food that takes little cooking time. Canned meat is good, as are crackers, hard cheese and granola-type cereals with powdered milk. Cooked potatoes will last a few days. Dehydrated soups with some carrots and tinned meat are great meals. Trying to cook pasta at a high altitude results in a pot of wall-paper paste. Bring lots of bread, but plan on eating it during the first few days. Chocolates, nuts and raisins are all good. You can purchase things like tin bowls, cups and utensils in the market in La Paz. Carry out your empty tins, regardless of what locals do.

In Pelechuco, you can hire a guide with horses, mules or llamas to carry some of the supplies. Ask people on the square – usually there is a clan of local men sitting on the benches watching you. Topographical maps of the area are poor, so a guide is highly recommended unless you are skilled in the Aymara language.

Be prepared to feed your guide and let him use other things like sleeping bags, tents and warm clothing. It gets very cold at night on this hike.

> ### ❖   LOVING THE LLAMA
>
> At maturity, a pack llama receives the *kawra pankara*, or llama flower, a string of woven wool that is attached to the hair on the llama's shoulders and on three consecutive places along its spine. Because they carry larger loads, male llamas are adorned with bigger llama flowers than females and the lead llama is always dressed in a rich head covering.

The average cost of a guide and two horses is $80 for the week. Try to have some gear available to give or sell him at the end of the week; usually you will have gotten to know him quite well. However, before you start the hike be certain that it is clear what is expected. Some things that should be clarified are the time to rise and quit, who does what chores, how far the guide must go and who negotiates passage through villages.

Some Quechua or Aymara words would be helpful as the guides from Pelechuco speak Spanish as their second language and misunderstandings are probable, especially if Spanish is also your second language.

If your guide uses pack animals, try to have a day pack with you for essentials. Pack animals move at a different speed than you, so your gear may be miles ahead or behind.

You can also book this hike with a guide from La Paz. (See *Tour Operators* in the La Paz chapter, page 71.)

RIO YARIAPU TO RURRENABAQUE: The route along Rio Yariapu to Rurrenabaque should be done as a guided hike. It starts in Madidi National Park and ends at Chalalan, just out of Rurre. Madidi Park was created in 1995 and covers 4.5 million acres of cloud and tropical forest, lowlands and savannah. This land is drained by raging rivers and dotted with pristine lakes. It is reported to have almost 1,000 bird species and 44% of the new world's mammal species. There is also a plethora of amphibians.

The hike starts with a couple of days of difficult jeep travel from Charazani to Apolo and then on to Machua. From there, the hike starts and seven hours later and 987 ft/300 m lower you will camp at Toma Alta. Another seven hours of walking will bring you to Piñalito, where birds such as falcons and papagayos are seen, as are capybaras and howler monkeys. The next few days you will descend into jungle with dense vegetation and along the way, pass Mamacona, Palo Grande, Eslabon and Pico Plancha. Just when walking becomes a bit much, you will reach the Tuichi River. The rest is a float, except for the rapids.

Once in Rurrenabaque you will have a few days in which to visit the *pampas* and maybe see an anaconda, cobra or boa constrictor. New Milenium Adventure Sports in La Paz offers this hike with local guides and porters (at least one of whom speaks English), all river transportation, cooking and camping gear (except for sleeping bags and backpack). Park fees are extra. See *Tour Operators* in the La Paz chapter, page 71, for details.

Climbing

Cordillera Apolobamba peaks can be accessed either from Pelechuco, Curva or Charazani. Although they are all around 18,000 ft/5,500 m, thousands (according to Yossi Brain) have not been climbed. If hiring a guide service, I would suggest Huayna Potosi in La Paz because Dr. Hugo, who helped Yossi Brain with a lot of the routes he describes in his book, is experienced in this area. Hugo is a local who speaks English fluently and who played in the mountains from the time he could tie a rope. See the La Paz section, page 125, for information on this company.

Chaupi Orco, the highest mountain in the Apolobamba at 19,700 ft/6,000 m, is on the Peru/Bolivia border. To get to the base of this mountain you must take mules from Pelechuco and hike for two days. It takes another day to get to the glacier and yet another to reach the summit. There are two routes up this mountain, with the east ridge joining the main route close to the top. You can ascend the main route and return by the east ridge. There is an approach from the southwest also, but it is longer.

Palomani Grande is the second tallest mountain accessible from Pelechuco. It stands at 18,977 ft/5,769 m and can be climbed in one day. Three routes are described in Brain's book, with one having a 60° section of incline with most of the route at a 50° incline.

Ascarani is north of Pelechuco. In 1969 a Spanish team explored the mountain, making 19 new ascents during the one expedition. Those who have climbed Ascarani give it high praise. Isolation. New ascents. Rock and ice. Thin air. The best of scenery.

◆ Adventures on Water

A **Tuichi River** expedition is difficult and follows in part the trail of the now cult figure Yossi Ghinsberg, an Israeli who, with three companions, was exploring the Tuichi (without the help of experienced guides). He lost his raft when it capsized while going over a high waterfall and was missing for over a month. They still haven't found the bones of two of his companions, though Ghinsberg himself was rescued. Ghinsberg's book is available in Rurrenabaque.

The rapids that make up the Tuichi are powerful and the water volume can be extreme. The jungle is thick and wildlife abounds. Traveling through is a wild adventure. This trip is offered by Explore Bolivia (☎ 303-545-5728, www.explorebolivia.com) with skilled and experienced staff. As in any third world country, you can always find a local willing to act as a guide if you pay the cash. However, I would suggest that you be careful.

It takes three days by jeep to reach Santa Cruz del Valle and another two-day trek with mules to reach the Tuichi River put-in spot at 3,355 ft/ 1,020 m. You will drop a total of about 2,300 ft/700 m during your descent to this river. It is not until day six of your journey that you actually are able to paddle. The first day on the river starts with a mild float that passes rocky beaches before throwing you into Surprise Canyon, where the rapids get bigger, going from a class II to a class IV the farther in you go. As you drop, the temperature gets warmer and the rapids appear more frequently. You then leave the canyon and float alongside the rolling hills of the Asariamas Valley.

The following day you will encounter large rapids that require technical moves to get through to San Pedro Canyon. The river becomes faster, narrower and more dangerous, moving from an average class III up to a class V. That night is spent in the canyon where monkeys and exotic birds are your only companions. The next day is an exploration/rest day when you can hike up the Ipurama River or just rest and prepare for the rush to come on the following day.

The canyon turns into a gorge and the rapids turn into class III and IV as soon as you leave camp. Those are the quiet ones. Next is the Gate of the Devil, class V, and the Gate of the Sun, class IV, the two stretches of hell that give the Tuichi its reputation. Those not skilled enough to be safe can portage these rapids.

The following day is a float by comparison, with a few class II and III rapids before the river widens and finally joins the Beni. The paddling section of the trip is over and wildlife viewing becomes the main focus as a motorized boat takes you down to Chalalan Lodge in the jungle, not far from Rurrenabaque.

Some of the above river run was described by the boaters of Explore Bolivia.

> ### ❖ HERBAL HEALERS
>
> The Kallawaya are naturopathic healers who have passed on healing traditions from father to son since before the Tihuanacan civilization began. They have their own language and have traveled from Ecuador to Patagonia both learning from others and healing. At the age of six or seven a boy learns how to collect and store plants. As he gets older he learns what plants are good for what ailments and how to relate to the patient so that he can prescribe a treatment that covers not only the physical but also the emotional aspects of the body. Most Kallawaya know the use of about 300 herbs, while the specialists know as many as 600. Women Kallawaya act as midwives and treat gynecological disorders. In the valleys between Pelechuco and Charazani, the Kallawaya inhabit six of the villages you will pass.

◆ Tour Operators

Explore Bolivia has a combination kayak/hike trip that starts with a pick up at the airport in La Paz. From there you tour the Tihuanaco ruins and go on to kayak Lake Titikaka for three days. The kayaking includes a visit to the ruins on Isla del Sol. The last week of the trip includes the Apolobamba hike. If you like everything done for you, this is a good option. Explore Bolivia also runs a two-week trip down the Tuichi, following in part the footsteps of Yossi Ghinsberg.

Huayna Tours, Calle Sagarnaga #398 at Illampu, ☎ 245-6717, berrios@mail.magalink.com is run by Dr. Hugo Berrios and his wife Damiska. Anyone who climbs in Bolivia will come upon Dr. Hugo somewhere. The company offers all the tours available with other companies, but their specialty is climbing. They will take climbers to any peak in Bolivia.

> ### ❖ THE ALTIPLANO
>
> Altiplano means high plain. It is high, but it is not a plain. In fact, it consists of volcanos, salt flats, dry rock formations and rolling hills. In Bolivia, the Altiplano runs from Lake Titikaka all the way to the Chilean border, a total of 551 miles/900 km, and it is about 122 miles/200 km wide. The climate is cold and dry and the vegetation is sparse. The grasses are spiky tufts that are tough to touch and unpleasant to sit upon. The trees are few. Quenua trees, which grow at elevations of up to 17,100 ft/5,200 m, are typical alpine trees. Because they are slow-growing, they are very dense and twisted.
>
> Animals of the Altiplano are usually of the camel family, although the highland fox is common. Birds are abundant and interesting. One, the rhea, is related to the ostrich and can be found in large numbers in Sajama National Park. There are others too; the egret, the ibis, the flicker and the mockingbird are often seen.

THE ALTIPLANO

The landscape of the Altiplano is exceptional. The climate can be bitter cold and the dryness can be irritating. But usually the temperatures are cool, even when the sun is out.

This information was provided, in part, by Tim Miller of Explore Bolivia.

Patacamaya

Patacamaya is a truck stop on the main road between La Paz and Oruro. It is also the junction where you branch off to go to Sajama or on to Tambo Quemado on the Chilean border.

◆ Getting Here & Around

Take any bus going east toward Oruro from La Paz. I used Atlas Bus to Oruro and they made me pay the full cost even though I was going only to Patacamaya. Later, I used Trans Salvador from Patacamaya to Oruro and they charged only part of the fare.

Buses going to Oruro stop at Patacamaya for a few minutes and it is usually easy to get a seat. The road is paved and in excellent shape. It is a major route for travelers heading out of Bolivia and into Chile.

If you're hungry, go to the Quirquincho restaurant. They make a great fried egg sandwich for 25¢ and coffee for less than a dime. The toilets are clean (although a long way out back) and the owners pleasant.

If you are coming here from Sajama, the mini-bus often leaves before 7 am, so you may not have time for breakfast. In that case, stopping in Patacamaya to eat is essential.

The mini-van to Sajama leaves the main road in Patacamaya daily at 1 pm. Be early so you are assured a seat. The driver I had did not charge for my bags when I went to Sajama, but he charged $1 for each bag when I returned. The one-way fare is $1.25 and the ride is three to four hours. Before going to Sajama, the mini-van goes all the way to the border town of Tambo Quemado to let off and pick up passengers at the border before returning to Laguna and Sajama. Should you be going to or coming from Chile by this route, there are basic places to stay in Tambo Quemado. There is also a large restaurant with a bar attached. Those staying at the border for the night may want to patronize the bar.

Those going into Sajama can get off the bus at Laguna and tour the church while the bus goes to the border. Make it clear to the driver to pick you up on his way into the village. The road into Sajama is mud, stretching for seven miles/12 km with not a twig for shade nor a trickle of water to drink.

If you get stuck in Patacamaya for the night, there are two *alojamientos* on the main road. They are both basic, clean and cheap.

Some people take a bus from La Paz going to Chile and get off at Laguna and the turnoff to Sajama. This means a 7.3-mile/12-km walk along the dusty road with almost no chance of a ride. The sun is dangerous at that elevation, so I really discourage walking in. But if you must, be sure to have a hat, some food and lots of water. It is a boring walk, but you can look at the mountain as you trudge through the sand.

◆ Adventures on Wheels

The road between the Sajama turnoff and Patacamaya is an archeological zone for the first 18 miles/30 km or so out of Patacamaya. Three areas have funeral monuments similar to those at Sillustani, Peru. These were built long before the Inca empire was established. The site closest to Patacamaya is exceptionally well preserved, the second is showing wear, and the third, called Pukara de Monterani Archeological Site, on the opposite side of the road from the other two, is excellent. The government is doing some restoration to these structures.

When the Tihuanaco civilization collapsed due to drought, the people formed small groups and migrated around the Altiplano. Many lived near or on the flat-topped mountains and built forts for protection against invading groups. Monterani is such a site. The mountain stands at 13,500 ft/4,050 m and has stone terracing and some burial towers left from that civilization.

Near the 100 Km sign along the road is a canyon with wind-sculpted rock that is excellent for exploration. If possible, take a tent and camp. Close to the Km 125 sign is a river with more interesting rock formations and a deep canyon. If camping, you can get off the bus and walk in. I do not know the water situation; assume you need to carry it. The alternative is to hire a jeep in Sajama or Patacamaya to get to the canyon.

If coming from Chile, the river with rock formations is between Km 45 and 50 and the canyon is at Km 75. The archaeological zone starts at Km 125.

The village of **Curahuara de Carangas** has a church that is fondly called the Sistine Chapel of Bolivia due to the huge wall murals inside. The paintings are reproductions of the Last Supper, the Final Judgment, Noah's Ark and Adam and Eve leaving the Garden of Eden. They were all done by Ciriaco Acuña in 1876.

The village of **Lagunas** is at the turnoff to Sajama and if you don't want to go to the border and back (and don't mind standing or crouching in a loaded *trufi* for the last seven miles/12 km) you can get off at Lagunas and have the driver pick you up later. In Lagunas, the 18th-century church has frescos, oil paintings and an altarpiece that is more interesting than anything you'd see at the border town of Tambo Quemado.

Sajama

Altitude: 13,815 ft/4,200 m
Population: 200

Sajama stands at a majestic 21,846 ft/6,549 m and is the highest mountain in Bolivia. The village of the same name is reminiscent of Tibet. It has the same mud brick huts, lack of electricity, high altitude and barren landscape. The entire mountain and village forms the Sajama National Park. The village is small and, when there are few tourists here, only one restaurant serves meals. If you need a meal, you will be sent to the place cooking for that day and there will be little selection.

There are a few places to stay, but they are basic with outhouses and communal cold-water taps for washing. Be certain to eat only food that is hot and drink water that has been purified. If purchasing bottled water, make certain the bottle has not been opened.

In winter (June, July and August) temperatures in Sajama can fall drastically to well below freezing. A warm sleeping bag is essential, along with some long-johns and warm hat. That is for sleeping. For daytime, a down jacket is highly recommended. In the summer (November, December and January) the temperature usually falls to around zero at night, but the days are warm enough to wear a cotton shirt and skirt or pants.

There are hot springs nearby and lakes teeming with wildlife. Mount Sajama is waiting to be climbed and three base camps make good destinations for hikers. A hill just out of the village is interesting to climb for the views. There are the Two Sisters Volcanos to visit and canyons on the main road (see above) that landscape photographers should not miss.

In my opinion, Sajama is one of the most exciting places in Bolivia to explore and those who miss it have missed a lot.

◆ Getting Here

See *Patacamaya* section, above.

◆ History

Sajama National Park was created on August 2, 1939 and was the first protected area in Bolivia. It covers an area of 217,000 acres/120,000 hectares and abuts the Lauca National Park in Chile. The mountain (volcano) itself stands at 21,500 ft/6,550 m and the area above 17,000 ft/5,200 m is covered in snow and ice year-round.

People have lived in the area for much longer than history can tell. The church is believed to be built over some pre-Columbian ruins and the landscape is dotted with burial towers like those seen on the road between Patacamaya and the border.

◆ Services

The **park office** is at the entrance to the village. You must stop in before entering the town and, as a foreigner, pay $1.25 entry fee no matter how long you stay or what you do. Locals pay 75¢. The park office has some maps, a few photos and some dusty critters on display. The stuffed condor has been robbed of his royalty as he sits in the corner staring at a stuffed puma that also needs re-crowning. Maps of the mountain are not available for purchase at the park office.

There is a clinic in town, but often it is closed with nobody there. It has equipment to deal with altitude sickness. If you are in serious need of medical help and no one is around, go to the park office. They will find the medical staff.

Long-distance **telephone** calls can be made from the booth at the park office, open 8 am to 7 pm daily.

Jeeps with driver cost $20 for two people and $35 for four people for six hours. Ask at the park office or at Restaurant Parinacota (on the square in town) for information about vehicles.

◆ Sightseeing

The **cathedral** in the center of town is a mud-brick construction believed to be over 200 years old. It is a photographer's paradise. Whether the church and mountains behind are captured in the morning dawn or evening dusk makes no difference. The place is worth a visit. The village, too, is interesting and fun to photograph. The colors are stark, the landscape rugged and the clay ovens picturesque.

You can walk to geysers, a lake and hot springs, but not all in one day. If you have a tent, there is excellent camping near the geysers. If not walking, ask your hotel owner about a tour. The usual recommendation is for a full-day tour, but a half-day is more than enough.

◆ Adventures on Foot

Hiking

GEYSERS: The geysers are five miles/eight km from town. Take the road past the church, across the creek, and up the valley on the other side. There are actually 130 pools in the area, some hot enough to boil eggs. The geysers erupt often and the colors of the landscape are interesting. Some of the plants seem as if they are from another planet, just because they are so green in such a barren landscape.

CERRO COMISERIO: A walk to Cerro Comiserio will help with acclimatization. Take the stone-lined trail behind the park office and head up the hill. The walk allows for excellent views of the entire valley plus a better view of Sajama volcano. If you are acclimatized, it will take an hour to reach the hilltop; if not, it will take three.

Climbing

SAJAMA: The summit of Sajama is 21,846 ft/6549 m and sits 8031 ft/2349 m above the village. It takes two days to reach the top and return. Sajama is often referred to as Bolivia's Chimborazo.

The first day of climbing is spent getting to one of three base camps, depending on which ascent – the north or the south – is to be climbed. At 4 am the following morning, the ascent is started as the summit should be reached before noon (the descent takes until almost dark). The climb is not very technical and may be attempted by those without too much experience or skill. The big factor is acclimatization.

If going up the north side late in the season, you may encounter the *nieve penitentes*, a field of ice crystals, some of which grow to a height of 10 ft/three m. If climbing the south ridge, there is enough room at the high campsite for about six tents.

There is enough equipment for rent at the park office for 10 people. It costs $10 per day. Four guides are available in the village and it is recommended that you use one. Juan Caballero has reached the summit of these mountains 33 times, so his skills are respected. Reynaldo is also highly recommended. A guide costs $50 per day and his fee can be shared by a group of climbers.

TWIN SISTERS VOLCANOS: Parinacota and Pomerata, along the Chilean border, can be seen from town. Parinacota is a perfectly shaped volcano and the slog up to the summit is more labor-intensive than technically difficult. Once at the top, regardless of which route you choose, you will find yourself at the rim of the crater looking down at least 329 ft/100 m. Although not as classic in shape, Pomerata is more technically challenging. The routes are long and the descent can be confusing. The summit of Parinacota stands at 20,822 ft/6,330 m and Pomerata is at 20,467 ft/6,222 m.

◆ Adventures on Water

There are two sets of **hot springs** near the lake. You will probably need specific direction (or a guide) to reach them. The springs are on the same road as the lake, but the turnoff is before the lake. **Kasilla Hot Springs** are five miles/eight km past the pink hotel toward the lake. The second hot springs, used mostly by locals, are half a mile/1 km farther along. They are smaller, cleaner and hotter.

If you can get someone to show you where the guide Ronaldo's place is, the springs are just past there on the creek. You must use the tuffed alpine grasses to hide behind when changing clothes or going to the bathroom.

◆ Adventures in Nature

To get to **Sajama Lake**, walk or drive past the pink hotel for about three miles/five km. The area is rich in bird life, especially flamingoes. Lots of rheas (called *suri* by locals) hang out near the water and the curious but cautious vicuña are everywhere. The lake is not as comfortable a place to camp as the geysers.

> ❖ **BIRDERS LOOKOUT**
>
> The *Soca cornuda* is a black bird with a yellow beak that lives only in high Andean freshwater lakes. It builds a nest by putting water vegetation into a mound and then perching on the mound. There are many at the lake.

Along the road to the lake signs lead to **base camp #1**. Close to the base camp road is another road that leads to the **quenua forest**. Quenua grows as a dense and twisted tree with red peeling bark. It does not grow very high, maybe 10 feet or so, but is the toughest tree on the planet.

The second base camp is reached from the road between Sajama and Laguna. There is a sign for that one also. The third base camp is reached off the main highway between the Chilean border and Laguna at the turnoff to Sajama. There are also two other hot springs along that road.

◆ Places to Stay

The pink building on the edge of town was to be a plush hotel built by Spaniards, but after spending $100,000 they ran out of money. The townspeople aren't anxious to see it open, as it will take tourist dollars away from locals.

There are places to stay around the square and along the main street. All are basic. Ask at the park office who is taking in guests on that particular day. Someone will always accommodate a foreigner. The cost is $1-$1.50 a night.

The **Eco Turismo Tomarapi** is reportedly open now and can accommodate up to 20 people at $25 per person, breakfast included. This was in a state of construction when I was there, but it is a brick hotel with thatch roof and private baths in each room.

On the square, **Restaurant Parinacota** has at least one room for rent. It's considered the best in town, with painted walls and a propane light. The Asian-style toilet is in a mud brick hut across the yard. Water is from a cold-water tap in the courtyard. Solar power generates electricity in the restaurant.

Oruro

Altitude: 12,197 ft/3,708 m
Population: 200,000

Oruro is an odd town. If you stay by the bus or train station, you will not get a good sense of the community. If you stay in the center of town for a day or so, your impression will change. Hotels here are either badly overpriced or they are deplorable dives. Since comfort and environment influence the impression you get of a place, in Oruro it is better to pay a bit more for a hotel and enjoy the city.

Oruro is best known for hosting the most traditional Carnival in the country. It occurs usually in February, but can be as late as the beginning of March, depending on when Lent, which is 40 days before Easter, occurs.

◆ Getting Here & Around

The train station is on Calle Velasco Galvarro and Aldana, ☎ 527-4605. Go there for information about schedules and reservations.

Going south, the express train leaves for Uyuni on Monday and Thursday at 3:30 pm. The slower train (Wara Wara) leaves Sunday and Wednesday at 7 pm.

The train arrives from Uyuni on Wednesday and Sunday at 6:25 am and Tuesday and Thursday at 8:25 am.

To get a ticket, some people line up as early as 5:30 am. Others make reservations a week in advance. The company does not sell tickets in advance, only reservations, so you still have to wait in line to get your ticket. (I waited in line for three hours during low season.) The cost to Uyuni is $5 for third class and $10 for first. There is little difference between the two. However, the train is the easiest way to get to Uyuni.

The bus station is about 10 blocks from the city center and a taxi there costs about 50¢ per person. La Paz buses go to Oruro every hour from 5 am until 10 pm daily. There is a 25¢ tax for using the bus station. Buses from Oruro to La Paz leave on the same schedule, every hour, all day. It is a four-hour ride to La Paz.

Buses going to and coming from Tarija stop on Avenida Ejercito at the east end of the city.

◆ History

1606	Town is founded by Judge Manuel Castro de Padilla.
1780-81	An Indian-led rebellion took place opposing treatment of miners.
1800	Mining changes from silver to tin.
1851	First Bolivian flag of the country is raised here.
1860	Simon Patiño is born. He marries a woman from Oruro and through tin mining he becomes one of the richest men in the world by the 1990s.
1914-1918	Tin was needed for the war effort and Oruro became rich supplying it.
1952	Rebellion led to mines being nationalized.

◆ Services

The **telephone office** is on Calle Bolívar across from the tourist office. It opens at 7:30 am and closes at 10 pm daily.

The **post office** is on the corner of Calle Adolfo Mier and Avenida Pdte. Montes.

Internet Bolívar on Calle Bolívar #687 has numerous machines, but they are slow. In general, Internet connection in Oruro is poor.

The **police office** is on Calle Bolívar, a block west of the square.

The **hospital** is on Calle Potosi and two blocks west of the train station.

The **tourist office** is just off the plaza on Calle Bolívar. It is a tiny kiosk that has some brochures and items of interest. However, do not arrive just before coffee break, lunch, siesta or closing or you will be given the bum's rush.

◆ Carnival

Carnival celebrations are a combination of pre-Columbian and Catholic rituals. Basically, it is a show of good against evil, with good always winning. Carnival was first celebrated in 1789 when it is believed that the Virgin of Socavon fought the devil and liberated Oruro. Through music and dance the people of Oruro re-enact this myth.

Carnival sees 37,500 dancers and musicians all dressed in expensive and elaborate costumes. Some of the masks cost well over $200 to make and the sequined dresses are equally as expensive. Each dance group must have its own band – which can cost anywhere from $700 to $1,000 for

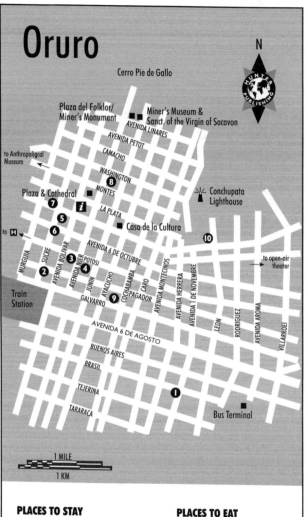

PLACES TO STAY
1. Hotel Bernal
2. San Miguel & Real & Hotel Restoria
3. Residencial Gloria
4. Palace Hotel
5. Hotel Sucre
6. Hostal Hidalgo & Hotel Monarca

PLACES TO EAT
7. Salteñas Potosinas
8. Gupers Restaurant
9. Ametauna Restaurant
10. Plaza Rancheria

the day – and each day of the Carnival requires the dancers to wear a different costume.

The best way to enjoy Carnival is to join a tour from either Sucre or La Paz. That way, you are there for the events but miss all the drink-fests that seem to start shortly after sunset.

Most things that reach perfection are practiced and Carnival is no exception. The first hint of Carnival starts on the first Sunday in November, when the dancers and musicians go to the Sanctuary of the Virgin of Socavon to give thanks for the opportunity to participate in the event and to ask small favors. December and January finds the revelers every Saturday parading in the main streets with a bit of drinking practice thrown in. Numerous marriages take place during the pre-Carnival events. In fact, there are so many brides on the square or driving around in decorated cars, it looks like a group event. Photographers are everywhere.

Two weeks before Carnival the party speeds up and the Sunday before Carnival in Oruro is almost as good as the real thing. If you can't get seats or a room during the main events, try the Sunday before.

◆ Sightseeing

Churches

There are 130 churches, temples and chapels in the Department of Oruro. Half of them are colonial structures, many of which incorporate both Indian and Spanish symbols. For example, there are pumas sitting close to saints or Amazonian plants beside thorns.

The **cathedral** on Calle Alfredo Mier and La Plata was built by Jesuits in the early 1600s, but its importance was replaced by the Sanctuary of the Virgin of Socavon, five blocks west of the central plaza. The first cathedral was destroyed and this second one was built in baroque and renaissance styles. The main chapel is built in the shape of a cross (not so unusual for Catholic churches). After the first church was demolished, its stone bell tower was relocated to the Sanctuary of the Virgin.

The Sanctuary of the Virgin of Socavon is the home of the patron saint of miners, a female counterpart to St. Michael. On the ceiling are paintings of her holding a sword as she defends the city from a dragon and a snake. The first sanctuary was built in 1781 and housed the Nuestra Señora de Copacabana, but she was moved to Copacabana and was replaced with the Virgin of Socavon.

The building also has an image of Mary with two cherubs that appeared by miracle in the late 1800s. The church was built on top of an Uru ritual center and over a mineshaft that is now a museum. The mineshaft at one time was believed to be the hiding place of Chiru, the Aymara version of Robin Hood, who stole from the rich to give to the poor. When he was shot by police, he repented any sins he had to the Virgin and, as soon as he died, Mary's image appeared. This story is recounted in one of the stained glass windows of the church.

City Sights

In front of the sanctuary is the huge **Plaza del Folklor** where the culmination of events occurs during Carnival. There is also a kids' cement slide that goes from the top of the hill down to the plaza.

Opposite the grand slide is a monument commemorating the miners and their part played in freeing Bolivian workers. It depicts a tunnel with an ore car, tracks and some miners with their hands raised in victory.

The hill behind the sanctuary is **Cerro Pie de Gallo** (Chicken-Foot Hill) and should be climbed (follow the steps) to get an excellent view of the city.

On the corner of Ayacucho and La Plata is the **courthouse**. Of course, the appropriately named Calle La Plata is lined with lawyers' offices.

The **Lighthouse of Conchupata** is on Avenida Herrera and Calle La Plata. Although it is in disrepair at the moment, this was where, on November 7, 1851, the first Bolivian flag was raised. The leader of the city, Manuel Isidoro Belzu, did the honors.

◆ Adventures in Culture

The **Religious Art Museum** (no phone) is on the upper floor of the Sanctuary of the Virgin and contains religious items made in honor of her. It's $1.50 to enter the church that displays many objects left after miracles were performed, the mineshaft and the art museum. There is a small gift shop at the Sanctuary beside the ticket wicket.

The mineshaft, now called the **Etnografico Museo de Mineros**, is far more interesting than the art museum. Miners feed Tio Diablo cigarettes and small amounts of alcohol, plus they decorate him with streamers and balloons. In return they get Tio's protection and guidance to the big ore-producing veins. At the opposite end of the mineshaft are artifacts from the early mining period in Oruro. Many of these are from the mine offices; I especially liked the old lead print machine and grandfather clock.

The **Cultural Museum of Simon Patiño** (no phone) is on Calle Ayacucho and Avenida Soria Galvarro, one block up from the street of the lawyers. The building was constructed in 1899 and made into a museum in honor of Patiño in 1970. It was originally his home but then the building was given to the university. Since universities and schools in Bolivia operate on almost no money, Patiño's home is pretty much the way it was left, with the addition of a lot of dust.

THE ALTIPLANO

> ### ❖ SIMON PATIÑO
>
> Born in Cochabamba in 1860 of poor peasant stock, Patiño married Alvina Rodriques who was from an Oruro peasant family. They had seven children.
>
> Simon struck it rich in iron and tin and become one of the richest men in the world. He sold most of his iron to the Germans during World War I. During the second World War, he remained loyal to the allies, although the Germans got lots of sympathy from the general population.

Patiño was known to pay his mine workers well, but otherwise he didn't contribute much to the poor. After becoming wealthy, he built the French-styled house in Oruro. He was like many self-made wealthy people in that they become ostentatious in an attempt to look refined.

A guided tour costs $1. Open hours must be guessed at; I went when it was closed but they took me around anyway.

The **Anthropological Museum** (National Anthropologo Museo of Eduardo Lopez Rivas) is in the south end of the city on Avenida España. A taxi costs just under a dollar for two people and a micro costs 15¢. Take the micro marked "sur" and tell the driver where you want to get off. The museum entry fee is 50¢. The displays here are excellent and include mummies found in the tombs on the road to Sajama as well as skulls that show how earlier people flattened the head of rich children for aesthetic reasons.

The park adjacent to the museum is well kept and the trees are labeled with local, family and scientific names. Behind the park and museum is a zoo.

The **Mineralogical Museum** (no phone) is at the Technical University at the south end of town. To get here, hire a taxi for 50¢ per person. Upon arrival, look for someone with a key to open the doors. The interesting displays include about 7,600 specimens in all. They include minerals – some in crystalline form and some with petroglyphs – and rocks of every type found in the hills around the city.

◆ Tour Agency

EBA Transturs, ☎ 242-2426, ebatrans@ceibo.entelnet.bo, have worked in 2001 with Dr. Allen from the magazine *Atlantis Rising*. The group toured through the villages described in the Pumiri road trip, above, and compiled an argument to support the fact that the Altiplano generally and this area specifically is the fabled Atlantis. For an interesting excursion, see these people. Their English is excellent.

◆ Places to Stay

Residencial Gloria, *around the corner from the palace, on Avenida Potosi near Bolívar,* ☎ 527-7250, *$,* has 13 rooms in a lovely old building that has been well kept and polished clean. The halls are bright and dotted with plants, and the rooms large and clean with high ceilings, wood floors and big windows. A small cafeteria sells snacks and drinks. The front door is always locked and you must ring the bell (*tocar el timbre*) to enter.

❖ HOTEL PRICING	
$	$10 to $20
$$	$21 to $50
$$$	$51 to $75
$$$$	$76 to $100
$$$$$	over $100

Residencial San Miguel, *Calle Sucre #331* ☎ 527-2132 *$,* charges $4.50 per person for a small room with bath. There are carpets in the rooms and rather glitzy bedspreads and curtains. However, the place is okay.

Residencial Real, *Calle Sucre #401*, ☎ 527-4722, *$*, is another basic place to stay. Rooms have private baths and TVs and there is a parking area. The owners will exchange dollars, but not travelers' checks.

Hotel Bernal, *Calle Brazil #701, across from the bus station, no phone, $$*, has a friendly staff and clean rooms. Consequently, it is usually full. The new place across the street from the Bernal is equally as good, but charges more. Other than these two, I'd skip the rest of the places around the bus station because they are either overpriced or deplorably drab.

Sucre Hotel, *Calle Sucre #510 and Avenida 6 de Octubre*, ☎ 527-6800, *$$$*, is a grand old place with friendly staff that keeps the hotel spotless. Room rates include cable TV, a telephone and a buffet breakfast. The wide halls feature original oil paintings on the walls, the floors are wood and the furniture is of good quality. Hot water comes from a boiler tank in the central courtyard and you must use cold water to get the right temperature. Rooms without private bath are small and located a fair distance from the communal bath. The hotel does not supply towels, nor is much English spoken.

Hostal Hidalgo, *Avenida 6 de Octubre #1616, around the corner from the Sucre*, ☎ 525-7516, *$$$*. Although it doesn't have the elegance of the Sucre, it certainly is a good deal. Rooms come with private or shared tiled baths, cable TV, carpet, chairs and tables. This hotel is much better than most for the price.

Hotel Monarca, *Avenida 6 de Agosto #1145*, ☎ 725-4300 or 725-4222, *$$$*, has moderately sized rooms with cable TV and hot water all day. There is a restaurant on site and underground parking is available. I found the management friendly and helpful.

Hotel Restoria, *Calle Sucre #370*, ☎ 525-8001, *$$$*, has single, double and triple rooms of moderate size, with night tables, cable TV and telephones, but the lighting makes them appear a bit drab. The baths are tiled and have separate shower stalls. English is spoken and breakfast is included. The old building has had quite a bit of care given to it and is a good alternative to the Sucre.

Palace Hotel, *Calle Adolfo Mier #392, on the corner of Potosi*, ☎ 527-2121, *smpalace@cotear.com, $$$$*, has singles, doubles and triples. The well-kept rooms, although not overly large, have writing desks, an electric heater and private baths. The price of the room includes breakfast and secure parking is available.

◆ Places to Eat

Salteñas Potosinas, *Calle Galvaro #6150*, has well-stuffed *salteñas* for 15¢ each – an excellent snack. *Rellenos*, fried dough stuffed with cheese, can be purchased in the markets near the miner's museum on Plaza Folklore. *Chicharon* (sausage) is served on Sundays only and is a great delicacy in Copacabana and Oruro. The other special dish is *langua peqanti*, tongue stew, which sometimes includes other "special" meats.

❖ RESTAURANT PRICING	
$	under $5
$$	$5 to $10
$$$	$11 to $25
$$$$	$26 to $50
$$$$$	over $50

THE ALTIPLANO

Ametauna Restaurant, *Calle Sonia Glavarro #1367,* ☎ *525-7703.* My *almuerzo* here consisted of a fresh salad, a soup spiced with a delicious blend of flavors, rice, potato and meat balls (this changes every day) and a dessert. It was excellent and the cost was 80¢ per meal. This place was the best I found while in Oruro.

Super Hamburguesas, *in front of the Entel building just up from Oggies on Bolívar,* is the popular Bolivian rendition of McDonald's, only this is 10 times as good. Super Hamburguesas has a second location at Avenida 6 de Octubre #5379. This restaurant has a lot of fresh vegetables that can be added to a hamburger or just eaten as a salad.

For the best hamburger go to **Plaza Rancherea** on Sundays at noon. It is on the corner of Calle Sonia Galvario. In a makeshift *tienda* vendors cook *churrascos* and serve them in a bun that has been partially dipped in the cooking oil. The bun is filled with freshly shredded veggies. This meal costs only 65¢, but plan on waiting at least 20 minutes because the lines are so long. You can also get a plate of *churrascos* with rice and salad at the same *tienda* for just under a dollar a plate. When you arrive at the plaza, just look for the crowd. That's where to eat.

Bravo's Pizza, *Bolívar between 6 de Octubre and Potosi,* has good pizza – a 12-inch veggie costs $3.50. Mugs of warmish beer are served with a huge head. If you are a beer drinker, ask for a small glass and pour your own.

Gupers, *Calle Junin and Pdte Montes,* ☎ *525-3815, is up one block from Plaza 10 de Febrero.* This popular place specializes in sweet and sour chicken. The restaurant also serves salads spiced with herbs.

I often used to go to **Govindo's Restaurant** run by the Hari Krishna, but it was not open on my last visit. Nor was the pub next door, the La Jaula. They may have been closed for renovations or just closed for good.

◆ Shopping

This is the place to purchase Carnival-related objects like masks or glittery hats and dresses. Places to buy masks are **El Kerquinacho**, Calle German Floriz #5379, and **Arco Irio** and **Ancestral Bordados** off Calle La Paz. Masks and costumes can cost anywhere from a few dollars up to hundreds.

Potosi

Altitude: 13,454 ft/4,090 m,
making Potosi the highest capital city in the world
Population: 125,000

Potosi is high. Your breathing and heart rate will be up and your energy down until you acclimatize. However, once you are comfortable in Potosi, you will be comfortable anywhere in Bolivia. Although it is not attractive, moving farther into the heart of the city reveals many treasures. And, if you are into history, Potosi is Bolivia.

During the summer months (October to March) the weather is rainy but warmer than in winter, when temperatures can drop well below freezing. One of the secrets of enjoying Potosi is getting a warm and comfortable place to stay.

◆ Getting Here & Around

If coming by bus, you will have a long walk up a steep hill to reach the main part of town. Taxis go into town and they are worth far more than their cost of 45¢ per person. The bus station is at Avenida Universitario. Some buses don't stop at the terminal but along the street close to the terminal. There is a 25¢ tax charged for using buses from the terminal.

Buses to Cochabamba leave at 6:30 pm, 7 pm and 7:30 pm daily.

Buses to La Paz leave at 6:30, 7 and 8 pm daily. **Copacabana Bus Company** offers a bus-cama to La Paz three times a week for $8 per person This bus has a foot section that folds down and seats that fold back to make a sort of bed. The bus is very quiet; even children know not to cry while on this bus. They do not pick up passengers once all seats are filled.

Buses to Oruro leave at 7 am and 7 pm. Those to Tarija go at 4 am and 4 pm and those for Tupiza/Villazon leave at 7:30 am, 6 pm, 7 pm and 7:30 pm. Buses to Uyuni leave at 11 am and 6 pm daily. Buses to Sucre leave at 7 am, 1 pm, and 5 pm daily.

The **Colonial Plus Car Company**, Calle Otero #121, ☎ 642-5101, has *collectivos* going to Sucre. It takes four hours and costs $3.50 per person.

To rent a car and driver for a private run, call **Silvero Mamani**, ☎ 718-16967 (cell). He is a fast driver, but quite safe.

There is an airport in Potosi but no planes fly there yet and the empty landing strip is a bit of a joke among the people of Potosi.

> ❖ **WORTH A POTOSI**
>
> The saying "vale un potosi" (it's worth a Potosi) became popular during the prosperous years of the city. Throughout the Spanish world and even beyond, "Potosi" meant that something was worth a fortune.

◆ History

Before the Spanish arrive, **Diego Huallpa**, a traveling local, discovers silver at Cerro Rico.

1545	Spanish arrive to mine the silver. Pilaviri Mine is opened and is still producing silver in 2005.
1630	Potosi is now the largest city in the Americas and even larger than London, England.
1672	The mint is built and produces coins for Europe and America.
1545-1825	Over eight million Indians die in the mines working for the Spanish under bad conditions.
1987	Potosi becomes a World Heritage Site.

THE ALTIPLANO

> ❖ **ACTIONS SPEAK LOUDER THAN WORDS**
>
> A Potosi priest saw mine workers coming to town at the end of a working period, their eyes like those of ghosts, their backs scarred by the lash. "I don't want to see this portrait of hell," said the priest. "Close your eyes then," someone suggested. "With my eyes shut, I see more," he answered. But he did nothing to stop the oppression.

◆ Services

The **telephone office** is on the corner of Calle Bolívar and Avenida Camacho and the **post office** is on Chiquisaca, one block down from the plaza.

The **police station** is on the central plaza.

ATMs and money exchange offices are set along the *prada* (el Bolívard), on Calle Tarija, and Avenida Comanche. **Banco Mercantil**, on Avenida Padilla and Moyos, changes traveler's checks but charges a commission. Should you need money wired to you, Western Union offices are found throughout Bolivia. ☎ 800-10-5057.

◆ Festivals

Besides the usual festivals like Christmas, Easter, Carnival and Todos Santos, Potosi has a couple of special ones.

Corpus Christi commemorates the institution of the Holy Eucharist and it is celebrated in a special way on the Thursday after Whit Sunday. (Whit Sunday occurs 50 days after Easter.)

The **Feast of St. Bartholomew** is celebrated August 24-26. The first day, called Chutillo, is when the people go to La Puerta, 3.7 miles/six km from the center, and raise a cross with great ceremony. The second day, Majtillo, brings a street parade with traditional music and dancing. On the third day, Tapuqullu, everyone joins the festivities and often visitors from around the world come especially to partake in the celebrations.

November 10, 1545, is the year that Potosi became a city. On that date, there are parades and, in the evenings, feasting.

◆ Sightseeing

In the City

I highly recommend a **city tour** so that you will learn details about the city that I cannot possibly put into this book. Many companies run city tours. I went with Aleida Fejardo Saavedra of Victoria Tours and was very pleased.

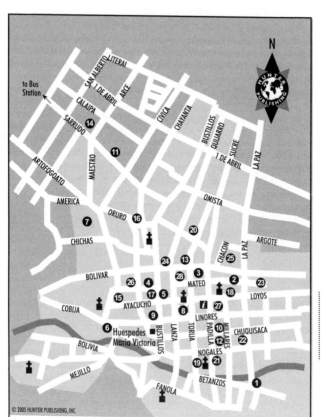

© 2005 HUNTER PUBLISHING, INC

Potosi

SIGHTS
1. San Marcos Café & Museum
2. Casa de Las Tres Portadas
3. Portada de Piedra Labrada
4. Compañión de Jesus
5. Casa de la Moneda
6. Arca de Cobija
7. Teatro IV Centenario
8. Plaza 10 de Noviembre

PLACES TO STAY
9. Residencial Sumaj
10. Compañión de Jesus
11. Residencial Tarija, Res. 10 de Noviembre, Res. Copacabana
12. Hotel San Carlos V
13. Hotel Felimar
14. Hotel Cima Argentum
15. Santa Clara Hostal & Restaurant, La Bodequita
16. Hostal Jerusalem

PLACES TO EAT
17. Manzana Magica
18. Café Potachi, Restaurant Kaypichu
19. Pollo Super Crock
20. Skyroom Restaurant
21. Restaurant La Boulivard, La Bode Guita
22. Pub Café Kuramy, Capricornio
23. Restaurant Doña Maria
24. Sumaj Orcko
25. La Teberna del Tio Anton
26. El Fogan Restaurant/Pub
27. Eli's Café
28. Candelaria Interet Café

> ❖ **MORE MONEY THAN SENSE**
>
> In 1639 a wealthy businessman lay dying. He called his lawyer
> so he could dictate his last will. He demanded that one fourth
> of his silver be used to build a latrine in the center of town, to be
> used by nobles and plebeians alike. Another fourth was to be
> buried in his yard and protected by four fierce dogs who were
> to be fed using money from his estate to buy the food. The third
> quarter was to be used to prepare a feast which would be left in
> the ditches so the worms could eat it. The final amount was to
> be used to adorn the asses of the town with jewels and gold
> vestments and then to have the adorned donkeys accompany
> his body to the grave.

The Mint, or Casa de la Moneda, is just off Plaza 10 de Noviembre on
Calle Ayacucho. It is open Tuesday to Friday, 9 am to noon and 2 to
6:30 pm, and on weekends from 9 am to 1 pm for guided tours only. Even if
you do not go to the mine, visit the mint and take the three-hour tour with an
English- , Spanish- or German-speaking guide. The museum is considered one of the best in South America.

> **AUTHOR NOTE:** *Ironically, the five boliviano coin now in circula-
> tion is minted in Canada. It is a miniature version of the Canadian
> "Toonie."*

The 200-room building, complete with courtyards and baroque decorations, is massive. It is constructed of carved stone, cedar wood, brick and
domed roofs covered in tiles. The outside walls are three feet thick and the
houses inside became residences of the early directors.

At the first courtyard near the entrance is a fountain with a stone mask
hanging above. Who the mask depicts is subject to great speculation.
Some think it is Bacchus, the Roman god of wine. The face looks like a
model who had too many drinks before sitting for the carving. Some claim
that the mask is a cartoon of President Manuel Isidoro Belzu who ruled at
the time of Independence. Still others think it is a representation of one of
the mint's directors, E.M. Moulon (the French artist who designed the piece
disliked Moulon). There are some who believe the mask is a mocking reaction towards Spain's greed. Today, the face has become the town's icon. In
the second courtyard is an upright sundial. Check your watch against it.

Other areas in the mint contain domestic and personal items that were
crafted from Potosi silver and used during Potosi's height. There are numerous coins from every era (1575-1953) and some interesting security
boxes or safes. Early coins were 90% silver, 10% copper and are odd
shapes. Coins produced later were stamped perfectly round and contained
80% silver and 20% copper.

The most interesting items from the past are the pressing machines, with
a series of wooden gears and axles that rotate with precision. The entire
set of wheels and gears is far too complicated to describe, but the source of
power was simple: four mules, attached to a drive shaft, going round and
round on the level below.

A bookstore offers some English-language books. Pick up the *Museum Guide of the Mint of Potosi*, an inexpensive publication with a lot of information. The translation from Spanish to English is excellent.

The **Museum of Santa Teresa**, open every day from 9 am to 12:30 pm and 3 to 6:30 pm, costs $3 per person for a guided tour. Each tour takes a minimum of two hours. Santa Teresa, originally a convent, was built in 1685. The outside of the building is adorned with three coats of arms, the center one being that of the Order of the Carmelites and the other two belonged to the building's founders. The woman responsible for the convent being established was Santa Maria de Jose para Jesus. She was from Paraguay. Her body is lying in a coffin at the monastery and is totally intact. This, people believe, is a miracle since no preservatives or embalming fluids were used. I didn't check to see if Maria really was all there.

The entering nuns had to have a dowry (some dowry items are displayed in the museum) equal to 2,000 pieces of gold, exclusive of the dress. The dress had to be very expensive and was given to the mother superior who did God knows what with it.

Frankly, while on this tour I started to imagine some wild scenarios that would be caused by sexual repression among 21 women living with a dead body and a huge pile of expensive dresses. It was an example to me of the weird forms that religious enthusiasm can take. These girls were sold into slavery by their families in exchange for credit in heaven.

The ornate church altar is covered in gold leaf. Some of the Christ statues are a bit gory but some of the paintings done by indigenous artists are interesting.

La Portada Torre de la Nave de la Comapñion de Jesus is the high Mogul-styled tower visible from around town. It was built between 1700 and 1707. The architect was Sebastian de la Cruz and he combined baroque with indigenous art but used the main design of the Arcs de Triomphe du Carrousel, a copy of the Arch of Severus in Rome. You can enter the tower on weekdays between 8 am and noon, and 2 to 6 pm. The cost is $1.50.

The **Arch Cobija**, on Avenida Cobija just past Calle Oruro, is a stone arch built during the peak of the silver mining period to draw a definite line between the Spanish and Indian sections of town. The Spanish, of course, lived on the upper levels. Just beyond the arch on the Indian side is a wall made from mixing calicanta, iron, chalk and egg white – it shows no sign of disintegration.

Mirador Pari Orko is the green monstrosity that can be seen from anywhere in town. Walk over and take an elevator to the restaurant at top. The views make it worth the effort. The mirador was not open when I was last in Potosi, but was rumored to be opening soon.

Tres Puertales, Calle Bolívar #1052-60, has three decorated doorways from the colonial period. The center one has an overhanging balcony like those along Avenida Ayacucho and Cochabamba.

San Marcos Café, Restaurant and Museum on Calle La Paz and Betanzos, ☎ 622-2366, is open every day from 8 am to midnight. However, the Textile Exposition is open only Monday to Saturday, 11 am to 3:30 pm and again from 6 to 7:30 pm.

THE ALTIPLANO

San Marcos Mill was built at the end of the 1800s at a time when the silver was no longer pure enough to extract without using tons of mercury. To do this, the ore had to be ground. The first machines used for grinding are now inside the café/museum, along with other equipment used in silver extraction.

Churches

Potosi has 34 churches. Originally nine were for the Spanish and 25 for the indigenous people.

The **cathedral** on Plaza de 10 de Noviembre was first built in 1564 but, after the center aisle collapsed, had to be totally reconstructed at the beginning of the 1800s. It took 28 years to complete. The final architect of the building was Fray Manuel Sanahuja. Inside, sculptures are by Gaspar de la Cueva and the gold moldings on the white background are all reminiscent of the Jesuit Missions out of Santa Cruz. The mausoleum is also worth checking out. Half-hour tours are offered every day except Sunday and at $1 are well worth taking.

The **Church of San Lorenzo** is behind the market on Calle Heros del Chaco and Bustillos and has the finest mestizo-baroque carvings in Potosi. They depict both Indian and Spanish culture. The floor inside is original and there is one nave. San Lorenzo was reconstructed in the 18th century, when the present façade was carved and the original chapel was removed. Inside are paintings by Melchor Perezde Holguin, one of Bolivia's more celebrated artists. This is probably the most photographed church in all of Bolivia.

The **Museum and Convent of San Francisco**, on Tarija and Nogales, was founded by Friar Gaspar de Valverde and built in 1547, making it the oldest convent in Bolivia. It was rebuilt, bigger, in 1707. The nuns will take you on a tour of the museum that houses religious pieces such as medallions of St. Francis, a sacred heart and 25 oil paintings by Gregorio Gamarro on the life of St. Francis of Assis. Just outside the vestry there are paintings such as the Flagellation (yuck) and the Holy Virgin. A wood carving between the two paintings represents Prayer in the Garden. Inside the vestry is a painting by Melchor Perez de Holguin. The outside entrance to the church was carved by Sebastion de la Cruz.

San Martin on Calle Moyos and Pizarro was originally one of the churches built for Indians who were forced here to work in the mines. It belonged to the Order of the Merced and was constructed in 1592. One wall on the inside is still of mud brick. The church of the mestizo-baroque design. Take note of the two door knockers, one set higher than the other. The lower ones were for people on foot and the upper ones were for people on horses.

The **Church of Bethlehem**, now used as the Omiste Theater, is on Moyos, just off the central plaza. It was originally established to take care of hospitals in Potosi and the Real de la Vera Cruz was run by them. Because of the work of the church, the Order of Our Lord of Bethlehem of Potosi was formed. In 1725 the building disintegrated under heavy rains, so Bernardo Rojas Luna and Saldana worked together to create the new one. Completed in 1753, the new building was used for the Faculty of Arts and Sciences for the University of Potosi and finally in 1862, it was made into the public theater. Its latest facelift won two prominent awards for architecture.

◆ Adventures on Foot

Cerro Rico stands at 17,049 ft/5,183 m and has a circumference of one league (over 18,000 ft). Called Sumaj Orko in Quechua, it is an impressive hill and I recommend a visit to its mine.

> ### ❖ LUCKY GIFTS
>
> It is customary to purchase gifts like coca leaves, fuel, boots, clothing or anything you feel you can afford to give to the miners. Your guide will assist you in this. The gift giving is thought to bring luck to the miners.

Run mostly now as a cooperative, the mine, even with all its improvements, doesn't look to me like an attractive place to work. The major difference from early days is that miners are looking for silver, lead and zinc instead of just silver. Apprentice miners must be 12 years old before they can start work here, and they must work three years hauling ore in backpacks to the pulley shafts where the ore is then hauled to the surface, before prospecting on their own. Apprentices earn between $4 and $8 a day, depending on the quantity and quality of the ore.

Some mines, like Rosario Bajo and Candalaria, are built on five levels and run only 658 ft/200 m deep, while others go 1,579 ft/480 m deep, passing through 17 levels on the way. The men work 12 hours a day and in an emergency are known to work around the clock. Presently, the 500 miners at Potosi supply 46 private processing plants owned by international corporations.

Health problems are rampant. Silicosis is common, as are stomach ailments. Arthritis of the neck and feet, felt by most working underground, is caused from the wet and cold conditions. Tuberculosis is also common. Because zinc and lead release a lethal gas under certain conditions, the men face the danger of inhaling the gas and dying within 15 seconds. The odor can be detected, but most often there is not enough time to escape the fumes.

Lagunas de Kari Kari is a hike that can be as long or short as you wish, ranging from a few hours to an overnighter. Most people walk a circle up to the lakes and then around Cerro Masoni. Walking up to San Sebastian Lake takes just over an hour and is recommended for birders even if you do not go past the rest of the lakes. If you do continue, take warm gear as rain/hail/sleet can fall at any time. Kari Kari itself is glacier-fed and it flows into Lake San Ildefonso, Lake Ray, Lake Reina and Lake Challviri.Twenty-two lakes were created to hold the water needed by the silver refineries; the lakes mentioned above are some of them.

To get to the trail, go east from the main plaza to Plaza Sucre. Continue up toward the fields until you can see the lake and a white plastered church. The trail becomes clear from there. Continue above the river on the east side. You will pass a small farming community with stone huts. Just beyond are some pleasant caves in which to eat lunch. Before you turn west to start your circumnavigation of the mountain, the valley narrows. Although long (12 miles/20 km), this is an excellent day hike.

La Puerta is 3.7 miles/six km from town along the road to Oruro. Follow Calle Antofagasta across the tracks and keep going. Along the road you will pass the Devil's Cave, made obvious by the red soil and rocks. The Puerta also has the chapel of St. Bartholomew that was built in 1598. Although buses travel here, it is best to walk at least one way. The walk allows you to watch local activities in a non-obtrusive manner.

◆ Adventures on Water

Tarapaya Lake & Hot Springs was revered by the Inca for its healing powers. Today, there are signs around the green-watered pool that warn swimmers not to enter due to dangerous currents. This volcanic hole is a perfect circle about 330 ft/100 m across that emits hot water, rather than lava. The walk to the public hot springs about a kilometer beyond the lake is spectacular.

To get here, take a bus from Potosi market to Tarapaya and ask the driver to let you off at the trail going to the lake. From there, walk along the upper ridge for as long as possible before going down again to follow the road to the pools. The last bus returns to Potosi at five in the afternoon.

Miraflores Watering Place is 1.2 miles/two km from Tarapaya and just beyond the public swimming area. Although not as popular as Tarapaya, it too can be visited for a long soak. Small restaurants offer meals.

There are changing rooms, a snack bar and three pools, each with water at a different temperature. One pool is Olympic-sized. On the far side of the river are some resorts.

◆ Tour Agencies

Jorge Gutierrez & Liliana Montes, Calle Cobija #90, ☎ 624-2377, take groups or individuals down into the mines. Jorge and Liliana work in their spare time at improving conditions for miners. Jorge's English is excellent.

Koala Tours, Calle Ayacucho #5, ☎ 622-4708, www.koalatourbolivia. com, offers the mine tour for $10 per person with a maximum of eight people. Fifteen percent of the tour fee goes toward the well-being of the miners. This company goes into the Candelaria Mine, one of the earlier mines dug hundreds of years ago. This is a five-hour activity. Rubber boots, jacket and helmet are provided at no extra cost. The headlamps are electric rather than calcium flame.

Andes Salt Expeditions, Plaza Alfonso de Ibanex #3, ☎ 622-5175, tourismo_potosi@hotmail.com, also has an office in Uyuni. They specialize in the Salar tours either from Potosi or Uyuni, and also run a mine tour, a trip to Tarapaya, a hike to Kari Kari and a city tour that includes a trip to the Casa de Moneda. The Salar trip can be done in two, three or four days and price depends on time. However, it is only the four-day tour that goes down to Laguna Colorado and Laguna Verde.

Victoria Tours, Chuquisaca #148, ☎ 622-2144, has the best city tour of all the companies in Potosi. The tour guides working for this company have a specialty where they learn everything available about their topic. Aleida Fejardo Saavedra is the guide that should be requested for a city tour. Her Spanish was such that even those without much Spanish could understand her and her English was excellent for those with no Spanish. She was humorous and knew her topics well.

◆ Places to Stay

Huespedes Maria Victoria, *Chuquisaca #148, no phone, $,* has a large colonial mansion with bright comfortable rooms set around a central courtyard. There are rooms with or without private bath. Antiques decorate the courtyard. A new section is being built and, during the

❖ HOTEL PRICING	
$	$10 to $20
$$	$21 to $50
$$$	$51 to $75
$$$$	$76 to $100
$$$$$	over $100

early stages of construction, an old passageway to the streets was found. It is now being restored. Breakfast is available in a heated dining room off the courtyard for an extra $1.50 for an Americano.

Residencial Sumaj, *Calle F. Gumiel #12,* ☎ *622-3336, $,* is very basic with dark rooms and only communal baths. Kitchen facilities are available, or you can order breakfast for a small fee. There is a TV room and Internet access on site. This is a backpacker's favorite.

Compañion de Jesus, *Calle Chiquisaca (no phone), $$,* has dull rooms; those at the back of the building are not worth the cost. This hotel seems to be in a constant state of construction. However, the showers are hot. Breakfast is included although it would be better to negotiate a lower cost for the room and skip the breakfast.

Residencial Tarija, *Avenida Serrudo #252,* ☎ *622-2711, $$,* has plain rooms with private bathrooms that are tiled and clean. The building is off the road so it has a better chance of being quiet. There is also a car park. Across the street are Residencial 10 de Noviembre and Copacabana, both basic and inexpensive.

Hostal Carlos V, *Linares #42, no phone, $$,* is a well-kept colonial house with rooms around a central courtyard. It is a step up from many hotels in town, although the rooms are a bit small.

Hostal Jerusalem, *on Oruro 143,* ☎ *622-4633, $$,* is a member of the International Hostelling Association. Set in a clean old colonial building, it offers large rooms, private bathrooms and hot water. The courtyard is dotted with flowering plants. Amenities include laundry service, TV, telephone, safe and luggage storage. The owners are helpful.

Hostal Felimar, *Avenida Junin #14 and Calle Bolívar,* ☎ *622-4357, $$,* is just off the *prada*. It has rooms with or without bath. Each room has a color TV and a fridge/mini-bar. The Felimar looks clean and comfortable, but the staff is not much interested in foreigners.

Santa Clara Hostal, *Calle Ayacucho #43,* ☎ *623-0092, $$$,* has clean and cosy rooms, all with private bath, closet, heater, large windows and cable TV (50 channels, some of which are in English). The Rosicler restaurant downstairs is convenient, as are the car park and laundry service.

Hotel Nuevo Milenio, *Avenida Universitario #450,* ☎ *624-3865, $$$$,* has single and double rooms. The hotel is done in oriental motif with four floors around a central patio that holds a restaurant. The place is clean and bright, but there is no elevator and four flights up in Potosi can be a challenge. Each room is carpeted and has color, cable TV and a phone. I found the staff near comatose.

Hotel Cima Argentum, *Avenida Villazon #239, four blocks up from the train station*, ☎ *622-3865, info@hca-potosi.com, $$$$$*, is a classy new hotel considered one of the best in the city. It has nine rooms – some hold up to four people, while others are suites complete with kitchen area and sitting room. The standard rooms have carpets, tile in the private bathrooms, hot water from a central tank, 50 channels on the television, telephones for national or international calls and heaters. Rates include breakfast and there is a discount offered for stays of longer than a week. An on-site restaurant is open from 7 am to 11 pm daily. This hotel also has nice cabins at Tarapaya and can arrange stays at them. They work with Andes Salt Expeditions so you can visit the salt lakes (or do any other tour) at your convenience with all arrangements made from the hotel. Rates: $33 single; $46 double, $52 apartment for two people; $60 apartment for three. An apartment has two rooms and one bathroom.

◆ Places to Eat

Potosi's *prada* is where most trendy restaurants and shops are located. No vehicles pass along the walkway, but the number of locals checking things out is amazing. The street is called, simply, **el Bolívard**.

❖ RESTAURANT PRICING	
$	under $5
$$	$5 to $10
$$$	$11 to $25
$$$$	$26 to $50
$$$$$	over $50

Manzana Magica, *Calle Ayacucho and Avenida Bustilla*, is a vegetarian restaurant with food made from organically grown veggies. The coffee, although *distilado*, is the best in town. Try to miss rush hours like *almuerzo* when the locals rush there to eat meals. Open 8 am to 10 pm, Monday to Saturday.

Café Potacchi, *Calle Millares #13*, ☎ *622-2759*, offers live music on Wednesday and Friday nights. It serves local dishes like llama steak and *quinoa* soup. You must order every item as a separate dish – steak does not automatically come with potatoes or rice. I recommend their *reichti*, a spiced potato done up Swiss-style. Most meat dishes are $2 and soup is $1. The convivial owner speaks English. A propane heater is kept going, so you can eat without chattering teeth.

Restaurant Kaypichu, *Calle Millares #16*, ☎ *622-6129*, is across the street from the Potacchi and is open Tuesday to Sunday, 7 am-1 pm and 4-9 pm. It has a pleasant atmosphere, is totally vegetarian and has good prices. Breakfast includes natural fruit juice, muesli, granola, yogurt or oatmeal. The café is operated by the same people who own the one in Sucre and it's every bit as clean and efficient.

Pollo Super Crock, *Calle Padilla #6*, ☎ *622-6938*, offers good and inexpensive chicken and chips. The staff is friendly and the building is warm.

Skyroom Restaurant, *Edificio Matilde, Calle Bolívar #701*, ☎ *622-0138*, is on the third floor (yes, you must climb the stairs) and offers the best *almuerzo* in Potosi for $2. Not only is the food good (indicated by the number of patrons), but the views are excellent. Cerro Rico stands as a backdrop for the red-tiled roofs of the village. Some English is spoken and there's an English-language menu.

Candelaria Internet Café, *Calle Ayacucho #5,* ☎ *622-8050,* is a groovy spot that offers traditional dishes, hamburgers and pizza, plus vegetarian meals for $1.50-$2. The Internet room on the third floor is very good, but the cappuccinos are not and I suspect they may be made from a mix. A craft shop sells weavings and Potosi silver. Their prices are average.

Santa Clara Restaurant, *el Bolívard #33,* ☎ *622-3746,* is open Tuesday to Saturday, 8:30 am-1 pm and 3-10:30 pm (on Sundays they open at 10:30 am, after church services). This restaurant is a chain. There is a second one on the Plaza (☎ 622-6547) and another inside the Casa de Moneda Museum. The pastries and ice cream are an excellent way to finish off any meal obtained elsewhere. It is a popular restaurant with locals.

Rosicler Restaurant, *Santa Clara Hostal, Calle Ayacucho #43,* ☎ *622-5270,* offers excellent service, international food, pleasant ambiance and a welcoming staff. This is a recommended place to eat, although the food is not cheap (but then neither is anything else about the Rosicler). During high season, a reservation is recommended.

Restaurant La Boulívard, *#852, no phone, in the back of the courtyard,* has a menu that is not for vegetarians. Their house special, called Plata de la Casa, includes beef, chicken, pork, llama and sausage. Prices are not listed; this a "treat-only" place that needs budgeting for. The ambiance is French and the food is of the same high quality found in good restaurants in France.

La Bode Guita, *el Bolívard, (no phone),* has a great *almuerzo* (some say it is the best in town) for $1.75. Offerings change daily. Locals patronize this place so getting here early is essential.

Pub Café Kuramy, *corner of Calle Chiquisaca and el Bolívard,* can be spotted by the bright blue door and an icon above of the five boliviano coin (the bi-metallic one minted in Canada) now in circulation. It's a great hangout for *gringos* to drink beer, eat hamburgers and stay warm. Some locals come here, too.

Restaurant Doña Maria, *Calle Mateos #81,* is upstairs and has an intimidating entrance. This is a local restaurant, serving only local foods at local prices. The food is delicious and, if you are sitting by the window, the view is also good.

Restaurant Capricornio, *el Bolívard #1,* is *gringo*-land, serving pizza, spaghetti, apple pie and other such things. They get the *gringos* because they know how to serve just a bit of what you left at home.

Eli's Café, *Linares #26,* ☎ *622-8609,* is open every day, even through siesta. It's set on the upper part of the plaza. The pastries are okay, but the coffee is not good. Have a beer instead.

Sumaj Orcko, *Calle Quijarro #46,* is an excellent restaurant serving both *almuerzo* and à la carte meals. A dish of *pique de la macho* (a spicy stew cooked with special sausage and served over French fries) is huge and delicious and costs less than $2. Unless you are ravenous, I'd suggest ordering the half-portion. Because of its popularity, Sumaj Orcko gets busy so try to eat here between rush times when you will get better service.

THE ALTIPLANO

◆ Shopping

Artesenia El Chasqui, Calle La Paz #1649, ☎ 718-36701 (cell), is a non-profit organization run by Rosario Angulo Martinez, a social worker with energy to spare. She has been recognized by numerous government officials and other organizations (far too many to list) for her endless efforts in promoting artistic works from the villages around Potosi.

I encourage all travelers to purchase something from this store, no matter how small. Every penny goes toward helping struggling artists.

The **Handicraft Market** is at Plaza Saavedra on Calle Sucre and Omiste, where numerous shops are located. Silver and Potosi weavings, called *bayetas*, are the desired products from Potosi. Prices are comparable to anywhere in Bolivia, although slight bartering is required (Bolivians do not like to barter much). If you are into silver, there are many items available. Besides jewelry, there are cake knives and lifters, letter openers, spoons and ornaments.

◆ Nightlife

El Fogan Restaurant/Pub, Calle Oruro and Frias, ☎ 622-4969, is open from 11 am until midnight. It is a good place to hang out in a relaxed atmosphere and many locals come here.

La Taberna del Tio Anton, Calle Simon Cachon #19, opens at 5 pm daily. It is situated in an old building, has great atmosphere and is popular with the quiet crowd.

La Bodequita is next to the Santa Clara Restaurant on El Bolívard. You must go to the back of the hall and then down stairs. It's an artsy place and has a good atmosphere – a great place for drinking hot rums.

Uyuni/Eduardo Avaroa National Andean Wildlife Reserve

Altitude: 12,069 ft/3,669.26 m
Population: 10,500

The main reason anyone comes to the desolate town of Uyuni is to travel to the Salar (salt flats) and lakes. Some use this route to get into Chile. The salt flats are the largest on the planet. They are located in a park – **Eduardo Avaroa National Andean Wildlife Reserve** – which welcomes 24,000 visitors a year to its 1.5 million acres/820,000 hectares of land.

The town of Uyuni has few things of interest for the traveler, but there are nice places to stay. Tourists, especially packer types, love to hang out on the main drag up from the railway station. It is a street that has been turned into a kind of plaza, lined with bars, cafés, pizza parlors and tour companies.

◆ Getting Here & Away

Trains continue south from Uyuni toward the border or north to Oruro. The Express goes north Monday and Thursday at 10:15 pm and the Wara Wara, the slow train, goes Sunday and Wednesday at 2:30 am. It takes about seven hours to get to Oruro from Uyuni on the fast train and nine on the slow one.

Buses to Potosi take seven to nine hours and leave at 10 am, 10:30 am and 7 pm daily. The road is not bad.

Buses to Oruro also leave daily but go in the evenings, at 7 and 8 pm. It takes four hours and all buses going to La Paz must pass through Oruro. Most people use the train for this section of their journey as it is more comfortable and interesting. Buses going direct to La Paz leave Sunday and Wednesday at 6 pm for the eight-hour journey.

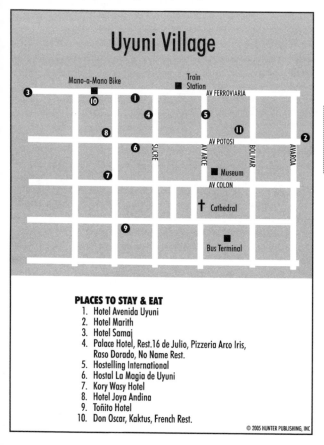

Uyuni Village

Mano-a-Mano Bike

Train Station

AV FERROVIARIA

THE ALTIPLANO

AV POTOSI

SUCRE

AV ARCE

BOLIVAR

AVAROA

Museum

AV COLON

† Cathedral

Bus Terminal

PLACES TO STAY & EAT
1. Hotel Avenida Uyuni
2. Hotel Marith
3. Hotel Samaj
4. Palace Hotel, Rest.16 de Julio, Pizzeria Arco Iris, Raso Dorado, No Name Rest.
5. Hostelling International
6. Hostal La Magia de Uyuni
7. Kory Wasy Hotel
8. Hotel Joya Andina
9. Toñito Hotel
10. Don Oscar, Kaktus, French Rest.

The route to Tupiza is serviced by 11 de Julio and they go Sunday and Wednesdays. It takes seven hours and costs $4. The road is not good. A jeep to Tupiza costs $7 and takes five hours. Belgrando and Bus Quechisla have jeeps going every day. The price and time is the same with all companies. The jeep leaves at 7:30 am and makes one stop in Atocha for lunch and vehicle change. You should purchase your ticket at least one day ahead as there is room for only 10 people. Regardless of what seat you get on the first leg of the journey (and what the company tells you), you will not get the same seat on the second leg, out of Atocha, unless you are very assertive. Once in Atocha, where you have an hour stopover, insist on choosing the seat you want for the next vehicle.

Atocha is also where you turn south to go to San Vicente should you wish to follow the Butch Cassidy and Sundance route. There are places to stay in Atocha if you have missed a vehicle heading south.

Chile is along the asphalt highway that goes to Iquique, Calama or San Pedro de Atacama. The border crossing is at Laguna Verde (Hito Cajon).

◆ History

Before tourists started to visit the reserve and salt flats, Uyuni was barely a hamlet. The National Reserve of Eduardo Avaron was established in 1973 to protect the three types of flamingos, the queñua forests and the area's archeological sites. It eventually included the area down to Laguna Colorada. The park has six levels of protection, ranging from areas to be used only for scientific study to areas that are open for tourism.

◆ Services

The **telephone office** is on Avenida Potosi just up from the clock tower.

The **post office** is on Avenida Cabrera, a block before the bus stop area.

The **police** are on Avenida Ferroviaria, across from the train station.

Banks are on Avenida Potosi, but they do not change traveler's checks nor is there an ATM in town. Bring American cash.

The **tourist office** is on Avenida Potosi, but it is useless. The staff were not even able to tell me if there was a nearby town called Pulacayo (it's down the road). For information, it is better to go to the park office under the clock tower.

The **park office**, Avenida Potosi #23, ☎ 693-2400, below the clock tower, sells a couple of English-language books about the area. A bird book I saw included descriptions of the reserve and its animals, plants, insects and special features. It sells for $5. Another good one is the *Travel Guide to Eduardo Avaroa National Andean Wildlife Reserve* by the Bolivian Conservation Association, for $6.

◆ The Land & Its Inhabitants

The salt flats cover an area of over 4,633 square miles/12,000 square km and are the largest in the world. They have an unusual amount of ulexite, a mineral used in the manufacture of borax, fertilizers and enamels for ce-

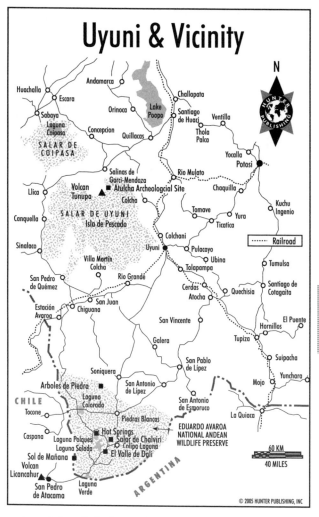

Uyuni & Vicinity

N

Huachalla

Escara

Andamarca

Sabaya

Orinoca

Laguna
Coipasa

Lake
Poopo

Challapata

Santiago
de Huari

Ventilla

Concepcion

Quillacas

Thola
Palca

SALAR DE
COIPASA

Yocalla

Potosi

Salinas de
Garci-Mendoza

Rio Mulato

Volcan
Tunupa

Atulcha Archeological Site

Chaquilla

Llica

Colcha

Tomave

Yura

Kuchu
Ingenio

SALAR DE UYUNI
Isla de Pescada

Ticatica

Canquella

Colchani

Sinalaco

Uyuni

Pulacayo

Ubina

Railroad

Villa Martin
Colcha

Rio Grande

Tolapampa

Tumulsa

San Pedro
de Quémez

Cerdas
Atocha

Quechisia

Santiago de
Cotagaita

Estación
Avaroa

Chiguana

San Juan

San Vincente

El Puente

Galera

Hornillos

Tupiza

Suipacha

San Pablo
de Lípez

Yunchara

Soniquera

San Antonio
de Lípez

Mojo

CHILE

Arboles de Piedra

Laguna
Colorada

San Antonio
de Esmoruco

La Quiaca

Tocone

Piedras Blancas

Caspana

Hot Springs

Laguna Polques

Salar de Chalviri

EDUARDO AVAROA
NATIONAL ANDEAN
WILDLIFE PRESERVE

Colipa Laguna

60 KM

Laguna Salada

El Valle de Dalí

40 MILES

Sol de Mañana

Volcan
Licancahur

San Pedro
de Atacama

Laguna
Verde

ARGENTINA

THE ALTIPLANO

© 2005 HUNTER PUBLISHING, INC

ramics and glass. Kollpa Laguna has a substance called kollpa, which is used by locals as a detergent.

These flats were originally part of Lake Minchin, an inland sea that once covered most of southwest Bolivia, including what is now Lake Titikaka. After Lake Minchin dried, the Uyuni and Coipasa flats were left dry, but Lake Poopo and Uru Uru were left with a thin layer of water. In the middle of the flats is Isla del Pescado, Fish Island. It is covered with cacti, some of which are over 26 ft/eight m high.

Along the Chilean border is a spine of mountains that range from Mount Linzor at 16,740 ft/5,089 m to Mount Uturunku at 19,763 ft/6,008 m. The two peaks that form an imposing backdrop around Laguna Colorada are Mount Chijlla at 18,780 ft/5,709 m and Mt. Pabellon at 18,085 ft/5,498 m.

Although there are a lot of lakes in the reserve, not much of the water is suitable for human consumption. The only river without salt is the Quetena. Most of the lake water has a high mineral content and toxic elements like arsenic. Laguna Verde is the lake with the highest arsenic content, while Laguna Colorada, with a depth of about 14 inches/35 cm, has a high salt content. Laguna Colorada also has the red algae called *Dunaliella salina* that gives the lake its red color, usually between the hours of 11 am and 4 pm when the winds increase and stir up the waters. This algae also gives the flamingos their pink plumage and the flamingo egg shells their orange hue.

There are often as many as 25,000 flamingos in the reserve and they create up to 5,000 nests every year. There are three flamingo species here. The **Chilean flamingo** is salmon-colored with reddish feathers on the upper wing. Its beak is whitish-pink with a black tip and its legs are blue-grey in color. The smaller **Andean flamingo** has a purple patch on its upper breast. It has a black beak with a yellow base and its legs are yellow with orange knees and toes. The **James flamingo** is smaller than the other two and the lower part of its body is black. It has a few pink feathers on the chest and its beak is yellow with a black tip.

Of the 190 different plants in the reserve, the most interesting is the **yareta** that grows about half an inch/one cm a year, making some of the bigger plants around 2,500 years old. The yareta looks solid and dense, bright green in color and firm to touch. The **queñua** tree, also interesting, grows at elevations from about 13,000 ft/4,000 m, all the way up to the snow line. This shrub has a red bark that peels and flakes. The ubiquitous grass seen on the Altiplano is called **ichu** and is spiky to the touch. It is often burned as a fertilizer. The **thola** plant seen dotting the landscape comes in six or seven varieties and is used by locals for fuel. Aside from these four there are the medicinal plants used by locals for curing everything from stomach ache to cancer. Those would have to be pointed out and described by your guide when on tour.

Of the wildlife species, the most common are the **vicuña**, the **vizcacha** (a high-jumping rabbit) and the **Andean fox**, which actually looks like a coyote.

There are some archeological remains, but they are of interest only to dedicated archeology buffs. There are *jaranas*, stone huts used by travelers to sleep in, *tambos* (trail markers), some rock paintings near the community of Quetena Chico and a ceremonial site lying in a depression between two volcanoes.

MOST INTERESTING SITES

Arboles de Piedra (trees of stone) is in the Pampa Siloli Desert. This collection of rock formations is interesting to explore and photograph.

Laguna Colorada is 37 miles/60 km long and turns a bright red after the wind comes up during the day. The red is caused from the algae growing on the bottom. The lake is home to many flamingos.

Sol de Mañana is the geothermic area where, if you visit early in the morning, you can see the boiling rock on the earth's surface.

Laguna Polques in Salar de Chalviri has hot springs. This salar also has mounds of white minerals that are different from anything found at Salar de Uyuni.

El Valle de Dali has a landscape that shows all the colors of the rainbow. It's an excellent spot for photographers and wildlife enthusiasts.

Laguna Verde turns a bright green after the winds start the waters moving. Here, the color change is due to arsenic content.

Volcan Licancahur and **Volcan Uturuncu** can be climbed if you choose the right tour company. This high-altitude experience will take you over 20,000 ft/6,000 m.

Atulcha, also called Chullpares, is an archeological site in a cave on Tunupa Volcano. It is interesting, but you must be acclimatized for the hike up the mountain.

THE ALTIPLANO

◆ Sightseeing

For a good introduction to the area, head to the **Uyuni Museum** on Avenida Arce. The greatest treasures here are four weavings (*chelapas*) from the Nor-Lipez culture (1200-1500). There are also skulls and pottery. At present, it takes less than a half-hour to go through the museum, but still it provides interesting information about a spectacular area.

◆ Adventures on Wheels

When choosing a tour company (there are 20 in Uyuni), you must first decide what you want to see and how long you want to stay away. Second, decide if you need the driver/guide to speak English. The other aspects of these tours are the same for everyone. Accommodations en route are usually basic, but adequate. Meals excellent; usually a cook accompanies you with bags of food, utensils, a propane burner and a tank. Beer or wine should be brought along in your baggage. A sleeping bag is also recommended, although most places will supply warm blankets.

❖ One-day tours will take you to the salt flats, Fish Island and back to Uyuni.

❖   Two-day tours will include everything the one-day tour offers plus the salt hotel, the salt mounds, and Tunupa Volcano. The volcano is exceptional in itself and there are some archeological areas nearby that could be of interest.

❖   Three-day tours include everything on the two-day tour plus San Juan, Laguna Colorada, the geisers, Laguna Verde and the chance to cross at the Chilean border to San Pedro de Atacama.

❖   Four-day excursions add a visit the Siloli Desert and the stone trees. You get more time at the geothermic areas, a dip in the hot springs, and a visit to the train cemetery.

❖   Six-day tour includes a night at Tunupa Volcano, the cave of the devil, Laguna Blanca and the opportunity to climb Mount Licancabur at 19,473 ft/5,920 m.

Tours run anywhere from $70 to $150, depending on how long you stay and what you visit. Be aware that the competition is great and the tour operators are desperate. They will often promise you a side trip to the moon to get your money. When first in Uyuni, talk to other travelers and see who is good and who isn't. This information changes often.

◆ Tour Operators

Although some guides are considered English speaking, many are not. It seems that if the guides can say hello, goodbye and thank you they are considered fluent. When going on a tour try to include in your group someone who has at least a smattering of Spanish and is willing to interpret.

> **AUTHOR NOTE:** *Tour companies do not include park fees in their prices. To enter the park costs $4 for foreigners, including entry to Fish Island, and it's $1 if going only to Fish Island.*

Besides the 20 companies in Uyuni that offer tours, there are also a number from La Paz, Potosi and Tupiza. The following are the ones with whom I spoke while in Uyuni.

Pucara Tours, Avenida Potosi and Calle Sucre, ☎ 693-2055, is owned and operated by the same people who run the International Hostel. I went on a four-day tour with Pucara and was pleased. The services they promised were actually given, the food was cooked fresh every day, the driver stopped whenever we wanted to take a photo and the guide was knowledgeable about the region.

Somja Jallpha Tours, Avenida Ferroviaria, ☎ 693-2410. These people speak English well. A one-day tour ($25) goes across the Salar to Fish Island and includes a hike to a lake partway up Tuñupa Volcano, the iron-laced volcano not far from Uyuni. From there, you can see the entire Salar. A two-day tour ($35) includes a night in a hostel near the volcano. Three days costs $65 and you see two islands – Fish Island and Bell Island, made of coral. Going for three days allows a trip to Atulcha, the archeological site that has mummies inside a cave. All tours include a visit to Yodadora Salt Plant. In the village you can watch people working with llamas, sheep, and quinoa. This company will take six people plus a driver and cook on each tour. Four-day tour prices are discounted during low season. The agency also give a complimentary t-shirt with a photo of the salar in front and their company name on the back.

Olivos Tours, Avenida Ferroviaria #23, ☎ 693-2173, olivostours@ hotmail.com, also books out of Marith Hostal on Avenida Potosi #61. This agency offers many combinations. A one-day tour includes a visit to Colchani, salt plant tour, Salar de Uyuni, Isla del Pescado and Cementario de Trains. Two-day trips add Conquesa, Chulparis and Tuñupa Volcano. On a three-day trip you also visit Laguna Atulcha, Cañapa, Laguna Hedeonda, Arbol de Piedra, Laguno Colorada, geysers, hot springs, El Valle de Dali (Altiplano landscape) and Laguna Verde. Four days, in addition to the above sites, will net you San Cristobal and a colonial church for $75 in low season and $95 in high.

Turismo El Desierto, Avenida Arce and Potosi, ☎ 693-3087 or 693-2953. This company is interested in pleasing the public and offers up to four days through and around the park. El Desierto also runs a trip up Mt. Lincancabur and will go to Tupiza to cover the Butch Cassidy route.

Toñito Tours, Avenida Ferroviaria #152 between La Paz and Sagarnaga, ☎ 233-6250 (in La Paz), www.bolivianexpeditions.com, has been in business for eight years. They are proud to keep their drivers employed year-round instead of contracting them for just one trip. Vegetarian meals are available. This tour can be booked in La Paz, but it makes the trip expensive. Better to book in Uyuni.

Toñito has one hotel in town and a second opening at Bella Vista on the other side of the Salar. The upscale Bella Vista location has an old burial tower and some groomed hiking trails for visitors to use while exploring, birding or photographing. Chris Sarage, one of the owners, also hopes to have mountain bikes for hire and to offer Salar treks with llamas.

Playa Blanca Tours, Ferroviara #304, ☎ 693-2772, playablancatours@hotmail.com, offers anything from one- to four-day tours. The staff was friendly and helpful. I spoke with one person who went with this company and he was especially happy with the meals.

Oasis Odessey Tours, Avenida Ferroviaria, ☎ 693-2308, has a flashy brochure and good-quality vehicles. The English spoken in the office was quite understandable and they were interested in trying to offer me what I wanted.

Tunupa Tours, Avenida Arce, ☎ 693-2823, does the usual trips and will take traveler's checks in payment – a bonus, since changing money in Uyuni is difficult.

◆ Places to Stay

Hotel Avenida Uyuni, *Avenida Ferroviaria #11*, ☎ 693-207,8 $, is across from the train station and was the first hotel in town. The owner opened 30 years ago with 24 beds and, due to the increase in tourism, now has 70 beds. Twenty-three rooms have private baths. There is a constant hum of activity at this excep-

❖ HOTEL PRICING	
$	$10 to $20
$$	$21 to $50
$$$	$51 to $75
$$$$	$76 to $100
$$$$$	over $100

THE ALTIPLANO

tionally clean property: someone washing linen, repairing cement, painting walls, cleaning windows. The only negative thing I could find is that sounds echo, but everything was certainly quiet by 9 pm. Rooms have tables and chairs and the walls are painted with an oil-base paint. The floors are all matching tile. There is a closed-in sitting area in the courtyard where guests can eat. Laundry costs 75¢ per kilo. This is a top-notch establishment. There is secure parking and hot water is available in the communal showers from 7 am to 7 pm.

Hotel Marith, *Avenida Potosi, #61*, ☎ 693-2174, *$*, is a short walk from the center (three blocks) and has 24 clean rooms around a central courtyard. This is a comfy place to stay, quiet and clean. Rooms have wood floors and painted walls. There are no toilet seats, but the shower water is hot. Laundry is 15¢ per item (two socks are considered one item).

Hotel Samaj, *Avenida Ferroviaria #96, corner of Calle Sucre*, ☎ 693-3099, *$*, was previously called Hotel Europa but management has changed hands and reputation. The new owner, Freddie Olvino Gomez goes out of his way to give guests all the comfort they need. There are 14 rooms, two with private baths. Rooms are plain, with wood floors, and the soft beds have 12-inch-thick mattresses and three heavy wool blankets for cover. There is a tiny kitchen that guests can use and a stove to boil water. A fireplace in the kitchen can be used on really cold days. There is a luggage deposit. People passing through Uyuni, who are not taking a room, can have a shower for 75¢. The water is heated by a gas water tank.

Palace Hotel, *Avenida Arce #7*, ☎ 693-2259, *$$*, has cool and quiet rooms with carpets and private baths for $6 per person or $2.50 for a room without bath. The price includes breakfast. The place is clean, English is spoken, and there is a rooftop salon for those wanting to get a good view. If you arrive late at night, ring the bell. There is someone available at all times.

Hostelling International, *Avenida Potosi and Calle Sucre*, ☎ 693-2228, *www.hostellingbolivia.org, pucara_tours@yahoo.com, $$*, is run by a native Uyunian, Vincente Ivor Nina Gallado (Ivor, for short). There are 13 rooms, eight with bathrooms attached. The beds have thick mattresses and the showers are always hot. Because Uyuni often has a water problem, Ivor installed a storage tank so the hostel never runs out. Each room has a cupboard where backpacks can be locked up. The hostel is bright and clean and your room rate includes breakfast. Parts of the hotel – like the TV sitting room and the reception area – are made of salt blocks. Hand-painted murals adorn the walls and the sitting rooms are tastefully decorated with a warm feel to them. There is also Internet access available and a kitchen that has everything, including a fridge and microwave. The dining room is separate from the kitchen. English is spoken. The hostel has been open since September, 2002. Once people know about it, rooms will be hard to get. The same man owns Pucara Tours, next door, and I know from experience that they run a good tour.

Hostal La Magia de Uyuni, *Calle Colon #432*, ☎ 693-2541, *magrano_uyuni@yahoo.es, $$$*, is a rustic, well-kept building with rooms around a grassy courtyard where a stuffed armadillo stands guard. The small rooms have carpets and private bathrooms. Three water tanks supply the showers for guests. Breakfast is included in the room rate. There is also a garage, laundry service, and Internet access on site.

Kory Wasy Hotel, *Avenida Potosi #304,* ☎ *693-2670, kory_wasy@ hotmail.com, $$$,* is run by Lucy Depares, a motherly figure who wants your every need met. All her rooms are carpeted and have small private baths with hot water that is available all day. The $10 per-person rate includes a buffet breakfast. The biggie is that Lucy provides hot water bottles for guests during cold weather. Plus, a doctor is on call. The hotel is built with cactus doors; according to local legend, anyone passing the night protected by these plants will have good luck. The stairs going to the upper level are steep, so hold the handrail. Lucy has a 4x4 available for four-day tours at $600. This price is for up to six people and includes a driver, a cook and all food. The hot water bottles go on the tour too.

Hotel Joya Andina, *Calle Cabrera #473, between Sucre and Comacho,* ☎ *693-2067, reservasjoyaandina@hotmail.com, $$$,* just up from the bus area, is brand new. It has 10 bright, tastefully decorated rooms, with matching bedspreads and curtains. Each room has a stereo system and TV, as well as a private bath. The showers are separated from the bathroom area and the hot water comes from a water tank. There are lights over the beds, clean scatter rugs, mirrors and a garage. Rates include a buffet breakfast. This is definitely a shining light in Uyuni.

Toñito Hotel, *Avenida Ferroviaria #60,* ☎ *693-3186, $$$$,* has 19 spacious rooms with private baths and queen-sized beds. They offer luggage storage and have the best book exchange in Uyuni. Rooms are comfortable, there's hot water all day, and the price includes breakfast.

◆ Places to Eat

Pizzeria Arco Iris, *Avenida Arce #27,* ☎ *693-2517,* is popular with tourists. Pizza is the big draw, but they also have cold Potosiña beer in a one-liter bottle for $1.75. Country and Western music plays (it's sometimes more welcome than pan flutes) and the service is good.

❖ RESTAURANT PRICING	
$	under $5
$$	$5 to $10
$$$	$11 to $25
$$$$	$26 to $50
$$$$$	over $50

Don Oscar, *Avenida Potosi,* offers a tortilla (actually an omelet) stuffed with tons of veggies for $1.25. Their fruit juices are thick. Don Oscar's is clean with no music blaring.

Kaktus, *Avenida Potosi, next to Don Oscar,* also has good omelets, called "omletts" on the menu. Kaktus is often full of tourists (an empty café is a bad sign), but they do play their music loud. Their fruit juices are also a bit thinner than those at Don Oscar's.

Restaurant Uyuni, *Avenida Potosi, next to Samaj,* has friendly staff, good food and clean tables, but don't look at the ceiling. A burger with fries is $1.60, one with egg and cheese is $1.15 and a pancake with chocolate is $1.25. This restaurant is far better than Raso Dorado on the square.

French Restaurant, *Aveninda Potosi,* is just one block from the square and has by far the best food in town. Thanks to Adriana Boon for trying this place first. The prices here are also exceptionally good. Everyone in town was talking about it.

Restaurant 16 de Julio, *Avenida Arce,* serves huge meals that have a lot of flavor. I recommend *silpancho*, a local dish that consists of a layer of rice with boiled potatoes covered with spicy fried meat. The meat is covered with an egg and the egg is covered with chopped onion and tomato. It was more than I could eat.

Raso Dorado on the square has had too many tourists. I ordered a burger that was served on an Inca bun (made of stone). When I brought this to the attention of the staff she at first argued with me saying that it was not stale. When I kept banging the table top with the bun, I think she decided to give me a new one for fear that I would chip the table. When she brought the second bun, she threw it on the table and said I could do what I wanted with it.

The No Name Restaurant, *Avenida Arce and Potosi,* ☎ *693-2670,* has great fries and thick fruit juices. The staff is friendly too. They have dried cactus on the doors for good luck. They will get it.

◆ Nightlife

The **Mano-a-Mano Bike Tournament** is held every Saturday at the Tuñito Hotel. The contestants choose a name for themselves, write it on a piece of paper and place it in a hat. There is a prize for the grooviest name. The names are drawn and two contestants enter the ring facing each other, each on a bike. The object is to make the opponent touch the ground with hands, feet or body while cycling past each other. The first one to touch the ground loses the match. Process of elimination is how the tournament proceeds. Gear is provided, including the Kona Mountain bikes. The cost is $4 per person. First prize is bragging rights in all of Bolivia, a Llama Mama t-shirt and a Minuteman Pizza.

The **bars** along Avenida Arce are where everyone coming back from a tour heads. Which bar? It matters not, as long as there is food, booze and service. The high after the trip is burned off before travelers head out of town.

The Yungas

The Yungas (the part around Cocha-bamba is also known as the Chapare) is located on the eastern foothills of the Andes, usually between 4,000 and 9,000 ft/1,250-2,700 m. It is

primarily steep jungle-covered mountains that eventually meet with tropical lowlands. The upper transitional forests are often called the eyebrow of the jungle in Bolivia. As you drop, the vegetation becomes thick and difficult to pass through unless there is a road. It is the wet climate of the Yungas (they get about 40 inches/100 cm of rain annually) that produces the heavy vege-tation. Canopied areas with lush, fast-growing grasses for undergrowth are common. As you get lower, large ferns are replaced with mosses, bromeliads and orchids.

The cultivated fields produce fruits and vegetables for highland resi-dents. Another region grows coca plants, legally. Throughout the Yungas, at all times of the year, birds and interesting insects are abundant.

The above information about the Yungas was provided by Tim Miller of Explore Bolivia.

Sorata

Altitude: 8,809 ft/2,678 m
Population: 5,000

This town, tucked into the hills of the Andes, is only four hours from La Paz by jeep and is one of the most popular destinations for the hiking and climbing crowd. They call it the Banff of Bolivia. The trails near town go to the impressive mountains of Illampu and Jacuma dotted with alpine lakes and hanging glaciers. Available accommodations are comfortable, the guiding services are excellent and the food is good, especially if you are into pizza.

I have given the details of a few hikes and climbs in the area, but this is only a teaser. Once you are in Sorata, speak with other travelers and those living in the area to learn of the latest climbing/hiking hot spot.

◆ Getting Here & Around

The road here is gravel and rock and narrow and winding. There is one high pass to be crossed between Achacachi and Sorata.

To hire a jeep from La Paz, work with a travel agent of your choice. Prices vary between $50 and $100 for the one-way trip into Sorata that takes four hours. A jeep leaving Sorata costs $30 to Achacachi and $50 or $60 to La Paz.

Buses leave La Paz every other hour. The two companies servicing Sorata are Transportes Larecaja and Flota Unificado Sorata.

You can also hop over to Sorata by *trufi* or taxi starting at the Peruvian border or at La Paz. From the border, the change places are Copacabana, Huarina, Achacachi and finally Sorata. Although this takes time, the vehicles are usually much smaller, making the passage safer than a bus ride.

A new adventure is to cycle to Sorata (my first choice). See *New Milenium Tour Company* in La Paz, page 74, for information on this option.

◆ History

The Sorata area has been settled for centuries. The early civilizations used the lakes above town for ceremonial purposes. There are rumors that Lake Chillata holds treasures of gold thrown in by locals to hide it from the Spanish.

The Spanish gold seekers were the first Europeans to come into the area and use it as a starting/stopping off point for access to the Amazon Basin and its gold-rich creeks and rivers.

Rubber was the next hot commodity and the same trails were used by slaves to carry latex into the hands of the Spanish.

◆ Services

The **telephone office** is on the square in front of Hotel Panchita.

The **police station** is opposite the telephone office, next to Residencial Sorata.

The **hospital** is up the hill from the square (take either set of steps) toward the right and along the main highway going to La Paz.

There is no **tourist office** in Sorata. The best information comes from **Louis** in Residencial Sorata on the square or at the **Associacion de Guias Turistica**, Calle Sucre #302 and just across from the Residencial Sorata.

◆ Adventures on Foot

Hiking

SAN PEDRO CAVE: The cave takes about three hours to reach walking at a leisurely pace. It is a 13-mile/22-km trip with a 987 ft/300 m change in elevation with the upward slope on the return. The cave is open from 8 am to 7 pm and there is a 50¢ charge to enter. You should have water, a flashlight and good walking shoes (boots are not necessary).

To reach the cave, follow the road past Altai Oasis toward the village of San Pedro. Walk on the trail above the river; the one beside the river disappears. At San Pedro, a sign directs you to the cave set at the bottom of a 148-ft/45-m marble cliff.

This is an excellent day hike and can be done without a guide.

CHILLATA LAKE: Also called Khotapata, this lake sits at 13,901 ft/4226 m above sea level and is at least an eight-hour hike from Sorata if you are carrying gear. That means you must spend a night at the lake. Or you could

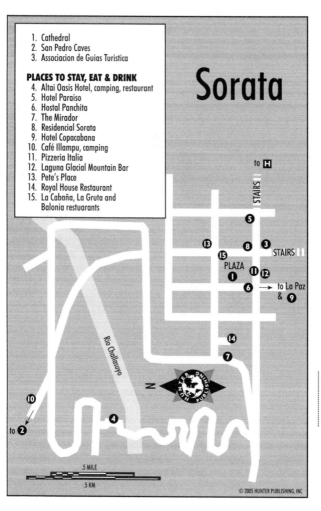

1. Cathedral
2. San Pedro Caves
3. Associacion de Guias Turistica

PLACES TO STAY, EAT & DRINK
4. Altai Oasis Hotel, camping, restaurant
5. Hotel Paraiso
6. Hostal Panchita
7. The Mirador
8. Residencial Sorata
9. Hotel Copacabana
10. Café Illampu, camping
11. Pizzeria Italia
12. Laguna Glacial Mountain Bar
13. Pete's Place
14. Royal House Restaurant
15. La Cabaña, La Gruta and
    Balonia restuarants

Sorata

THE YUNGAS

spend two nights at the lake and do a day hike up to **Glacial Lake** (16,530 ft/5,025 m), on the col between Illampu and Ancohuma mountains. It is believed that the glacier on the col once flowed down to Chillata Lake (see below for details on that hike).

Chillata is a sacred body of water where visitors are not welcome during a new moon because the Kallaway hold secret religious ceremonies at that time. Up until 1995, no tourist had visited here.

Because of the maze of trails leading from Sorata to the mountain villages, it is highly recommended that you hire at least one guide and, if you want luxury, hire a porter with a mule too. However, if you strike out on your own and ask villagers along the way, you may be lucky and get to the lake without problems. Boots, rain gear, a tent, a warm sleeping bag, food for two or three days, and a sun hat are essential for this hike.

Leave the village of Sorata and head up toward the hospital, taking the stairs outside the hospital gates. Continue along that road. At the fork, take the trail to the right (a left will take you above a water cistern and to another trail, although eventually the two trails come together). A small footbridge leads onto a ridge. Veer to the right once you are over the bridge. Note that there is no vehicular traffic on this road due to landslides and washouts. Switchback up the ridge and then cross it. Follow the road past a sign saying "Beinvenidos, Unidad Educativo Jumoco." The road has been washed out about 1.8 miles/three km farther along, so it is better to follow a trail where locals go down to the River Lakataya and over this second bridge. If you continue along the main road toward Quilambaya and try to cross the river at the washout, you will not be able to unless water levels are low.

Work your way up the hill to the village of Colani (10,339 ft/3,143 m). Unless you are acclimatized, you will breath twice for every step you take here.

Continue along the main road that goes east and parallel to Rio Tusca Jahuira. If you become uncertain about the way, you can either hire a guide or ask people along the way. This is not an isolated trail.

After 4½ to six hours and a 3,550-ft/1,000-m elevation gain, you will come to a bowl with the lake tucked inside. The mountains around are fairly steep and dotted with alpine grasses. You may spot tiny black patches that are the remains of ceremonies. The lake is deep and steep near the shore. Illampu can be seen in the background.

There are some ruins on the hill at the far side of the lake.

GLACIAL LAKE: Laguna Glacial, also called Lichikhota, sits 17,000 ft/ 5,130 m above sea level in the col between Illampu and Ancohuma mountains. From Chillata, continue south and hook up with a small road that leads to Titisani Mine site (often the base camp for climbers going onto Illampu). From there, the terrain becomes more rugged with jagged outcroppings and talus slopes. The lake is in the saddle between the two peaks. The closer to the lake you get, the windier and less-vegetated the environment becomes. Soon, lichen takes the place of grasses and Lake Titikaka becomes visible in the distance. The glacier pours itself into Laguna Glacial. In the other direction you can see the clouds of the Yungas.

> **AUTHOR NOTE:** Going to Laguna Glacial should be attempted only in good weather. If it is foggy, raining or snowing, the trail becomes slippery and dangerous and the way becomes difficult to find. Besides, why go to so much work when all you will see is a white blur?

Climbing

The best months to climb are June, July and August.

Ancohuma (21,141 ft/6,427 m) and **Illampu** (20,947 ft/6,368 m) form a massif with about 30 peaks over 16,500 ft/5,000 m high. This is an impressive landscape for any climber. Most people make base camp at the Titisane Mine site or Aguas Caliente and climb from there. You will need at least one guide and porters with mules are highly recommended. There are outfitters who arrange everything before you arrive in Bolivia and then there are the guides who can be hired in Sorata or La Paz.

Some of the peaks, like Pico Schultze, have amphitheaters with 200-ft/60-m walls to climb and the pitch on Huayna Illampu is 70°. Reaching the summit and getting back down will take skilled climbers up to 10 hours for some routes. For in-depth descriptions, see Yossi Brain's book, *Bolivia, a Climbing Guide*.

To reach base camp at Aguas Caliente, hire a jeep, porters, mules and guides in Sorata. The jeep will take you to the village of Ancoma. From there it is a three-hour walk to Aguas Caliente (15,000 ft/4,600 m). The name of the site is not quite accurate as the water is anything but hot.

If making Titisani or Laguna Glacial the base camp, you must hike most of the way, which takes days. See directions for hiking to Laguna Glacial, above. This is considered by the guides in Sorata to be the best way to access Illampu.

◆ Tour Operators

Associacion de Guias Turistica (Association of Tourist Guides), Calle Sucre #302, ☎ 213-6698, guiasorata@hotmail.com, is an organization that hires qualified guides, rents equipment and arranges everything needed for trekking in the area. The administrator, Eduardo Chura, can speak some English and will help with arrangements. The association has 18 qualified guides and 25 porters. The work these men manage to get through the Association supports over 50 local families, about 250 people. The cost to hire one of these men is $15 per day, a two-person tent costs $4 per day, and a sleeping bag runs $2.50. The association also has cooking equipment and utensils for rent. Although most of the guides are good, the one who was especially recommended to me was Toribio Quispi.

Trekking Guides, Calle Villavicencio #116, ☎ 213-5044, guiasorata@hotmail.com, also offers guided trips into the mountains. If the Association of Tourist guides is not able to meet your needs, try these people. They hire only local guides.

◆ Places to Stay

Altai Oasis, ☎ 715-19856 (cell), $, has a variety of accommodations including camping on their five acres of rainforest on the banks of Rio Challasuya. Two buildings suitable for families or larger groups have kitchens, bathrooms, patios

❖ HOTEL PRICING	
$	$10 to $20
$$	$21 to $50
$$$	$51 to $75
$$$$	$76 to $100
$$$$$	over $100

and lofts for bedrooms. One cottage has three bedrooms. Other buildings have either two or three bedrooms with shared bath. Standard rooms cost $3 per person and the cabins run $5. Campers ($1) have a covered cooking area and a private shower spot right on the river. The on-site restaurant is good. The well-tended grounds at Altai Oasis contain a menagerie of animals that were mistreated or abandoned and then rescued by Roxana and Johnny Resnikowski. Johnny speaks German and English.

Hotel Paraiso, *Calle Arce just up from Residencial Sorata*, ☎ *213-6671, $*, has clean carpeted rooms with closets, big windows and fairly soft beds. The private bathrooms are tiled to the ceiling and some have huge tubs. You can order breakfast at the hotel; a continental is $1.50 and an American is $1.75.

Hostal Panchita *$, on the plaza next to the church.* To enter the hostel either go through the Entel office to the back or go to the side of the building and in the first door. There are 11 basic but clean rooms, all with shared bath. There are two floors, each with a bathroom. Rooms are set around a central patio that has a small garden. The owner is friendly and helpful. There is also a luggage storage facility, hot water all day and laundry service.

The Mirador, *Calle Munecas #400*, ☎ *289-5008, $*, has the best view in town from the patio, which looks toward San Pedro Cave. Rooms are large and clean with windows that overlook the valley. The owners are friendly and breakfast is available. This is a good deal.

Residencial Sorata, *on the plaza*, ☎ *213-6672, resorata@ceibo. entelnet.bo, $$*, is an old trading house once called Casa Gunter. It was built by the Richter family in the 1830s. In the late 1980s, Louis Demers from Québec, Canada became the manager. He had toilets installed, floors painted, furniture rearranged and everything cleaned to a whistle. Gardeners rejuvenated the plants and Louis built a gazebo. Today, there are 11 huge rooms with high ceilings, antique furniture and private baths that cost $6 per person. Sixteen smaller rooms around the building have shared baths. The rooms rent for $4 per person. In addition to a garden restaurant and a formal dining room, there is a reading room and a TV room with a fireplace. Staying here is comfortable. It is also interesting for history buffs and antique lovers.

Hotel Copacabana, *$$$, on the way into town.* This is the best place to go if you are in search of entertainment and a good bar.

Kon-Tiki Tours, ☎ *719-38889 (cell), kontikisorata@yahoo.com*, is owned by Ermanno and Silvi Antonini. They have a house along the road to the cave with five rooms overlooking the Sorata Valley. It is peaceful, but a little way from town. There is also a small restaurant at their place. They are not open during low season.

Camping at **Café Illampu** is possible for $1 per person. To get there, take a taxi (truck) or walk toward San Pedro Cave. It's about a 45-minute walk from the center of town. Staying here would assure you first choice of the baked goods hot from the oven. I have no contact numbers for this place.

◆ Places to Eat

Pizzeria Italia, *Plaza Enrique Peñaranda #143*, has branches in Copacabana and Rurrenabaque. They are open from 7 am until 9 pm daily. Besides the thin-crusted pizza with thick toppings, they serve spaghetti, lasagna, tortellini and ravioli of very high quality. As a bonus, for dessert they serve real Italian ice cream.

❖ RESTAURANT PRICING	
$	under $5
$$	$5 to $10
$$$	$11 to $25
$$$$	$26 to $50
$$$$$	over $50

❖ CHEFS STEP OUT ON THE PLAZA

At one time there was a prosperous restaurant in the Residencial Sorata but hard times fell and all the highly skilled chefs had to move on. Most just went around the corner to the plaza and opened their own places. Pizzeria Italia is one such place.

Restaurant Altai Oasis is on the porch of the main house and they serve excellent goulash for a mere $3.50 per serving. The steak, on the other hand, was tough. Breakfast and coffee were great. To get to Altai Oasis, walk from town to Rio Challasuyo on the way to San Pedro Cave. The food and hospitality of the owners will make the walk worth the effort.

Café Illampu is along the road that goes to San Pedro Cave and about half an hour past Altai Oasis on the cave side of the valley. They specialize in German pastries, whole-grain bread and great coffee. They also have a book exchange. The café is closed on Tuesdays. I have no contact numbers.

Laguna Glacial Mountain Bar on the plaza has happy hour every day between 6 and 8 pm. They make excellent cappuccinos and pastas, but it's the vegetarian meals that are a feature. The owner is one of the skilled chefs who worked at the Residencial Sorata before opening his own business.

Pete's Place, *Plaza Enrique Peñaranda #13*, ☎ *289-5005*, is famous for curried dishes made with spices imported from England and mixed with skill by the cook. At least one stop here is necessary. Pete's is open daily from 8:30 am to 10 pm. While enjoying curried chicken (highly recommended) you can scan maps and books for trails you may want to hike.

Royal House Restaurant, across from the market on the dead-end side street, serves a good *almuerzo* for less than $2 per person.

La Cabaña, **La Gruta** and **Balonia** are all located around the square and make up the rest of the relocated chefs from Residencial Sorata. All are good and, during peak season, usually full.

◆ Shopping

Artesania Sorata, Plaza Enrique Peñaranda, ☎ 811-5061, cnsorata@ceibo.entelnet.bo, has a wide assortment of handmade dolls, wall hangings and hand-knitted sweaters for children and adults. They also have a large supply of postcards. The English spoken here is excellent.

Coroico

Altitude: 5,757 ft/1,750 m
Population: 3,500

Coroico is tucked into a hill in the rainforest that is lush with vegetation and teeming with birds at all times of year. The town is small, quiet and a good place to rest (after coming down the Road of Death). There are some short hikes, a few interesting villages in the vicinity and some exciting whitewater rafting. Coroico and the surrounding villages make up one of the few places in Bolivia where you will see an African influence. Africans who were brought as slaves to work in the Potosi mines and survived the ordeal came down to transport rubber and quinine in the Yungas.

◆ Getting Here & Around

The best way to get to Coroico, 59 miles/96 km from La Paz, down the Road of Death is to take a **bicycle** from La Paz. Once in Yolosa at the bottom of the hill, three miles/five km from Coroico, your support vehicle will drive you to your destination. It takes seven hours to cycle from El Cumbre, just 16 miles/26 km from La Paz.

If cycling is not your thing, the next best way to get here is to **walk** along the Takesi or Choro trails, on an ancient paved road that is steep enough to cause knee damage and require that you rest in Coroico. It takes three or four days to walk to Coroico from La Paz.

Trufis and **taxis** leave El Cementario in La Paz about once every hour for Yolosa. From there you must catch a bus, *trufi*, taxi or truck, or you must walk the last three miles/five km up the hill to Coroico. If you arrive in Yolosa late and can't get to Coroico, there are some basic *alojamientos* in town. You should book hotels ahead during peak season.

Totai Tour, ☎ 221-2391; Palmeras, ☎ 221-9442; Yungeña, ☎ 221-3513, run scheduled trips all the way to Coroico (rather than stopping in Yolosa) and back. It takes three to four hours by bus and costs $2.

If you take a **bus** from La Paz, the vehicles coming downhill must ride on the outside of the road so that the driver can see how close the tires are to the cliff edge. Quite often, drivers misjudge exactly how close they are. Taking a bus or truck uphill is much safer as those vehicles must drive on the inside, close to the cliff wall. I would ride a *trufi* rather than a bus, and a taxi rather than a *trufi*. The smaller the vehicle the better, it seems.

A bus from Yolosa takes 15 to 16 hours to reach Rurrenabaque and costs $10. It leaves Yolosa around 3 pm.

Caranavi is three to four hours from Coroico and Yucumo is five or six hours from Caranavi. Small trucks go every day from Yolosa to Caranavi and they leave around 11 am.

◆ History

Coroico was first located on the Coriguayco River where gold-seekers settled. But local natives didn't like foreigners and they often attacked the miners, who sought refuge farther into the jungle. While searching for a spot, a storm arose and the men were forced into a cave for protection. The cave was just below the spot where the present church is located. The men lived in relative peace until the War of Independence. At that time 5,000 Aymara attacked the 500 residents of Coroico. However, the village's location atop a hill gave its residents enough of an advantage that they forced the Aymara to withdraw.

As Bolivia grew, districts were formed and Coroico became the capital of North Yungas in 1899. At that time fruit, coca and wood were grown on large land holdings and the produce was exported to La Paz. Then, in the early 1950s, a revolution occurred and land reforms forced a redistribution of the land. Today, Coroico still produces coca, fruit and wood for those in La Paz. It is a relatively prosperous area because it is so close to a major city.

◆ Services

The **telephone office** is on the plaza on Avenida Guachalla. There is a second office on Calle Heroes del Chaco.

The **post office** is across from the Bank of Bolivia, just a few feet from the plaza on Calle Heroes del Chaco.

There is a **bank** on Calle Julio Zuazo Cuenca, on the plaza and across from the post office.

The **hospital** is on the upper road going to Sol y Luna. From the plaza, follow Linilla Rafae Miranda all the way out.

The **tourist office** is on the square, but I found the young woman quite surly and uninformed. For accurate information, go to the office of Inca Land Tours, also on the square, opposite the cathedral. That gal will open the office even during siesta if she knows you want something.

THE YUNGAS

◆ Festivals

October 20th is the day when Coroico became a village. This is the biggest celebration the town has.

The **Coroico Coffee Festival** in mid-June has been a celebration since 1998 and all the coffee-growing communities in the area participate.

❖ BOLIVIAN BREWS

Bolivian coffee grown in Coroico is the best in the country and is served at Alexander Coffee shops, where it is sold by the bag under the name Alexander Coffee. Royal Bolivian Coffee, available in the Tarija area, is also good. The best thing about most Bolivian coffee is that all the caffeine isn't roasted out of it. The lighter the roast, the higher the caffeine content. Be aware that Haiti Coffee, sold in La Paz, is a heavy roast; I don't recommended it.

◆ Adventures on Foot

TOCANA: The village of **Tocaña** is 14 miles/23 km from Coroico. You can walk here along a dirt road in the heat, but I suggest taking either a taxi or a truck at least one way. If you go to the village, poke around for a few hours and walk back, it will take you all day. Be certain to have sunscreen, a hat, water and good shoes.

Tocaña is an Afro-Bolivian settlement of about 50 families. The village is surrounded by rocky terrain. There is a school and the Audubon Society has posted teachers here under the sponsorship of the School Yard Ecology Education Initiate, whereby children learn about the natural environment. This is important around Tocaña. Of the 1,375 species of birds found in Bolivia, about one third can be found in this area. Tocaña is also one of the villages where it is legal to grow coca. A potato grown exclusively in this area carries the same name as the village.

THREE WATERFALLS: Tres Cascadas is a 4.3-mile/seven-km, half-day walk (don't believe the official tourist sheet that states you can walk to and from Tocaña in three hours). To get to the waterfalls, follow the road up toward Hotel Esmeralda and El Relincho, where horses can be hired. At the sign pointing toward the horse coral, go straight up the hill to Hermita Calvario, a small chapel, and the aqueduct. Follow the trail down to the waterfall that cascades through the jungle, dropping about 49 ft/15 m into a pool where you can dip. This is a popular hike. Birds, again, are a big draw.

CERRO UCHUMACHI: The summit of Cerro Uchumachi is a popular place to go on June 21st for the winter solstice. People go up on the 20th and camp overnight so that they can see the sun rise. As a day hike, it takes four to six hours round-trip. Follow the same trail as you do for Tres Cascadas, except, at the chapel, go to the right. Behind the chapel is an easy-to-find trail through dense vegetation to the top of the hill, where there are three crosses.

MURURATA BRIDGE: Puente Mururata can be reached by following Avenida Ayacucho out of town past the Cerro Verde hotel until you come to a trail that goes off the road and down the hill. Follow it to the river. The bridge is just off the trail. Go upstream if you want a dip in the pools. The downside of this hike is that you must climb back up the trail to return to the village.

◆ Adventures on Water

Rio Coroico has two possible runs, one for average rafters and kayakers and the other for the more skilled thrill-seeker. The first run passes through Class III rapids and is a six-hour paddling session. There are only a few challenging spots and the drops and rapids are minimal. However, the lush jungle is a draw for birders as they can concentrate on the wildlife rather than running the boat. The trip starts at Puerte Carmas and goes to Puerto Chaña. On the way it passes the impressive waterfall of Puerto Leon. The cost is $65 for a six-hour day.

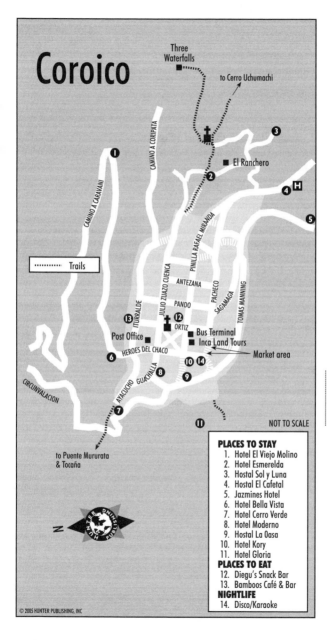

Coroico

Three Waterfalls

to Cerro Uchumachi

El Ranchero

CAMINO A CORIPATA

CAMINO A CARAVANI

H

.... Trails

PINILLA RAFAEL MIRANDA

JULIO ZUAZO CUENCA

ANTEZANA

PANDO

PACHECO

SAGAMAGA

TOMAS MANNING

ITURRALDE

ORTIZ

Bus Terminal
Inca Land Tours

Post Office

HEROES DEL CHACO

Market area

AYACUCHO

GUACHALLA

CIRCUNVALACION

NOT TO SCALE

to Puente Mururata
& Tocaña

N HUNTER PUBLISHING

© 2005 HUNTER PUBLISHING, INC

PLACES TO STAY
1. Hotel El Viejo Molino
2. Hotel Esmerelda
3. Hostal Sol y Luna
4. Hostal El Cafetal
5. Jazmines Hotel
6. Hotel Bella Vista
7. Hotel Cerro Verde
8. Hotel Moderno
9. Hostal La Oasa
10. Hotel Kory
11. Hotel Gloria
PLACES TO EAT
12. Diegu's Snack Bar
13. Bamboos Café & Bar
NIGHTLIFE
14. Disco/Karaoke

THE YUNGAS

The second trip has some Class IV rapids and, during high water, Class V. This stretch has many areas where rapids come close to rock-garden status and the shoots are narrow and swift. There are pools and holes, drops and surfing waves (for kayaks) with a few easy eddies to pull into when the rush gets a bit much.

Rio Unduavi is another possible run, but is farther and harder to reach from Coroico. The lower section of the river has everything up to Class IV water. The advantage of going to this river is that it is a bit more isolated than the Coroico.

◆ Adventures on Horseback

El Relincho, ☎ 719-23814 or 719-59072 (cell) can be found on the road between the Esmeralda Hotel and Sol y Luna. Renoldo, a gentle man, and his unassuming wife Gladys, operate this family business. Gladys is the cook and I can attest to the quality of her food. This company comes highly recommended. There horses cost $6 per hour for guided rides. The owners require two days notice for overnight trips. Their prices are reasonable and the family tries hard to please.

You can circumnavigate Uchumachi Mountain on horseback. This is a two-day trip that passes small villages such as Chocayo, Arapata and Chuso. The first night is spent at Chuso. The second day you ride on to Santa Barbara and back to Coroico via Cruz Loma. The cost is $70 per person with a minimum of four people and a maximum of eight. Food is supplied but you must have a tent. If you don't have one, Renoldo can put up a tarp. Another trip Renoldo offers is a three-day ride to La Paz along the Chustipata Trail. The cost is $100 per person, with a minimum of four people.

◆ Adventures of the Brain

Spanish lessons in Coroico are near total immersion as there is little chance to use English (not that there is much English anywhere in Bolivia). Courses are offered by **Dula and Jose Parija**, Calle Panckeko, ☎ 243-2067.

◆ Tour Operators

South America Rafting, ☎ 715-00556, southamericanrafting @hotmail. com, is in Coroico just one block from the plaza. If you make up your mind at the last minute to raft or kayak, you can book with them. They offer trips down the Zongo River (which they classify as difficult) and down the Tuichi River (intermediate).

El Relincho, ☎ 719 23814 or 719 59072 (cell), has horses for hire and can be found on the road between the Esmeralda Hotel and Sol y Luna. See *Adventures on Horseback* for a description of their most popular rides.

Inca Land Tours, on the square, ☎ 719-81990, has jeeps that can go to Uagante for $24 per person, to Tocaña for $25 per person, and to Rurrenabaque for $30 per person, with a minimum of four people. All fees include a guide. The Rurrenabaque excursion takes 11-12 hours and is much safer in a jeep than in a bus. This will change as road conditions improve. A jeep can take four to seven people.

Tours Palmeras, just off the square near the market (no phone), has an impressive timetable but buses go only when full. My experience with this company was that the driver was competent and careful, important factors when traveling the Road of Death.

◆ Places to Stay

There are many places to stay in Coroico that are not mentioned here. I have taken the better of the mid-range places and named a few high-priced ones, but there are numerous budget digs around the market that seemed safe and clean enough.

❖ HOTEL PRICING	
$	$10 to $20
$$	$21 to $50
$$$	$51 to $75
$$$$	$76 to $100
$$$$$	over $100

La Casa, *Alidad Linares #3511,* ☎ *022-1360, lacasa@ceibo.entelnet. bo, $,* has very basic cement-floor rooms with or without private baths. The place is pleasant and overlooks the valley. If there are more than one of you, try to get the double room overlooking the Yungas – the view worth staying for.

Hotel Kory, *Calle Casella #6020,* ☎ *243-1311, koryhostalcelia@ hotmail.com, $$.* Rooms at the Kory are big and clean with tiled floors, closets, and tables and chairs. If staying longer than three days, the hotel offers a discount. There is a swimming pool and a nice patio with flowers. The owner changes traveler's checks without charging a commission and laundry service is available. Bicycles are available for rent at $7 per day. The owner has a wealth of knowledge about the area, but he speaks only Spanish. The restaurant makes excellent banana shakes and serves vegetarian and international foods.

Sol y Luna, ☎ *236-2099, www.solyluna-bolivia.com, $$.* Prices vary depending on the accommodation you choose, a basic room, a cabin or a luxury cabin. There are five rooms in the main building, six cabins for rent and camping in the garden for $2 per person. Firewood is 75¢ per bundle. It is a 30-minute walk uphill from the plaza to the hotel. This is a holistic place offering tarot card readings and lessons as well as massage therapy. It has a meditation room devoid of distracting furniture. There is also a pool and hot tub ($6 per hour) that holds up to three people. The on-site restaurant serves mainly vegetarian dishes. As a sideline, the hotel also sells ceramic jewelry that is made locally ($6 for a plain necklace).

The Moderno Hotel, *Guachalla #32,* ☎ *715-20411, $$,* is a well-kept building just off the square. It has 21 rooms and is run by a jovial chap who tries hard to please his guests. The rooms are clean and pleasant, the shower water comes from a tank and the floors are tile. There is a pool and parking.

Buena Vista, ☎ *715-69237, $$,* is just 329 ft/100 m off the square and overlooking the valley to the east. The mountains can be seen through the huge windows opposite the beds. This is a hacienda-style building, bright and well decorated with 11 rooms that can hold 21 people. The clean rooms have soft beds and ceramic tile floors. There are gold taps in bath-

THE YUNGAS

rooms and hot water is supplied from a tank. A sitting area is located on each floor, and there's also a racquetball court and a restaurant on site. This is a good deal.

Hotel Cerro Verde, *Avenida Ayacucho #5037,* ☎ *719-57592, cerrove@ hotmail.com, $$,* is a new place built in colonial style. It has fairly large, clean rooms with private baths and is quiet. There's a pool, a well-tended garden, and a view that is worth every penny you pay for the room. The people are friendly. This is a good place to stay close to town.

Esmeralda Hotel, ☎ *213-6017, reservas@hotelesmeralda.com, $$$,* is the most popular place to stay in Coroico. The 31-room hotel has large rooms with foyers and balconies, tiled bathrooms, soap, towels, toilet paper, closets and seven TV channels. The hot water is supplied from a water tank rather than an electrical shower heater. The owner will either pick you up in town or pay for a taxi if you stay at the hotel. This is a bonus because the walk up the hill is at least half an hour and, with luggage, could be longer. Laundry service is available for $1 a kilo. But it is the grounds at this hotel that are exceptional. Interspersed among the vegetation are board games, videos, fooze ball tables, pool tables and a great butterfly collection. There is a large pool with a sauna nearby. Food in the restaurant is served buffet style and is in the top 10 for quality. An all-you-can-eat breakfast costs $2, lunch is $2.50 and supper is $3. The owner speaks English, German and Spanish and is knowledgeable about the area.

Hotel Gloria, ☎ *240-7070, www.hotelgloriabolivia.com, $$$,* has seen better days. At one time this hotel was a classic, with high ceilings, heavy chandeliers, dark wood cupboards and four-piece baths. Then it went into a period of decline. However, the management is now remodeling and Hotel Gloria should, in the near future, be a good place to stay once again. Since Gloria is a chain in Bolivia, there are special rates for those booking at three hotels in different locations. The bougainvillea is as old as the corner stones and seems to dominate the center of the front yard. The hotel is at the bottom of the hill (follow the stairs down from the plaza) below the soccer field. The on-site restaurant serves okay food in a colonial dining room.

Hotel Viejo Molino, *.6 miles/one km along the road to Santa Barbara,* ☎ *220-1519, viejomolino@vaimatours.com, $$$$,* is a five-star hotel with everything in the rooms to make you comfortable, including TV, private bath and matching décor. Your breakfast is included in the price. There is a sauna and restaurant on site.

Jazmines Hotel, ☎ *222-9967, $$$$, on the road between Yolosa and Coroico and just .6 miles/one km from the center of Coroico,* is a four-star, two-storey building surrounding a pool. The hotel is clean and luxurious and has a restaurant, racquetball court, tennis court, beach volleyball and three pools.

◆ Places to Eat

In addition to the hotel restaurants, there are numerous places to enjoy a meal.

Diegu's Snack Bar *(no phone), on the square,* offers an egg sandwich with a banana milkshake for less than $1.50. They are open fairly early, around 7:30 am, and stay open until around 9 pm, depending on the amount of people in the restaurant. The food is good, the place is clean, the kids are cute.

El Cafetal *(no phone), up the hill beside the hospital*, is run by a flamboyant Frenchman who, true to his culture,

❖ RESTAURANT PRICING	
$	under $5
$$	$5 to $10
$$$	$11 to $25
$$$$	$26 to $50
$$$$$	over $50

serves the best meals in town. You can also stay on the premises for $3.50 per person without private bath if you can't make it home after your meal. The restaurant overlooks the valley and this is good because it takes time to eat with the French. While the owner prepares your meal, you need to sip on wine and gaze at the landscape. A hamburger with fries costs $1.50, spaghetti, lasagne and soufflés cost $3.50-$4. A bottle of Bolivian wine is around $7. They also carry things like Johnny Walker whiskey that sells for $3.50 a shot.

Bamboo Bar, Calle Iteralde, just two blocks from the square, is a great place for a Mexican dinner. The food is good, the service cheerful and quick. They serve, among other dishes, vegetarian burritos and tacos and they have a happy hour every day from 6 to 7 pm. This is one of the better places to eat in Coroico. There is live music on the weekends. The restaurant is part of the same business as the Don Quixote Hotel.

◆ Shopping

Artesanias Arco Iris on the square has good quality jewelry, some made with lapis lazuli, others made with silver from Potosi. It is all unique. They also sell local coffee beans and a few small woven purses. Coffee from Caranavi, just a few miles away, is used by the best coffee shops in Bolivia.

◆ Nightlife

There are two discos in town, both close to the entrance of the village on the road to La Paz. The name of the road is Tomas Manning and the name of the most popular disco with the Bolivians is La Tropicana (the other disco is referred to as "the disco"). But just hanging out in the plaza with a beer attracts attention in Coroico. Most foreigners go to the restaurants and poolside bars when in need of entertainment.

THE YUNGAS

Las Colinas

Sucre

Altitude: 7,829 ft/2,380 m
Population: 210,000

Sucre is a town that sparkles like a diamond in the dry brown mountains surrounding it. Although it is the official capital of the country, it is in facto the judicial center while the seat of government is in La Paz.

There are many cycle and horse trips that can be made from Sucre. Some people come to see the famous dino tracks right on the edge of town, while others come to purchase the exquisite and unique Inca textiles made in the villages nearby.

◆ Getting Here & Around

Buses to Potosi leave at 7 am, 1 pm and 5 pm. To Uyuni, they leave at 7 am and 1 pm. Those to Villazon and Tupiza leave at 1 pm, La Paz at 5:30 pm, Cochabamba at 6:30 pm and Santa Cruz at 5 pm. Tickets for the Sunday market in Tarabuco can be purchased in town or at the bus station. Bus tickets can be purchased in the center of town (Calle Arce #95 on the corner of San Alberto, Real Audiencia, Office #4, ☎ 644-3119) for the same price as those at the bus station.

Daily flights with all the major airlines run between Sucre and La Paz, Cochabamba, Santa Cruz and Yacuiba. Those to and from Cobija and Trinidad go only once a week. See page 49 for airline contact information.

A **taxi** from the airport to the center of town is about $2 for up to four people. Colonial Plus Taxi Service, Avenida Ostria Gutierrez, ☎ 642-9750, has vehicles for hire. They also run a *trufi* to Potosi. The cost of a private taxi is $30 a day for travel on the main roads. If you need a taxi to go to Potolo during the rainy season, the fare may be a bit higher ($130).

A fast driver is **Silverio Mamani**, ☎ 7181-6967 (cell). Another good honest driver is Martin Espendola. He charges about $15 for a full day on paved roads. For a day on the road to Potolo he charges closer to $60 or $70 during dry season. Call ☎ 42000 and ask for number 21.

◆ History

1540	Sucre was established by Pedro de Anzures and called Chiquisaca.
1609	First Bishop in Upper Peru was established.
1625	First (third in the Americas) university is built here.
1825	Sucre is renamed after the first president, Antonio, Jose de Sucre. Declaration of Independence is signed at Liberty House on the plaza.
1991	City is declared a World Heritage Site.

◆ Services

The **telephone office** is on the Plaza 25 de Mayo along Avenida Ayacucho.

The **police station** is on Plaza Zundonez along Avenida Olañeta between Junin and Bustillo.

There is a **tourist office** on Calle Argentina and Olañeta. The official office is in the Casa de Cultura on Calle Argentina. It is useless.

Laundry, Calle Loa #407 and Avenida Siles, close to the central market, ☎ 642-4066, is open daily, including holidays. They can have your clothes ready within two hours if needed.

◆ Sightseeing

Casa de la Libertad, on the main plaza, is where the declaration of independence was signed on Aug 6, 1825. Inside are portraits of past presidents, military decorations and documents, one of which was signed by Simon Bolívar. Tour the Senate room where the legislative assembly convened for over 50 years. The original carved chairs and tables are still in place. Today, the University of St. Francisco Xavier uses the room for its senate meetings.

Glorieta Castle was built by the Prince and Princess of Glorieta, a name endowed to Francisco Argadoña and Clotilde Urioste by Pope Leon XIII for their charitable work in Bolivia. Most of the family fortune came from the profits of the Huanchaca mine, close to Uyuni. The castle was built between 1893 and 1897 using European styles, so you can see hints of gothic in the clock tower, renaissance in the furniture, baroque dotted throughout and neoclassic designs in the pink marble and wood. The building was used as a military base from the 1950s until recently. Restoration is in progress and the results are good. The grounds have a man-made lake, a miniature railroad, fountains, gazebos surrounded by marble statues, even an outdoor dining room.

To get here, take minibus #4 from Calle Ravelo and Arce. It's a half-hour ride. You can also walk the 3.7 miles/six km along Avenida Argentina (it changes names) to Destacamento Chuquisaca (passing Otto-Chiquisaca on the way) or rent a bike from Joy Ride Tours (Calle Oritz #14, ☎ 642-5544, www.joyridebol.com). The house is open daily, 8:30 am-noon and 2-6 pm, and costs $1 to enter.

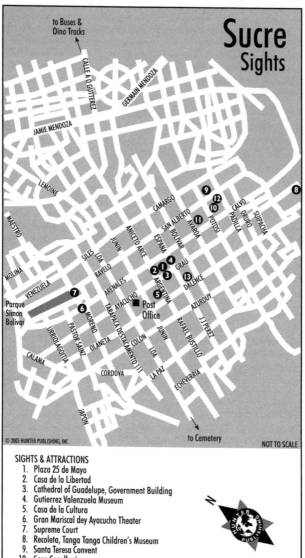

SIGHTS & ATTRACTIONS
1. Plaza 25 de Mayo
2. Casa de la Libertad
3. Cathedral of Guadelupe, Government Building
4. Gutierrez Valenzuela Museum
5. Casa de la Cultura
6. Gran Mariscal dey Ayacucho Theater
7. Supreme Court
8. Recoleta, Tanga Tanga Children's Museum
9. Santa Teresa Convent
10. Casa Capellanica
11. Santa Clara Convent
12. Indigenous Art Museum
13. University Museum (Charcas, Anthropological, Contemporary Art)

◆ Adventures in Culture

Festival de la Cultura, FSCC@pelicano.cnb.net, holds an annual two-week arts festival at the beginning of September. It involves classical, jazz and rock music events. Theater, drama, opera and ballet are performed. There are showings of contemporary paintings and plastic art, as well as a cinema to watch and literature to listen to. Some of the events are in the theater while other events are performed on the streets or in the plazas.

Masis Cultural Center, Calle Bolívar #561, ☎ 645-3403, losmasis@ pelicano.cnb.net, is a center where kids come to learn traditional music from a master of the art, Roberto Masis. The center is open daily at 6 pm. There is no charge, but a donation is appreciated. The money goes directly to the kids – often for snacks or refreshments, and sometimes toward the purchase of instruments.

If you wish to purchase a pan flute or churango, the ones for sale in the shop are of excellent quality – all are handmade under they eye of the master, Roberto. He and his group of musicians have over 20 recordings, all of which can be purchased at the shop.

Music lessons can be had at the reasonable cost of $20 per month for three lessons a week. The teacher will be either Roberto himself or his son Roberto. This would be a group lesson.

> **AUTHOR NOTE:** *CDs purchased on the street usually will not work on your players at home. They are good only for the computers on which they were made.*

The **Museum of Natural History**, on Plaza 25 de Mayo, is on the main floor of the building. The entrance fee is $1.25; open hours are Monday to Friday, 8 am-noon and 2:30-6 pm, Saturday, 9 am-noon and 3-6 pm.

Upstairs is the **Dr. Alfredo Gutierrez Valenzuela Museum**, which features a collection of Louis XV and Louis XVI furniture, some of which belonged in the Castle of La Glorieta (see above). There is also a collection of gold-trimmed/painted vases, crystal, marble carvings and porcelain pieces. Open Monday to Friday, 8:30 am-noon and 2:30-6 pm; Saturday, 8:30 am-noon and 3-6 pm.

The **Anthropological Museum**, Calle Bolívar #698, ☎ 645-3285, has three sections: colonial art, archeological artifacts and contemporary art.

The museum is not cluttered and it takes about two hours to see everything. It's open Monday to Friday, 8:30 am-noon and 2:30-6 pm, and Saturday 8:30 am-noon. The cost is $1.50.

The **Ecclesiastical Museum**, Calle N. Oritz #61, ☎ 645-2257, is open Monday to Friday, 10 am-noon and 3-5 pm, and on Saturday until noon only. It's housed in a cathedral that was built in 1559. This museum is one of the richest in Bolivia with every type of jewel possible, many of them stuck to garments of long-gone priests. There is one diamond, displayed in a case of its own, that is worth more than the Hope diamond. It takes about two hours to visit this museum without rushing.

The **Recoleta** and the **Tanga Tanga Child's Museum** is on Calle Polanco #162, ☎ 645-1987. It is open from Monday to Friday, 9 am-noon and 2:30-4:30 pm. The cost is 75¢.

Founded in 1600 by Francisco de Morales, the courtyard of the convent has a cedar tree that is said to be 1,000 years old and that was declared a historical monument in 1956. The church beside the convent was built a hundred years or so after the convent and its choir loft is designed in 17th-century baroque style, with carved chairs and backboards. The walls behind the chairs are carved to match. The heavy rich wood is local cedar.

The Tanga Tanga museum is up the side stairs from the central courtyard and is made with every child in mind, regardless of age. It's open Tuesday to Sunday, from 10:30 am to 6:30 pm and costs just over a dollar to enter. The museum's four floors symbolize the four areas of Bolivia; the Altiplano, the valleys, the Chaco and the Amazon. A library and reading room are on site. There is also an outdoor cafeteria, theater and park.

Santa Clara Convent, Calle Calvo #212, ☎ 645-2295, is open Monday to Friday, 9 am-noon and 2-6 pm. It was built by the Franciscan Fathers in 1636 and is now filled with religious art. The big draw is the pipe organ, built in 1792 and reported to have the best sound of all organs in the country. The pipes are encased in an ornate brass holding.

The Indigenous Art Museum, Avenida San Alberto #413, ☎ 645-3841, is open Monday to Friday, 8:30 am-noon and 2:30-6 pm. On Saturday it is open only until noon. Entrance fee, $2.50. If you are not on a tour, they will give you a pamphlet written in English describing the museum. You may not take your pack into the museum.

There are 12 rooms in the museum that feature Tarabuco and Jalq'a weavings. They have examples of weavings used for religious ceremonies and weavings from specific areas/villages. A room downstairs demonstrates what archeologists believe the people were like before recorded time. One section has instruments, bows and arrows, jewelry and baskets. Weavers, dressed in traditional clothes, demonstrate style and technique and are there to be photographed.

The ASUR Indigenous Art Association is an organization that has managed to revitalize the art of weaving in Bolivia and their attempt has resulted in many of the people getting a fair price for their product. They have a shop on site.

Museo Sacro Jerusalen, Avenida Camacho and Avenida del Maestro, is open 9 am-noon and 3-6 pm on Monday, 4-8 pm, Tuesday to Friday, and 8 am-noon on Saturday. Entry costs $1. The church was built in honor of the Virgin of Candelaria in the early 1600s.

❖ **LEND A HAND**

Nanta Educational Center, Plazuela Cochabamba #315, ☎ 645-2523, is a non-profit organization that works with under privileged kids. They depend solely on donations and volunteers. Their brochure says they will take volunteers for one week or one year, whatever suits the person. If you have skills in teaching especially in the elementary areas, photography, with video equipment, music, organizational skills for expositions, fund raising, advertising or anything similar, they can use you.

Festivals

Tarabuco is a village just 37 miles/60 km from Sucre and its Sunday market is a must. The villagers come from miles around to trade, eat and gossip while tourists come to shop, photograph and gawk. Although there are places to stay in the village, there is nothing going on except for the Sunday market so it is best to take the tourist bus from Sucre out in the morning and return at midday.

Getting there and back is easiest by tourist bus. Tickets ($1.50) can be purchased at almost all hotels and at the office on Calle Arce #95 at the corner of San Alberto, Real Audiencia, Office #4, ☎ 644-3119.

◆ Adventures on Foot

The **Cal Orck'o dinosaur tracks** are just 3.7 miles/six km from the center of town, in a quarry that is still being mined. Even though the workers looking after the tracks just found the first dinosaur bone the day I was there, they can't convince the local company or the government to leave the largest paleontological site in the world to paleontologists.

The tracks come from now- extinct animals walking across a mud field. Because of tectonic movement, the once flat land has been pushed up so that it looks like a wall. On this wall are over 5,000 dinosaur impressions and fossils belonging to 290 animals dating back some 68 million years. Slabs of old lake bed sometimes slide off the wall, revealing even older tracks.

The Dino Truck, operated by **Abbey Path Tour Operators**, ☎ 645-1863, leaves the plaza in front of the cathedral every day at 9:30 am, noon and 2:30 pm. The cost for the ride out and back is $1.50 and the cost to enter the site is $3 per person. If you wish to walk one way and take the truck the other, you will be charged for a two-way ticket. Guides speak English well and were as entertaining as the tracks themselves.

If you wish to walk to the tracks, follow Avenida Ostria Gutierrez past the bus station and past the intersection for the road to Tarabuco. Continue along the main road (the name changes) for about an hour or so and you will see the quarry on the hill alongside a huge slab of rock that leans on an upward slant. It is an interesting walk through residential and light industrial areas.

Two other sites have tracks nearby. One is at **Calancha**, just 4.3 miles/seven km from town, and the other at Nucchu, 14 miles/23 km from town. Calancha has about 80 prints dating back 65 million years. However, the best ones are at Cal'Orcko.

◆ Adventures on Wheels

There are a few places recommended for riding a bicycle from Sucre. These routes take between three and seven hours and, because of elevation, are not easy unless you are fully acclimatized. If going with Joy Ride (see *Tour Operators*, below), they can take you to the top of a hill in a truck so that you aren't exhausted before you start. Or you can rent a bike, get trail descriptions and head out on your own.

K'atalla, or the **Seven Waterfalls**, is five miles/eight km north of Sucre on the Quirpinchaca River. The ride is mostly downhill going there, but 70% uphill coming back. This is an easy route and no guide is needed. The owners of Joy Ride will provide a map when you rent your bike.

The **Loyola to San Juan to Aranjuez** trip is an all-day ride that covers about 18 miles/30 km. It is 100% downhill if you go on a tour. The driver will take you to the top of the hill across the valley from Cerro Obispo and overlooking the Chullchuta River. The cycle down to the river is easy. It is not too steep and the scenery is excellent. It takes a couple of hours for those who want to admire the scenery and less than an hour for those racing. At the bottom of the hill is a spot where you can have a snack, load the bikes and go to the next hilltop. From there you can cycle back to Sucre with just 5% of the ride being uphill.

You can eliminate the second hill run if you're short on time. See Joy Ride for information and recommendations that will suit your skill level.

◆ Adventures of the Brain

Academia Latin America, Calle Dalence #109, ☎ 646-0537, www. latinoschools.com, is run by Sandra del Corral de Maldonado. This language school has been in South America for about 14 years and the one in Bolivia has been around for five. They give a placement test before setting you up with a group. Usually, students take one month of lessons, studying four hours per day, five days a week. They also live with a family. The cost is between $5 and $7 per hour for lessons and $12 per day for room and board.

> **AUTHOR NOTE:** *You may want to pay by the week rather than for an entire month, just in case you are not happy. Also, I suggest you find your own home to live in, rather than booking through the school. That way, the family gets a better cut.*

Fox Language Academy, Calle San Alberto #30, ☎ 644-0688, offers conversational Spanish for beginners. They have a home-stay program and run cultural excursions so that the student will be able to practice while a teacher is around to help with grammar. The cost is just over $5 an hour. This is a small school, but certainly not inferior to others in town. Fox also teaches classes in Quechua.

Cultural Institute of Bolivia, Calle Avaroa #326, ☎ 645-2091, www. icba-sucre.edu.bo, is affiliated with the Goethe Institute of Germany. They offer 45-minute classes and as many as eight a day can be attended. The staff speaks English, German or French in addition to their own language. The cost is $6 per lesson for individual classes, $4 if there are two students and $2.50 per person if there are three to five in the class. You get one free lesson for every 16 you take. They have a minimum of 12 lessons per course, but this could be completed in a very few days if only survival Spanish is wanted.

For those staying longer, home-stay programs can be arranged. There is also a good library for students, with books, tapes, magazines and newspapers in Spanish, German and English.

LAS COLINAS

◆ Tour Operators

Joy Ride Motor Bike Tours, Calle Oritz #14, ☎ 642-5544, www. joyridebol.com, use Honda XR 400s for their tours. To go on this tour you must have a motorbike license and be serious about riding. If you do not have a valid license you can ride but you must leave a $1,000 deposit to cover costs if there should be an accident. The bikes are not automatic; they have a clutch. A two-day trip to the Altiplano is an extreme-type trip. You can start riding in the morning when the temperature is 19° F/ -7°C. This is cold. Insurance is included in the price.

Joy Ride also has bicycles, Raleighs and Konas (16 gears) with front-end suspension. You can rent bikes and go on your own for $2.50 an hour or you can join one of their guided and already scouted-out routes that cost anywhere from $12 to $39. These trips last three to seven hours. To cycle up hills, you should first be acclimatized. This is an excellent way to enjoy the area. There are waterfalls and small villages to visit. Some tours include a motorized lift to the top of a hill.

Candelaria Tours, Calle Estudiantes and Oritz, ☎ 648-1601, www. candelariatours.com, 8:30 am-12:30 pm and 2:30-6:30 pm daily, opened in 1975. Candelaria offers specialized tours such as to weaving centers or archeology sites. They also run Hacienda Candelabra, 13 miles/22 km from Tarabuco. You can stay at the hacienda and be introduced to skills like baking in a clay oven or weaving. Ecla Canyon is nine miles/15 km from the hacienda; if you wish to visit the canyon, you must stay at the hacienda overnight, spend the next day hiking and return to Sucre the following day. The historical tour that goes with the hacienda stay includes a lecture on topics like the granaries, the chapel and events that occurred during the land reforms of 1952. Returning from the hacienda, you will stop at the Sunday market in Tarabuco. English, German and Italian are spoken by the guides.

Eclipse Travel, Calle Avaroa #310, ☎ 644-3960, offers hiking tours around Sucre from three hours to four days. The most interesting and difficult sites to reach are the Maragua crater and Potolo. Due to the variety of things to see in the Maragua crater area, there are numerous hikes from which to choose.

Tourismo Sucre, Calle Bustillos #117, ☎ 645-2936 or 646-0349, offers tours to Maragua crater, Chataquila, Potolo and the Chaunaca pre-Inca trail. The cost is $10 for half a day and $18 for a full day. These tours do not operate during rainy season. This company also has a half- or full-day city tour.

◆ Places to Stay

Katalla Camping, ☎ 771-28627 (cell), $, is five miles/eight km north of Sucre near the Seven Waterfalls. It's a rustic place tucked into the vegetation where camping costs $2 per person and a basic cabin costs $3.50. There is a fully supplied

❖ HOTEL PRICING	
$	$10 to $20
$$	$21 to $50
$$$	$51 to $75
$$$$	$76 to $100
$$$$$	over $100

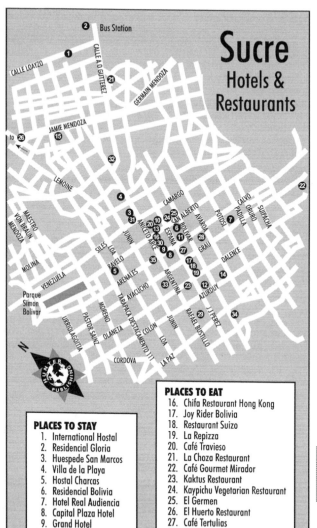

Sucre
Hotels & Restaurants

Bus Station

CALLE LOAYZO
CALLE A.O GUTIERREZ
GERMAIN MENDOZA
JAMIE MENDOZA
to 26
LEMOINE
MAESTRO
VON BRAUN
MENDOZA
MOLINA
VENEZUELA
Parque
Simon
Bolivar
SILES
LOA
JUNIN
RAVELO
ARENALES
PASTOR SAINZ
MORENO
OLANETA
TARAPACA DESTACAMENTO 111
URRIOLAGOITIA
COLON
CORDOVA
LA PAZ
AYACUCHO
ANICETO ARCE
CAMARGO
SAN ALBERTO
BOLIVAR
ESPAÑA
AVAROA
GRAU
POTOSI
CALVO
ORURO
PADILLA
SUIPACHA
DALENCE
ARGENTINA
AZURDUY
JUNIN
RAFAEL BUSTILLO
J J PEREZ

N

NOT TO SCALE

© 2005 HUNTER PUBLISHING, INC

LAS COLINAS

PLACES TO STAY
1. International Hostal
2. Residencial Gloria
3. Huespede San Marcos
4. Villa de la Playa
5. Hostal Charcas
6. Residencial Bolivia
7. Hotel Real Audiencia
8. Capital Plaza Hotel
9. Grand Hotel
10. Hotel España
11. Hostal Indepencia
12. El Hotal de su Merced
13. Premier Hotel
14. Del Rosario Hostal
15. Hostal Paulista

PLACES TO EAT
16. Chifa Restaurant Hong Kong
17. Joy Rider Bolivia
18. Restaurant Suizo
19. La Repizza
20. Café Travieso
21. La Choza Restaurant
22. Café Gourmet Mirador
23. Kaktus Restaurant
24. Kaypichu Vegetarian Restaurant
25. El Germen
26. El Huerto Restaurant
27. Café Tertulias
28. Café Berlin
29. Gnadenlos Café
30. Café Capota, Snack Pascana
31. La Taverne
32. El Virgelito Restaurant
33. La Milaneza
34. El Solar
35. Pata Ti Chocolate

kitchen and a bench-style dining suite. Hammocks hang around the porch and a comfortable games room offers dominos, ping pong and cards.

The **Hostel**, *part of the Hostelling Association of Sucre, Calle Guillermo Loayzo #119,* ☎ *644-0471, $*, is one block from the bus station and, like the hostel in Uyuni, is a fine place. In addition to regular rooms, they offer a colonial bedroom for two for $20. It has a larger-than-average bathroom with a Jacuzzi tub. Everything here is colonial. The colonial furniture throughout is glittering white and interspersed around the colonial building are balconies overlooking a flower garden. There are ceramic tiles on the floors and the cheaper rooms without bath have lockers. The bathrooms and the kitchen are spotless. The dining room is huge and there is laundry service. The only drawback is the location, about a 20-minute walk down to the plaza.

Residencial Gloria, *Avenida Augusto Gutierrez #438, across from the bus station,* ☎ *645-2847, $*, has 15 rooms and rates include breakfast. It is bright and clean, with wood floors, large windows, a patio and clean communal bathrooms.

Huespede San Marcos, *Calle Arce #233,* ☎ *606-2087, $*, is just three blocks from the plaza, tucked back off the street where it is quiet. The 14 rooms (with and without a private bath) are set around a flower garden. They are large and nondescript, with wood floors and tiled bathrooms. Best of all is the fully equipped kitchen that is as clean as the rest of the place, plus a porch where one can relax. This is a real deal.

The new **Villa de la Playa**, *Calle Arce #369,* ☎ *642-2577, lisis208@yahoo.com, $$*, is run by Ruth Cabrera. It can accommodate 12 people in all. There are two, two-bedroom suites that have a kitchen, living room and bathroom. Ruth also has two tiny rooms on the patio that can be rented by students for long-term stays. Upon arrival, you must ring the doorbell as the house is kept locked. The place is spotless. Ruth is friendly and helpful and guests (including me) do not like to leave. The patio has a sitting area and a hammock. This is a real deal. I suggest you e-mail to make reservations.

Hostal Charcas, *Calle Ravelo #62,* ☎ *645-3972, $$*, has three floors of rooms set around a central courtyard. Rooms are of average size, clean and fresh. The water is so hot that cold needs to be added when showering. If you need a guide or information on schools, ask to see Elva Ines de Bueno, ☎ 644-1892. She is knowledgeable and helpful and, if not working at the hotel, may be your guide on a tour to Potolo. She knows the area well.

Residencial Bolivia, *Calle San Alberto #42,* ☎ *645-4346, $$*, has rooms with or without private bathrooms. The rooms are large, clean and have wood floors. This is a good deal.

Del Rosario Hostal, *Calle Azurduy #151,* ☎ *644-0464, $$$*, has rooms around a central courtyard. Though small, they do have cable TV, telephones and private bathrooms. The hostel is near the cemetery.

Hotel España, *Calle España #138,* ☎ *644-0850 or 646-0295, hoespana@cotes.net.bo, $$$*, offers rooms with private bathrooms and breakfast included in the rate. Located around a covered central courtyard, the rooms are large and clean, with wood floors and matching décor. They also contain writing desks and VCRs.

Grand Hotel, *Calle A. Arce #61*, ☎ *645-1704 or 645-2461, $$$*, has been in Sucre since 1960. It is a grand old place, modeled after the one in Paris. All rooms have private bathrooms and cable TV. The restaurant is always busy for lunch with the business crowd and the staff is friendly and attentive.

Hostal Indepencia, *Calle Calvo #31*, ☎ *644-2256, $$$$*, has singles, doubles, triples and suites. The price includes a buffet breakfast. This is a lovely place with large bright rooms, great colonial architecture, color TVs, mini-bars, Internet service and a restaurant. There is a flower garden in the patio and ceramic tiles in the halls.

Premier Hotel, *Calle San Alberto #43*, ☎ *645-2097 or 645-1644, $$$$*, is a four-star hotel that includes a buffet breakfast in its rates. Spacious rooms are set around a bright and cheery courtyard. They have a king-sized bed, double dresser with mirror, tiled bathroom and plush carpet, as well as a stocked bar and cable TV. The hotel is clean. The restaurant, La Candela, has formal décor and is open to the public. There is safe parking inside the premises and laundry service is available.

El Hotal de Su Merced, *Calle Azurduy #16*, ☎ *644-2706 or 644-5150, $$$$*, is an immaculately restored colonial house. Tastefully decorated rooms are set around a central garden and all have private bathrooms. Some include a small sitting area. There is laundry service available and a restaurant where the complimentary breakfast is served. Special diets will be catered to.

Paola Hostal, *Calle Colon #138*, ☎ *644-1419, $$$$*, is another finely restored colonial mansion that has plants and pottery around its lush garden. The inside courtyard is tiled and sparkles. Rooms are large and comfortable, with cable TV, sitting areas, stocked fridges and Jacuzzi tubs in the tiled bathrooms. Breakfast is included and special diets can be accommodated.

Capital Plaza Hotel, *Plaza 25 de Mayo #28*, ☎ *642-2999 or 645-3242, www.capitalplazahotel.com, $$$$$*. This old hotel was built in 1917 and has been continually restored and remodeled so it can offer modern luxury. Moderately sized rooms are carpeted and have comfortable beds and night tables. The bathrooms are tiled. There is a central courtyard, a formal restaurant and piano bar on site, plus a pool and business center with free Internet access. You can change traveler's checks here and the staff can arrange car rentals.

Hotel Real Audiencia, *Calle Potosi #142*, ☎ *646-0823, real_aud@ mara.scr.entelnet.bo ,$$$$$*, has rooms and suites. Room rates include a buffet breakfast and the hotel offers a small discount if you stay longer than one night. This is the classiest hotel in Sucre and it offers a pool, saunas (both dry and wet), and a terrace with a view of the entire city. Free transportation to and from the airport is available. A well-kept flower garden is a good spot to sit. The huge rooms have a sitting area, TV, private bath and a fully-stocked fridge that even includes some Para Ti chocolate. Bedroom furniture is made of cherry wood and the bathroom has everything, including a hair dryer. The hotel is close to the Indigenous Art Museum.

LAS COLINAS

◆ Places to Eat

Joy Ride Bolivia, *Calle Nicolas Oritz #14 at Sucre*, ☎ *464-5455 or 462-5544*, has a groovy restaurant that serves espresso coffee (from a machine). They also offer fruit with yogurt and granola for breakfast. Their pancakes served with cane syrup can't be beat. The restaurant

❖ RESTAURANT PRICING	
$	under $5
$$	$5 to $10
$$$	$11 to $25
$$$$	$26 to $50
$$$$$	over $50

opens at 8 am so they are one of the few places that provide gringos with breakfast at a time when they want to eat it. Joy Ride also stays open at night until the last partier staggers down the street. There is an outdoor patio that has overhead heaters that are turned on during the cold weather. There's live entertainment on weekends. There is a useful travelers' bulletin board in the main restaurant area.

Chifa Restaurant Hong Kong, *on the plaza on Avenida Emilio Mendizabal #754*, ☎ *644-3962, and at Plaza 25 de Mayo #46*, ☎ *644-3272*. They have real Chinese food at both locations. The stir-fried veggies are a treat and the sweet and sour dishes are also well done in a Hong Kong style, rather than the bastardized American style. The portions are good and the prices are reasonable, $2-$2.50 a meal.

La Repizza, *Calle Nicolas Oritz #78*, ☎ *645-1506*, is popular with locals for lunch, but skip their pizza – it is all crust and not that good a crust either. Their lunches offer three good salad choices, as well as vegetarian lasagna, chili and spaghetti. Crêpes are on the breakfast menu.

Café Gourmet Mirador, *Calle Iturricha #281, at the Museo de los Niños, Tanga Tanga*, ☎ *644-0299*, has a new cook and menu. It is a highly recommended place to have a snack after or between museum visits. The cold cappuccino lathered in thick sweet cream is excellent.

Restaurant Suizo, *Calle Nicolas Oritz #42*, ☎ *642-3985*, is a clean little place that offers both Swiss and Bolivian foods. I had their curried chicken that was well presented and tasted just as good as it looked. The gypsy kabob was tasty too, but the Greek salad was nondescript. Both meals cost $3 and the salad was just under $2. Portions are adequate, but not large. They have live music on Saturday nights.

Café Travieso, *Calle Arce #237*, ☎ *644-7979*, has metal folding chairs and tables with tablecloths. Although the décor isn't the Hyatt, the food and prices are. They serve lasagna for $1.75, ravioli for less and tortellini for $1.50. They also have goulash or schnitzel and if you order in the morning you can have fondue. All the food I had here was excellent. This is a real find.

La Choza Restaurant, *Avenida O. Gutierrez #119*, is open at 8:30 am and does not close in the afternoon. It has a bamboo theme and each table is in a separate little cubicle. Their soups are less than a dollar and meat cooked on the grill runs from $1 to $1.50 per meal. On weekends they offer a special *chicharron* (sausage) in two portion sizes for $1 or $2. The place is spotless and the meals are tasty.

El Huerto Restaurant, *Calle Ladislao Cabrera #86*, ☎ *645-1538 or 642-9579*. To get here you will need to take a taxi, but your meal will make the fare worthwhile. El Huerto's is noted mostly for meat dishes like steak done on the barbecue. Although I never ate here, every taxi driver in the city recommends it.

Kactus Restaurant, *Calle España #176*, ☎ *644-7376*, opens every day at 7 pm. It's a small place that will soon have to be expanded because of its popularity. There is an extensive menu and I never heard "no hay" to any request. The meals are huge. Try the sweet and sour barbecue ribs for less than $4 – they are exceptional in flavor and size.

El Virgelito Restaurant, *Calle Cruz Verde #51 off Arce*, is not fancy but its Italian dishes are. This is off the main routes and usually patronized by upper class locals (and me).

Kaypichu Vegetarian Restaurant, Calle San Alberto #168, ☎ 644-3954, serves *almuerzo* Tuesday through Saturday in a tastefully decorated room (sadly, the seats are backless stools). The food is excellent and comes from a spotless kitchen. Breakfast here is the best in town, but the coffee at Joy Ride was better. The staff is friendly and useful; some speak English. There are piles of *Time* magazines (in English) around for the homesick. Open Tuesday to Sunday, 7:30 am-2 pm and 5-9 pm.

El Germen, *Calle San Alberto #231*, ☎ *7713-1940 (cell)*, claims to be open from 8 am to 10 pm, but I often found it closed during those hours. It serves all vegetarian foods and excellent pastries. Along with a coffee, nothing could be better. There is also a book exchange.

Café Tertulias, *Plaza 25 de Mayo #59*, ☎ *642-0390*, is popular with travelers who come for a late-afternoon beer. The restaurant opens from 9 am to noon and then again from 4 pm to midnight. The food is more sandwiches and salads than full meals, although they do serve pasta and meat dishes.

La Milaneza, *Calle Argentina #49*, ☎ *642-2775*, specializes in fast food *Milaneza*. *Milaneza* is a meat that is pounded thin, breaded and fried. It is just as quick to cook as hamburger.

El Solar, *Calle Bolívar #800*, ☎ *645-4341*, serves local and international cuisine. Open since 1977, it has a reputation of serving the best *pique de la macho* in town ($4).

La Posada Café Restaurant, *Calle Audiencia #92*, ☎ *646-0101*, has an inside dining room and an outside patio. They have a different *almuerzo* every day. They are open Monday to Saturday, 10 am-10:30 pm, and Sunday, 11 am-3 pm.

Café Berlin, *Calle Avaroa #326*, is a good place to have your early evening beer and snack. Recommended are the Swiss-styled potatoes (*rellenas*) that are spiced and fried. However, it is the pastry that I really liked.

Gnadenlos Café, *Calle Bustillas #121*, ☎ *644-8258*, is open for breakfast around 8:30 am and serves granola with fruit and yogurt. This is always a draw in hot weather. They have a lot of vegetarian choices too. The owners also exchange books, arrange tours and know where there is a good Spanish teacher.

La Taverne, *Calle A. Arce #35*, ☎ *645-3599*, is both a restaurant and a cultural center where the French language is taught to local children. The restaurant is open daily from 8 am to noon and 6 pm until 11 pm. They specialize in French dishes and you have the choice of sitting inside under subdued light or out on the patio in the sun. Videos in French can be viewed on Wednesday, Friday and Saturday evenings at 7 pm for 50¢. There is often live music in the patio during the day.

◆ Nightlife

Alaska Disco, Arce #4325, is fairly new, clean and not too loud. Since it is just up from the plaza, you get the quieter crowd (older than 20) patronizing the place.

Joy Ride Bolivia, Calle Nicolas Oritz #14 at Sucre, ☎ 464-5455 or 462-5544, is the *in* place to meet other *gringos*, drink beer and talk about things like travel, bikes and entertainment preferences, or just tell jokes. The bar sponsors a lot of specialty nights, like "Hawaii Night." They also bring in live entertainment on the weekends. For an idea about some of their crazy nights, go in and have a look at the photos on the walls. They are a fun bunch.

◆ Shopping

Ajllay Wasi Arts and Craft Shop, Calle Audiencia #17, opens daily from 9 am-12:30 pm and 3-7:30 pm. It is just around the corner from Joy Ride and sells high-quality weavings for groups of women not involved with the co-op at the Indigenous Art Museum. Some smaller *chulpas* sell for $30-$40, a good price for good work.

Para Ti Chocolate, Calle Arenales #7, ☎ 645-5689, www.chocolates-para-ti.com. If you come to Sucre and fail to taste the chocolate you are missing a main feature of the city. Visiting Bolivians take these chocolates home as gifts. The main shop is less than 100 ft/30 m off the square. Para Ti put out its first chocolates 50 years ago from a factory that had three machines. A few years later, it had 20 machines that produced chocolates. Some Para-Ti are made with a variety of grains melted into the chocolate for flavor and nutrition. Grains used include amaranto, one of the original cereal grains of the Inca, and quinoa, a grain grown in the Altiplano.

> ❖ **BANG FOR YOUR BUCK**
>
> Quinoa can be puffed like popcorn, ground into flour, made into a paste or used as a cereal like couscous and is the only vegetable that has all eight of the essential amino acids.

The shop at the **Indigenous Art Museum**, San Alberto #413, ☎ 645-3841, does not allow you to take your pack into the store. They sell Jalq'a waistbands for $18 and good-quality *chulpas* for $30. Their selection is large and they often have numerous pieces of the same design. They are an Inca Pallay Co-op and purchase only from members.

Inca Pallay Co-op, Calle Bolívar #682B, ☎ 646-1936, is an association with locations in Sucre and La Paz. It helps weavers and artists from the Tarabuco and Jalq'a areas by putting their products on the world market for a fair price. They also give workshops and help administer them for local artists. The association manages the Indigenous Art Museum in Sucre (see above). On Sundays in Tarabuco, they occasionally sponsor traditional dancing demonstrations. The price of an average-sized *chulpa* runs $30-$40 for those from the Tarabuco area. You'll also find some wood carvings and silver products.

Ananay Craft Store, Plaza de la Recoleta, ☎ 644-0299, www. artesaniasdebolivia.com, carries, among other things, unique and creative ceramic pieces. I found a woven vest that was of better quality than some I saw in specialty shops in La Paz. The price was also higher. If looking for something different, stop in.

> ❖   **A TASTY OFFERING**
>
> Ch'alla is a wine made specifically as an offering to Pacha Mama, Mother Earth. It is sold in markets. During a festival, locals sprinkle ch'alla on a floor or field in Pacha Mama's honor.

Tupiza

Altitude: 9,704 ft/2,950 m
Population: 30,000

If you travel between Tupiza and Uyuni (the most common route used by travelers), the dry landscape goes from bleak desert dotted with plastic bags to hills that are carved by the wind, the debris creating sand dunes. A true desert is in the making. Once past Atocha the landscape becomes Grand Canyon-like, except the rock is loose conglomerate that is easily eroded by wind and rain. A few miles farther, the earth and sandstone turns red and the landscape is rugged and dry. The scenery grows more and more dramatic the closer one gets to Tupiza. If coming from Tarija, the route is on another of Bolivia's death roads. But the landscape is stunning and, as you cross the two high passes, you should see lots of wildlife.

Once in Tupiza, pull out your hiking boots as you will not be able to resist entering the canyons and ravines that are in the area. If you are not a hiker, try riding a horse the way Butch Cassidy and the Sundance Kid did. If none of those activities are interesting, try visiting the Kallawaya naturopath living in town, ready to help with some of your ailments or just to give advice on how to live.

The longer people stay in Tupiza, the better they like it. The climate is dry and warm, the people are relaxed and happy.

◆ Getting Here & Around

Most people come to Tupiza by bus or jeep. The mountain road into Tupiza from Uyuni is rough, but not the worst in the country.

There are daily buses to Potosi that leave at 7 pm and cost $4 for the seven-hour ride. There is one bus a day going to La Paz that leaves around 7 pm (but check because times change). The trip is 14 hours and costs $8 per person.

Numerous buses leave daily for Tarija, but if you want a day-time bus, you must wait until one of the companies has enough passengers to warrant the trip. Crystal frequently offers day-time trips at $7 for the nine-hour ride. The distance is 133 miles/218 km along another "Road of Death." Wise travelers will consider hiring a jeep, available through one of the tour offices. If going into the Chaco, to Argentina or Santa Cruz, you must get to Tarija to make connections.

◆ History

The indigenous history of Tupiza is sparse due to the fact that most of the architectural and cultural remains disappeared even before the arrival of the Spanish. The **Chicha Indians** dwelled in the area but were absorbed by the **Inca** when they moved through on their way to places like Chile and El Fuerte in Samaipata. The Chicha called the area Tupesa, a word that is believed to mean red rock.

The **Spanish** arrived on the heels of the Inca but found little reason to stay and so moved on to Chile. In 1574 **Captain Luis de Fuentes** officially founded Tupiza while on his way to Tarija, the wine capital of Bolivia. He left behind a few Spaniards who established some fairly large ranches.

After independence, mining companies moved in and developed silver, tin, antimony and lead mines. During the late 1800s, Tupiza got its best break. Butch Cassidy and the Sundance Kid decided to make off with some of the mine's payroll. Little did the locals know the benefits in tourism that would result.

◆ Services

The **telephone office** is on Calle Senador Aramayo and Calle Avaroa.

The **post office** is on Plaza Indepencia on Calle Sucre.

The **police** station is on Plaza Indepencia.

A **money changer**, Cambio Latin America, Calle Avaroa, #154, ☎ 694-2985, charges 4% off the official rate on travelers' checks. She changes euros, Argentinean, Chilean, English and Peruvian money. She does not change Canadian currency. If you change more than US $100, she offers a discount on the commission. She is fast and efficient. The money changer across the street charges a higher commission.

The **hospital** is on Chichas between Calle Avaroa and Florida.

◆ Sightseeing

Casa de Aramayo is an old estate that is going to ruin but still offers interesting exploration and photographic opportunities.

Carlos Victor Aramayo, grandson of Avalino Aramayo (1809-1882), the man whose bust stands in the main plaza, was a tin and silver baron who owned the richest mine in the area before the revolution in 1952. It is also the company that Butch and Sundance robbed in their last job before meeting their deaths.

To get there, cross the river at the south end of the city by the bus station and walk north until you are at the unfinished bridge that has no entrance or exit (only a center). From there, walk east toward the mountains. Once past the football field, you will come to the Aramayo estate with the remains of many buildings.

◆ Adventures in Culture

Kallawaya Medicine Man is on the north side of the river across from the incomplete bridge (there is a center, but no on or off ramp).

Silvino Paredes Ricana comes from a Kallawaya family in the north of Bolivia. He has three beds and a special bath that he uses for his patients. For some conditions, he takes patients to the Salar de Uyuni where he uses special mud packs. This treatment is usually for digestive disorders, but his specialty is blood pressure disorders. He is an interesting man. However, you must know a fair amount of Spanish to understand what he is saying.

The **Museum** on Calle Sucre is upstairs and next door to the military map office. It is they who have the key to the museum, which is open from 8 am to 6 pm. There is no charge to enter. The museum has one room packed with artifacts from the area.

◆ Adventures on Foot

There are many trails from Tupiza. The few described here are the easiest to access. However, once you become familiar with the area, ask around about other trails.

> **AUTHOR NOTE:** *All these hikes require proper boots and you should carry at least two liters of water. Wear sunscreen and a peaked hat to shade your eyes and cover your head. Some snacks are a good idea.*

ELEPHANT HILL: You'll see why Cerro El Elefante got its name as you walk this route. To get there, cross the river at the south end of town just past the bus station and walk north, or cross on the pedestrian bridge that is at the north end of the market and walk northeast. There is a good view of the elephant-shaped terrain from the pedestrian bridge. The cross on the top of Cerro La Cruz can also be seen. Go through a gap in the hills to the right of La Cruz. Once through the gap, there is a wide valley or wash-out, populated by goats mostly.

Head for the elephant's trunk. About halfway into the valley and to the left are some hobbit-like formations made from rock and red clay. One is a gigantic doorway where you can start making your way over the hills to another washout with a road running through it. There is no clear route from the stone doorway straight over the hill to the road on the other side. We went through and followed a dry creek-bed up and to the right. In the heat of the day, it was a grunt to get over the top. Staying in the channel generally keeps you out of the hawthorn bushes, but means you have to do some rock clambering and climbing. Once you are on the road, head left and pass through a smaller gap onto another road. Continue to the left on that road, through a highway checkpoint, down to Tupiza.

Should you continue farther up the valley in front of the elephant (rather than going through the hobbit-like doorway), you end up in an amphitheater surrounded by a high ridge.

Approaching the trail from the opposite direction is easier for a circular route. To do this, walk out of town through the market, following the railway tracks. Follow the road that goes to Potosi, past the highway roadblock, past Escuela Genolieva and Bar and Pension Dos Hermanos. The road splits. Stay right, past another bar/pension and the highway checkpoint. A large washout will come from the right. Follow this into the hills. Four by fours have gone here. A second washout will flow into the first after about 15 minutes. Follow it to the top of the hill. You must go up into the hills before you come to the front of the elephant's snout.

Once at the top of the hill, pick your way down, veering toward hobbit land. You must go to the bottom on the far side of the doorway. You can return to town by walking down the gravel to the gap in the hills. This should take about three hours, depending on how much time you spend doing other things besides walking.

When in the valley, regardless from which direction you enter, you can follow a trail up to the elephant on the far side of the valley. There is a waterfall up there during wet season. This is a nice four- to five-hour exploration.

GOBLIN CANYON: Cañon del Duende is at the beginning of this trail, but a little farther is the Valle de los Machos and beyond that the Cañon del Inca. Go in as far as you like and return by the same trails.

To reach the trailhead, walk south of town past the bus station. When the road turns east at the tracks, you turn south. Don't cross the tracks and don't cross the bridge going over Rio Tupiza. Continue south. This route runs beside the railway tracks and will eventually hook up with a road. Walk along the road for about an hour, past a swimming pool (it's clean and costs only 50¢ for the day – there is a smaller pool beside the main one for children). Continuing along the road, walk up the hill and, when you see a trail down below on your right, cut across land to meet it. Follow it back in the direction of town. You will find yourself in a gravel wash that has been used as a landfill. It is disgusting, but walk through a gate of high conglomerate pillars and you are in the canyon. The rocks on the wash where you are walking get bigger the farther in you go and the red fins of the mountains close in. This is a spectacular spot.

After walking for about a half-hour you will encounter a rock on the passage blocking the way. During high water this would be a waterfall. Although you can free climb past the obstruction, I don't recommend it.

DEVIL'S DOOR: Puerto del Diablo is close to town and popular for a day hike/photo session/horse trip. Walking in this dry landscape seems to leach the water out of your cells, so keep drinking. You should drink at least two liters every four hours.

To hike, cut across town toward the Mirador. Once on the street called Sanado Aramayo, turn south. You will pass a small park. Continue weaving your way through the streets past a children's park and then to the military practice grounds. Stay on the same path until you reach the garbage

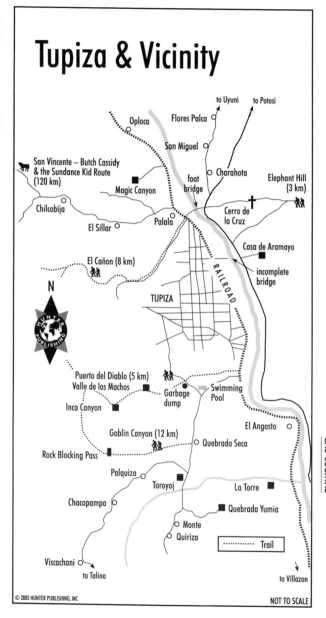

Tupiza & Vicinity

to Uyuni
to Potosi

Oploca
Flores Palca

San Miguel

San Vincente – Butch Cassidy
& the Sundance Kid Route
(120 km)

Charahota

Elephant Hill
(3 km)

Magic Canyon

foot
bridge

Chilcobija

Cerro de
la Cruz

El Sillar
Palala

Casa de Aramayo

El Cañon (8 km)

incomplete
bridge

RAILROAD

TUPIZA

N

Puerto del Diablo (5 km)
Valle de los Machos

Swimming
Pool

Inca Canyon

Garbage
dump

Goblin Canyon (12 km)

El Angosto

Rock Blocking Pass

Quebrada Seca

Palquiza

Toroyoj

La Torre

Chacopampa

Quebrada Yumia

Monte
Quiriza

.... Trail

Viscachani

to Talina

to Villazon

LAS COLINAS

© 2005 HUNTER PUBLISHING, INC

NOT TO SCALE

dump. Turn just before the dump and follow that trail into the hills, canyons and conglomerate fins. It's about three hours before you come to a waterfall. But going beyond the fall is also recommended. As you get to the Valley de los Machos you may (with the help of a guide) be able to find some Chichas Indian rock paintings. The rock formations in this area are like nowhere else in South America.

EL CANON: El Cañon is reached by following Calle Chiquisaca until opposite the Mirador (with the huge Christ figure). Turn left along a washout that soon closes in. This area is especially known for its splendid cactus that blooms in a flaming red or creamy white around mid-December.

◆ Adventures on Water

The pool next to the bus station is popular with local kids. They charge 50¢ for half a day. Another pool is on the road to Cañon del Duende (see above). The second pool has a large deck, clean water and charges 50¢ for the day.

◆ Adventures on Horseback

Taking a horse on the trail of Butch Cassidy and the Sundance Kid from Tupiza, where the two planned their first Bolivian robbery, to San Vincente, where the two died, is an adventure. See *Tour Operators*, below, for a list of outfitters who can saddle you up.

Before going on the horse trip, be certain to watch the 1969 movie starring Robert Redford and Paul Newman portraying the life, Hollywood-style, of the two men. Also read Bruce Chatwin's book, *Patagonia*. He tells the story well. Villa Hermosa Tours offers this trip, as do other tour companies in town.

◆ Tour Operators

The advantage of taking the tour from Tupiza is that, as a home base, Tupiza is a nicer place to stay than Uyuni.

Valle Hermoso Tours, Avenida Pedro Arraya #478, ☎ 694-2370, in the hotel of the same name, offers numerous tours. This company is best known for its horseback trips that go from half a day up to four days. The horses are gentle, the saddles are padded with sheepskins, and the guides know how to handle and care for animals. The English spoken at Valle Hermoso is excellent. Horses rent for $2.50 an hour. Hermosa offers tours to Puerto del Diablo, the Valle de los Machos, and across the Bolívar Valley to Angosto, where you will pass through two natural tunnels, one for vehicles and the other for trains. The classic four-day trip covers the route of Butch Cassidy and the Sundance Kid. If you have time, this excursion, like Uyuni Salt Lake, is a must.

Tupiza Tours, Avenida Chichas #187, ☎ 694-3001, www.tupizatours. com, is in the lobby of the Mitru Hotel. They offer anything from a half-day tour by jeep or/and horse to a four- or five-day trip ending in Uyuni. A half-day jeep trip with a full group of six people can cost as little as $7 per per-

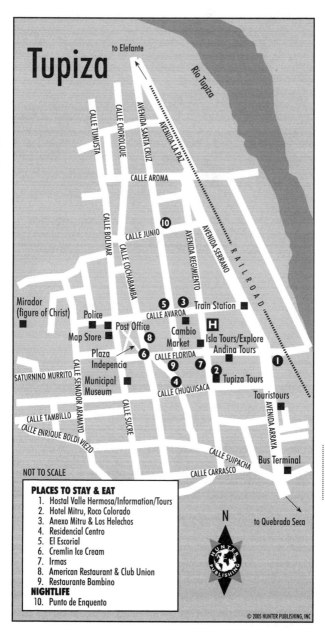

Tupiza

to Elefante

Rio Tupiza

RAILROAD

CALLE TUMUSLA
CALLE CHOROLOQUE
AVENIDA SANTA CRUZ
AVENIDA LA PAZ

CALLE AROMA

CALLE BOLIVAR
CALLE JUNIO
⑩
CALLE COCHABAMBA
AVENIDA REGIMIENTO
AVENIDA SERRANO

Mirador
(figure of Christ) ■

Police ■
Map Store ■
Post Office ■

⑤ ③ Train Station ■
CALLE AVAROA

H

⑧
Cambio
Market
⑥
Plaza
Indepencia
CALLE FLORIDA
⑨ ⑦

Isla Tours/Explore
Andina Tours ■

❶

SATURNINO MURRITO

Municipal
Museum ■
CALLE CHUQUISACA

❷ Tupiza Tours

CALLE SENADOR ARAMAYO

❹

CALLE TAMBILLO
CALLE SUCRE

CALLE ENRIQUE BOLDI VIEZO

Touristours ■

AVENIDA ARRAYA

CALLE SUIPACHA

Bus Terminal ■

NOT TO SCALE

CALLE CARRASCO

to Quebrada Seca

N

HUNTER PUBLISHING

LAS COLINAS

PLACES TO STAY & EAT
1. Hostal Valle Hermosa/Information/Tours
2. Hotel Mitru, Roco Colorado
3. Anexo Mitru & Los Helechos
4. Residencial Centro
5. El Escorial
6. Cremlin Ice Cream
7. Irmas
8. American Restaurant & Club Union
9. Restaurante Bambino

NIGHTLIFE
10. Punto de Enquento

© 2005 HUNTER PUBLISHING, INC

son. Horse trips can last three, five or seven hours or take up to two days. Rates are $20 per day, including food.

Isla Tours, Calle Florida (Avenida Ferrovairio and Uyuni), ☎ 7183-2712 (cell), has offices in Tupiza and Uyuni. They offer the same tours as everyone else in Tupiza, but they try to compete by cutting their prices and, of course, their meager profit margin. This is one of only two agencies in town that is not attached to a hotel.

Explore Andina Tours, Avenida Chichas #220, ☎ 694-2633, is on the main floor of Roca Colorada Hotel. They offer a number of tours, including a city tour, a tour to Uyuni, a two-day Butch Cassidy tour, and up to three days on a horse. Andina also has a number of different vehicles for rent. Using a vehicle in this area seems fairly safe to me and this is one place in Bolivia where driving would have advantages.

Touristours, Avenida Pedro Arraya, ☎ 694-4534, tourslossalares@ hotmail.com, offers all the usual tours plus an exceptional trip to the village of San Pablo de Lipez, in the municipality of Portulos, near the Argentinean border. The tour can be as short as four days or as long as 12, and part of it may be done as a llama caravan. You will be involved with Los Ripes indigenous group. San Pedro village (16,500 ft/5,000 m) has mud brick structures with thatched roofs. For this trip one must be prepared for full cultural immersion.

The people running this office are sincere and interested in promoting their cultural background. If you have even an inkling of interest in these types of trips, talk to them. Their prices are comparable to everyone else in town.

◆ Places to Stay

Hostal Valle Hermoso, Avenida Pedro Arraya, #478, ☎ 694-2370, $, is a five-minute walk from the bus station. Its rooms are clean with tile floors and windows overlooking a small courtyard. There is a rooftop patio and a dining room where, if you order ahead, breakfast can

❖ HOTEL PRICING	
$	$10 to $20
$$	$21 to $50
$$$	$51 to $75
$$$$	$76 to $100
$$$$$	over $100

be served. A TV and VCR allow you to watch *Butch Cassidy and the Sundance Kid*. Luggage storage and laundry service are also available.

Residencial Centro, Avenida Santa Cruz #287, ☎ 694-2705, $, has basic rooms and good rates. The place is clean, the walls are painted and bougainvillea decorates the courtyard. Parking is available and there's a guest kitchen area.

Anexo Mitru, Calle Avaroa, ☎ 694-3002, $$, next to Los Helechos, has a plethora of rooms with various prices and options – with or without private bath, with or without TV, etc. This hotel is part of the Mitru Hotel (below) and if you stay in the annex you get to use the pool (in the Mitru itself) for $1.25 per day (non-guests pay $2). Laundry costs $1.15 per kilo and ping pong will set you back 75¢ for half an hour. Baggage storage is available.

Roco Colorado, Avenida Chichas and Chuquisaca, just up from Mitru, ☎ 694-3016, $$, has spacious rooms with large windows and nice-sized bathrooms. There is even a curtain around the shower stall. Cable TV is usually included. The place is clean. Breakfast is offered in the dining room downstairs (all rooms are on the second floor). It costs $1 for a continental and an Americano that includes scrambled eggs runs $1.25.

Hotel Mitru, *Avenida Chichas #187*, ☎ *694-3001. www.tupizatours. com, $$$$*, has a lovely flowered patio and a pool. A two-room suite is $20 for one and $35 for two. This includes a large bedroom with tile floor and cactus wood furniture. The curtains all match, the bathroom is large and has a separate shower stall, and cable TV is in the sitting room just off the bedroom. The sitting room has a couch, chair and coffee tables. These suites are a luxury for Bolivia. Towels, shampoo and breakfast are all included in the price. The hotel has rooms with private bath that cost $5.50 per person, and simple rooms without baths go for $2.50 per person. However, there is a 75¢ per-day fee to use the pool. Other amenities include laundry service ($1 a kilo), luggage storage, a book exchange and a safe car park. There are presently 110 beds available and a new addition will be completed soon.

◆ Places to Eat

Los Helechos, *Avenida Avaroa*, ☎ *694-3002*, can have sullen waitresses, but the food is good and the restaurant is clean. An egg sandwich is 50¢ and a banana milkshake is 60¢. The shakes are strong on banana and the sandwiches have lots of onion.

❖ RESTAURANT PRICING	
$	under $5
$$	$5 to $10
$$$	$11 to $25
$$$$	$26 to $50
$$$$$	over $50

El Escorial, *Avenida Avaroa and Santa Cruz,* has their menu on a sandwich board on the street. The portions are not large (I had to order two pieces of chicken) but the flavor was good. The service is quick.

Cremlin Ice Cream, *Avenida Cochabamba and Calle Florida, on the square,* is the most popular parlor in town. The best dish to try is the papaya split. The prices are low.

> ### ❖ ORDER A TUPIZA SPECIAL
>
> Tupiza has some unique dishes to try. *Tomales* are made with spiced llama meat. *Humintas* is a sweet corn dish that has ground and cooked corn mixed with a spiced cheese. The mixture is wrapped in leaves and cooked in an oven. *Pelado* is a large-kernel corn cooked with peppers, onion, a little beef, garlic, chili and rice.

Irmas, *Calle Florida,* has a sign in English painted on the wall, below the red and white sign that says "Agency Cascada." Irma is always in the *tienda* "Frial Castro" that is located just below the sign. You must order your meals two hours ahead of time. A full supper includes everything that an *almuerzo* would include and costs $2.50. Breakfast is $1.25. You get to eat in her dining room and this should give you a sense of Bolivian home life. The big payoff is the excellent food (including vegetarian).

American Restaurant, *on the plaza,* is named after its clientele. It serves a small pizza for 75¢ and a large for $1.25. The place is always full of tourists looking for the usual North American foods. I was not all that impressed with the food or the portion size.

◆ Nightlife

Punto de Enquento, Avenida Santa Cruz & Calle Arandia, is the karaoke bar where the young crowd goes on Saturday nights. The other popular, but nameless, place is at the bottom of the stairs that lead to the mirador on the hill where the Christ figure, which can be seen from anywhere in town, is located. These dance bars open at 8 pm, but nothing really starts happening until after 9 or 10 pm. The cover charge is under 50¢ and traditional music is played.

Line dancing is the most popular dance at the moment in Tupiza. The open-air sports center in town across from the train station often has dance competitions on Saturday nights. Check with your hotel owner for information.

Villazon

Altitude: 11,332 ft/3,445 m
Population: less than 2000

The border town of Villazon is a grubby place that at one time was filled with Bolivian migrants heading for Argentina, with its better standard of living. Today, the floods have reversed and the Bolivian expatriates are returning home.

Villazon can be reached by rail or by bus. It has a few places to stay and eat, and some money changers. The exchange rate is better in Bolivia than Argentina. However, this could change as the economies change.

The border crossing is easy. Walk from the plaza to the frontier, get your exit stamp, go a few more feet, and get your entry stamp to Argentina.

◆ Getting Here & Away

Buses to or from Tarija take eight hours. There is one bus in the morning and the rest go at night. There are many buses to Tupiza, three hours away. This is probably the best destination from the border.

The **trains** run between Villazon and Tupiza three times a week and take the same time as the bus. This service is threatened by privatization of the rail service.

◆ Places to Stay & Eat

I suggest you stay at the **Hotel Plaza** *on the square,* ☎ 596-3535, $$. It has clean rooms with bath and color TV. If this is not an option, there are cheaper and more basic places to stay near the bus terminal.

For food, try the **Chinese Restaurant** opposite the bus terminal. The other place to eat is at Hotel Plaza.

Tarija

Altitude: 9,099 ft/1,854 m
Population: 120,000

Tarija has many plazas that are clean and vegetated due to the almost tropical climate. A wide boulevard runs along the river and, in general, the area looks prosperous. This is due to the numerous successful vineyards and wineries in the area, plus the fact that in the past, when the Argentinean economy was better, many people from Tarija worked there for high wages. People of Tarija are known for their songs and dances accompanied by the many varieties of drums.

Tarija has a lot of beggars, which is surprising as the city looks better off than most Bolivian cities. Many of the beggars are refugees from the recent economic crash in Argentina.

Tarija is a great place to hang out and rest after some tough travel. It sees few tourists and has yet to be discovered. However, the hotels are good and the restaurants numerous.

◆ Getting Here & Around

Most **buses** between Tarija and Tupiza travel at night but occasionally, when the volume of passengers allows it, Chrystal Bus Company offers a day trip. You must go to the bus station in Tupiza and see if there are enough people going. The cost for the trip by bus is $7 per person. Although it's just 134 miles/218 km, the journey takes anywhere from seven to 10 hours, usually with a couple of half-hour breaks to fix the bus or have dinner in Tojo.

Buses to Potosi via Uyuni take about 20 hours. Buses direct to Potosi take 14 hours and cost $10 per person. They have only night buses, the earliest leaving at 5 pm. Camargo, 111 miles/182 km north of Tarija on the road to Potosi, can be reached by taking a bus to Potosi. You will have to pay for the entire way even though you are getting off at the halfway point. The trip is long and through the mountains. It is best to go by jeep.

Buses to Villamontes ($7) take 12 hours to go 158 miles/258 km. The slow time indicates that it is another treacherous road. A hired taxi takes 10 hours and costs $130 for up to four people (see Suzie at Dinar Travel, ☎ 664-8000, if you wish to do this). You can find a taxi to do the run for a lot less; ask around.

Trains leave Wednesday and Saturday for Santa Cruz.

Planes fly to and from Villamontes on Friday and Saturday. Planes to or from Santa Cruz go every day during the week and cost $75 per person. Planes do not fly if it is raining.

Taxis in Tarija cost 45¢ per person, anywhere within city limits. Tarija has all one-way streets, and every corner has a huge sign indicating the name of the street and numbers in that block. This makes getting around easy and safe.

LAS COLINAS

◆ History

Tarija was founded on July 4th, 1574 by **Captain Luis de Fuentes y Vargas**.

In 1810 Tarija declared its independence from Spanish rule, though Spain ignored the declaration. On April 15th, seven years later, the citizens of Tarija, under the leadership of **Moto Mendez**, won the **Battle de la Tablada**. However, it didn't win them independence. It was at this time that the village was named for Francisco de Tarija, who was the first Spaniard to enter the valley.

Shortly after independence, Argentina realized the value of the fertile lands around Tarija so the governors asked the people of Tarija to unite with Argentina, but the people opted to stay with Bolivia. Every person in Tarija seems proud of this, though considering Argentina's overall greater prosperity and stability, one has to wonder. Finally, in 1825 Bolivia won independence from Spain and Tarija, in turn, concentrated on being Bolivian.

◆ Services

The **telephone office** is on Calle Virginio Lema and Daniel Campos, just one block up from Plaza Sucre.

The **post office** is next door to the telephone office on Calle Virginio Lema.

Internet access is everywhere, but the office on Plaza Sucre at Calle Bolívar is about the fastest. Many machines have curtains around them so no one can see what the operator is looking at.

The **police** station is on Avenida las Americas, between Calle Ballivan and Juan Misae.

The **hospital** is on Calle Cochabamba and Avenida Santa Cruz. **Medical Clinic** - Infirmary Varas Castrillo, Calle Alejandro Corrado #176, ☎ 664-2051, cell 7186-0163, has a diagnostic lab and blood bank. They can do electro-cardiograms and general practice. The clinic is open 24 hours a day. A general examination costs $7.

There's a **tourist office** on Plaza Luis de Fuentes, at the corner of 15th de Abril.

La Esmeralda Limpieza, Calle La Madrid #157, ☎ 664-2043, does **laundry** for $1 a kilo. The wash is done by machine and can be ironed if you wish. They also offer dry cleaning.

◆ Festivals

Besides the usual festivals like Carnival and Christmas, there are numerous events that mostly celebrate the production of wine. Viva Tours, ☎ 663-8325, offers four-day tours for most of these festivals.

The **Festival of the Grapes** takes place in February/March in Concepcion Valley, an area that has grown to be the center of Bolivia's grape-growing region. The date changes every year and is dependent on the growing season. The queen of the grape is crowned during this festival.

Carnival, in Tarija, starts two Thursdays before Carnival proper. The first Thursday is the celebration of the *compadres* (men) and the second is the celebration of the *comadres* (women). The *comadres* day is most important. This is when the ladies of the city parade through the streets with special cakes that sit in baskets decorated with fruits, flowers, cheese or other sweets. A week later Carnival starts with the devil being brought to the main square in a cage. Once he is liberated, the festival can begin. The final day is celebrated with the funeral of the *Momo* (monkey) King, who is recreated as a puppet. He is taken to Villa Abaroa, placed in a cardboard carton and drowned in lots of *chicha* and wine before being burned.

April 15th and 16th is **Efemerides de Tarija**. It celebrates the Battle of La Tablada, when, in 1817, citizens of the area won a battle against the Spanish. They were fighting for independence. The celebration includes a rodeo in memory of the city's *gaucho* connections. There is also the **Fair of Southern Bolivia**, which features a huge display of items produced or hand-made in the area. The event is patronized by people from all of South America and is one of the biggest in the country.

The end of March or the beginning of April is the Pascua Florida, or **Easter**, celebration. In Tarija, things are done just a bit differently than in other areas. On Good Friday the women don white dresses and parade to the cathedral while chanting a mournful sound commemorating the death of Christ. On Sunday, the cathedral is decorated with roses and other flowers, and rose petals are strewn on the ground. The Procession of the Resurrection occurs when the people parade to the church carrying a statue of Christ that symbolizes his rising from the dead.

Fiesta of the Virgin of Chaguaya is a long celebration that occurs between August 15th and September 10th. This religious festival takes place in the village of Chaguaya, 37 miles/60 km from Tarija. Many pilgrims come walking to the site where the virgin was supposed to have been seen.

Fiesta de San Roque is between August 15th and September 12th, with the main feast day being August 16th. San Roque is the patron saint of Tarija. Although there are parades every Sunday for the entire month, the main celebration (different than feast day) occurs on the first Sunday in September when the people of the city carry a statue of the saint through the streets in a dramatic procession to the cathedral. Since San Roque was the saint of dogs, the people of Tarija adorn their dogs with colored ribbons.

You will notice that the dogs of Tarija are well taken care of and many have ribbons around their necks. This is an indication that the dogs have had all their shots (in honor of San Roque).

The **Fiesta of the Virgin of Guadalupe** occurs on the first Sunday of October when the Virgin is paraded through city streets to a field on a small hill near the town. She is placed on a makeshift altar to watch the re-enactment of a battle that took place on May 17th, 1735. It was then that groups of men made up of the Matacos, Cuñas and Chiriguano (indigenous groups) fought over the possession of the Virgin.

The information about the festivals of Tarija was given to me by Viva Tours in Tarija.

◆ Sightseeing

In Town

Miradora de la Loma is on the hill at the west end of Avenida Domingo Paz and Corrage. Stairs lead to the park and viewpoint on top. The views of the city are good – ignore the numerous lovers. Below the hill you can see the Capilla de San Juan de la Loma, a historical church that has been well maintained and glitters in the sunlight.

Casa Dorada, Avenida Ingavi and Calle Gran Trigo, is a museum and a cultural center. Built at the end of the 1800s for Moises Navajas, the building was declared a museum in 1903. The architecture, and the building's statue of liberty standing over the main entrance and flanked by statues of Victorian women, make Casa Dorada exceptional. Inside are Persian carpets, crystal chandeliers and mirrors framed in gold leaf. It is worth a walk through. Open Monday to Friday, 8 am to noon and 3 to 6 pm. The entry free is $1 per person.

The **Archeological Museum**, Calle General Trigo #0402, ☎ 663-6680, is part of the university and has archeological, paleontological and historical sections. Among the 500 fossils are the bones of the only Andean elephant ever found in South America. The archeological section has over 5,000 pieces that include jars, pots, arrowheads and spears. Admission, 25¢. The museum is open Monday to Friday, 8 am to noon and 3 to 6 pm. On weekends, it opens at 9 am.

Churches

The **cathedral**, Calle Madrid and Avenida Campero, was constructed in 1810 by the Jesuits and was declared a cathedral in 1925. The interior features oil paintings and silver and gold chalices, many inlaid with precious stones. The glass windows in this cathedral depict local peasants working in the fields.

San Juan de la Loma on San Juan Hill is a lovely white plaster church that is an historical relic. This is where the Spaniards signed a treaty of surrender on April 15th, 1817 after the Battle of Tablada, a field just outside the city. The battle was led by Moto Mendez. You can visit his house, which is now a museum, in San Lorenzo (page 201). To get to San Juan de la Loma, walk along Avenida Domingo Paz to the church.

Iglesia San Francisco, Avenida Madrid and Calle Daniel Campos, was built in 1606 and is considered the oldest church in Tarija. The library and archives, housed in the college next door, hold over 15,000 books. The church itself has some of the city's best oil paintings.

◆ Adventures in Culture

There are about 120 sites featuring rock paintings in this area, some with as many as 200 individual paintings. Some of these works are about 500 years old, while others are suspected to be up to 3,500 years of age.

The Methfessels (father and daughter), unofficial specialists in the rock paintings of Bolivia, became interested in the paintings many years ago.

Lilo, the daughter, took photographs and made cards from the images that she in turn sold in her Tarija shop. As the father and daughter continued research, they realized that they had found some important archaeological treasures that were unknown to Bolivian scientists. The Methfessels registered their finds with the Archeological Department in La Paz. They also participated in the International Rock Art Symposium that took place in Tarija. This father and daughter team has been instrumental in getting these anthropological treasures brought to international attention.

The Methfessels will take you to some of the paintings, but they have strict rules. You can photograph the paintings, but you may not touch them, sprinkle water on them to make them brighter or walk on them. Call them at ☎ 664-2062 and see my review of their services under *Tour Operators*, below.

◆ Adventures on Foot

INCA TRAIL: The Inca Trail in the Cordillera Sama Biological Reserve (see below) was used long before the Inca arrived, but it has not been studied and its age is not known. This paved trail is steep and often used by locals to get from the highlands down into the valleys. It can be walked in eight hours, but this leaves little time for exploration. It is best to spend at least one night in the reserve. While walking you will see archeological remains such as drainage troughs, platforms, an old bridge and structural walls made from huge slabs of rock. Rock paintings can be seen in six different locations and to find them you will need a guide.

The trail starts at Tajzara, near the Great Lake. The lake is surrounded by sand dunes. Across the main highway from the lake is Copper Hill, where queñua trees manage to survive at an elevation of 16,000 ft/5,000 m. These trees grow to a height of 10 ft/three m and have twisted trunks that seem to peel from the sun.

As you start to cross the Sama range, you will pass waterfalls and mountain streams on rugged terrain. The trail descends to the village of Calderillas. From there it goes to the Calderilla River ravine and down into the village of Pinos along the road to Tarija.

A private vehicle must be taken to the trailhead and another must be arranged for pickup at the end. The best time to hike is between April and September, when the trail is driest. There is camping at the lakes near the main road. You must have your own equipment for this. The village of Iscayachi, at the point in the road just before it drops into the Tarija Valley, has a fairly decent hotel. You could start from there in the morning and hire a taxi to take you to the trailhead. There is a campsite in Calderillas and Pinos has a restaurant.

FOSSIL WALK: The hills and fields around Tarija, especially along the way to the airport, are riddled with fossils from the Pleistocene era. It is illegal to take any of these fossils out of the country, but it is fun to hunt for them. Because of the sedimentary and conglomerate rock and clay, the fossils are not hard to find. It was in this environment that the huge elephant bones now in the Archeological Museum in town were found. Take water and a sun hat as the area is excruciatingly hot.

To get here, take a bus going to the airport and get off when you can see the cliffs, gulches and open fields just above the town. From there, you can follow the pipeline or just roam.

◆ Adventures on Water

Man-made **Lake San Jacinto** is six miles/10 km out of Tarija (buses leave from the Palace of Justice every half-hour or so and cost 20¢). Get off the bus at San Jacinto and walk across the bridge that spans the dam. At the lake you can hire rowboats for a trip across the water and back. Numerous food stalls line the road to the top of the hill.

◆ Adventures on Wheels

Tarija is surrounded by interesting villages that are worth a ride to visit.

Tomatita village has a park on the banks of the Guadalquivir and Erquis rivers. The area is shaded with eucalyptus trees and the river is dotted with swimming holes. There are restaurants and *tiendas* on the main road and on the street by the river. A private pool on the opposite side of the highway is far cleaner than the river – you can play in the pool all day for just 75¢. The park has covered huts for picnics. To get here, catch a bus (20¢) marked A or B along Avenida Domingo La Paz. Along the road to San Lorenzo, near Tomatita, are numerous restaurants offering local dishes.

San Lorenzo is an interesting colonial village beyond Tomatita. Wave down a bus marked San Lorenzo in Tomatita or catch it along Avenida Domingo La Paz in Tarija. The fare is 25¢ from Tomatita and 30¢ from Tarija.

There is no place to stay here, but there are a couple of eateries on the square. The **Museum of Jose Eustaqueo Moto Mendez** (hero of the war for independence), costs 25¢ to enter. This colonial house is almost as it was when Mendez lived there. Stairs leading up to the bedrooms and balcony are made of red brick boxed in wood and the doorway to the bedroom is low. The bedroom furniture remains, but no linen has been kept. On the main floor is a collection of swords and wooden stirrups, as well as some written materials praising Mendez.

Following the road two miles in the opposite direction from the children's park will take you to the village of **El Picacho**. It is a lovely walk through farmland along a shaded road. El Picacho is on the river and there are small pools in which to wade and one large rock in the middle of the river that is the pride of the locals. From El Picacho you can take a minibus to **Corana**, where there are more swimming holes. Or you can return to Tarija.

There are no places to stay in these villages, but there are places to eat and drink. Minibuses and collectivo taxis return from the square in San Lorenzo back to Tarija. Or you may take a minibus along the main highway from Corana back to Tarija.

◆ Adventures in Nature

Cordillera de Sama Biological Reserve (35 miles/60 km from Tarija on the road to Tupiza) has two regions, the Altiplano or puna grassland and the inter-Andean valleys. It covers a total of 270,000 acres/108,500 hectares. One of the main purposes of controlling this area is the provision of unpolluted water to Tarija and surrounding villages. The rivers delivering this water are the Tolomosa, Camacho and Guadalquivir.

The puna grasslands are in the higher and drier part of the reserve and are characterized by sparse vegetation and dominated by spiky grasses. There is often a frost at night in this environment, even during the warm periods of the year. Acidic bogs are common and attract many birds like plovers and snipes. The wetlands include four permanent lakes that account for 3,200 acres/1,300 hectares of land. They are home to 41 bird species, three of which are threatened flamingos. Also, 80 migratory bird species pass through every year. Plant life in the area is delicate and includes such species as the yareta (looks like a bright green clump of moss) that grows about half an inch/one cm a year.

Archeological sites in the reserve include remains of forts and rock paintings. See Carlos and Lilo Methfessel in Tarija for tours, ☎ 664-2062.

Tariquia Biological Reserve is about 125 miles/210 km from Tarija on the Bermejo River where it meets the Rio Grande de Tarija. Access is through the village of Bermejo, on the river of the same name. The reserve butts up against Baritu Park in Argentina.

The most common wildlife species protected in the reserve are the Amazon River turtle, the Jucumari bear, the jaguar, the carpincho (caiman) and the giant anteater. The reserve is in a mountainous area with steep cliffs along the Bermejo River system.

The above two reserves are managed by **PROMETA**, Calle Alejandro del Carpio in Tarija, ☎ 664-5865, in conjunction with the National Protected Areas Service (**SERNAP**). For more information about these areas, contact PROMETA.

◆ Adventures of the Vine

Tarija is the wine center of Bolivia and the vines grow at the highest elevations in the world. There are a total of 5,700 acres/2,300 hectares of vines planted in the Tarija Valley. Because the grapes get more ultraviolet light at that elevation (8,000 ft/1,500 m), the flavor is more aromatic. A visit to at least one winery is a must.

Wine making in Bolivia was started between 1550 and 1570 by the Augustinian missionaries, who needed wine for religious purposes. Later, the mining industry of Potosi desired a stronger liquor than wine to stave off the cold and misery of their environment. The people of Singani village started distilling the wine and made a liquor that was about 40 proof. Singani, indigenous to Bolivia, is still being produced and is the alcohol used in a cocktail called a chufley. Singani can also be enjoyed straight. The grapes they used then and still use today are a muscatel variety. Singani was de-

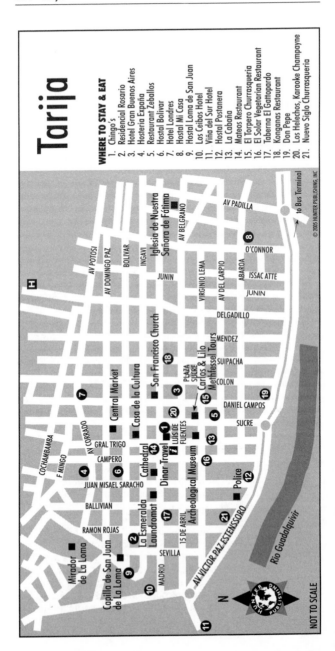

Tarija

WHERE TO STAY & EAT

1. Chingo's
2. Residencial Rosario
3. Hotel Gran Buenos Aires
4. Hostería España
5. Restaurant Zeballos
6. Hostal Bolívar
7. Hotel Londres
8. Hostal Mi Casa
9. Hostal Loma de San Juan
10. Los Ceibos Hotel
11. Viña del Sur Hotel
12. Hostal Postanera
13. La Cabaña
14. Mateos Restaurant
15. El Torpero Churrasquería
16. El Solar Vegetarian Restaurant
17. Taberna El Gattopardo
18. Konganas Restaurant
19. Don Pepe
20. Los Helechos, Karooke Champoyne
21. Nuevo Siglo Churrasquería

© 2005 HUNTER PUBLISHING, INC

NOT TO SCALE

clared an appellation of origin on May 4th, 1992 and is considered an exclusive product of Bolivia.

Although the wines have not reached the level of quality that the French or even some of the Argentinean and Chilean wines have, a wine-tasting tour is fun. Concepcion and Kolberg are the most popular brands of wine in the country, but that does not mean that they are the best. Try many – they are inexpensive – and decide for yourself. For a tour of the wineries, contact Viva Tours (☎ 663-8325, visatour@cosett.com.bo).

◆ Tour Operators

Dinar Travel 2000, Avenida Gral Trigo #579 on Plaza Luis de Fuentes, ☎ 664-8000, susyqui@olivo.tja.entelnet.bo. This company's owner, Susi Ouiroga, speaks excellent English and can help with just about any travel problem. If you have questions about travel in Bolivia before you arrive, e-mail her. This company is very honest.

Carlos and Lilo Methfessel, Calle Sucre #665, ☎ 664-2062, methfess@olivo.tja.entelnet.bo, are probably the most knowledgeable people in Bolivia in regards to rock paintings and engravings. Their place is under the sign marked Consolado de Alemania (German Consulate). They offer half- and full-day tours to the rock painting sites for $25 a half-day, $50 for a full day, with a maximum of 10 people. A full-day tour will take you to three sites. On both tours you must have good walking shoes and be able to walk for about an hour. All garbage must be carried out.

The company offers longer tours, too. For a two- or three-day tour you must book at least two days in advance. The three-day tour costs $200 per person and includes all meals and accommodations.

Viva Tours, Calle Sucre #615, ☎ 663-8325, visatour@cosett.com.bo, does a combination wine and archaeological tour that includes seeing some rock art. However, their big draw is a combination river/hiking trip on waterways in the El Chaco area in southern Bolivia that takes from four to 12 days. These trips include going into the Tariquia Biological Reserve along the Rio Grande or to Aguarague National Park. They visit cultural groups such as the Guaranies and Weenhayek.

◆ Places to Stay

Residencial Rosario, *Calle Ingavi #777 and Avenida Ramon Rojas*, residen_rosario@latinmail.com, ☎ 664-2042 or 663-6710, $, would be my first choice for an economical place to stay. It is squeaky clean with rooms around a central courtyard that has a well-tended garden. The

❖ HOTEL PRICING	
$	$10 to $20
$$	$21 to $50
$$$	$51 to $75
$$$$	$76 to $100
$$$$$	over $100

LAS COLINAS

17 rooms have large windows, tiled floors, bed lamps and clothes racks. Those with bath also have TVs. There is hot water all day, luggage storage, safe deposit and laundry service. In the lobby is a pop and water dispenser. This is a family-run hotel that has been in business for 15 years. The owners are friendly and helpful.

Hostal Hogar, *Calle Victor Paz Estenssoro, across from the bus station* ☎ *664-3964, $,* has excellent rooms with or without private bath. This family-run establishment is whistle clean.

Hostal Club Social, *Calle 15 de Abril #271,* ☎ *664-2107, $$,* is close to Plaza Sucre in a rambling old building that has seen some classy days long ago. Rooms are large and have a foyer separate from the main bedroom. Each has cable TV and a telephone, large windows and storage closet, but rather narrow beds. All the bathrooms in the building have recently been remodeled and tiled. Rates include breakfast. The hotel has an interesting display of masks. There is also a games room, a restaurant and a bar. It is clean.

Hotel Gran Buenos Aires, *Calle Daniel Campos #448, near Avenida 15 de Abril,* ☎ *663-6802, hotelgranba@hotmail.com, $$,* offers single, double and triple rooms, all carpeted and all with baths. Rates include breakfast, cable TV, fan, fridge and a large closet (with hangers). The bathrooms are tiled and a gas water heater supplies the showers; towels are provided. The windows are small but adequate. The hotel offers room service, and has an Internet café, a pizzeria and a beauty parlor. This is a good spot, but it has seen better days.

Hosteria España, *Calle Alejandro Corrado #546,* ☎ *664-3304, $$,* has accommodations with and without private baths. The rooms are cleaned regularly and well laid out, with large bathrooms, cable TV, desks, closets and fresh towels. The hotel has a nice courtyard, but you must ring the bell to get the door unlocked.

Residencial Zeballos, *Calle Sucre #966,* ☎ *664-2068, buenaireahoteles.tarija.com, $$,* is a family-run establishment. Its flowered patio has an 80 year-old grape vine acting as the roof. The grapes, when ripe, are there for guests to enjoy. Rooms have large windows, tile floors, head lamps over the beds and telephones. Those with private baths have a TV also. Rates include breakfast. This is a good choice and the owners are friendly.

Hostal Bolívar, *Calle Bolívar #256,* ☎ *664-2741, $$,* has large rooms with baths around a central courtyard. You'll notice that it's cheaper to get two single rooms than one double. Go figure. The floors are tiled and there is cable TV and a phone in all the rooms. The hotel is clean and well maintained.

Hotel Londres (London), *Calle Daniel Campos #1072,* ☎ *664-2369 or 664-2033, $$,* has large, clean and pleasant rooms with tiled floors and TVs. Pictures hang on the walls and some rooms have balconies. The shower water is supplied from a tank. Breakfast is included in the price. There is a sitting area on each floor and a roof-top terrace on the 7th floor, but no elevator.

Hostal Mi Casa, *Calle O'Connor #138,* ☎ *664-5267 or 663-6020, $$,* is comfortable and well decorated with tiles and rich, dark wood. The large rooms have closets and cupboards, lights over the beds and telephones. Breakfast is included in the room rate. The bathrooms are big and showers are separated from the rest of the bathroom. The water comes from a gas-heated water tank. There are 11 rooms in this Spanish hacienda-styled building. The travel-tour service can arrange jeep and micro bus tours. The staff is exceptionally helpful and pleasant. Mi Casa is fairly close to the bus terminal.

Hostal Martinez, *Avenida La Paz #251 and Avaroa*, ☎ 664-0222 or 663-6518, *hos_mart@oliva.tja.entelnet.bo*, **$$**, is the best bet in the mid-range. Rooms are large, tastefully decorated with matching accessories (even a bed skirt), tile floors, quality furniture and soft beds. The rooms with triple occupancy are actually two rooms with a bath in-between. Breakfast is included in the room rate. The staff is friendly and helpful. This is a good deal.

Hostal Loma de San Juan, *Calle Bolívar, in front of the San Juan Church*, ☎ 664-4522 or 663-6101, **$$$**, is the hidden gem of the city. Enclosed by a high wall covered in creeping vines, this tiny hotel offers rooms that look out on the old church or into the gardens. Rooms are large, with soft and clean carpets, rich wood cupboards, tables and chairs, color TVs and large soft beds with bed lamps. There is both a bath and shower in the tiled bathroom that has huge mirrors, and shampoo and soap provided. A buffet-style breakfast is included in your rate. A flower garden surrounds a clean pool and lawn chairs are lined up on the deck. A covered patio is at one end of the pool. Bottled water and fruit is supplied daily. If you like small, elegant and quiet, this is the place.

Hotel Los Ceibos, *Calle Victor Paz Estensoro and La Madrid*, ☎ 663-4430, *ceibohot@cosett.com.bo*, **$$$$**, is, for me, the swankiest place in town. A large and inviting foyer is filled with chairs, couches and desks and the staff is friendly and cooperative. The pool is large and clean and surrounded by a flower garden. There is a bar and restaurant, laundry service and a safe for valuables. Each big room is clean, with tiled bathrooms, comfy beds and tasteful décor. For the price, this is a good deal. Large suites consist of two rooms with an en suite bathroom, a large living room and a fully supplied kitchen. This goes for $70 and will hold up to four people.

Viña del Sur, *Zona Miraflores*, ☎ 663-2425 or 664-9041, *vinasur@olivo.tja.entelnet.bo*, **$$$$$**, is the pride of Tarija. The hotel, built in 2000, sits on a hill overlooking the river. It has rooms and suites, a small shop, restaurant, pool, gym and sauna. Rooms have wide windows, a modern heater/cool air fan, cable TV, fridge, mirror and double closets. The bath is fully tiled and the place is very clean. The staff is helpful and pleasant. Buffet breakfast is included.

Hostal Postanera, *Avenida Los Americas, corner of J.M. Saracho*, ☎ 664-2851, *www.hostal-postanera.com*, **$$$$$**, is an upscale hacienda built in an exquisite architectural design. The rooms are large, everything matches in the décor, and plants dot the halls. Each room has cable TV, closets, cupboards, and tables and chairs. Rates include a buffet breakfast (and they cater to vegetarians).

LAS COLINAS

◆ Places to Eat

La Cabaña, *Calle Gran Trigo #435, (no phone)*, is a well-kept property with a thatched roof. The tables are covered with linen tablecloths. The restaurant offers a smorgasbord of good food and you pay by the kilo.

Mateos Restaurant, *Calle Trigo and La Madrid, just off the main plaza (de Fuentes)*, has fine décor complete with an indoor fountain. Mateo's salad bar (part of the *almuerzo*) offers three or four varieties of salads that you can have before soup. There is usually a choice of

❖ RESTAURANT PRICING	
$	under $5
$$	$5 to $10
$$$	$11 to $25
$$$$	$26 to $50
$$$$$	over $50

main course foods that include chicken Milanesa or lasagna. They make real mashed potatoes (not instant) and include cooked veggies with the main course. The *almuerzo* cost $2.50 and the pop was $1 extra.

El Torpero Churrasqueria, *Calle V. Lima #226 and Daniel Campos, across from the Entel office*, is a popular place for *pique de la macho*, a meat stew loaded with spiced sausages. Locals often bring their instruments and play at this restaurant. El Torpero is set in a flowered courtyard away from the street.

El Solar Vegetarian Restaurant, *Calle V. Lima and Campero*, tries to look new wave with bold colors and oddly shaped furniture. In Bolivia, the vegetarian trend hasn't caught on yet and the beef-eating locals often poke fun at those patronizing vegan eateries. El Solar has a limited menu, but the food is good.

Cafe Mokka, *Calle15 de Abril on Plaza Sucre*, is popular. Although their bread can be a bit stale, it is of better quality than breads offered at many other places. The food is good and moderate in quantity. The sandwich with fries that I had cost $1.75 and was stuffed with cheese, tomato, lettuce, onion and meat.

Taberna El Gattopardo, *Calle La Madrid #318*, ☎ *663-0656, on Plaza Luis de Fuentes*, has tourism figured out. It is open from 8 am until midnight every day, including holidays. You can sit on the street or inside at the open windows or deep inside where the décor is pleasing and the beggars can't get at you. The restaurant has an à la carte menu and offers dishes like omelets and spaghetti. Prices are higher here than at places patronized mostly by locals. This is a popular restaurant with the over-21 crowd, both local and tourist. The food is good and the portions almost adequate.

Konganas Restaurant, *Calle Virginia Lima and Avenida Suipacha #786*, ☎ *611-2452*, offers set meals like spaghetti or goulash for about $2 per plate. The inside of the restaurant is dimly lit and nicely decorated. There is also an outdoor patio and tables on the street so you can watch the action on Plaza Sucre. The food is good, but the portions are small.

Don Pepe, *Calle David Campos #138*, ☎ *664-2426*, is a classy place. Waiters are dressed in black and white, drinks are watered down and meals are excellent. Steaks are smothered in salty mushroom gravy, cooked as requested. The service was excellent, the music classical and everything was clean.

Chingo's, *Plaza Sucre*, ☎ *664-4864*, is where young locals come to drink and party. They celebrate football game losses and wins, graduations, weddings and christenings, or anything else they can think of. Occasionally, they even eat. The steak specialty at $3.50 is good. Go here if you want to hang with the local younger crowd.

Nuevo Siglo Churrasqueria, *Avenida Los Americas #888,* ☎ 664-6488, has good meat. The steak is recommended, but the best dish is *piquante de gallina* (chicken).

Los Helechos, *Avenida Avaroa, half a block up from the train station*, offers breakfast of meusli, yogurt and fruit. This is fairly uncommon in Bolivia. They also have pizza and hamburgers, chicken and omelets, desserts and beer. The prices are good and so are the meals – especially breakfast.

◆ Nightlife

Karaoke Champayne, 15 de Abril #274 and Calle Sucre, is a dark and dingy place where all sorts of sins can be indulged, especially being inebriated. The place is popular with locals.

◆ Shopping

Artesanias Andaluz, Calle 15 de Abril, between Avenida Daniel Campos and Calle Sucre, ☎ 664-3709, offers well-crafted leather articles, straw weavings from the same type of grasses that are used to make Panama hats, and I got a butterfly collection (11 mounted) for $20. This is the best shop in Tarija for souvenirs.

Café Royal, Calle Ungavi #371 and Avenida Gran Trigo, sells local coffee beans that cost anywhere from 75¢ to $2 per kilo, depending on quality. It has a grinder, if you need it. Coffee is a good gift for friends and this is a place to replenish your own supply.

Camiri

Altitude: 8,224 ft/2,500 m
Population: 3,000

Camiri, also known as the capital of black gold, is an oil-boom town connected to the Chaco, though it is really tucked into the foothills almost 6,000 ft/2,000 m above Villamontes. The greater height makes the climate pleasant. The people are friendly and often take the time to chat.

◆ Getting Here & Away

Buses coming from the south start at Yacuiba, on the southern border. One leaves in the morning and then a number of buses leave at night. You can catch these buses either at the border or in Villamontes.

There are shared taxis between Villamontes and Camiri. The last one leaves around noon going in either direction (see *Villamontes*).

Numerous buses go to Santa Cruz from Camiri, but only one leaves during the day (8 am). There is no bus terminal in town. The bus companies are all on Calle Bolívar and Cochabamba. Most buses leave for Santa Cruz around 7 pm and the cost is $7 per person. The company with the most comfortable buses is Guzman and their buses (two of them) leave at 7 pm.

LAS COLINAS

◆ Places to Stay

Hotel Oriente, *Calle Comercio #78*, ☎ *952-2564*, *$*, has 22 rooms plus a garden and sitting area. The reception and patio are decorated with old instruments and Bolivian hats. The rooms are clean and the owner is friendly. Consequently, they have many return guests. There is also a car park. The hotel was the first in the town and is about 50 years old, but the present owner has had it for about 10 years. There are connections to Che Guevera: Che stayed in the owner's uncle's place and the uncle remembers him.

Hotel Sun, *Avenida Busch #39*, ☎ *952-4444*, *$*, has 30 beds in clean rooms. Breakfast is included in the price. The owners are helpful and pleasant. The first tourists they ever had were two Canadian cyclists with whom they still communicate.

Alojamiento Londres, *Avenida Busch #154*, ☎ *952-2726*, *$*, is basic and the communal bathrooms fall under the primitive category. This is more a Bolivian guy's place. However, Che Guevera stayed in room #4 during his run through to Valle Grande. There are elders of the village who remember Che's visit.

Residencial Primer, *Avenida Busch #60*, ☎ *952-2204*, *$$*, is a nice place and the owner is friendly and helpful. All rooms have large windows, towels, toilet paper, a large closet, balcony and remote control for the cable TV. Those with air conditioning and TV cost a little extra. There is a lounge area.

J. R. Hotel, *Avenida Sanchez #247*, ☎ *952-2200*, *$$*, has 17 large rooms and a pleasant sitting area on every floor. Each room has air conditioning, cable TV, private bath, gas-heated hot water, big windows, telephones, tile floors, towels and curtains that match the bedspreads. The price includes breakfast. There is also a restaurant, bar and car park on site.

Samaipata

Altitude: 5,000 ft/1,520 m
Population: 20,000

Samaipata is a colonial village tucked into the hills above Santa Cruz and overlooking the sandstone mountains of Amboro National Park. To visit Samaipata, you need time. The place makes you slow down and enjoy a tea at the Vesperes Garden Café or a cake from the German bakery. The comfortable climate and spectacular surroundings bring out even the most bored person's desire to explore.

There are long and short hikes around Samaipata and there are historical horse routes that can be followed. Visits to Amboro and the ruins of El Fuerte are a must. Whether you like to use a guide or go it alone, the area is perfect for exploring.

Places to stay are varied, but most are upscale in comfort while moderate in price. Samaipata is also trying to compete with Santa Cruz for culinary excellence and is giving them a good run.

◆ Getting Here & Around

Micros and shared taxis go from Santa Cruz to Samaipata. A shared taxi with four passengers costs $3.50 per person and takes about three hours. Vehicles leave Santa Cruz from Calle Omar Chavez and Soliz de Hulguin, around the corner from the old bus terminal. There is a daily bus that goes to Cochabamba along the old road and passes through Samaipata. It leaves from the bi-model station at 4 pm.

From Sucre there is one bus a day and it passes through Samaipata during the night. From Cochabamba there is a bus that passes daily but, again, it is a night bus. Going to Cochabamba, you should purchase a ticket through one of the tour agents or go to Mairana, 10 miles/16 km down the road from Samaipata, and catch the bus there as it does not stop in Samaipata if it is full.

◆ History

The present Samaipata was founded in 1680. There are two theories as to the meaning of the name; one from the local culture means a "resting place," while the word from the Tihuanacan language means a "marriage place." About 20 years ago, Europeans started buying property here. It seems they now own half the town. You know what that means – hot showers, real coffee, good bread, English.

◆ Sightseeing

The Plaza in Samaipata is the most interesting in all of Bolivia. It has stone works that are reproductions of the carvings at El Fuerte.

On the east side of the plaza a circular step sits in front of a sculpture. Stand at the side of the circle and say something to the statue and then stand in the center of the circle and say the same thing. You'll hear an echo when you are in the circle. This phenomenon came about by accident.

El Fuerte is open daily, 9 am-5 pm. It is the second-largest ruin in Bolivia and during its time must have been quite an impressive city. The first excavations started in 1951 and after the importance of the fort was realized, it was declared a national monument. More excavations didn't occur again until 1974 and then again it was left until 1992.

The site's main ceremonial center is a huge carved outcropping 658 ft long by 18 wide and 82 high (200 x 60 x 25 m) with niches that at one time held gold-plated statues. There was a virgins' quarters that held about 2,000 virgins and a grand plaza. There are signs of buildings lying under the present structures that indicate an earlier civilization having been there prior to the Tihuanacans and Inca.

The center has three creatures carved into the top of the outcropping. The first is the snake that, to the Inca and pre-Inca civilizations, represented the underworld. The canals that are part of the snake carvings are believed to have carried blood, water or *chicha* during religious ceremonies. The second animal, on the lower top surface of the rock, is a puma, which represented life on earth. A photograph taken in 1945 shows the outline in the rock of three cats, rather than just one. Because the rock is so soft, the image has been worn away by weather. The final image, near the puma, is of the condor that represented the afterlife, or life in the heavens. The seats carved into the south-central side of the rock suggest people sat there to watch ceremonies.

Located just south of the ceremonial area was the Five Bakers' Temple. This site is under the care of Stonewatch (an organization that monitors and protects significant stones worldwide). One of the reasons for their interest in the ruin is that the sandstone on which it sits is thought to be like a sponge. During rainy season the rock is saturated and during dry season the water seeps out of the rock onto the ground. There are only two or three places in the world where this occurs.

Although the site isn't breathtaking, it is impressive and should not be missed. There is an elaborate wooden infrastructure built around the rock, with viewing platforms. Take binoculars.

Much of the information I received about the ruins came from the works of Hugo Buero and Oswald Rivera Sundt and was told to me by Olaf Liebhart of Roadrunners.

To get to El Fuerte you can take any vehicle going toward Santa Cruz and get off at the road that leads uphill to the ruins. There is a sign. The walk from the road is 4.3 miles/seven km. This is a long haul with good views. Alternately, you can join a tour.

Another option is to take an overnight horse trip to the ruins. This includes spending one night close to the headwaters of the Pirai River. On the second day you would arrive on Cerro del Inca and walk down to the ruins. The ride back to Samaipata is in a vehicle. The cost is $155 per person if two people go and $123 if three or more go.

◆ Adventures in Culture

If visiting the small museum in Sampaipata, your entry ticket covers both the ruins and the museum. You cannot pay for only one place. However, the museum is worth it. And to appreciate the ruins, you need information. Foreigners pay $3, while locals pay $1.75. The museum is open Monday to Saturday, 8:30 am-12:30 pm and 2:30-6:30 pm. The ruins are open daily, 9 am-5 pm.

The museum has a scaled model of El Fuerte in one room with photos of what it looked like when it was first found.

◆ Adventures on Foot

CERRO INCA: Walking to this hill is recommended because it gives a view of the entire site of El Fuerte. From the hill you can see the carved ceremonial outcropping, the place where the grand plaza stood and the field where the huge administrative building may have been.

From the ruins where the fence is located, follow the trail downhill and away from the parking lot. When you come to a fork, go to the left and continue down to the river. Cross the river on dry rocks; the wet ones are slippery. Go straight up from the river. At the top, the red rock walls near Amboro National Park and clouds over the rainforest can be seen. The curious condors in this area seem to like to keep an eye on people.

Roadrunners Tour Company (see *Tour Operators*, below) in Samaipata will rent a GPS with the route of this climb mapped out. If you feel you would like to use one, see them in town. You must leave your passport as security.

> ### ❖   TRUMPET OF DEATH
>
> Trumpet flowers, common to the valley are white or pink in color and look like trumpets. They are beautiful to look at but deadly to eat.

CERRO DE LA PATRIA: To get here from the center of town follow the signs uphill to the Campeche Cabins. Cross the soccer field in front of Campeche and walk along the edge of the forest until you come to a road. Follow it to the end and then head up the mountain. Be aware that snakes like to curl up in the grass. On top of the hill is a wire fence. Cross it and go left. After a short distance there are some stone circles, actually Inca silos. Return by the same way. This is a two-hour walk.

CONDOR HIKE: For those with a strong leg and determined spirit, this hike will take you to where condors meet, nest and bathe in natural rock pools. However, the hike is about four hours straight up (don't forget the heat) to a ridge where these magnificent birds hang out. You may do this either as a long one-day trip or as a two-day trip with an overnight at La Pajcha Waterfall.

Pieter at La Vispera has found this spot, developed the route and knows the easiest way to get there (although no way is really easy). You must see Pieter in order to do this hike.

The one-day trip costs $41 per person for a group of two, $31 per person for a group of three and $26 per person for a group of four. The two-day trip costs $72 per person for a group of two, $55 per person for a group of three and $45 per person for a group of four. Prices include a guide and transportation. Meals and gear are extra.

LA PAJCHA: This three-tiered waterfall drops about 115 ft/35 m and is tucked into a cathedral of vegetation. The falls end in a cool pool beside a sandy beach. The pool is just made for swimming. If you have a tent, it is possible to camp here. However, it is difficult to reach on your own. It is advisable to join a tour or hire a private taxi that will take up to four people for $30.

To get there, take the road going south from Samaipata for 25 miles/ 41 km and walk about five miles along a path through the jungle. There is a sign indicating the turnoff. The walk will reveal some interesting vegetation and some birds, but nothing as compared to what is in Amboro. There is a fee of 75¢ to enter the falls area.

LAGUNA VOLCAN: This clean little lake is tucked into a flat area above the village of Bermejo. To get there, take a bus going toward Bermejo and get off .6 miles/one km before the village. A sign indicates the turnoff. Walk uphill to the north (toward the park) for two to three hours. There is a cost of 75¢ to enter the area.

LAS COLINAS

QUIRUSILLAS: This is a place to spend a laid-back weekend in a relaxed community and/or to visit the lake. Quirusillas is 18 miles/30 km from Samaipata on a secondary road going south. It sits where three valleys meet. A nine-mile/15-km circular route goes from the village to the lake and back. This lake is where the community gets its water supply.

The ridge above the lake offers views of Vallegrande Valley (southwest) 34 miles/55 km away, Mairana and Samaipata (northeast). To the southeast is Postrer Valle, where Che Guevera fought one of his less famous battles.

◆ Adventures on Wheels

SALT ROAD TO SUCRE: This is a 4x4 trip along an old salt trade route that goes 276 miles/450 km. It takes about four days with camping along the way. It can include a side excursion to the colonial and historic town of Vallegrande. Sunday is market day in Vallegrande.

But first there is a stop at **Mataral**, where there are some 10,000-year-old rock paintings. From Vallegrande, you drive to Pucara where you can take another side-trip to La Higuera, where Guevera was killed. From there you climb out of the humid climate of the forest and get the cooler valleys of the foothills near Tarabuco and then go on to Sucre.

AMBORO NATIONAL PARK: Amboro is accessed from the new road between Cochabamba and Santa Cruz. It is about 62 miles/102 km (three hours by car) west of Santa Cruz. You can also get to Amboro from the old road that passes through Samaipata. There are two main areas to visit, the fern grove and the higher canyon area.

Four major rivers pass through the park. The **Yapacani**, a major tributary to the Amazon that can get as wide as 2,600 ft/800 m in places, serves as a park border. Another important river is the **Surutu** that passes close to Buena Vista and has hiking trails along its banks. These rivers also offer canoeing and rafting opportunities.

Macuñucu Tropical Forest is a popular destination because of its 132-ft/ 40-m waterfall that has a swimming pool at the bottom and a cave system nearby. Hugging this waterfall are some of the 2,961 species of plants that have been identified in the park, belonging to a total of 200 families. The most impressive are the 33-ft/10-m arboreal ferns that date back about 300 million years. They are in the rainforest. But the trees include everything from pine to palm with many serving as hosts to about 100 varieties of orchids and bromeliads.

Within the forests and along the rivers are 127 species of mammals and 815 species of birds (60% of the country's total). These include the more common rock hens, blackbirds and condors. Over 100 species of reptiles have been identified and 43 species of bats.

There are three ways to get into the park. At the western end, a 4x4 road leads from Mairana on the highway toward Cochabamba. It goes eight miles/13 km to La Yunga, from where you can walk into the forest along a track.

If you continue by jeep along the road back toward Samaipata, it goes another 11 miles/18 km to Lautas and then up to Los Alisos or back down to

Samaipata. These are difficult roads and not recommended during rainy season. The walking trails that go between the curves on the road are great for seeing wildlife.

The second entry point into the park is from Achira Cabins, six miles/ 10 km east along the road toward Santa Cruz from Samaipata. The road into the park is a four-wheel-drive track that goes to Abra los Toros. From there you can start hiking into the fern forest. There are also the remains of an Inca fortress along the way.

The southwestern part of the park is where giant ferns, mosses and bromeliads are located. Five hundred orchid species have been found in the rainforest here, along with with numerous plants that are often used for medicine by naturopaths (like the cats claw, used to fight cancer).

> ❖ **MOSES CACTUS**
>
> Yucca is the tall plant that has a bunch of white flowers on top. The shape of the cluster looks like a beard, so locals call the plant the Moses cactus.

The center of the park has deep canyons formed by swift rivers. Mountains rise up above these canyons and many are dotted with bamboo groves. The lowlands of the northern area are rich in bird life. One of the rarer birds in the area is the quetzal, with its 3.5-ft/one-meter tail feathers of the kind used by the Aztecs in Mexico to make Montezuma's cape.

For a good trip, I suggest hiring a guide or a tour company. They know where to go, how to get there and what to look for. If you are interested in the fern forest, you will get rain; if you are interested in the rugged rocks and canyons, you will get heat. A tour company can help you make decisions and make certain you see most of what you would like to see.

◆ Adventures on Horseback

CHE GUEVERA TRAIL TO VALLEGRANDE: Every October, Bolivians visit the school where Guevera was killed. They celebrate the anniversary of his death. Che is more of a mythological than political hero, as he is in the rest of the world. No one knows his real story or is interested in his communist ideology. He gave his life trying to fight the establishment. Plus, he was handsome. These are the important facts.

This horse trip takes anywhere from six to nine days and covers about 80 miles/130 km of trail. La Vispera (see *Tour Operators*) has horses and tents for rent; they charge $100 for the trip. The route follows a secondary road from Samaipata to San Juan del Rosario, past La Pajcha waterfall, and on down to Postrer Valle. Some of the villages en route are 600 years old and not a part of our electronic age and lifestyle.

Eventually, you must cross two passes to reach Tierras Nuevas and then cross over to Vallegrande, close to La Higuera, where Che Guevera died. From the ridge, you will be able to see the ravine where the battle took place. You can visit the school room in the village where he was shot.

In Vallegrande where Guevera's body was put in storage (and on display) is the **Che Guevera Museum**. The tomb of Tania, Guevera's friend, is in the graveyard. Guevera's grave under the tarmac is now empty because his body has been sent to Cuba. The body was kept in the laundry room in the Knights of Malta Hospital before it was buried, and that room, too, is open for view. This is also where Rodriguez (CIA agent) brought the dead body of Che out and held him up so he appeared still alive (complete with open eyes) for journalists to photograph. You can purchase copies of the photos taken during this event.

Hotel Ganadero, Calle Bolivar #115, ☎ 492-2176, is clean and the place to stay in town. However, there are two other choices I can recommend: **Alojamiento Teresita**, Mendosa #107, ☎ 492-2151, and **Residencial Valle Grande**, just up from Teresita (no phone). Both are good and a bit cheaper than the Ganadero. Should you be here during a festival and can't find a room, locals will offer you their home. Ask around.

From Vallegrande, there are two routes back to Samaipata. Pieter, from whom you rented the horse at La Vispera, will advise you because the conditions (and thus the route) depend on what time of year you travel.

❖ THE LIFE & DEATH OF CHE GUEVERA

Che Guevera was born in 1928 in Argentina. He suffered from asthma and because of this was unable to participate in many children's games. Instead, he read from his father's collections of Marx, Engels and Freud. As a university student, Che became anti-Peron, although he never participated in the demonstrations that called for Peron's fall.

Guevera studied medicine and specialized in dermatology in general and leprosy in particular. But he was a restless sort with socialist ideals, so in 1949 he took his famous motorbike trip north, working along the way at everything from ditch digging to practicing as a doctor in specialized clinics for leprosy. In 1951 he arrived in the United States.

He came to Bolivia in 1952 to be part of the revolution that was occurring at the time. But he found it an opportunists' revolution (not pure enough) and refused to participate. Instead, he went to Guatemala where he earned a living writing travel articles. At that time he became an even purer socialist and rejected most forms of communism. He lived with Hilda Gadea, an Indian and Marxist who helped Che with his indoctrination. She also married him.

In 1954, Che met Raul and Fidel Castro in Mexico City and followed them to Cuba where he studied guerrilla warfare. He became ruthless in his methods of ruling, shooting, without question, those who turned against Castro or the revolution. He hated a turncoat. He also hated cowards, so he shot them too. With this type of dedication it didn't take long for Che to become Fidel's top man.

After the success in Cuba, restlessness and desire for revolution continued to drive Che. He divorced Hilda and married Olidia. Together they visited the Congo in Africa and then Che came to Bolivia believing that the country, because of its poverty, was ripe for insurrection. Also, the 12-year-long so-cialistic rule of the MNR was over and the generals were back in power, rolling back the clock, in Che's opinion. Bolivia also bordered five countries, so the spread of the revolution would be easy. Che entered Bolivia on November 1st, 1966. The miners were on strike but he failed to see this as the place to start. Possibly, this was his great error. Unions have leaders and Che wanted to be the leader. Instead, he formed a guerrilla training camp in Santa Cruz that attracted a few men but got no sympathy or support from the locals.

In the meantime, the US, still smarting about the Cuban Rev-olution and the Bay of Pigs, was tracking Che. A CIA agent by the name of Felix Rodriguez worked with the Bolivian army in the hunt. The first thing they did when they got in the vicinity of Guevera's army, in order to get support of the locals, was drop pamphlets from the air saying they would pay $4,200 for the capture of Guevera. Rodrequez then led a 650-man bat-talion into the area near Vallegrande.

Between March and August 1967, Che and the Bolivian mili-tary had skirmishes, but nothing serious happened until Au-gust 31, when the army killed about one third of Che's men. They also captured Che's best soldier, Paco. Che retreated and his asthma started to cause him great discomfort.

During his retreat toward the south, Che went to Alto Seco to buy food and spend the night, but he learned that one of the locals had gone to inform the military of his presence. So Che and his men went to Loma Larga, a ranch between Alto Seco and La Higuera. The peasants living there fled. Che contin-ued on to Vallegrande, but he found that there, too, most of the villagers were absent. Shots could be heard in the dis-tance and Che quickly surmised that they meant the Bolivian military was hot on his tail. So he and his men moved toward Valle Serrano, south of Rio Grande. He thought that if he got across the border into Paraguay he would be safe.

The group was camped on the Yuro River when an old lady passed by. Che paid her to keep quiet about their presence. However, it was an old woman who told the military that she heard voices of men on the Yuro River near San Antonio. It has never been confirmed that it was the same lady, but chances are good that it was.

The final battle started along the Yuro River. Che was shot in the leg and, as he retreated, he was hit several more times. His follower, Sarabia, picked him up and ran. Che lost his hat. Sarabia sat down in an open area and tried to defend Che. They both shot at the military but the army circled them, filling Che with bullets. He could no longer hold his gun and fire at the same time. At one point, Che shouted that he was worth more alive than dead. He surrendered. The battle ended at 3:30 pm with Che being taken prisoner. Carried on a stretcher to La Higuera, Che was placed in a school house where he lay in the dirt, arms and legs tied, hair matted, clothes torn, bullet wounds adding to his discomfort. He was also having trouble breathing. Rodriguez arrived in a helicopter. He took some photos of Che and of his diary and then, against the advice of his bosses, gave the orders to execute Guevera. Rodriguez also warned the firing squad not to shoot Guevera in the face because he wanted it to look like Guevera had been killed in battle. As Che stood facing the firing squad his last words were, "Know this now, you are killing a man."

After Che died, Rodriguez took Che's Rolex watch and later showed his souvenir to newspaper reporters. He also stored the body in the laundry room of the hospital. When journalists wanted proof that Che was still alive, the military men brought the body out and held Guevera up so he looked like he possibly could be alive. His eyes were still open. The journalists took their photos. However, when the reports went into the Pentagon, there were discrepancies. The Pentagon wanted Guevera alive and the journalists reported that he was alive. If he had died in battle as Rodriguez told the Pentagon, he should have been dead 24 hours before the time that was reported on his death certificate. Rodriguez, tried to cover his tracks. In doing this, he had Che's hands cut off to prove this was the right man. He buried the rest of Che in an unmarked grave under the tarmac of the airport at Vallegrande. As for the newspaper reports, everyone knows that journalists never get anything correct.

◆ Tour Operators

Roadrunner, ☎ 944-6193, is run by Olaf Liebhart and his partner, Frank. They are a wealth of knowledge about the area. They rent GPSs, with a number of different routes keyed in, for $10 per day. You must leave your passport as a guarantee. Roadrunner charges $10 per person for a day trip to El Fuerte (up to four people). The price drops with more people. It also runs trips into the north end of Amboro National Park for two days. These cost $50 per person, with a minimum of two people, and $30 per person if there is a group of five. The $2.50 park entry fee is not included in the price of the trip.

Gilberto Aguilera, Calle Sucre #2, ☎ 944-6050, is the most respected guide in the entire village. He takes individuals or groups to Amboro National Park, Las Cuevas and La Pajcha. Gilberto is often hired by tour agencies in town and his knowledge of the area is second to none. If you book with an agency, ask if Gilberto can go along as your guide.

Michael Blendinger, Calle Bolívar, across from the museum, ☎ 944-6186, mblendinger@cotas.com.bo, offers all the usual tours and is willing to customize a trip to meet your needs. Michael is a biologist who speaks English, German and Spanish; his English is exceptional. Michael is a landscape photographer and specializes in birding tours. He offers a trip into Amboro where, during dry season, you leave your gear with donkeys

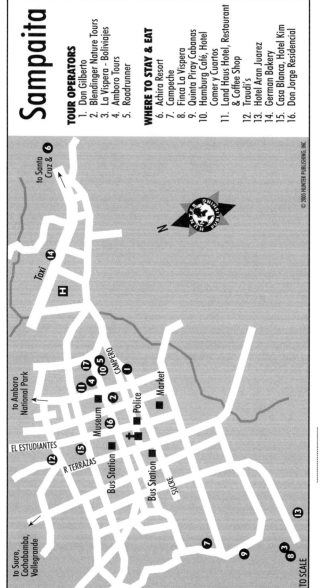

Sampaita

TOUR OPERATORS
1. Don Gilberto
2. Blendinger Nature Tours
3. La Vispera - Boliviajes
4. Amboro Tours
5. Roadrunner

WHERE TO STAY & EAT
6. Achira Resort
7. Campeche
8. Finca La Vispera
9. Quinta Piray Cabanas
10. Hamburg Café, Hotel
    Comer y Cuartos
11. Land Haus Hotel, Restaurant
    & Coffee Shop
12. Traudi's
13. Hotel Aran Juarez
14. German Bakery
15. Casa Blanca, Hotel Kim
16. Don Jorge Residencial

to Santa Cruz & 6

Taxi

to Amboro National Park

EL ESTUDIANTES

Museum

R TERRAZAS

Bus Station

Police

Market

Bus Station

SUCRE

to Sucre, Cochabamba, Vallegrande

NOT TO SCALE

LAS COLINAS

N

© 2005 HUNTER PUBLISHING, INC

that take a different route as you go through a gorge just big enough for a human to pass. Michael does a lot of photography and some photos have been on exhibition at the tourist office in Santa Cruz.

La Vispera rents horses for $3 an hour. They will also take you on a six- to nine-day trip from Samaipata to Villegrande and back to Samaipata or on to Sucre. Pieter at La Vispera runs a 4x4 trip that goes along the old salt trade route to Sucre. This is a four-day excursion (see above). Pieter will also hike from his place cross-country up to El Fuerte, arriving at the ruins from the backside. The only downside of this trip is that, after hiking all day, the final lap is an upward slog. However, what you will see is worth 10 slogs. The cost is $24 per person (minimum of two people) and the price drops to $8 per person if 15 people go.

A one-day trip into Amboro National Park for two people costs $28 per person, while an overnight trip costs $140 per person. This includes cooks, pack mules, meals and camping equipment, plus an English-speaking guide. It does not cover the $2.50 park entry fee, a sleeping bag or mat. One trip done by this company for the first time ever was a hike across the park from La Vispera, an 18-day trip. Ask about it.

Amboro Tours, Calle Bolívar #43 (across from the museum), ☎ 944-6293, is operated by the ex-director of Amboro National Park. They offer three trips into the park that take from one to three days. The first is to the volcano, the second is through the fern forest and the third is along the Rafael River to the Devil's Tooth.

◆ Places to Stay

Samaipata streets often lack names. However, the community is small enough that locating hotels and restaurants is easy. If you need direction, ask a local.

❖ HOTEL PRICING	
$	$10 to $20
$$	$21 to $50
$$$	$51 to $75
$$$$	$76 to $100
$$$$$	over $100

Mi Casa, *across from Casa Blanca, $,* has no phone and only five rooms with either private or shared baths. The rooms are basic, with bamboo and thatch roofs and brick floors.

Chilo Residencial, ☎ 944-6014, *$,* is freshly painted. The central courtyard has been spruced up and everything is clean. Hot water is available all day and some rooms have TV. This is a good deal.

> **AUTHOR NOTE:** *I would stay at the three hotels around the square – the Paola, Familiar and the Rosario – only as a last resort.*

Hostal Kim, ☎ 944-6161, *$,* has basic clean rooms set around a small courtyard. They come with or without private bath. This is a small and friendly place. The entrance is inviting, decorated with plants and trees.

Don Jorge Residencial *just down from the Hamburg,* ☎ 944-6086, *$,* has clean basic rooms with bath. This is a good deal.

La Vispera, ☎ 944-6082, www.lavispera.org, *$/$$,* is .5 miles/one km uphill from the center of town and is run by Dutch ex-pats, Margarita and Pieter. La Vispera is highly recommended, especially for a long rest. The rooms are exceptional and the gardens could be classed as the botanical garden of Samaipata. Margarita and Pieter have lived in Bolivia for 19 years. They speak Dutch, German, English and Spanish and can arrange tours, answer questions, take time to have a tea or rent you a place to stay. The food here is excellent (see *Places to Eat*).

Room rates are higher for advance reservations. The rooms are clean and comfortable with soft beds and shared bathrooms. Kitchen facilities are available and tiled porches allow you to sit and enjoy the hummingbirds buzzing around or view the distant hills dotted with white haciendas. Cabins have bedrooms, living/sitting rooms, fully supplied kitchens, private bathrooms with gas-heated water and a private porch. A **camping** area has two gas-heated showers, separate toilets in a modern tiled building, a full kitchen and a barbecue pit. If the conditions are good, Pieter can supply wood for a campfire. Tenting costs $3 per person if you have your own tent and $4 per person if you use one of theirs.

I noticed dozens of hummingbirds and the other birds I was unable to identify were numerous. Ornithologists stay at La Vispera to work.

Pieter and Margarita will arrange your pickup from the airport in Santa Cruz for a small fee. Should you wish to spend a night in Santa Cruz and then visit a few hot spots on the way to Samaipata, that too can be arranged. This must be negotiated with Pieter or Margarita.

❖ HOT POTS

There are clay ovens throughout Bolivia that people still use for cooking. The one above the garden at La Vispera was built by Pieter. The ovens sit on a layer of bricks that have an eight-inch layer of salt beneath. The salt helps get and keep the temperature of the oven high by reflecting heat. To make the oven, the first layer of mud is mixed with straw and placed on a wooden frame. The mud is covered with strands of straw placed in the same direction. When this dries, a second layer of mud is laid and a second layer of straw is placed with strands going in the opposite direction to the layer below. This process is repeated until the clay/mud is nine to 12 inches thick. A fire is made inside and burned for four hours until the temperature reaches about 1,300°F/700°C. The fire is then hot enough for the oven to be used for 24 hours. To maintain a cooking temperature after that, a fire is built for one hour a day.

Land Haus Rooms, ☎ *944-6033, $$,* is up from the square three blocks and at the same place as the restaurant. Follow the signs. Rooms and cabins here hold anywhere from two to seven people. They have a private bathroom, TV, sitting area, full kitchen and a patio with a barbecue pit. Larger, more expensive cabins have fridges, two-burner stoves, double beds, separate shower stalls in the bathrooms, a dining/sitting area and fireplaces.

The yard is manicured and has old trees and flowering bushes, including a grape canopy over a large picnic table. The patios are all tile and flagstone. A swimming pool and dry sauna can be used for $20 per group for up to four hours. The sauna is large and well made and sits beside a massage mat (bring your own therapist) and a cold shower. Guests may pick fruit from the trees in the yard, which is peppered with hammocks. The two big pluses to this place are its proximity to town and the café and restaurant on the premises. This allows you to eat, drink and roll into bed all in one smooth movement.

If coming from Sucre, the bus will let you off at the bottom of the road and you need to walk only 500 ft/150 m to the hotel. German and English are spoken.

Quinta Piray, ☎ 944-6136, quinta-piray@cotas.com.bo, $$, is another top-notch place. It's set on the hill overlooking town. The large piece of property has maintained gardens and a lawn dotted with white plaster cabins topped in red tiled roofs. The cabins hold anywhere from two to six people; the large ones have two bedrooms and two bathrooms. Some have fireplaces and all have barbecue pits. They are self contained and hospital-clean. Rates vary from $20 for two, mid-week, to $130 for six during a holiday. This is a gem of a place. To get here, follow the hill to the right at the fork that leads to La Vispera and Traudi's.

Traudi's, ☎ 944-6094, $$, is across the way from La Vispera. Rooms come with or without bath and private cabins are available for larger groups. The semi-detached cabins (row houses) are clean and comfortable. There is a large pool for guests to use and a kitchen where breakfast can be ordered in advance. This place is peaceful, with sheep and horses mowing the lawns. If you wish to be left alone and never bothered, except for a cleaning lady wanting to fix up your mess, this is the place. The area has lots of birds and frogs to watch during the day and fireflies at night.

Casa Blanca, ☎ 944-6076, $$$, has three floors of spacious and clean rooms around a central courtyard. All the rooms have private bath and those from the second floor up are new. They have nice furniture, soft beds and tiled floors. Breakfast is included in the rate.

Hostal Campeche, ☎ 333-6607, www.campechebolivia.com, $$$, is a member of the International Hosteling Association. Up on the hill, the cabins are built on a slope overlooking town. Room rates range from $12.50 per person in the middle of the week to $120 for a six-person cabin during holidays. Some accommodations have only a room with a private bath, while the bigger places are two-bedroom, two-bathroom cabins with fully supplied kitchens, living and sitting rooms and a terrace with a built-in barbecue. There's a café and restaurant on site. The cabins have a lot of stonework around them and the rooms are bright.

Hotel Comer y Cuartos, $$$, is a new building just up from the Hamburg. The rooms are clean and moderate in size. The cost is $20 for a room with bath and $10 for a room without. This place can be a bit noisy when table tennis is being played in the main foyer.

Hotel Aran Juarez, on the highway at the entrance to the village, ☎ 944-6223, $$$, is the hotel that was robbed by the followers of Che Guevera during his fatal trip into the area. From the hotel, the bandits moved to the hospital and relieved them of valuables and medical equipment (which the bandits were really going to need) before heading down to Vallegrande. For visitors today, the hotel is clean, free of militant communists and comfortable.

Achira Sierra Resort, *six miles/10 km from Samaipata on the road to Santa Cruz*, ☎ 352-2288, $$$, www.achiraresort.com, is the Bolivian version of Club Med, except that it caters to larger groups. The smallest cabin (except for the honeymoon suite), holds four people and the largest holds 18. Each place is self-contained and the grounds have a pool, tennis court, volleyball court, ping pong, a games room, mini golf, shuffle board, a restaurant and a bar. Rates run anywhere from $15 for a single to $95 for the largest cabin. A campsite on the 14-acre property is tucked into an orange grove and is equipped with tables and barbecue pits. The cost is $2 per person, per night.

◆ Places to Eat

Hamburg Café, ☎ 944-6153, is decked in antiques and has a nice ambiance. It carries only Bolivian wines. The curried chicken was exceptional, but the omelet was less than ordinary. The Milanesa should have had an extra dish of vegetables with it. However, all dishes run about

❖ RESTAURANT PRICING	
$	under $5
$$	$5 to $10
$$$	$11 to $25
$$$$	$26 to $50
$$$$$	over $50

$3.50, a definite bargain. The Hamburg also has an Internet café with one machine. Internet access is via phone lines in Samaipata, so the service is slow. Also, it is available only from 7 pm to 7 am on weekdays and all day on weekends. The cost is about $2 an hour. The café's book exchange has a strange policy. All books exchanged must be the same size and in the same condition as the one taken. The literary content is irrelevant.

La Vispera will give you a breakfast in their Garden Café as long as you order ahead. The cost for pancakes and coffee is $1.50. They also serve muesli with fresh fruit and yogurt. Their lunchtime specialty is soup with scones and they claim it as the best in the village. I found the garden irresistible. The Garden Café is also open for theme suppers and offers traditional Dutch meals once a week. This includes *hutspot*, or red cabbage. Rhubarb pie is available almost all the time, as are herbs for tea picked fresh from the garden.

Land Haus Restaurant, Café and Artists' Shop, ☎ 44-6257, landhaus@cotas.com.bo, is close to the center and is the best restaurant in the village. It serves real filtered coffee, not espresso watered down. The owner is a professional chef and his baked goods go well with the coffee. The restaurant is open Thursday to Sunday, 6 pm-midnight. There is a salad bar offered on weekends. The house specialties are German dishes. The food is good, the portions large and the prices reasonable ($5 each). Vegetarian fare is available. The family comes from a line of chefs so good food is a way of life.

The **German Bakery** carries fresh French bread, numerous kinds of cookies and chocolate brownies; it sells all the teas and conserves made by Margarita at La Vispera.

Chakana Restaurant, *on the plaza*, has a good *almuerzo* for $1.50 per person. I had spaghetti with a white sauce, salad, soup and dessert. I could not eat it all, even though it was delicious. They also make vegetarian

LAS COLINAS

dishes and pizzas and are open early enough to offer breakfast. This place is popular with foreigners.

◆ Nightlife

The **Mosquito Rock Café Disco and Bar** is owned by the son of the owners of Land Haus. The bar has a yellow Volkswagon on the roof and a car motif inside. Next door is the Pizzeria Las Alturas. I understand that the cost for pizza delivered to the bar is a tad high.

La Disco, in town, is open Friday, Saturday and Sunday nights and on holidays. It plays the music of "today" and is the happening-est place in town.

◆ Shopping

La Vispera sells herbs grown in their garden. Margarita sells fresh herbs to some of the best restaurants in Santa Cruz and she dries some and sells them to the public. They are used as teas or as medicinal plants to alleviate the symptoms of diarrhea, rheumatism and circulation problems. Other herbs are mixed with oils and used for massages. Margarita also sells mango chutney and rhubarb jam.

Pieter has **maps** of the local terrain for $6 each.

The **Land Haus Artists' Shop** sells ceramics; the paint is made and firing is done on the premises so you can watch the process. These unique designs show the blending of European with Bolivian styles. The owner also raises and sells Bolivian cactus. There is every kind ever grown in Bolivia.

Michael Blendinger, Calle Bolívar, sells some of his landscape photos in his tour agency/craft shop. The photos are both mounted on postcards and sold as larger images. He also has good-quality crafts and weavings done by people living in the villages around Samaipata.

Carmen Luz is a contemporary artist living in Samaipata. Some of her work is available at the Hamburg Restaurant. Her studio is near the end of the street that goes along the side of the plaza. There is a sign. She also offers Spanish lessons for $5 an hour. This is steep but the lessons are good.

Cochabamba

Altitude: 8,329 ft/2,523 m
Population: 620,000

Cochabamba, the Garden of Bolivia, boasts the world's most comfortable climate; warm dry days with clear blue skies and cool nights. The elevation is low compared to the Altiplano, so the wind doesn't bite. But it is high compared to the Chaco and Amazon, so the breeze is fresh. Cochabamba is a medical center and has the most advanced labs and clinics in the country. The town also claims to have the best *chicha* in Bolivia.

These are good boasts, but there is more. Cochabamba's proximity (three hours by bus) to Torotoro National Park makes the town one of the best bases for muscle-powered adventures. This is not generally known, so you will not be crowded off a river or hiking trail. Cochabamba is also within three hours by bus or three days by foot from Villa Tunari, where an animal refuge and park are located. There is a lake in the center of town where birders can add new species to their lists. There are the caves of San Rafael to explore and Cerro Tunari, the highest peak in the district, to climb.

If you are coming from the Amazon and heading to the Andes, Cochabamba is the perfect place to acclimatize.

In my opinion, Cochabamba has been horridly undersold. This is probably because the name comes from two Quechua words: kjocha, meaning swampy, and pampa, meaning plain. It is anything but a swampy plain.

◆ Getting Here & Around

LAB, ☎ 800-337-0918 (US), 800-10-3001 (Bolivia), www.labairlines.com, **TAM**, ☎ 244-3487, www.tam.com.br, and **AeroSur**, ☎ 231-3233 or 336-7400, www.aerosur.com, have daily flights to and from other major centers like La Paz and Santa Cruz. Up to six flights a day run to and from La Paz. The cost is $50 per person one way. There are also at least two or three flights a week to faraway places like Riberalta, Puerto Suarez or Cobija.

A **taxi** from the airport to town costs $3.50 for up to four people. There is a radio taxi right at the airport door; if you walk out to the road and hail one, it will cost about $2.

Buses. There are eight going to Santa Cruz between 7:30 am and 9 pm daily, 10 going to La Paz between 8:30 am and 10 pm daily, two to Oruro at 9 am and 7:30 pm daily, four to Sucre between 4:30 pm and 7 pm daily and one to Potosi at 6 pm daily.

◆ History

1542	First colonists arrive in the valley habited by Quechua.
1571	Cochabamba declared a city by Viceroy of Toledo.
1574	Foundation stone laid for plaza by Sebastian Barba de Padilla. The city was called Villa Orapeza but the name never took.
1810	City declared independence from Spain.
1812	Men of Cochabamba fought Spaniards and when the number of men declined, the women took over to fight and won the battle.
1825	Independence for South America is won.
1952	Land reforms won by the poor.
2000	War of water is fought and won.

LAS COLINAS

◆ Services

The **telephone office** is on Avenida Ayacucho and Calle Bolívar.
The **post office** is on Avenida Ayacucho and Avenida de los Heroinas.
The **police station** is on Avenida Ayacucho and Calle Aguirre.

Money is available through any of the town's many bank machines. Traveler's checks can be cashed by paying a fairly high commission (3%).

The **tourist office** is on Calle Colombia between 25 de Mayo and España.

IAMAT Medical Center is at Edificio Servimed, 5th floor, Calle Baptista #777, ☎ 428-2192, or Clinica San Pedro, Calle Aurelio Melean #154 (no number available).

◆ Sightseeing

The **cathedral** on the plaza was built by Domingo del Mazo in the 1570s, making it the oldest in the city. It has an indigenous baroque façade in a colonial structure. The columns at the entrance are the most interesting parts, with flowers, vines and cherubs. The paintings inside are colonial in style and displayed in hand-carved wood frames. The altars, of which there are three, are carved from wood and adorned with gold. The central altar is embossed with decorative silver. This church is almost always open.

◆ Adventures in Culture

Museum Casa Santivañez, Calle Santivañez between Avenida Ayacucho and Junin, is open Monday to Saturday, 9 am-12:30 pm and 3-6 pm. The cost to enter is 50¢. It houses the National Library of Science and Technology. Under the administration of the Patiño Society of Geneva and the city of Cochabamba, the house is a cultural center and technical library.

Cultural Center and **Patiño Mansion**, Avenida Potosi #1450 and Avenida Portales, are open every day for one-hour guided tours only. The English-language tour starts at 5 pm and the Spanish at 3 pm. The cost is $1.50 for foreigners, 75¢ for locals. The English tour guide was especially good at describing the architectural styles of the mansion. After the tour you can visit the **Contemporary Art Museum** in the basement. It is well lit, uncluttered and a treat to visit. The art that I saw was varied in style and medium. In 1999, there were 78 Bolivian artists displayed at the museum.

The center is maintained by the Simon I. Patiño foundation in Geneva, Switzerland.

> ### ❖ THE SIMON PATINO FOUNDATION
>
> The foundation is huge in Bolivia. In memory of Simon Patiño, a native of Cochabamba who became the richest man in the world during the early part of the last century, the foundation was formed to help Bolivians. It pays for scholars to be educated in countries that are most advanced in a particular field, such as medicine or nuclear science. The payback is that the students, once they have completed their education, must give seven years of labor back to Bolivia. However, the foundation is having a hard time forcing scholars and doctors back into their own country. Less than half of the Bolivian students who became doctors on Patiño's money came back to Bolivia.

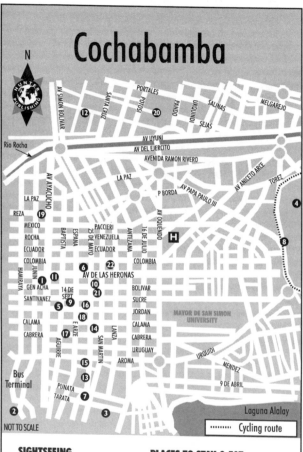

Cochabamba

SIGHTSEEING

1. Casa Santivañez
2. Monumento a las Heroínas
3. Mercado de Ferias
4. Cristo de la Concordia
5. Archeological Museum
6. Casa de la Cultura
7. Artisans Market
8. Teleférico
9. Cathedral
10. San Francisco Convent
11. Ranabol Tours
12. Fitzcarroldo Tours

PLACES TO STAY & EAT

13. El Salvador Hotel, El Dorado Hotel, Canada Hotel
14. Hostal Florida, Hostal Jordan II
15. Papichin Restaurant
16. City Hotel
17. Hotel Mary
18. Hotel Los Angeles, Sucre Manta, Espresso Café
19. Regina Hotel
20. Anteus Hotel
21. Cesar's Plaza Hotel
22. Los Leás Pizza Parlor

But the foundation also supports a medical clinic in Bolivia. They run an experimental farm. They help pay for public housing and they publish books. They run a research station for genetic improvement in agriculture. They also maintain one of the larger libraries in the country.

The **Archeological Museum**, on the plaza at Avenida Aguirre and Calle Jordan, is open weekdays 8:30 am-6:30 pm, and on weekends until noon. It is closed on all holidays and during Carnival. Admission is $2. Displays include about 20,000 pieces of rocks, shards, pottery, weapons, weavings, skulls, and so on, from the cultures of every group ever to live in Bolivia going back as far as 5,000 years.

Quillacollo, nine miles/15 km from Cochabamba, is known for its festival celebrating the miracles of the **Virgin of Urkupiña**. On August 15 every year, pilgrims walk from Cochabamba to the colonial church where the Virgin is housed. Apparently, a young woman tending her flock on the hill nearby had some visions of the Virgin. The fiesta is started with pilgrims and worshipers climbing the hill to where the Virgin was first spotted. Once they have prayed, they take a piece of rock with them to insure health and wealth in the future. Back in the village, people dance, eat and drink.

The **colonial church** on the plaza is the second attraction of the village. Inside are numerous items left in appreciation of the miracles performed by the Virgin. The Sunday market is when the artists of the area sell many of their handmade crafts.

To get to Quillacollo, catch a minibus from Avenida Ayacucho and Aromas. The half-hour journey costs 25¢ each way. Should you wish to stay in Quillacayo for the night, there are two places just 2.5 miles/four km north of town. **Eco Hostal Los Nuevos Inkas**, ☎ 446-1505, charges $12 per person for a room with bath. **La Posada de los Cisnes** (no phone) charges $10 per person for a room with bath.

Villa Albino and the Pairumani Estate is 12 miles/20 km from Cochabamba. This is where the Patiños are buried in an ornate marble mausoleum. On the property is yet another house that Simon Patiño built, this one for his wife. Mansion tours are offered in English or Spanish at 2 pm daily. The cost is $1.50 for foreigners and half that for nationals.

Incallajta Ruins are 86 miles/140 km from Cochabamba and about 12 miles/20 km in from the old road to Santa Cruz. This Inca fort is interesting, although not as spectacular as El Fuerte or Tihuanaco. To get there from Cochabamba you must take a bus going to Epizana or Totora and get off at the turn-off to Collpa and Pocona. From Collpa you must walk five miles/eight km uphill to the site. The bus trip alone takes about 2½ hours. The easiest option is to take a tour or hire a jeep in Cochabamba. The last choice is to stay in Tortora and hire a vehicle or take a bus to the turn-off for the ruins.

Pocona is the village 5.5 miles/nine km south of the junction to the ruins. The village is dominated by colonial architecture with cobbled streets and old wooden doors. The center for the Assistance for Tourists is here and offers the service of guides for the ruins. There's also a small medical center and general information about Incallajta. At the center is a small archeological museum that has some pieces excavated at the ruins.

◆ Adventures on Foot

CRISTO DE LA CONCORDIA: On Avenida Rubin Dario, this statue of Christ can be seen from anywhere in the city during the day. At night he is lit up bright as day. This is the symbol of Cochabamba. It is the biggest statue of Christ in South America, standing at 132 ft/40 m from feet to forehead and weighing about a million pounds/two million kilos. It is a nice climb to the top of the hill, and the view of the city spreads farther with each step. If the one-hour climb is not your thing, take the cable car up for a mere 25¢ and walk down. Inside the statue base is a restaurant patronized by everyone who has made the climb.

LAGUNA ALALAY: The lake, located along Avenida Ruben Dario and Avenida 9 de Abril, is flanked by the hill and Parque Progreso, by the Campo Ferial and by the country club. A paved walking trail and cycling road encircles the entire lake.

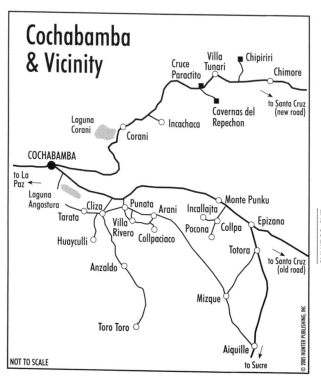

Cochabamba & Vicinity

Villa Tunari
Cruce Paractito
Chipiriri
Chimore
to Santa Cruz (new road)
Cavernas del Repechon
Laguna Corani
Incachaca
Corani
COCHABAMBA
to La Paz
Laguna Angostura
Cliza
Punata
Arani
Incallajta
Monte Punku
Tarata
Villa Rivero
Pocona
Collpa
Epizana
Huayculli
Collpaciaco
Totora
Anzaldo
to Santa Cruz (old road)
Mizque
Toro Toro
Aiquille
to Sucre

NOT TO SCALE

LAS COLINAS

© 2005 HUNTER PUBLISHING, INC

Parts of the lake are swampy and perfect for birds. There have been over 150 bird species seen at the lake, some examples of which are the white-tufted and silver grebe, the puna ibis, Andean gull, the grey-bellied shrike-tyrant and the yellow and blue tanager.

SAN SEBASTIAN HILL: La Coronilla is just up from the bus terminal and above Avenida Roma. San Sebastian park is across the way. The hill has stone steps up to a monument of powerful women in battle, arms raised in defiance and with children hugging their legs. This is in memory of the women who fought to defend the city after the men had been defeated during a battle against the Spanish in 1812.

CERRO TUNARI: Cerro Tunari is a 17,000-ft/5,200-m cone-shaped peak in the Cordillera Oriental that can be seen from Cochabamba. Two routes ascend the mountain, one from the north and the other from the south. If going from the north, you will have to stay overnight and have camping equipment. See Ranabol Tours (☎ 458-3039 or 717-17097, ramiroc15@ hotmail.com) on Avenida Ayacucho about doing this trip. They are able to show you more than just the hike up the mountain.

The climb from the south requires that you go along Avenida Ayacucho (or take bus #103) for 5.5 miles/nine km and ask to be let off the bus at the park. Follow the trail going up. In about an hour you will come to some picnic tables and more trails. Pick any one that goes up. The climb is steep. As you ascend, the vegetation becomes sparse and llamas and birds will be your only companions. The black scree makes the hillside look a bit barren. Watch also for the mountain finch, the cone bill and Torrent ducks.

If going by the northern route you will need to go to Quillacollo and then on to Chaqueri, halfway to Morochata. The best way is to take a taxi or join a tour. Taking buses will use up all your hiking time.

Chaqueri is at about 13,158 ft/4,000 m, so the change in elevation to the summit is not much. On this side, you may be lucky enough to spot condors. The hike to the summit takes five or six hours; coming back down is three or four. You can see the higher peaks to the north and the city of Cochabamba to the south.

◆ Adventures in Nature

Laguna Angostura is 10 miles/17 km from Cochabamba, situated between the old road that goes to Santa Cruz and the road that goes to Tarata. On the way to Tarata, you will pass the western and southern sides of this man-made lake. On the lake are three large hotels with restaurants and bars that overlook the water. There are boats for hire.

Liruini is five miles/eight km past Quillacollo and its **hot spring** is reputed to cure kidney and liver disorders. The springs are in a bathhouse and are fairly clean.

Should you want to stay in Liruini, try the **Janajpacha Hotel**, ☎ 446-1234, on the road toward Quillacollo near the hot springs. It charges $9 per person for a room with private bath and all meals.

◆ Adventures of the Brain

Escuela Runawasi, c/o Hinojosa, Casilla 4034, ☎ 424-8923, charges $1,000 for a six-week total immersion language class with a maximum of three students who are working at the same level as you. The classes can be in Spanish or Quechua, and the cost includes room and board, 20 hours of instruction per week and all materials. The school also offers advanced classes for those wanting to study literature, rather than language.

The school is 2.8 miles/4.5 km from the city center and most home-stay residences are in the same neighborhood.

Normally, the classes are composed of three students. However, for those with no Spanish, the school may use larger groups while others may have one-to-one communication. Once some Spanish is learned, the student may be put into a group. Some prefer grammar while others prefer conversation and these distinctions are accommodated.

Home stays can accommodate individuals or families. Some can provide private bath. If special accommodations are required, the information needs to be sent to the school prior to arrival. The host family provides all meals and non-alcoholic drinks. Laundry can be done by the student or by the host family for $1.50 for 12 pieces (a pair of socks is one piece).

Anyone arriving with children can enroll the child in a class but the school does not take kids under 15 in its adult classes. There is also a day care or kindergarten that costs $50 for a month of half-day care.

◆ Tour Operators

Ranabol Tours, Avenida Ayacucho #112 and Heroinas, ☎ 458-3039 or 717-17097 (cell), ramiroc15@hotmail.com or ranabolraf@hotmail.com, offers the best in outdoor adventure for the area. Romero offers a three-day bike trip to Samaipata, and a four- to seven-day canoe trip through the selva from San Francisco down to Rio Negro. His four-day hike from Cochabamba to Villa Tanuri runs through incredible landscapes and includes stops at the Repechon Cave to see bats and the guacharo, the only bird ever found in a cave occupied by bats. Romero also does three- to four-day hiking, caving and canoeing trips to places like Torotoro National Park, Carrasco National Park, Amboro National Park and Isiboro-Secure Park. In Torotoro, he will take you to the Humajalanta Cave, where stalagmites and stalactites form structures like the Sauce Tree, the Christmas Tree and the Concert Room. Geologists believe these caves were at one time under water. There is one four-day trip that includes rafting, trekking, rappelling and mountain biking. It ends at a hotel where you can shower, eat, drink beer and massage your muscles. He also does a lot of spelunking and can arrange obstacle courses for eco-challenge types.

If paragliding is your thing, Ranabol Tours will take you where you can fly. This is the only company in Bolivia that I know of to offer such an activity to tourists. Flying over the Andes! How romantic.

Romero offers rafting, mountain biking, trekking and rapelling down waterfalls or any combination of sports for a custom trip. He has most equipment you may need and his prices are around $30 a day. Some trips have a minimum age as some of the trips can be demanding. Romero is skilled and knowledgeable, especially about Torotoro. He even knows some English. He comes highly recommended.

Fitzcarraldo Expeditions, Avenidas Aniceto & Padilla #225, at the Casa Internacional, ☎ 424-2431, tombol@hotmail.com, offer kayaking/canoeing trips lasting four to eight days; some may include hiking. They travel on easy-to-paddle jungle rivers so you have the pleasure of enjoying the wildlife, rather than trying to stay afloat. This company is very safety conscious. You can hook up with them in Vallerroel or Santa Cruz.

Their shortest trip runs along the Ivirgarzama River near Villarroel, a village directly south of Trinidad. It costs $330 per person if three people go and drops down to $270 if five people sign up. Another excursion is for five days on the Isarzama River, not far from Cochabamba. It ends at Villarroel, where there is an eco-lodge for visitors to use. The cost of this all-inclusive trip is $390 per person if three people go and $300 if five people go. If tropical rainforest is your desire, take the trip along Snake River (named because of its curves, rather than its resident reptiles) through Bolivia's Green Hell for either five or eight days. The river passes through the most southern section of the Amazon Basin and, for part of the time, you are in the steaming jungle with a view of snow-capped mountains in the distance. The cost, depending on duration and group size, is $489-$889 per person.

◆ Places to Stay

El Salvador Hostal, *Calle Montes #E0420, on the corner of 25 de Mayo,* ☎ 422-7303, $, has rooms with or without baths. They are large and bright. All rooms have cupboards, tables and chairs, cable TV, telephone and some have balconies. The place is clean, the owner pleasant. This is my first choice for a room in Cochabamba.

❖ HOTEL PRICING	
$	$10 to $20
$$	$21 to $50
$$$	$51 to $75
$$$$	$76 to $100
$$$$$	over $100

Hostal Florida, *Calle 25 d Mayo #583,* ☎ 425-7911, floridah@elsitio.com, $. The rooms are not big but the cable TV gets about 30 channels, including CNN in English. Those with wood floors are better than those with carpets. The big draw here is the center courtyard.

Residencial El Dorado, *Calle 25 de Mayo #1034,* ☎ 422-1940, $, has 25 exceptionally clean rooms around a central courtyard. The floors are tiled and each room has a small desk and chair. There is a separate TV room and a small snack place where you can get soft drinks, tea or a sandwich.

Hostal Jordan II, *25 de Mayo between Uruguay and Cabrera,* ☎ 422-5010 or 422-4821, $$, has single, double and triple rooms. All have private baths with separate shower stalls, cable TV, carpet, large windows and writing desks with chairs. Those not facing the street are a little darker.

City Hotel, *Calle Jordan #341 between 25 de Mayo and Esteban,* ☎ 422-2993 or 422-9575, $$, is a favorite hangout for local artists and musicians, who often jam together in the bar on weekends. The uncrowded rooms have carpet, cable TV, telephones and private bathrooms that have both tubs and showers. The hotel is clean. Some rooms at the back of the hotel have nice views of the city. The new restaurant has more vegetarian dishes than meat choices and is open 24 hours a day.

Mary Hotel, *Calle Nataniel Aquirre #601 and Cabrera*, ☎ 425-2487 or 425-2488, *$$*, has moderately sized rooms with clean carpets, tiled bathrooms, cable TV and closets. The single rooms are a good size, but some rooms have small windows so they appear a bit dark. There is an operating elevator.

Hotel Los Angeles, *Calle E. Arce #345*, ☎ 423-4523, *$$*, is a good deal. The rooms are big, bright, clean and have large windows. Each has a lounge chair, a desk and a mirror. Each floor has a sitting area in the hall.

Canada Hotel, *Calle 25 de May #1000 on the corner of Montes*, ☎ 455-3315, *$$$*, has 30 rooms and an elevator that works. The rooms are large and comfortable with a separate sitting area. The bathrooms are tiled and have separate shower stalls. The windows are large, the halls wide, the doors solid wood. This is a clean place. There's an on-site bar and restaurant for breakfast (included). There is enclosed parking.

Regina Hotel, *Avenida Reza between España and the Prada*, ☎ 425-7382 or 422-9163, *hregina@netbol.com*, *$$$$*, has large, bright rooms with private bathrooms, cable TV, telephones and small sitting areas. There is also laundry service, a safe for valuables, private parking and a restaurant that serves both continental and American breakfasts.

Anteus Hotel, *Avenida Potosi #1365*, ☎ 424-5067, *hotelanteus@hotmail.com*, *$$$$*, is a small and friendly place with good monthly rates. It's across from the cultural center. Rooms here have private bath and cable TV. Purified water is supplied daily. There's a safe, private parking, laundry service, bicycle rentals and gym and the proprietors will change guest traveler's checks. There is a restaurant on the premises and an Internet café next door. During high season, make advance reservations.

Cesar's Plaza Hotel, *Calle 25 de Mayo #5210-223*, ☎ 425-0045, *$$$$*, is a first-class hotel close to the central plaza. They offer a 20% discount if you stay two days or more. The rooms are spacious. There's a sauna, travel agency, beauty parlor and handicraft shop. The price includes breakfast and Internet access.

Hotel Diplomat, *Avenida Ballivian #611 near the Prada*, ☎ 425-0687, *www.diplomat.com*, *$$$$$*, has rooms and suites. Each of the 86 rooms, on 15 floors, has a private bathroom, large bed, mini-bar, cable TV and air conditioning. They are carpeted, spacious and have small sitting areas. The hotel, situated in a middle class area just off the *prada*, offers free transportation to and from the airport. There is also a business center with Internet access. There are two restaurants and a bar on site.

Gran Hotel Cochabamba, *Plaza Ubaldo Anze E-0415*, ☎ 428-2551, *cbbhotel@bo.net*, *$$$$$*, offers rooms, a suite and a presidential suite. It's an elegant old place that has been restored numerous times so the latest conveniences are offered while the charm is retained. Each tastefully decorated room has cable TV, large mirror, clean carpets and a spacious bathroom. The grounds have a swimming pool and there is a central gazebo where drinks or meals can be enjoyed. There is also a restaurant and separate bar. English, French and German are spoken by the staff.

LAS COLINAS

Portales Hotel, *Avenida Pando #1271, $$$$$,* is a first-class, five-star hotel that is part of a chain with other hotels in Santa Cruz and La Paz. It has three restaurants, a bar, two swimming pools, a dry sauna, a Turkish bath, gym, Jacuzzi, racquetball court, hair dresser, cable TV, business center and a doctor on call.

◆ Places to Eat

La Suisa Restaurant, *Avenida Ballivian #820*, ☎ *425-7102 or 425-7103.* This elegant restaurant has waiters in black ties ready to supply your every culinary wish. A separate bar features elevator music cranked low. Original oil paintings grace the walls and the décor features heavy

❖ RESTAURANT PRICING	
$	under $5
$$	$5 to $10
$$$	$11 to $25
$$$$	$26 to $50
$$$$$	over $50

wood paneling and stained glass windows. The meals keep the tone. Appetizers are free. Soup is about $1.75 and steak $5.50. A bottle of wine is $9, but the menu showed no prices for cocktails. This is probably the most elegant restaurant in Cochabamba; because of its good food and ambience, it has managed to stay in business for 15 years. Open Monday to Saturday, 11:30 am-2:30 pm and 6-11 pm (11:30 pm on Friday and Saturday).

Papichin Restaurant, *Aroma #402 and 25 de Mayo,* is a clean local eatery that serves highly recommended *chirascos*. If this doesn't suit your taste, there is also an à la carte menu. A typical *almuerzo* runs at $1.75. However, they serve only one beer per customer per meal. If you want to drink more, you must go elsewhere as this is a family restaurant.

Sucre Manta, *Calle Esteban Arce #356,* just behind the cathedral, serves traditional food from Sucre using grandma's secret recipes. This restaurant is a favorite with everyone. Prices are low, food is good and a pianist plays during lunchtime.

Espresso Café Bar, *Calle Arce #340,* ☎ *425-6861,* serves cappuccino and espressos. This tiny café is a favorite for those hanging around the square. The shop also has some pastries, although the coffee, with its huge glob of sweet cream, is the real draw. Open 8 am-1 pm and 3-10 pm daily.

❖ ODE TO THE SPUD

There are 1,290 varieties of potatoes produced in Bolivia and the country is the world's largest per capita consumer of the vegetable. One variety, called the ñojcha, is used to test the value of a new daughter-in-law. If the young lady can peel the plant's funny curves and shape without losing too much of the potato, she will make a good wife.

Burger King, *Avenida America #620,* ☎ *445-1525,* is where homesick North Americans go. The restaurant has air conditioning, clean bathrooms and the usual North American hamburger. The prices, too, are North American.

Los Leñas Pizza Parlor, *Avenida San Martin #179, between Bolívar and Heroinas,* ☎ *450-0674,* is a funky two-story pizzeria that cooks excellent thin crust pizza in a traditional clay oven. The cost is between $3 for a small to $6 for a fully loaded family size. The restaurant is open for lunch and stays open until after 10 pm.

Fratelo's Bar and Restaurant, *Pando #1143 and Recoleta,* ☎ *440-2050,* has good pasta and fish and is popular with the younger, rowdier crowd. Open 11 am-2 pm and 6-11 pm.

Casa Nuestra, *Calle Oruro #389 and Antezana,* ☎ *452-2038,* is classy in appearance and service. However, some of the portions are on the scanty side. Although dishes like the lasagne are laden with cheese and the size is also fairly good, the price is $5 per serving. Fettuccini is $3.50 and the portion was moderate. The pasta of the house, which I didn't try, goes at a hefty $10 per plate. Once they sort out their portion size to price, it will be a good place to eat.

◆ Nightlife

Acha Theatre on Calle España just off the plaza is the local concert venue where performing arts are presented in an elegant hall. The building was constructed in 1578 in the convent of St. Augustine and is the most famous concert hall in the country. The acoustics seem to be especially designed for the performing arts. You will need to look for posters or visit the tourist office for information about performances.

Portales Hotel, Avenida Pando #1271, has a casino where you can pull the arm, play black jack or try your luck at the roulette wheel. When you've won enough money you can go across to the disco and dance up a storm with the more affluent of Cochabamba's population.

Avalon Restaurant and open-air bar is on Avenida Potosi, next door to the Cultural Center. It is the Bolivian version of a rave club that is often manned on weekends by popular disc jockeys.

◆ Shopping

The **Cancha Market** across from the Laguna Alalay is the largest market in the area. It offers everything from local foods to modern dresses (no Christian Doir though). If you need to walk and are tired of the small market on 25 de Mayo, then have a look. The grounds are fairly new, built in the 1990s I believe.

Vicuñita Handicrafts, Avenida Rafael Pabon #777, ☎ 425-5615, near the airport, will ship goods anywhere in the world. As their name implies, they have some upscale vicuña and alpaca products. They have a similar shop in Santa Cruz.

Tarata

Altitude: 9,046 ft/2,750 m
Population: 30,000 people in the village and surrounding countryside.

Tarata is a colonial village just 21 miles/35 km from Cochabamba, tucked into hills that are farmed to their tops. The village should be on every architectural-photographer's dream list. Some of the houses have doors that date back to the 1890s, while others are from 1907 and 1911 (signs above indicate when the door was built). The houses on which the doors hang are just as picturesque, with flowered balconies and stone façades. At one time some of these buildings were home to famous Bolivians such as Mariano Melgarejo, Esteban Arce and Rene Barrientos Ortuño (president of Bolivia from 1964-1967). Barrientos' house is just one block off the plaza.

Tarata also has some excellent weavings and is known for its fine *chicha* production. If you see a red or white flag hanging on a pole outside a house, it means there is *chicha* for sale. You can go in and purchase some or sit and enjoy a glass with the local *chichaleros*.

To get to Tarata, take a *trufi* from Calle 6 de Agosto just up from Avenida Republica in Cochabamba. Returning, the first bus leaves half a block from the square at 5 am and the last one leaves at 7 pm. It takes about 45 minutes to get to or from Cochabamba and costs 50¢.

◆ Services

The **tourist office** is on the main square. This is one of the best offices in the country. The staff was helpful and knowledgeable as to what tourists want, whether it be a place to stay, something to do or finding a phone.

◆ Sightseeing

San Pedro Church, on the main square, was built in 1605 and its organ is original. Inside is an urn with the ashes of Esteban Arce, who led a revolution in 1810 while trying to get independence for Bolivia. The church also has the skull of Mariano Melgarejo, one of Bolivia's most corrupt presidents and notorious drunks.

The **Convent and Church of Franciscan** (near the Cabañas los Piños) is also called the Temple of San Severino or the College of the Apostles of the Missions of Guarayos. It has an urn that was used by the patron saint of Tarata, San Severeno, the saint of rain. The convent's library has over 8,000 books, sermons and documents pertaining to the administration of the missions run by the Franciscan Fathers in Bolivia. The saint's day is celebrated in the village on the last Sunday of November with processions leading from the church, around the village and back again.

The **stone bridge of Melgarejo** was once over the Pilcomayo River. It now seems to be a bridge over a depression in the land. Mariano Melgarejo was president of Bolivia from 1864 to 1871. He had the military under his command, even though he was a notorious drunk who signed some of the most bizarre treaties in the country's history. He once signed a treaty with

Brazil in the hope of getting water rights to the Atlantic Ocean. This resulted in Bolivia giving Brazil 39,537 square miles/102,400 square km of its prime land and Melgarejo getting a horse (so he could ride to the ocean). Melgarejo also sold parcels of land that didn't belong to him. He insisted that the Indians pay a large amount of money to prove ownership of their land. When they couldn't do this, the land was confiscated and sold to the Spaniards wanting to settle in the area. The logic of this alone shows the insanity of the man. The uprisings that resulted from the confiscation of land were bitter. Melgarejo was eventually overthrown and, later that same year, murdered in Lima, Peru.

Melgarejo's house is three blocks past Plaza Esteban Arce and the Church of San Francisco. When facing the church, go left and then right at the corner, so that you walk past the side of the church. Continue for three blocks and turn right again. A sign indicates the house.

On the plaza is the **Palacio Consistorial** that contains photos and paintings of important leaders from Bolivian history who were born or lived in Tarata. There are also some documents that have the signatures of Bolívar and Melgarejo. Other buildings on the plaza have the old hanging balconies and picturesque doorways.

◆ Places to Stay & Eat

Alojamiento Municipal is right by the bridge going over the Calicanto River. It is reached along the main road going to Cochabamba. The rooms are simple and the cost is $4 per person. There is no phone.

> **AUTHOR NOTE:** *If you want help in finding the hotel (or a phone), go to the tourist office on the main square.*

The only place to eat in the village is at the **market** near the Church of Franciscan. The *churascos* sold here are excellent – a full meal of more than I could eat was about 50¢. Other traditional dishes are *aloja*, a drink similar to *chicha* but without alcohol, and *chanca de conejo*, a soup made with rabbit, potatoes, green onion, green beans, yellow chilies and tomatoes.

◆ Shopping

Huayculli, 4.3 miles/seven km from Tarata, is the center for local ceramics. The best pieces are items used in the kitchen such as plates, pots and cups. These ceramics are among the finest quality in the country and Bolivians often travel a long way to purchase them.

The last Sunday of every month is **market** day in Tarata and villagers come from miles around to sell or trade their goods and handicrafts.

◆ Mizque

Mizque has cock fights and a watered-down version of the running of the bulls in Pamplona, Spain. This happens during the festival of **Señor de Burgos**, held on the second weekend of September each year. The week before the festival is the religious procession in honor of the Virgin of Mercy. In 1767 the town built three convents as well as the Inglesia Matriz, under the administration of the order of San Juan de Dios. They may have been hoping for a large influx of religious fervor. My theory is that so many guys got wiped out during the running of the bulls that the church had to build convents for the widows.

Mizque is four hours from Cochabamba. Buses ($2) leave from 6 de Agosto and Republica around noon and return every day at 3 pm. You also get here from Tarata or Sucre (but the bus arrives in the middle of the night and you must pay full fare between Cochabamba and Sucre).

There are five basic **hotels** in the village. All charge about $3 per person for a room without a private bath.

From the village, you can hike to **Kuri Canyon** (493 ft/150 m deep). This is where the Bridge of the Liberator, used by Simon Bolívar, spans over the canyon. Also, you can walk to **Pajcha Pata waterfall**, which drops about 411 ft/125 m, and visit the cave paintings in Aguada and Tablada. For these two trips you will need a guide. One can be hired in town for $10 to $30 per day.

Torotoro National Park

Altitude: 9,211 ft/2,800 m
Population: 500

The big draw to Cochabamba is Torotoro National Park, where there are dinosaur prints, fossils galore, a river gorge, a lake with blind fish, rock paintings, caves and insignificant ruins. Hiking can be done almost anywhere in the park's 41,000 acres/16,570 hectares, which is dotted with deep canyons, hanging valleys and waterfalls.

Due to the earthquake in 1998, when many places in the village were destroyed, there are mostly new-styled buildings in town – not very interesting, but adequate. The locals have a deal among themselves as to who will feed a *gringo*. Ask where you are staying and they will direct you to the producing eatery.

◆ Getting Here & Around

Torotoro is difficult to reach. There is a bus direct from Cochabamba on Thursday and Sunday that leaves at 6 am and returns on Friday and Monday. Catch it on Avenida 6 de Agosto and Republica in Cochabamba and on the plaza in Torotoro. The trip is seven hours in all with the last 24 miles/ 40 km on a horrid track that occasionally, during rainy season, becomes impassable. This section takes three hours during dry season. It is highly recommended to take a tour to this park.

When you first arrive at Torotoro, you will be encouraged (forced?) to pay your $2.50 park fee. This is a one-time cost and covers all the time you are in the park. You can also hire a guide who will charge about $10 per day for up to four people.

◆ Adventures on Foot

DINOSAUR TRACKS: The tracks on Cerro Huayllas are easy to find. Walk from the plaza down to the river, cross where everyone crosses and then walk upstream for less than 300 ft/90 m. Follow the track on the left that goes uphill. Nearby are three-toed dinosaur tracks stomping across the landscape. If you return to the river and go a bit farther upstream, you will find more tracks. These prints were made around 70 million years ago. Some were left by three-toed meat-eaters that grew to about 23 ft/seven m in size. Their prints are usually about 10 inches/25 cm wide. The four-toed Sauropods, vegetarians who grew to around 33 ft/10 m high, are responsible for the larger prints. Once the animals walked across the mud, leaving their prints, the mud dried, solidified and petrified. Then tectonic movement forced the land upward, thus giving the appearance that the tracks are walking uphill.

ROCK PAINTINGS: Batea Cocha is a spot where the rushing water during rainy season has smoothed and sculpted rock to form what looks like washbasins in the stone (thus the name). Just before the basins, on the wall to your left, are rock paintings. These are from Inca times. One image looks like it could be a snake, but the paintings are faint and some damage has been done to them. This section of the river is downstream from the dino tracks.

Just a bit farther downriver are a series of waterfalls and a canyon where the cliffs along the river's edge plunge 987 ft/300 m into the earth. To get to the canyon, walk along the road to Cochabamba for about 20 minutes and, at the curve, follow the trail on the left. Another 20-minute walk will bring you to a set of stone steps that lead to the river. At the bottom, continue following the river downstream. Going to the canyon is a two-hour walk, one way.

FOSSILS: The **Tarya site** is about an hour's walk west from the town. As you head up the trail that winds up the mountain, check the river beds for fossils of turtles, fish, seashells and algae. Scientific research has discovered bones from about 55 mammal species that lived during the middle Pleistocene period. Some of these fossils are believed to be 350 million years old.

UMAJALLANTA CAVES: The caves are 5 miles/eight km from Torotoro, about a two-hour walk, one way. See the park office for explicit directions but, generally, you will head in a northwest direction along the road, past the turnoff to the mountain with fossils, and past some four-toed dino tracks belonging to one of the vegan dinos (these tracks seem to be less directed than the ones near the town). Shortly after, you will see the cave entrance.

The cave itself was carved by the Umajallanta River that disappears at this point and comes out again at Torotoro canyon. Inside is about three miles/five km of explored cave area with more yet to be explored. A guide may be useful and a flashlight is essential. As you enter the cave, the passage seems okay, but then it narrows and sometimes becomes only 10 feet wide. Some of the stalagmites and stalactites have been broken and taken by visitors who do not have enough weight in their backpacks. There are vampire bats, but they bite only during a full moon or when tourists threaten to break the rock formations. As you work your way into the cave you will come to a small lake. This is where the blind fish are supposed to be.

◆ Place to Stay

The village of Torotoro has a few basic places to stay and even a nunnery that can give you a bed. The most popular hotel is the **Charcas**, ☎ 413-3927, that charges about $3 per person for a clean room with a communal bathroom and clean showers. The water supply is often sparse and always cold and the electricity is on only two hours a day.

Villa Tunari

Altitude: 1,000 ft/300 m
Population: 1,000

Villa Tunari is three hours by bus from Cochabamba to the east on the northern highway that leads to Santa Cruz. Most of the residents in the immediate area live mostly by farming.

At one time this was a rich cocaine center and the main street with its lush hotels and glitzy restaurants is a relic from that period. Now, the village is mainly patronized by workers from aid agencies and the animal shelter. However, it is in the Chapare region where the American drug enforcement agency is adamant on stopping the drug trade. This has resulted in hardships for the locals.

◆ Getting Here

Buses leave from Cochabamba or Santa Cruz at 7:30 am, 9:30 am and 7 pm and 8:15 pm daily. It takes seven hours by *flota* to get to the village from Santa Cruz and three hours from Cochabamba.

◆ Adventures (without cocaine)

Inti Wara Yassi Community (Villa Tunari Animal Shelter), ☎ 04-413-6572 (ask for Nina, the administrator) on the new road to Cochabamba, www.intiwarayassi.org or www.geocities.com/refugiobolivia/, is an animal rehabilitation center that takes volunteers for a minimum of two weeks to work with rescued animals. Prospective volunteers show up, make a deposit ($70) to guarantee their stay and start working. The deposit pays for accommodations and kitchen use. Volunteers who leave before the two weeks of committed time, lose the deposit. If they stay longer, they are made even more welcome than they were when they first arrived and they pay only $2.50 instead of $5 a day for their stay.

As a fundraiser, volunteers often make a meal and sell it to the other volunteers. They give the profits to the shelter. This money is used to purchase food, new cages and equipment for the animals.

Volunteers can also work at the new station near Guarayos, on the road to Trinidad, but they must first turn up at Villa Tunari. The cost to work at the second station is a deposit of $45 for the first two weeks.

Non-volunteers can visit the shelter, go on a tour and make a donation toward animal upkeep. The cost of a tour is about $1 per person. You pay $2 for the privilege of using your camera and $3 if you want to use a camcorder. This money does not go toward the upkeep of the animals. Instead, it goes to the landowner.

To get to the shelter from Cochabamba, take a bus heading to Santa Cruz and ask the driver to let you off at the park, rather than the village. Enter the first building on the left. This is called the Casa. There among armadillos and toucans you will find a volunteer or two who will direct you. If coming from the village, walk along the road toward Cochabamba. Once you are over the bridge that crosses Rio Espirito Santo, turn right.

The shelter's aim is to rehabilitate animals that have spent time in captivity. They get pumas, Jeffries cats, monkeys, birds and turtles.

> ### ❖ GATO'S GAIT
>
> Gato is the famous puma who was taken away from a circus. The circus trainers had him jumping through a ring of fire. Because Gato was bitten and given a bad diet, he became crippled in his back legs. When the cat came to the shelter, he could not walk. A volunteer started him on a physio program. The result was that the volunteer stayed nine months and Gato can now walk. Gato has two volunteers who spend all day walking in the jungle with him. Although he can go on his own, Gato is always kept on a leash.

After a volunteer has been assigned an animal, it is that person's job to care for it, keep records, maintain a rehab routine and train a new volunteer to replace him/herself. Bolivians are usually assigned baby animals because babies must stay with their people 24 hours a day. If it is a monkey, for example, that means taking it to bed.

The program is popular and there are usually 25-50 volunteers here at any one time. Often, these people become so involved that they stay a long time, over a year. The job is seven days a week and each day includes all your waking hours.

A veterinarian working at the shelter first checks newly arrived animals. If no immediate medical attention is required, the animal is then put into quarantine for 40 days to prevent spread of disease. A rehab program is designed for each individual animal. For example, toucans living in captivity often can't walk, so they go on a program to get their feet working again. Birds like hawks can learn to fly as long as their wings have not been cauterized after clipping.

LAS COLINAS

◆ Places to Stay

Hotel San Martin, *Avenida Integration*, ☎ *411-4115*, *$$*, has plain rooms around a central garden. Each room has a private bath and a fan.

Hotel Las Palmas, *Avenida Integration #777*, ☎ *411-4163*, *$$$*, has cabins on the San Mateo River. They charge $24 for a cabin that holds two people or $10 per person for a room with private bath. The on-site restaurant is noted for its fish dinners.

The Toucanes, *Km 162 on the highway*, ☎ *411-4108*, *$$$*, has cabins on the Chapare River. This well-kept place has palapa huts around the grounds for guest use.

El Puente Jungle Lodge, *2.4 miles/four km along the road toward Cochabamba*, ☎ *445-9392*, *$$$*, offers cabins that take two people. They are fully contained and include a private bath, fan and breakfast. There is a pool and restaurant.

◆ Places to Eat

The Palmas, *Km 161 along the highway*, ☎ *411-4163*, is known for its fish dinners. **San Silvester**, *.6 miles/one km farther*, has excellent steak. Both restaurants are clean and the prices are reasonable.

◆ Nightlife

Jazmin Bar, Restaurant and Karaoke, *Calle Chiquisaca*, is the most active place in town. Drinking, eating and singing all in the same place is often beneficial, but sometimes the singing can put you off your food.

The Chaco

Santa Cruz

Altitude: 1,438 ft/437 m
Population: 1,200,000

Santa Cruz is usually windy, often flooded and always hot. The streets, unless they have a boulevard, are all one-way but travel is confusing.

The main thoroughfares go in circles and are called *anillos* (an-EE-yos). Between these circles, streets form a grid, sometimes pie-shaped. Since there is no other town in Bolivia that is quite as confusing to get around as Santa Cruz, a compass is essential. All the major intersections are adorned with a statue, usually of a person with historical importance. These are used as landmarks. There is also the large Christ figure on the second *anillo* at avenidas Banzer and Cristobal de Mendoza. The people of Santa Cruz are proud of their Christ.

Santa Cruz is the economic capital of Bolivia. Much of it is new. You will see, on the highway to the airport for example, the big showrooms of John Deere, Caterpillar, Volvo, Ford and so on. These are the installations of corporate giants that are supplying the agriculture and petroleum industries. Both industries are conspicuous in the sur- rounding countryside. For example, there are few small farms. It is agribusiness growing vast fields of soy and sunflowers for oil. The tractors and silos are huge. Some large holdings are Mennonite, and members of these groups can be seen in their straw hats and bib jeans.

There is a kind of independence movement in Santa Cruz that would like to cut La Paz off as the corrupt middleman in dealings with the corporations and banks so that Santa Cruz could get more of the benefits of capitalism.

Tourists use Santa Cruz as a base from which to visit Noel Kempff National Park (see page 287) in the Amazon or to explore the Pantanal. Others head over to Samaipata and Amboro National Park, while culture seekers visit the unique Jesuit missions. Birding is big in the area. Regardless of your interests, you will find Santa Cruz rich in culture, history and art, with good food and comfortable hotels.

◆ Getting Here & Around

LAB, ☎ 800-337-0918 (US), 800-10-3001 (Bolivia), www.labairlines.com, and **AeroSur**, ☎ 231-3233 or 336-7400, www.aerosur.com, have daily **flights** from La Paz to Santa Cruz via Cochabamba for $60 per person. The flight is half an hour from Cochabamba and just over an hour from La

Paz. There's also a direct one-hour flight from/to Tarija twice a week. It beats the dangerous bus trip across the mountains down to the flatlands. The flight over the Amazon from Santa Cruz to Trinidad goes daily in a small plane.

The airport in Santa Cruz is the only international airport in the country besides the one in La Paz. Should you not want to fly into La Paz because of its high elevation, coming to Santa Cruz from out of the country is an alternative. Numerous companies – like Varig, Continental and Lan Chile – fly into Santa Cruz from places like Miami, Florida, Santiago, Chile and Lima, Peru. The airport is nine miles/15 km from the center of town and a taxi ride there costs $10. Public buses go from the airport as far as the second *anillo*, a few blocks from the main plaza, and charge $2 per person.

Buses from Santa Cruz to Villamontes take anywhere from 12 to 18 hours during a good dry spell. If the roads are bad it takes longer. The daytime bus leaves at 8:30 am and costs $10 per person. Night buses leave between 5 pm and 7 pm. The road is paved as far as Abopo, after which it becomes a mud-hole. The road picks up again at Camiri which means most of the trip is through the mud hole.

Buses to Trinidad in the Amazon take 12 hours during dry season. In the height of rainy season, you must fly. These buses all travel at night, leaving Santa Cruz between 5 and 8 pm. The fare is about $10 per person.

There are two roads to Cochabamba and both are on a paved highway so travel is fairly quick. It is a 12-hour ride whether you take the old or new road. Only one bus a day takes the old road through Samaipata, while numerous buses go along the new.

Sucre is about 16 hours by bus from Santa Cruz, as is Puerto Suarez on the Brazilian border. Most people take a train to Puerto Suarez.

Many buses around Santa Cruz are a bit road worn so comfort is minimal. Bolívar Bus Line is a good company, but their windows often leak. Copacabana Bus in other parts of the country is excellent, but the scam out of Villamontes (see page 268) makes me want to avoid them. Ask other travelers or locals as to who is giving the best service. This changes all the time.

Trains go to Yacuiba on Monday, Wednesday, Friday and Saturday at 1 pm. The super Pullman costs just under $10, while the second class costs $2. Children under three do not pay and those up to age 11 pay only 50%. I'm happy to report that the cost of a ride to San Jose is much less than a ride to the border (some bus companies charge for the full distance to the end of the line, even if you get off earlier).

Trains to Quijarro on the Brazilian border leave every day except Sunday at 3:30 pm and the cost is $14 for a super Pullman or $2.50 for second class.

There is also a ferrobus night train that goes to the border and leaves Tuesday, Thursday and Sunday at 7 pm. A bed costs $35 per person all the way to the border and a semi-bed (which, in reality, is a reclining seat), costs $30. This includes air conditioning, TV, food and bathrooms.

Those people wanting to visit the missions can take a train to San Jose de Chiquitos, the first village along the circuit, and then bus it the rest of the way. If going super Pullman class, all meals and some soft drinks are included in the fare. There is toilet paper in the bathrooms (for a while any-way) and supper is served in a dining car. The trains are comfortable, though you must endure watching Spanish-language kung-fu videos.

A large train/bus station called the Terminal Ferraviaria, on the third *anillo*, is where buses, trains, tickets and schedules can be obtained. The compound is often called the "bimodal." Hawkers outside sell traditional foods. Taxis are not allowed within the gates. Considering that train tickets can be purchased only on the day of travel, the lines are well managed. Note that some people make a living by standing in line and selling their places to others who arrive later. This is an accepted practice.

Transportation from the bimodal to the center of town costs 45¢ per person by taxi. Buses cost 15¢, but luggage can be a problem. Taxis in town cost 45¢ to anywhere within the first two *anillos*. It is a half-hour walk, without a pack, from the bimodal to the center of town. The climate is hot, so to walk with a pack would require a few beer stops on the way.

Taxis can be hired for the day from Rembarto Artegoa, radio mobile #99, ☎ 422-2020 or 716-196-682 (cell). He charges between $25 and $30 for a full day, gas included, and can take up to four people.

◆ History

Santa Cruz de la Sierra was founded by explorer Nuño de Chavez in 1560. He was a Spaniard who named the city in honor of his own city, Extremadura in Spain. But the Bolivian version was later renamed after the third president, Andres de Santa Cruz, the man responsible trying to unite Peru and Bolivia into one country. Originally built on the plains of Grigota near the village of San Jose de Chiquita, 135 miles/220 km east of its present location, Santa Cruz was destroyed by local Indian tribes within three years. The town was moved to Rio Guopay, and by 1595 it was moved again to Rio Pirai, where it now sits. The city quickly became the center of religion for missionaries of all orders. It has been known by four different names; Santa Cruz de la Sierra, San Lorenzo de la Frontera, San Real Lorenzo and San Lorenzo of the Ravine.

◆ Services

The **telephone office** is on Warnes #82, just off the plaza. Telephone booths on the streets take the shapes of various local birds. I especially like the pelican.

The **post office** is on Avenida Bolívar and 21 de Mayo.

Internet service is available at many places. Try the one at Avenida Ayacucho #208, ☎ 333-7981, upstairs. It has the fastest machines and the room is cool inside.

Money exchange is done on the plaza at the Western Union office. They charge a mere 2.5% commission for travelers' checks but give the going bank rate minus .01 peso. Bank machines charge a minimum of $2.50 per transaction so unless you can take out a large amount at one time you may still be better off with travelers' checks or cash. There is no commission charged for cash.

THE CHACO

A **clinic** that is recommended by IAMAT is **Clinica Angel Foianini**, Avenida Irala #468, ☎ 623-2465. The director is Jorge Foianini. The main hospital in the center of Santa Cruz is on Avenida Canoto (the 1st *anillo*) between Avenida Ibanez and Rafael Peña.

◆ Sightseeing

Plaza 24 de Septiembre seems to be as busy a place as the cathedral flanking its side. I read, in numerous places, that sloths live in the trees around the plaza, but look as I did I found nothing. It seemed to me that the locals were laughing at me as I searched.

The **Zoological Park** on Avenida Cristo Redentor has animals like wolves, wild dogs and wild pigs tucked into jungle vegetation and is considered one of the better zoos in Bolivia. Don't believe it. The climate is not conducive to the health of all the animals (like the bear or the llamas) and because Bolivia is strapped for cash when it comes to the care of animals, they don't have adequate housing. This zoo would be a great project for the Villa Tunari group who rescue damaged or mistreated animals and put them on rehabilitation programs. The zoo is open daily from 9 am to 8 pm and admission is $1.

Rio Pirai at the end of Avenida Roca and Coronado has a resort atmosphere, with numerous places to eat, drink beer, enjoy the sun (or get out of it) and play with locals in the 104°F/40°C temperatures.

A park area close to the river has dry forest, grassland and a small marsh. Birding is excellent in the mornings, although the afternoons can be a waste of time as some birds, like the locals, prefer to rest during the height of the heat.

The **Botanical Gardens** are seven miles/12 km from the center along Avenida Suarez Arana, on the road to Cotoca, east of the city. The gardens are a haven for birders. This is a fairly new park and work is ongoing. The area covers some of the most important dry forest in the country, along with grassland and a small marsh so the variety of birds is large. Most of the many plants are labeled and park benches are scattered around.

Parque Arenal and **Municipal Ethnographical Museum** is between Vaca Diez, 6 de Agosto and Caballero, four blocks north of the plaza. Walk along Calle Chiquisaca and you will come to it. The park's famous ceramic-tile mural, La Gesta del Oriente Boliviano (The face of the eastern Bolivian), was created in 1969-71 by the artist Lorgio Vaca. It shows many people as they march along waving banners.

The museum has a grand collection of musical instruments like handmade violins and drums from the missions area.

❖ SYMBOLIC DANCE

One of the dances indigenous to the region and often practiced on the streets of Santa Cruz has the dancers with ghost-white faces parading through traffic on stilts. This display is supposed to depict the conquering of pagan deities by Christianity.

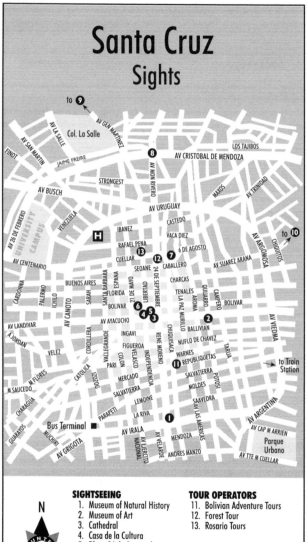

Santa Cruz
Sights

to **9**

AV GEN MARTINEZ

Col. La Salle

AV LA SALLE

AV SAN MARTIN

FINOT

JAIME FREIRE

STRONGEST

AV BUSCH

AV 26 DE FEBRERO

UNIVERSITY CAMPUS

VENEZUELA

H

AV CENTENARIO

CARDININA

PALERMO

ICHILO

AV CANOTO

AV LANDIVAR

A JORDAN

VELEZ

M SAUCEDO

M FLORES

CHARAGUA

GUARAYOS

MUCHIRI

Bus Terminal ■

AV GRIGOTA

8

AV MON RIVERO

AV CRISTOBAL DE MENDOZA

LOS TAJIBOS

MAXOS

AV TRINIDAD

AV URUGUAY

IBANEZ

CASTEDO

VACA DIEZ

RAFAEL PENA

CUELLAR

13

12

7

6 DE AGOSTO

CABALLERO

AV SUAREZ ARANA

SEODANE

CHARCAS

BUENOS AIRES

ESPANA

SANTA BARBARA

FLORIDA

SARAH

BOLIVAR

AV AYACUCHO

4

3

CORDILLERA

VALLEGRANDE

FIGUEROA

VELASCO

COLON

PARI

CATOLICA

IZOZOG

MERCADO

SALVATIERRA

LEMOINE

PARAPETI

LA RIVA

AV IRALA

AV VELARDE

AV EJERCITO NACIONAL

MENDOZA

ANDRES MANZO

TENALES

AROMA

LA PAZ MURILLO

BALLIVIAN

NUFLO DE CHAVEZ

WARNES

REPUBLIQUETAS

SALVATIERRA

MOLDES

SAAVEDRA

AV LAS AMERICAS

AV ARGENTINA

QUIJARO

CAMPERO

BOLIVAR

AV VIEDMA

TARIJA

POTOSI

AV CAP M ARRIEN

Parque Urbano

AV TTE M CUELLAR

to **10**

CHIQUITOS

AV ARGOMOSA

to Train Station

2

INGAVI

RENE MORENO

CHUQUISACA

INDEPENDENCIA

11

SEOANE

24 DE SEPTIEMBRE

LIBERTAD

21 DE MAYO

1

N

HUNTER PUBLISHING

SIGHTSEEING
1. Museum of Natural History
2. Museum of Art
3. Cathedral
4. Casa de la Cultura
5. Plaza 24 de Septiembre
6. Chiquitas Art
7. Arenal Park
8. El Cristo
9. Zoological Park
10. Botanical Gardens

TOUR OPERATORS
11. Bolivian Adventure Tours
12. Forest Tour
13. Rosario Tours

1 MILE

1 KM

© 2005 HUNTER PUBLISHING, INC

THE CHACO

The **Museum of Natural History**, Avenida Irala #565, ☎ 436-6574, is open 9 am to noon and 3 to 6 pm daily. Admission is $1.25. Exhibits include rocks and gemstones found in the area as well as fossils and dead amphibians (often in jars of formaldehyde). But the big display is the insects. The roach display has 3,500 species, some whose ancestors go back about 320 million years.

Historical Churches

Plaza 24 de Septiembre on Calle Ayacucho and Avenida 24 de Septiembre has a brown-brick **Basilica Menor de San Lorenzo** dominating one side. It is an imposing building, the most recent in a long line of cathedrals on this spot. Built by Mercedario Fray Diego de Porres in 1605 under the directorship of the Viceroy of Teledo, the cathedral was reconstructed by Bishop Ramon de Herbosos in 1770. Finally, in 1835 Marshal Andres de Santa Cruz (third president) wanted something worthy of the city so, under the guidance of French architect Felipe Bestres, the new cathedral came to be. It is nice to see brown brick rather than stone as the architectural base.

Go inside whenever the doors are open. The altar is of worked silver originally from the Jesuit mission of San Pedro de Moxos, as are four hand-carved wooden confessionals with intricate paintings over the wood. The ornate interior of the cathedral is quite a contrast to the exterior.

The **Carlos Gericke Suarez Museum**, attached to the cathedral, is divided into four rooms, one featuring silver, one jewelry, one paintings and one woodwork. All rooms have relics from the Jesuit Missions farther east as well as gold and silver workings from the 18th century. The museum was named after a university professor from the area whose silver work was used as an example of craftsmanship throughout the 17th and 18th centuries. The museum is open Tuesday, Thursday and Sunday, 10 am to noon and 6 to 8 pm.

◆ Adventures in Culture

Casa de Cultura de Raul Otero Reiche, on the plaza, is used as a cultural theater, offering plays, concerts, movies, exhibits of photography, sculpture and contemporary paintings. The theater halls are lined with old paintings and there is also a library featuring regional publications. Try to get tickets to a concert while in town. Watch for posters at the entrance.

The **Museum of Art**, Avenida Sucre and Calle Potosi, ☎ 334-0926, is in the same colonial building as the tourist office. The artwork is good, mostly contemporary sculptures. There are numerous rooms, some with works of young artists not yet famous and other rooms with works of artists like Lorgio Vaca. There is usually a new display of Bolivian work every six months or so.

Chiquitas Art at the Santa Cruz Museum of History, Avenida La Casona and Calle Junin, just in front of the post office, ☎ 332-4620, is open Monday to Friday, 9:30 am to noon and 3:30 to 7 pm. The art display has works that blend old styles with contemporary ones. This is a permanent exhibition.

◆ Adventures on Foot

Hash House Harriers is a club of runners who usually have a fun run once a week in Santa Cruz. A hash run goes like this. There is a route, fixed by one of the club members, that the runners must follow. However, the runners don't know where the route goes or what the markers are. The runners start running and, as they figure out the markers and are able to follow them, they holler "on-on" in Spanish, of course, and everyone follows. This is done at a jogging pace. When the run is finally over, everyone usually congregates for a few hours of socializing. In Santa Cruz they welcome anyone, members and non-members, from the ages of zero on up. They run on Mondays at 5:30 pm and have a dinner after the run. The contact persons are Jim Bibb, ☎ 558-5003, jimbibb@its.com.bo; Susan Guillen, ☎ 355-0000, susan.guillen@bg-bolivia.com; and John Naphan, john.naphan@transredes.com.

Lomas de Arenal del Palmar is 9.8 miles/16 km east of the city along the highway to Palma Sola. This odd landscape, nestled in the tropical jungle, is a desert complete with sand dunes and a tiny lagoon that is good for swimming. Originally designed to be part of the sewage system, opposition from locals resulted in this area becoming a park instead. The sand is believed to come from erosion of surrounding rocks. Bird activity is high. There are trails and a camping facility. To get here, catch the Palmar micro from Calle Grigota and Cañoto, or take a taxi (less than $5).

Las Cuevas is a set of waterfalls between Samaipata and Santa Cruz along the old highway. To get to the falls, catch a minibus going toward Samaipata. Ask the driver to let you off for the walk to Las Cuevas. It is barely half an hour from Santa Cruz to the turnoff. The walk starts along the river that crosses the highway. Go about 650 ft/200 m upstream and follow a trail uphill on your right. At the top, face the valley and hike to your left (not right, or you will fall off the hill). Continue along the ridge until you come to a road. Follow this back down to the highway. The reason most people do this hike is to watch for birds. Bring your reference book, binoculars, some water, sun hat and bird list. The place literally twitters.

◆ Adventures on Water

There are two public swimming pools in Santa Cruz and, with the heat, you may want to patronize them. The first, called **Aqualand**, ☎ 385-2500, is seven miles/12 km on the highway going north toward Trinidad (see below). The other, **Pescina de Santa Cruz**, is three miles/five km along the old highway toward Cochabamba. This one is an ordinary pool for those wanting only to swim. The entry fee is 50¢ and open hours are about 9 am to 6 pm daily.

Aqualand at Km 12 on the northern highway just past the Viru Viru Airport (not to be confused with the swimming pool, above) is 16 acres of water fun. It has a capacity to hold 5,000 people and employs up to 60 lifeguards during high season. Inside is the usual water park with slides and a wave pool. A sandy beach surrounds the pool. A lazy river section has gentle waves and current for those wanting to float along. A speed slide attracts high rollers, while the kiddy slide sees more sane visitors. A family raft that carries a number of people down the slide together is popular. This is the only water slide park of its kind in Bolivia. The entry fee is $10 and open hours are Friday to Sunday, 9 am to 6 pm.

◆ Tour Operators

Bolivian Adventure Tours, Avenida Chiquisaca #561, ☎ 336-4848. Ana Maria Garcia, who runs the company, speaks English very well. The tour agency's specialty trip is a run down the Beni River on a luxury boat, *Reina de Enin*. The other big offer is a trip to Noel Kempff Park for three days at a cost of $600 per person (all-inclusive) with a minimum of two people. Their final area of expertise is a trip to Amboro National Park at a cost of $70 per day, per person. Bolivian Adventures can also take you on a three-hour city tour or around the Jesuit missions for a couple of days.

Hombre y Naturaleza is mentioned numerous times in regards to trips around the Pantanal both in the north and in the south. There are also stations in the mission circuit and one at Charagua, south of Santa Cruz and 46 miles/75 km from the Paraguayan border. Contact them in Santa Cruz at ☎ 923-2239, hynb@bibosi.sca.entelnet.bo or prowames@cotas.com. bo. Their English is perfect, their Spanish is even better, and they will assist in planning a trip to meet your needs. They are a NGO and their entire focus is on preserving the environment.

Forest Tour Operator, Calle 24 de Septiembre #22 at Libertad, ☎ 337-2042, offers a number of outdoor adventure opportunities. Their specialties are three days on a ranch, four days in the Pantanal along the Paraguay River and a two-day hike at Robore, just outside the mission town of San Jose de la Chiquitas. Their trip into Amboro National Park can include a horse, hike or bike trip. The company is willing to adjust itineraries to suit your needs. Because of their flexibility, the Robore hike can be included with a mission tour plus a visit to the hot springs. They also offer a hiking trip to Santiago de Chiquitos. One of their more interesting aspects is that they teach forest survival courses. You can rent a jeep for about $130 a day for up to four people. I found them helpful and cooperative, although a bit expensive.

Rosario Tours, Avenida Arenales #193, ☎ 336-9977 or 336-9656, adventura@cotas.com.bo or rosario_tours@cotas.com.bo. Rosario Baldomar is the owner of this tour agency. She offers many tour combination trips, but her best go into Amboro National Park and the Pantanal. There are also the city tours and shopping tours around Santa Cruz. The four-day trekking trip in Amboro requires a minimum of three people. It runs $245 per person, including food, transportation, accommodations and a Spanish-speaking guide (an English-speaking guide costs more). You can also go for three days and two nights at a cost of $145 per person.

The Pantanal trip runs four days and three nights. If staying in the five-star hotel, the cost is $487 per person and the tour is all-inclusive from Puerto Suarez (which can be reached by train). If staying in the hostel, the cost is $374 for one, $246 (each) for two people and $206 for three people. This trip includes a visit to the Cave of Motacusito, which has vampire bats inside, a boat trip through the Santa Tecla Forest area, a trip down Rio Paraguay to Brazil and a stop at the Laguna Caceres on the way back.

Rosario's mission tour takes four days. It's all-inclusive and costs, depending on your hotel selection, $480 per person (minimum of two people) or $280 per person (minimum of four people and a maximum of seven). English- and German-speaking guides are available. The English-speaking guide with whom I spoke had good command of the language.

Wildland Tours, 3516 NE, 155th Street, Seattle, WA 98155-7412, www. wildland.com, takes travelers into Noel Kempff National Park starting with a pickup in Santa Cruz. In six days they cover both areas of the park and transportation services are included. Their specialties are in guided hikes, bird watching and photography. This is a company that will do everything for you except click your shutter. See page 45, *Outfitters Who Do All the Work*, for more information on this company.

◆ Places to Stay

Residencial Ballivian, *Calle Ballivian #71*, ☎ *332-1960, residencialballivian@ yahoo.es, $*, has rooms set around a large courtyard that's well maintained and full of plants. There are lots of toilets and sinks around the building (no private bathrooms) and hot water is available all day.

❖ HOTEL PRICING	
$	$10 to $20
$$	$21 to $50
$$$	$51 to $75
$$$$	$76 to $100
$$$$$	over $100

The kitchen can be used until 9 pm, when it is shut down so the noise won't disturb other guests. The owners are friendly and helpful.

Hotel Sara, *Calle Sara #85 between Calle Ayachuco and Avenida Junin*, ☎ *332-2425 or 337-2524, $$*, has large rooms, all with private bath, TV, ceiling fans, reading lights and soft beds. The rooms are cleaned daily. The owner uses solar panels for electricity so the hot water is usually cold. A continental breakfast is included in your room rate.

Los Pozos Hotel, *Calle Quijarro #431 and Caballero and 6 de Agosto*, ☎ *332-1245, $$*, has a number of rooms on three levels around a central courtyard. The hotel is just one block from the Parque Arenal. The rooms are large and all have private baths. Everything here is clean.

Hotel Bilbosi, *Avenida Junin #218*, ☎ *334-8887, $$*, has a travel service and complimentary Internet access. Rooms have fans or air conditioning (additional cost), dressers, chairs, soft beds, tiled floors, mirrors, large bathrooms and luggage holders. This is a clean and pleasant place.

Excelsior Hotel, *Calle Rene Moreno #70*, ☎ *332-5924, $$$*, is directly across from the cathedral, so it's handy to the square. Rooms have private bath, air conditioning, TV, towels and telephone and come with a continental breakfast. Each has attractive wall murals painted by local artists and some rooms have built-in desks that have been painted in modern design.

Hotel Copacabana, *Avenida Junin #217*, ☎ *336-2770, $$$*, is a three-star property that offers rooms with air conditioning (more expensive) or a fan. Located on three floors around a courtyard that doubles as the restaurant, each room is small and clean and features large windows, tasteful décor, mirrors, TV and soft beds. The price includes breakfast. Bathrooms

THE CHACO

have a separate shower stall and towels; toilet paper and soap are supplied. The rooms with air conditioning are larger and have a fridge/mini bar.

La Siesta, *Calle Vallegrande #17*, ☎ *334-9775, www.hotel-lasiesta. com, $$$$*, has 44 small bright rooms with tiled floors, cable TV, cupboards, air conditioning and a separate shower stall in the bathroom. The price includes a continental breakfast, use of the pool and Internet access. There is also a safe, garage, restaurant, money exchange and laundry service.

Hotel La Paz, *Calle La Paz #69*, ☎ *332-1728, hotellapaz@cotas.com. bo, $$$$*, has good rates. The 16 rooms are set around a well-maintained courtyard. The place is spotless and the owner is friendly. A single room is small, but the doubles are huge – some have sitting rooms. Rooms have soft beds, large closets, cable TV, telephones, air conditioning and a fridge/bar and breakfast is included. There's a travel agency on site, a safe deposit service and a car park. Many tourists stay here and repeat guests are common. Reservations are advisable during high season.

Globtrotter Hotel, *Calle Sarah #49*, ☎ *337-2754, $$$$*, is a quiet little place that includes breakfast in the rate. Rooms are large and clean, with air conditioning, cable TV and a fridge/bar. I think the price is a bit high.

Gran Hotel Santa Cruz, *Calle Rene Mareno*, ☎ *334-8811, www.gran-hotelsantacruz.com, $$$$$*, is the classiest place in eastern Bolivia. What first strikes your eye when entering the large marble foyer are the three carpets lying under leather couches. The rugs are genuine, handmade Persians. The hotel has six floors, with 110 rooms in all.

There is a large pool at the back flanked by a bar. Above the bar is a gym and sauna, both wet and dry. The rooms are huge, with wall-to-wall windows, 80 TV channels, mini fridges, double beds, telephones in the bedrooms and bathrooms, full-length mirrors and safes in the closets. A larger, more elegant room has a sitting area with leather couches. There are also Jacuzzis and bidets in the ballroom-sized bathrooms. The halls are thickly carpeted and interspersed with oak writing desks. The entire building has central air conditioning and/or heating, security monitors and underground parking. To date there has never been a robbery from a car in the parking area.

Canciller Hotel, *Calle Ayacucho #220 between Colon and Velasco,* ☎ *337-2525, hotelcanciller@entelnet.com, $$$$$*, is a four-star hotel that has over 40 rooms plus a presidential suite. The rooms are spacious, use the modern magnetic strip card to open the doors, and have air conditioning, mini-bar and a sitting area. On site there is a restaurant, swimming pool, laundry service and Internet access.

◆ Places to Eat

Casa del Camba, *Avenida Cristobal de Mendosa #539*, ☎ *342-7864, www. casadelcamba.com*, opened in 1986 and is the best restaurant in Santa Cruz. It should be experienced by everyone at least once. A taxi here will cost $1 for two people and as you pull up a waiter

❖ RESTAURANT PRICING	
$	under $5
$$	$5 to $10
$$$	$11 to $25
$$$$	$26 to $50
$$$$$	over $50

Santa Cruz
Hotels & Restaurants

1. La Casona Bistro	12. Shanghai Bar
2. Residencial Ballivan	13. Peru Restaurant
3. Los Pozos Hotel	14. Texas Rodeo Grill
4. Globetrotter Hotel	15. Canciller Hotel
5. Casa de Camba	16. Hotel Sara
6. Alexander, Mr Café, Yogen Fruz	17. Copacabana
7. El Chico	18. La Paz
8. La Esquina del Pescado	19. Bibosi
9. Restaurant Barbablu	20. La Siesta
10. Restaurant Vegetariano	21. Hotel Excelsior
11. La Carreta, El Gato	22. Gran Hotel Santa Cruz

N

© 2005 HUNTER PUBLISHING, INC

dressed in a straw hat, white shirt and black pants will open the car door and show you the way inside. "Inside" is outside, an open courtyard with covered areas in case of rain.

The restaurant has a long list of Argentinean, Chilean and Bolivian wines. The most expensive was $14.50 per bottle. We ordered a steak with sausage and shish kabob, served with rice. The meat, cooked on the brazier in front of us, was done to perfection. There was more than we could eat. The cost in total was $30 (price on bill was also displayed in US dollars). The restaurant holds about 800 people and by 8:30 pm (on a Monday night), it was half-full. Unless you come early, as we did, you may want to make reservations. This can be done online.

Alexander, *Avenida Monseñor Rivero #400*, ☎ *337-8653*, is as good here as it is in La Paz. They make a cheesecake with baracuya topping that I highly recommend, while some of my friends prefer the cheesecake with strawberries. Baracuya is a fruit that has a tart, lemon-like taste. Alexander is in the center of a three-block, up-scale string of cafés and bars near the university and court house. It is a nice walk from the central plaza.

Pastic Ceria Café, Avenida Monseñor Rivero #328, ☎ 333-4410. The best pizza in town is made here. You can watch yours being made from scratch and stuck in the wood-fired oven to bake. This place has the same owners as Restaurant Barbablu, below.

Mr Café, *across the street from Alexander on Avenida Mons. Rivero #260*, gives strong competition to Alexander with excellent pastries and top-notch service. The thick sweet cream put into the coffee (if you want it) is so good I was tempted to tell them to forget the coffee and just serve the cream. They also offer some mean pasta dishes for anywhere between $3 and $7.

La Casona Bistro, *Calle Arenales #222*, ☎ *337-8495*, is a little Mexican place that serves both snacks and full international meals. The atmosphere is a big draw. Plus, it is not far from the main plaza.

El Chico, *Calle Libertad #350*, ☎ *333-0027*, is a Tex-Mex bar and restaurant chain. They have good burritos and pizza and also carry an entire line of Mexican foods. Open Monday to Thursday, 11 am-midnight and on weekends until 1 am (on Sundays they close at 3 pm).

Restaurant Ria Lia, *Calle Murilla #40*, ☎ *336-8183*, has an incredible buffet. Come hungry. When I was there they had 46 veggie dishes, both hot and cold. Besides that, there were five meat dishes that could be included on your plate (some locals just loaded up with meat) and three juices from which to choose. All this sells for $2 on Sundays and $1.50 the rest of the week. They are open from 11:30 am until 3 pm. A *boca libre* sign means all you can eat. Come early to eat here because Bolivians know about it too.

❖ **BREAKFAST BUNS**

Uñape is a small bun that has a doughy center filled with cheese. These are often sold around the bus stations during breakfast time.

Leonardo's Restaurant, *Calle Warnes #300, just down from La Vieja Café and Bar,* is situated in a huge colonial mansion. It offers one of the classiest atmospheres in Santa Cruz.

La Esquina del Pescado, *corner of Sarah and Florida,* looks like it takes up an entire block but, in fact, it is three places side by side. It is famous locally for its food. To get food, you must give your order to the man at the cash box beside the barbecue. He will take your money and give you a numbered receipt. You then find a place to sit, either on the street or in one of the three restaurants. Someone will pick up your receipt and your meal will miraculously appear. The fish is good and often there are five or six choices. The cost is around $2 per meal. They start serving at 9 am and stay open till late in the evening. Saturday and Sunday are the most popular days and often the wait for a table is 15 minutes.

Burger King, *Avenida San Martin & Calle Siete,* ☎ 342-8410, *or Calle Rene Moreno and Avenida Andrez Manzo,* ☎ 337-1292, has not been run out of town by local restaurants – yet. If you want a touch of home, a sparkling clean bathroom, Arctic-quality air conditioning and a Whopper Combo for $3, then this is the place. If you're economizing, a simple burger with ketchup, mustard and one dill pickle is less than a dollar. With cheese, brings the price up to a full dollar. They also have a chef's salad for $2.25, hot apple dessert for 85¢, and two pieces of chicken for $3.25.

Restaurant Vegetariano, *24 de Septiembre #351,* ☎ 332-1794, is open every day from noon to 3 pm and again from 6 pm to 8:30 pm. This highly recommended place offers a buffet full of organic vegetables.

La Carreta, *24 de Septiembre,* ☎ 332-1794, has a nice ambiance with an open fireplace and an open-air patio. For example, ravioli is $1.50, sweet and sour pork is $1.75 and a filet is $1.25. The restaurant is patronized by many Bolivians.

Restaurant Barbablu, *Avenidea Ejercito Nacional #150,* ☎ 334-4037, is known for its home-made pasta and is recommended by locals. When we were here, lots of people were eating, but many more were taking orders home. Barbablu's second place is on Avenida Monsenor Rivero #328, ☎ 333-4410. It specializes in Italian pastries. The coffee is excellent also.

Rincón Brazilero, *Calle Libertad #358,* ☎ 333-1237, sells food by the kilo. I did not try it, but it comes highly recommended by aid workers in Bolivia.

Yogen Fruz, *Calle Cañada Strongest and Monseñor Rivero,* ☎ 337-7221, has the entire line of frozen yogurts, plus ice cream. The shop is tiny, but the air conditioning is great. This is a real treat – far better than some of the other franchises that come out of North America.

El Gato, *24 de Septiembre #285,* ☎ 333-2040, has a good buffet that offers ravioli, spaghetti with mushrooms, chicken, meats and salads. The cost is by weight. Half a kilo is about $1.75 with a minimum charge of $1. The buffet is available every day from noon to 3 pm, after which meals can be ordered from the menu. This is a popular place.

Shanghai Bar and Restaurant, *Avenida 26 de Febrero #27 (in the 2nd anillo),* ☎ 352-3939, is where one should go for Chinese food. The sweet and sour ribs are excellent – similar to those I have tasted in Hong Kong.

THE CHACO

The atmosphere is classy, rather than tacky. The only drawback is the location, a little way from the center of town.

Peru Restaurant, *Avenida San Martin and 9 Oeste Equipetrol*, ☎ 336-0296, offers the best ceviche in eastern Bolivia, as well as other dishes such as filet mignon. The portions are large and the food excellent, but prices are high, about $5 per serving. Diners are given a complimentary dish of salted corn chips before their meal. There is a rather ordinary eating area in an open patio, plus an elegant inside area that sets the tone for a romantic evening.

Chalet la Suisse, *Calle los Gomeros #98*, ☎ 343-6070, has been recommended by many for its trout, llama, quinoa and hot peppers (among other well known Bolivian and European dishes). They also have fondue dishes with either meat or cheese.

Michelangelo, *Avenida Chiuisaca #502 and Sulvatierra*, ☎ 334-8403, is open Monday to Friday for lunch and Monday to Saturday for dinner. This is considered one of the better restaurants in town.

Texas Rodeo Grill, *Calle Aruma, in the Urbar Barrio, outside the second anillo*, ☎ 352-2244, is in Hotel La Quinta and is open noon to 2:30 pm and 6-11 pm. They specialize in grilled meats and Mexican food. This is where the Hash House Harriers often go after their weekly run. I take that as a sign that the food is very good.

◆ Nightlife

La Taberna, Calle Monseñor Rivero #281, ☎ 345-3949, is a tapas bar that is popular with local yuppies. It specializes in paella made with meat, fish or vegetables.

The Irish Pub on the main plaza in the Bolivar Shopping Mall is by far the best place to fraternize with the local ex-pats, but the cost is high. A drink or a meal costs the same here as it does in North America. The pub overlooks the square and is decorated with numerous old photos of Ireland and a great poster showing famous literary characters like James Joyce and Jonathan Swift. The music is usually good but a tad loud, the lights are dim and the service is moderately quick.

◆ Shopping

Manos Indigenas Artist Shop, Calle Cuellar #16, ☎ 337-2042, has handmade works from the Guarayos, Chiquitos and Ayores indigenous groups of eastern Bolivia. There are ceramics from Cotoca and Huayculi, wood carvings and jute bags, masks and even a few instruments (although I cannot determine the quality). This is an excellent place to browse. The shop is off the main tourist areas, so you must be interested in indigenous art in order to seek it out.

Artesanias Pewter Palace, 24 de Septiembre #76, ☎ 333-8916, is filled with wooden bowls, leather items (hats especially), and pewter and silver pieces. Prices are comparable to other shops in town, but this shop has a good selection. Open 8:30 am-9 pm daily.

Inca Products, Avenida Cañoto and Landivar, ☎ 333-7049, incaproduct@hotmail.com, has a large selection of wood, pewter, copper, silver, alpaca wool and leather products. English is spoken and your purchases can be shipped anywhere in the world – for a price, of course. Open Monday to Saturday, 9 am-8 pm, and Sunday, 10 am-5 pm.

Joyeria Andrea, Calle Junin #177, ☎ 334-2435, is a classy shop that specializes in bolivianite, or ametrine, as it is also called. A semi-precious quartz, bolivianite comes in purple or yellow and looks to me a lot like amethyst. This jewelry shop was the first to work with the stone and some of the pieces they have for sale are exquisite.

Arte Campo, Monseñor Salvatierra #407, ☎ 355-9133, is a co-op that carries the work of mission artists and distributes it around the country. Please stop into their store and maybe make a purchase. The bags for sale come from seven different groups of artists and each group has its own specific art design. The dyes are from plants and the material is from the garabata plant that women gather from the forest. The money from the sale of bags alone helps support the families of 200 women.

◆ Jesuit Mission Tour

Altitude: 1,363 ft/410 m (average)

The Jesuit missions near Santa Cruz are unique and different from anything else you will see in the world. They are mostly constructed with wood beams and ceilings that have been polished and carved into different patterns using baroque designs interspersed with images of local plants and animals, such as vines, pineapples and armadillos. The plaster walls have been painted in intricate designs using natural colors of the Amazon area. The buildings have been restored.

DISTANCES BETWEEN MISSIONS	
Santa Cruz to San Jose	162 miles/265 km
San Jose to San Rafael	80 miles/130 km
San Rafael to Santa Ana	15 miles/25 km
Santa Ana to San Ignacio	28 miles/45 km
San Rafael to San Miguel	24 miles/40 km
San Miguel to San Ignacio	22 miles/36 km
San Ignacio to Concepcion	111 miles/182 km
Concepcion to San Xavier	38 miles/62 km
San Xavier to San Ramon	32 miles/52 km
San Ramon to Santa Cruz	88 miles/143 km

THE CHACO

A tour of the missions can be done with a company, by rented jeep or by public transportation. If going on your own and using public transportation, start in San Jose and end in Concepcion. This is because of the train schedules. Traveling from Santa Cruz to San Jose, the train leaves in the afternoon and arrives in San Jose before midnight. Going to Santa Cruz by train from San Jose means you must catch it at 2 am and arrive in Santa Cruz a bit before noon. Sitting around a train station in the middle of the night is not very appealing.

You must carry either Bolivian or American cash as there are no bank machines or places that will accept traveler's checks on this circuit.

History

Declared a UNESCO site in 1990, the 10 missions that were built in the territory we now call Bolivia were constructed between 1692 and 1760. Others were built in Argentina, Brazil, Paraguay and Peru.

When the Jesuits came, they not only brought religion but they also offered the semi-nomadic societies in the area a school, hospital and religion complete with impressive ceremonies. The Jesuits gave the people a place to express their art forms by carving and painting. But most of all, the locals were attracted to the church because of the music.

Father Martin Schmid came here in 1729. He was a dedicated musician originally from Switzerland. He started designing the missions in the unique fashion, with huge halls and high ceilings, built with mud brick covered in plaster and painted. Each wood beam is made from a single tree trunk and carved by local artists of the time. Schmid also started and directed choirs, made musical instruments like flutes and violins, and copied thousands of sheets of music.

Schmid was obsessed with music and even the construction of the missions is believed to symbolically represent musical keys that metaphorically allow the architecture to resonate with music. This I was told.

❖ **NOT LITTLE PEOPLE**

The indigenous people were called Chiquitos, not because of their size (*chiquito* means tiny in Spanish), but because of the size of the doors to their houses. The doors were made small to keep the excruciating heat out, the cool in.

In 1767, King Carlos III of Spain expelled the Jesuits from Bolivia and the missions fell into disrepair. See the somewhat sanctimonious de Niro movie, *The Mission*, about this closure. The leaders of the Roman Catholic Church took a lot of these items because they felt the riches would be better appreciated by white people in big cities. However, in 1975 restoration of the missions started under the leadership of architect and priest Hans Roth, and with the help of Father Godofredo Trenker. What inspired Roth was that while he was poking around the area, he came across 5,000 pieces of hand-written music. Some of the music pieces were by Zipoli Domenico, a famous European composer who lived from 1688 to 1726. It is now believed that Father Schmid had brought this music with him, as well as pieces copied from other composers such as Vivaldi and Corelli. It was this music that was used to teach the local people how to sing and

Mission Tour

N

Noel Kempff Mercado

Urubichá
Santa Maria
San Pablo
Ascención
Zuruquizo
SAN FRANCISCO XAVIER
Santa Rosa de la Mina
San Ramon
CONCEPCION
Totaicito
Carmen Ruiz
Panorama
SAN IGNACIO DE LOYOLA
SANTA ANA
SAN RAFAEL
SAN MIGUEL DE VELASCO
San Juan de Lomerio
La Manga
San Rafaelito
El Recreo
El Cerro de Concepción
Estación Quimone
SAN JOSE DE CHIQUITOS
San Juan de las Taperas
Roboré
Aguas Calientes
to Puerto Suárez
Los Troncos
Pailón
Buena Vista
Santa Cruz de la Sierra
La Guardia

...... Railroad

61 MILES
100 KM

THE CHACO

© 2005 HUNTER PUBLISHING, INC

play. After Roth found the music, he spent the next and last 30 years of his life helping with the restoration of the missions.

Adventures in Sound

All the missions are involved in a new music program and sponsor a bi-annual festival that is of an international standard. The event includes renowned musicians from Spain, Bolivia, Argentina, England, Italy, Germany and France playing with local symphonies. The first concert, held in 1998, was such a success that the organizers decided to have it every other year. The next festival will be in 2004. For detailed information about the festival, contact Festival International de Musica Misiones de Chiquitos, Casa Municipal de la Cultura Raul Otero Reiche, Casilla #3673, Santa Cruz, ☎ 332-2476.

As a lead-up to the festival, missions present concerts on the last Saturday of every month. In July and August, performances are Saturday at around 8 pm, with a few early morning sessions as well. The touring musicians are both Bolivian and visitors who will later participate in the festival. There is no cost for you to go and listen. Ask at the tourist office in Santa Cruz for schedules or ask at the missions as you travel the circuit. Participating missions are Santa Ana, San Ignacio, San Rafael, San Miguel, San Jose, Concepcion and San Javier. All the music is classical.

❖ VIOLIN VILLAGE

Those very interested in music, and specifically in the violin, should visit the village of Urubicha on the road to Trinidad. Although not part of the missions, the village plays a musical role. To get there, take a bus from Santa Cruz going to Trinidad and get off at Asuncion. From there, take a micro to the village. There are basic accommodations available and places to eat.

There, under the guidance of priests, children learn to play classical music very much as their ancestors did. They memorize the notes and often play three different instruments. There are over 200 children who form the village choir and orchestra. The students play (practice) every day and come for lessons in-between classes at school.

The interesting thing is that these children, whose ancestors were first introduced to the music 300 to 400 years ago, now play the same missionic baroque music with pride. They also play their own traditional music with passion. Many of the young students take part in the biannual festival of music.

The village violin maker claims he can't make the instruments fast enough to keep pace with the demand.

Mission San Jose de Chiquitos

This is the first (or last) village on the mission circuit. The train from Santa Cruz arrives here around midnight, but the village, being in the hottest area of Bolivia, is wide awake in the cool of the night so walking to the center is not dangerous. There are also taxis available at the train station.

San Jose is a dusty, dry town that seems more like an outlaw's hideout than a religious center. Even the mission is what you would see in an old Western movie.

The town of Santa Cruz de la Siera was first built at this location in 1592. The village was later moved to the banks of the Guopay River and then again to its present site. However, some people remained near the village of San Jose and the mission prospered.

THE MISSION: The Mission of San Jose de Chiquitos was built in 1697. It features high wooden ceilings and attractive carved wood pillars and doors. A ghoulish figure of Christ bleeding on the cross sits at one of the side altars. Some of the front façade has the original paint and is not as glittery as the rest. The ladder to the bell tower is held together by grooves and wooden pegs, rather than nails. This is how it was originally made. The beauty of this mission is the stonework and the block-long front face. It is the only mission in the country made of stone.

ADVENTURES ON FOOT: If you have the time, walk to the base of Turubo Hill, the hill with some vegetation beyond the village. You will see paths going up to the top. To reach the base of the hill will take about 15 minutes from the plaza.

PLACES TO STAY & EAT: The owner of **Hotel Turubo**, *on the plaza*, ☎ 972-2037, $, scrutinizes her clients carefully before she rents a room. The moderate-sized accommodations have mosquito screens on the windows and the communal bathrooms and showers are clean and well kept. The Turubo offers a basic breakfast but no juice, just Nescafé coffee. However, the *salteneria* just one block north has good food.

Victoria Hotel, *to the side of the mission (no phone)*, $, can hold up to 35 people and, during festivals, you can negotiate for a hammock or even a spot for your tent. Rooms come with or without private baths, and those with private facilities can accommodate three people. The small rooms have fans and are spotlessly clean, with cement floors and small windows. There are hammocks in the patio area and a car park. The owner was friendly and went out of his way to accommodate me. Breakfast can be negotiated into the price.

Alojamiento San Jose, *Avenida Mons. Carlos Garicke*, ☎ 972-2106, $, is under new management. It currently has 12 rooms – five with private baths – and an additional four are being built around a tended garden area. The rooms are basic and clean. The new owner is friendly and cooperative.

Hotel Denisse, *Avenida Mons. Carlos Gerike Suarez*, ☎ 972-2230, $$$, has rooms with and without baths and air conditioning. Breakfast is included in the rate. The hotel is clean, comfortable and the beds are soft. Bolivian businessmen patronize the Denisse.

Rafa, on the road to San Ignacio, has the best supper in town. For lunch, go to **Los Yescas** or **Casa Pyla** – both are excellent. To find them, walk along the side street by the Turubo Hotel away from the church. They are within a block of each other.

THE CHACO

GETTING HERE & AWAY: The **bus** leaves from Calle Oriental and 24 de Septiembre daily (except Sunday) at 1 pm for San Ignacio. The five-hour journey costs $4. The **train** for the border leaves around midnight. The train to Santa Cruz, in the opposite direction, leaves at 2 am.

Mission San Rafael

San Rafael was founded by Father Jose de Arce, the same priest who started the mission at San Francisco Javier. This mission was started in 1693 and it was moved from its original site to the banks of the Sapoco River in 1705. It was completed in the mid-1700s and from then until the expulsion of the Jesuits it was home to over 5,000 people. Today, that number has fallen to 1,000.

THE MISSION: The church itself is one of the more ornate on the circuit, with decorative painting on the outside covering almost every inch. However, I didn't find it gauche. San Rafael is the saint whose image is inside, over the main altar. He made it big with locals because he was believed to be a symbol of one of their own gods who lived in the forests. Both the saint and this god carry fish.

PLACE TO STAY: The town itself is tiny and dusty, but there is one place to stay right on the corner of the plaza. It's basic, but if you can get no farther it is comforting to know the bench in the plaza won't be your home for the night.

GETTING HERE & AWAY: If you come by bus from San Jose de Chiquitos you will have to spend the night. Should you go on to San Ignacio you can take in this mission by returning via taxi (about $25 for two people). That way, you can also stop at Santa Ana and San Miguel. If coming the opposite way by bus, this loop in the circuit can be done either from San Ignacio or by staying at San Rafael for the night.

Mission Santa Ana

THE MISSION: Santa Ana is the smallest of the missions and the most authentic. Built in 1755 by priests who came specifically to help with a smallpox epidemic, it was administered by Jesuits for only 12 years before they left. During that time Father Julian Knogler set up a college that taught wood carving, a craft for which the area is now famous. The paintings on the walls of the buildings are of angels, flowers and musicians playing violins and singing, but the building overall is less ornate than other missions. This simplicity makes it appealing. The bell tower is a simple three-storey structure that sits on four posts and has two bells on the top storey. The bells are still rung before mass every day.

PLACE TO STAY: Hombre y Naturaleza (based in Bolivia) and Amigos de Doñana (based in Spain) are NGO societies dedicated to the promotion and preservation of the natural world. They offer a fairly basic and comfortable place to stay next to the north side of the plaza on Calle Bolívar, ☎ 343-6968. It costs $9 per person per night for a dorm bed, $10 if breakfast is included. Private rooms with double beds cost $8 per person. Bathrooms are communal.

TOUR AGENCY: Hombre y Naturaleza offers half-day guided trips to the museum and gardens for $5-$8 per person, depending on how many are in your group. Guides offer information about museum exhibits and the plants in the garden. The group also offers 4x4 trips to dry forests, mica mines and to Santa Teresita, the Precambrian rock that stands 1,645 ft/500 m high. Should you have a specific interest, talk to these people. They will try to help. Contact them in Santa Ana at caloping@teleline.es or mamencill@hotmail.com; in Santa Cruz at ☎ 923-2239, hynb@bibosi.sca.entelnet.bo or prowames@cotas.com.bo. Their English is good and they will assist in trip planning.

GETTING HERE & AWAY: If you take the bus from San Jose de Chiquitos, you will have to get off at San Rafael and take another bus to Santa Ana. For exact times of buses contact Hombre y Naturaleza (see above). You may also take the bus from San Ignacio direct to Santa Ana (see San Ignacio section for information).

Mission San Miguel de Velasco

San Miguel can be visited from San Ignacio or you can get off the bus from San Jose and spend a night at the one basic *alojamiento* in town. San Miguel is a small, dusty town but interesting enough. Some believe that this mission, on the inside, is the most beautiful of them all. Plan on visiting the carving shops also. There's one at the side of the mission and another just out of town on the road to San Ignacio.

THE MISSION: To get inside, go into the yard by a side gate beside the bell tower and ring the bell of the priest's door.

The mission was started by Felipe Suarez and Gaspar Fernandez de Campos in 1718 and was dedicated mostly to the arts. However, in 1748 the simple adobe church was reconstructed under the direction of Martin Schmid and Father Juan Mesner and in 1765 it was finally inaugurated. At that time it was dedicated to San Miguel. It took 200 workers every day from about 1750 until 1765 to complete the construction, carvings and paintings of this building.

Inside the church, the front altar is carved wood from floor to ceiling, painted in gold glitter so that the polished wood pillars go almost unnoticed. The pulpit is the finest in all the missions. The confessionals are intricately carved and painted in gold and red. The walls too are painted with floral designs interspersed with pictures of different saints. The building's main structure is the original one.

SHOPPING: The **Artist's Workshop**, on the road going to San Ignacio and just up from the church, has carvings for sale. They are mostly reproductions of mission pieces. Because the co-op in town carries work from all the missions, the workers feel that it is better for you to purchase from the co-op and, in turn, keep more people employed. The wooden angel that is used by the missions as a logo was created by an artist from this village.

GETTING HERE & AWAY: If coming from San Jose de Chiquitos by bus, you can get off at San Miguel. To get from there to San Ignacio or San Jose de Chiquitos, you must take a taxi (there aren't many in San Miguel). The best way to visit San Miguel is via San Ignacio, where you can hire a taxi for $10 for two people, round trip.

Mission San Ignacio de Loyola

San Ignacio is a town of about 20,000 people, although I find this hard to believe as the area never seems crowded or busy. However, the action revolving around the bi-annual music festival is obvious and the tourist office strongly promotes these events. The town is one of the more lively mission towns and the places to eat are a bit more varied.

San Ignacio's biggest fiesta besides the usual religious holidays is July 31, when the town celebrates San Ignacio Day.

THE MISSION: Started in 1748 by Miguel Areijer and Diego Contreras and finished in 1761, this mission was the biggest of the group and had the largest congregation until Santa Ana and San Rafael were built. During that time, the arts and skills of the locals were promoted and goods were exported to places as far away as Europe. The economy was healthy and the people had time to study music.

The mission was closed in 1767 when the Jesuits were expelled, but saw a brief revival in 1790 when a traveling priest came. Then the mission closed again until, in 1930, it became a college under Monseñor Bertoldo Buhel. The college served all of Bolivia. Finally, in 1984 the Jesuits returned to Bolivia and the mission started to thrive again.

When Hans Roth started photographing and recording the condition of the missions, San Ignacio's main building was in a bad state. Roth started the present restoration (there were seven restoration attempts in 250 years) on some missions, but it wasn't until 1997 that San Ignacio was worked upon. The altars, pulpits and confessionals – all from the original church – have been spruced up a bit. These pieces of carved wood have inlaid mica for decoration. However, even with restoration, the clock in the tower does not work.

This mission is one of the most active in the festival of music.

SHOPPING: The **tourist office** on the square has a small showroom with weavings and wood carvings, some painted and some varnished. These exceptional pieces are reproductions of original mission items. The cost for some of the moderately sized items is under $30.

SERVICE: The **money exchange** on the plaza changes cash only.

ADVENTURES ON FOOT: Marilandia is a 5,000-acre/2,000-hectare forest on the edge of town, past Laguna de Guapoma on the road to San Miguel. It has self-guided trails, and you can also walk up the hill that has the Stations of the Cross for views of the town and surrounding area. The hill is the only one that can be seen from town.

ADVENTURE ON WATER: A reservoir at the edge of town is the local swimming hole. Walk left from the Casa Suiza hotel when going toward the plaza and follow that street to the reservoir.

Laguna de Guapoma is a clean lake that lies between San Ignacio and the village of San Miguel. This great swimming spot is used by everyone. It can be reached by taking a taxi or getting off the bus on your way into San Ignacio coming from San Miguel. In the heat, you may like a swim before getting a place to stay in San Ignacio.

PLACES TO STAY: Hotel Oriental, *24 de Septiembre and Cochabamba*, ☎ 962-2150, *$*, is across from the San Ignacio and near the bus stop. It has a lovely garden with grapefruit and lime trees. Large rooms – with or without private bath – have big windows, fans, tables and chairs and hot water. This is a good deal.

Alojamiento El Riabe, *Calle Sucre #491*, ☎ 962-2586, *$*, has large rooms with tiled floors, tables and chairs, but rough mattresses (you would need a sleeping bag). The communal bathrooms are clean.

Hotel Palace, *on the square*, ☎ 962-2073, *$*, has a well-tended garden in the patio area. The small but clean rooms all have a private bath.

Hotel Plaza, *Plaza Principal*, ☎ 962-2035, *$$*, is next to the mission that runs it. The 11 clean rooms have private bath with towels supplied, fan, large windows, decent-sized mirror and tiled floors. Breakfast is included. This hotel offers a lot of information about Noel Kempff park.

Casa Suiza, *a few blocks up from the bus station*, *$$*, is spotless. The rooms and bathrooms are large and the beds are comfortable. A good breakfast is complimentary. There is a book exchange and a garden. The guest book is full of recent information on where to go and how to get there. The hotel is quiet. To find Casa Suiza, walk from the bus station toward the plaza and turn left on Calle La Paz that passes along the south side of the plaza. Continue for four blocks. You will not see the sign painted on the side of the hotel until you are across from it.

Hotel Guapomo, *Calle Sucre*, ☎ 962-2095, *$$*, is beside the cross that stands in the middle of the road. The rooms are of average size with soft beds, tiled floors, large windows and a ceiling fan. It's clean.

Hotel San Ignacio, *Calle 24 de Septiembre and Cochabamba*, ☎ 962-2157, *$$$$*, has a flavor of Hawaii that is a contrast to the dryness of San Ignacio. This hotel offers both regular rooms and larger rooms that feature a loft with extra beds. All rooms have a TV, a bar, sitting area, soft beds and tiled floors. The bathrooms each have a separate shower stall. A well-tended garden and pool are flanked by a thatch-roofed bar. Hammocks are interspersed around the courtyard. The place is exceptionally clean and tastefully decorated.

Hotel La Mission, *Plaza 31 de Julio, Calle Libertad*, ☎ 962-2333, *$$$$$*, is actually Swiss-owned and -operated, offering rooms and more expensive suites. All rooms have air conditioning and cable TV. There is a bar and restaurant, a pool and a professionally tended garden on the premises. Breakfast is complimentary. The pillars (support beams) at the entrance to the hotel are carved wood, similar to those in the mission.

PLACES TO EAT: The Social Club on the plaza offers a buffet lunch, including a pitcher of lemonade, for $1.50 per person. The buffet has at least three salads and two meat dishes and sometimes more. The eating area is set around a huge courtyard.

Hotel La Mission, *Plaza 31 de Julio, Calle Libertad*, ☎ *962-2333*, has cold beer and excellent food in moderate-sized portions. I recommend their pasta with Alfredo sauce for less than $4. The service is good and the staff friendly but not overbearing. The music was Vivaldi and the bill was manageable. What a treat.

Restaurant Venicia, *on the corner opposite the mission*, has been recommended by many as the best place to eat. However, I found the drinking customers a bit obnoxious as they hollered comments to the women riding around the square on their motorbikes.

GETTING HERE & AWAY: The **bus** companies by the main station near the market in San Ignacio will tell you that buses go to Concepcion or San Jose only on Monday, Wednesday and Friday. This is not true. A first-class bus leaves from a different station every evening at 7:30 pm. It takes four hours to reach Concepcion. To find that station, walk three blocks past the square along the same side as the tourist office and away from the Venicia Restaurant. Turn left one block past the hospital and walk for half a block.

Concepcion

Concepcion first became a Jesuit village in 1699 with Father Lucas Caballero as the priest/missionary. In 1722 Father Juan de Benavente moved the village to its present site. The priests knew to introduce music to the locals if they wanted to catch their attention, but they also introduced a written language with grammar and vocabulary rules.

Somewhere between 1730 and 1753 (there are conflicting dates) Martin Schmid started the construction of the mission church. It is believed that the building was completed in 1756 and within the next 10 years the village grew to 713 families with 3,276 people. At that time, eight different languages were being used. It was shortly after that the Jesuits were expelled from the country.

In 1950 the church at Concepcion was declared a national monument and in 1975 restoration began. This was completed in 1982 and nine years later the mission became a cultural site recognized by UNESCO.

THE MISSION: Because of conflicts and power struggles among the priests, the town was not established until 1719 and then its permanent location was not decided upon until 1722. The mission itself was not completed until 1756 and restoration was done in the 1970s under the directorship of Roth.

The mission has an attractive bell tower with a circular staircase that is held up by spiral support poles. The altar is partly decorated with inlaid mica to give it glitter. The most interesting part of the church is the pews. Each has a scene carved from the bible with the book it comes from recorded below. The Old Testament scenes are in the back half of the church and the New Testament scenes are in the front. The pulpit is of carved silver, as is part of the altar. A contemporary painting depicts the restoration with images of a logging truck and a guy with a chainsaw.

The **Mission Museum** on the plaza is open from 8 am to noon and 3 pm to 6 pm daily. Admission is 75¢. The house was donated to the mission by ex-president Hugo Banzer. In the central courtyard is a wooden sugarcane press. These are seen around the country and it is good to know what they are.

The museum has many original mission pieces. One set of plaster statues of Mary, San Pablo and San Ignacio are exceptional in their artistic quality (so I am told). Note the carving at the entrance to one of the rooms that has a saint with his finger up his nose.

ADVENTURE ON FOOT: Trek through the jungle to look for birds, amphibians and monkeys. Just five miles/eight km from Concepcion is the **Piedra de Santa Teresita**, a rock that stands 1,650 ft/500 m high. It is a Precambrian granite hill and the area is especially rich in bird life. The hike takes a minimum of three hours (some of it driving) and is considered to be of medium difficulty.

ADVENTURE IN NATURE: The **Pachanga** is a man-made water hole only 6.7 miles/11 km from town. It can be visited at any time of day. The area is rich in birds like the heron and the vulture, not to mention some of the smaller song birds that are ubiquitous in the long grasses.

ADVENTURE ON WATER: **Zapoco Dam**, 1.8 miles/three km from town, was originally built to supply electricity, but this did not happen. Instead, the reservoir is used for water activities such as swimming. The landscape has been spruced up by local authorities and now it is a park. It's a pleasant place to visit, with palapas and barbecue pits for you to use. There is a chance to see capybaras at this place. The water-bird life too is abundant. During rainy season you can sit near the area where the water comes into the dam, with your back against a rock, and experience a natural Jacuzzi.

TOUR AGENCY: Hombre y Naturaleza (based in Bolivia) and Amigos de Doñana (based in Spain) are NGO societies dedicated to the promotion and preservation of the natural world. They offer six different excursions that focus on science and conservation. The excursions are flexible. For example if you are interested in frogs, they will take you to an area where you may find frogs. Depending on which excursion you choose and how many people go along, the cost can be anywhere from $120 for one person for an overnight trek to Puerto Pedrito to $6 for four people on a guided hike to the Pachanga. Contact Humanos y Naturalesas, in Concepcion at ☎ 964-3074 or mabubones@yahoo.es; or in Santa Cruz at ☎ 923-2239, hynb@bibosi.sca.entelnet.bo or prowames@cotas.com.bo.

PLACES TO STAY: Hotel Grandero, *on the side street that leads to the cemetery, a half-block west of the plaza, $,* has a courtyard scattered with hammocks. The rooms are large and plain, with high ceilings, fans and private bathrooms.

Colonial Hotel, *Calle Nuflo de Chavez #7,* ☎ *964-3050, $$,* has the largest armadillo hide I have ever seen. The rooms are large, with tile floors and private bathrooms, and are placed side-by-side in a row that is in traditional Chiquitos housing style. A large patio for communal use has ham-

THE CHACO

mocks, a clay oven and a thatch roof, also traditional. Breakfast is included.

Hombre y Naturaleza, *$$*, has 12 biological stations in Bolivia. Those in this area are at Concepcion, Santa Ana, Puerto Suarez and San Matias. To get to the station in Concepcion, walk along the north side of the plaza for two blocks. The station is an inconspicuous place with a few signs on the wall of the porch. Walk through the gates around to the back. Rooms here have basic bunk beds in a four-room cabin that costs $6 per person. It is in a quiet compound that has a fairly good reference library and a small museum with objects rescued from villages in the surrounding area. The volunteers are friendly and some speak English.

El Escondido, *Calle Pando*, ☎ *964-3110 $$*, is, as its name implies, a hideaway. This is a true little island in the jungle only six blocks from the main plaza. The hotel was recommended by many travelers as the best average-priced place on the mission circuit. It has 12 rooms around a maintained garden, all with tiled floors and private bath. They feature mission-styled trim painted on the walls. The place sparkles. The owner, a pleasant lady who is highly respected by both her fellow townspeople and foreigners, offers complimentary breakfast to her guests. She goes out of her way to make you comfortable.

Hotel Las Misiones, *on the plaza*, ☎ *964-3021, $$$*, has an attractive flowered courtyard. All rooms have bathrooms, some have beds upstairs in a loft, all have hand-quilted bedspreads and dried flowers in the bathrooms. The property is well maintained and painted with designs like those at the church. The furniture is hardwood and there is a sitting area in each room. Rooms come with or without air conditioning and breakfast is included.

Gran Hotel Concepcion, *Calle Aurelio Roca Llado*, ☎ *964-3031, $$$$*, is an elegant place that has housed important people like the presidents of Spain and Colombia (you will see pictures of them in the foyer). The hotel is built in colonial style with the rooms around a garden and attractive patio. The rooms are clean and rather plain, each with a wooden cross hanging over the bed. The elegant décor is reserved for the foyer. There is a kidney-shaped pool and French colonial furniture. Most of the furniture and books are antiques. All rooms have a fan and breakfast is included in the price.

PLACES TO EAT: Restaurant Buena Gusto on the plaza is situated in a lovely flowered patio. It opens at 8 am and offers an excellent *almuerzo* with lots of salad and good soup. The lemonade was a bit too sweet and the bread was bad, as usual, but the service made up for those two faults.

GETTING HERE & AWAY: Buses come and go to San Ignacio every day. Buses to Santa Cruz leave at 7 am, 2 pm, 6 pm, 10 pm and 11:30 pm. A number of different bus companies are located in the same block on the same street, just up from the plaza.

Mission San Francisco Javier

This mission was built in 1691 by Jose de Arce and another Jesuit priest by the name of Antonio Rivas. San Francisco Javier is the patron saint of the

Chiquitos. The mission was not built on its present site to begin with, but was moved four times before it finally found its permanent home in 1708.

This mission is between Concepcion and the mission of San Ramon on the main highway. Neither are popular stopping places and should be visited only by those really interested in missions. Since there are a number of buses going and coming from Concepcion, it is not difficult to get a ride after stopping in this village.

Villamontes

Altitude: 2,253 ft/685 m
Population: 3,000

This is the hottest place in Bolivia. Not only is it hot, but it is dry and dusty. The only draw to the village is the canyon that you pass when traveling overland from Tarija and an excellent museum dedicated to the Chaco War. Although some people are friendly, Villamontes caters mostly to the young oil patch workers. If you can, spend the night in Camiri, as it is far more appealing than Villamontes. And, Che Guevera slept in Camiri.

◆ Getting Here & Around

Yacuiba is 100 km/60 miles from Villamontes and has the closest airport. It is easy to catch either a bus, *trufi* or taxi up to Villamontes. Most people who fly from Santa Cruz to Yacuiba are traveling down to Argentina. **TAM** (☎ 244-3487, www.tam.com.br) and **SAVE** (☎ 212-1548) airlines fly between Yacuiba and Santa Cruz daily, usually leaving Yacuiba at 7 am. There is one on Friday that leaves at 10:30 am.

There is only one **bus** traveling from the border to Villamontes and then on to Santa Cruz each day. It leaves the border at 8 am. However, there are many *trufis* going. Once in Villamontes, you can spend the night, take a collectivo to Camiri (a much better option) or take a night bus to Santa Cruz. The duration of that trip, 294 miles/480 km, is anywhere from 12 to 16 hours on good days and a bit longer if the road is really wet.

Copacabana is the only bus company that goes to Santa Cruz during the day. If you do not get on at the border town of Yacuiba (the beginning of the line), you will be charged a lot for a seat. You must pay $10.50 for the entire distance between Yacquiba and Santa Cruz. If you reserve your seat in Villamontes, you must pay an extra $8 for the girl to make the reservation. That is double the cost of a seat from Yacuiba to Villamontes. This means that if you got a ticket at the border all the way to Santa Cruz, you would pay $10.50, but if you get on at Villamontes (two hours closer to Santa Cruz) you pay $18.50 for the same seat. A night bus with a different company is another option. Night buses leave between 5 pm and 7 pm daily.

Also consider taking a shared **taxi** to Camiri. The last taxi goes around noon. The Nancahuazu Transport is a collectivo/taxi and can be found at the crossroads between Villamontes, Paraguay and Santa Cruz and just up from the bus station. From Camiri, take a day-time bus to Santa Cruz or get on a night bus with Guzmar, that charges the highest in price but is by far the most comfortable. You must book a seat early as the buses (two go every evening at 7 pm) fill quickly.

Spending the night in Camiri is a good option. It sits a bit higher than Villamontes and thus is cooler. Set in the hills, it is also aesthetically more attractive. It has great places to stay, and the people of Camiri are far more pleasant than those in Villamontes.

The bus from Villamontes to Tarija goes along another road of death that, in part, follows the Pilocomayo River and Canyon. The scenery is spectacular, the trip long and difficult for the drivers.

A **train** goes to Santa Cruz on Tuesday, Thursday and Saturday. It takes 12 hours minimum and the cost is about $12 per person, first class. It leaves late in the afternoon, usually around 5 pm.

◆ History

Prior to the arrival of the Spanish, the area was sparsely inhabited by **Guarani Indians**. After the Spanish arrived, it became a small army outpost, a hot and dusty place where no one wanted to be. During the Chaco War in the 1930s, General Bernardino Bilboa Rioja and Major German Busch won the territory from the Paraguayans. They also managed to secure some of the Chaco that is closer to Santa Cruz. Today, it is a hub for oil exploration and, due to this, the cost of things in Villamontes is a bit higher than it should be.

◆ Festivals

Festival dates change because they are always held on weekends. For exact dates, contact either Susi at Dinar Travel in Tarija, ☎ 664-8000, susyqui@olivo.tja.entelnet.bo, or Viva Tours, also in Tarija, ☎ 663-8325.

Villamontes Farmers' Fair, in August, has a display of all the products grown and raised in the area. The three-day fair is a tribute to the *gaucho* of the Chaco area and is honored by a rodeo. There's also music, dancing, parades and lots of food.

The **Fish Festival**, also in August, is a wild time, with dancing, plays showing historical events, storytelling and general praising of the culture that revolves around fishing in the Pilcomayo River. The fair is celebrated with lots of eating and drinking. The fishing area for the festival is up from the canyon on the river.

> **AUTHOR NOTE:** Due to climatic changes, the Pilcomayo River is now host to the *piraña*, the meat-eating fish found mostly in the Amazon Basin.

◆ Adventures in Culture

The **Museum of Military Heroes of the Gran Chaco** is west of Plaza 6 de Agosto in an old colonial house complete with a wide porch where you can often see the keepers of the museum (soldiers) fast asleep. There is a 50¢ charge to enter the museum. In the yard (by far the best part of the museum) are dugouts, bunkers and the remains of bullet-riddled machinery used in the Gran Chaco War.

Inside the museum are photos of heroes and other characters, as well as medals and other memorabilia. The locals around Villamontes are very proud of their museum. I recommend going there if you are in town for a while. It is the highlight of Villamontes.

◆ Places to Stay

Residencial Raldes, *Calle Cap. Manchego #171*, ☎ *672-2088* or *672-2545*, *$*, is a fairly basic place that charges $4 per person without private bathrooms (two rooms share one bath). The rooms are cleaned daily, but the beds are the hardest I've slept in while in Bolivia and the hot water was almost too hot.

❖ HOTEL PRICING	
$	. . . . $10 to $20
$$	. . . . $21 to $50
$$$	. . . . $51 to $75
$$$$	. . . . $76 to $100
$$$$$	. . . . over $100

There is a large courtyard, swimming pool (popular with local kids) and a few rooms with private baths. The bottled water sold at the *tienda* attached to the hotel was the highest price I paid in all of Bolivia.

Hotel Avenida, *Avenida Mendejarco between Calle Ismel Montes and Avenida Ingavi*, ☎ *672-2106* or *672-2412*, *$$$*, is clean and friendly. There are private baths, air conditioning, cable TV and fridges in all the rooms.

El Rancho Hotel, *Barrio Ferravianio*, ☎ *672-2140* or *672-2059*, *rancho@olivo.tja.entelnet.bo*, *$$$$*, is the classiest place in town. When getting off the bus, this hotel is in the opposite direction from the plaza along the main street. All rooms have large tiled bathrooms, air conditioning, cable TV, fridges and soft beds. The place is clean. Beds have stereo sets in the headboards. There's a large shaded patio and a swimming pool out back that's accompanied by an open-air restaurant and bar. There is also an inside restaurant at the entrance to the yard.

La de Aladino. While walking along the main road toward the plaza you will notice a sign pointing to a motel. When you get to the motel, you will notice that it is securely guarded. This place rents rooms by the hour. I didn't get a price because they didn't believe that I wanted a room for 24 hours, but they did look at my husband with great respect.

◆ Places to Eat

Pizza Place on the plaza (two places side-by-side) has great pizza, is open all day and has pleasant owners.

❖ MUSIC OF CHACO

Long ago, musicians and singers of the Chaco were important and respected. The musicians kept the rhythm of the work going while they played. Also, the songs were a record of historical events. Over the years, the songs developed until, today, they are more satirical than historical.

Carlos Miguel Palmo, born in the Chaco in 1966, is Villamontes' musical hero. He has played in Argentina, Tarija and Santa Cruz and has two recordings with traditional music from the Chaco published by Habana Records, Calle 25 de

THE CHACO

Mayo, #1667, Barrios San Martin, Tarija. The recordings include Argentinean, Bolivian and Paraguayan music and feature Escondido, La Queca and Bolivian Zamba.

Bolivian Zamba is different than Brazil's. The music, with a good beat, is played on the guitar, a violin and drums. The drums are long and thin and beaten with two sticks. **Yacuiba** is the border town between Bolivia and Argentina. It is hot and grubby, standing at 2,072 ft/630 m above sea level. Yacuiba was the second city ever established in the department and at one time was considered the capital of the area. However, an earthquake in 1881 destroyed all the colonial structures so Tarija became the capital. Today, Yacuiba is made up of modern places only.

The second week in September the town celebrates for three nights at one of the best folk festivals in Bolivia. Musicians come from Argentina to join the Bolivians in this event. It is excellent.

The Pantanal

The Pantanal covers over 81,000 square miles/210,000 square km of wilderness, an area larger than Greece. It is considered the world's largest wetland and is one of the richest wilderness areas on the planet.

The Pantanal spreads across Bolivia, Brazil and Paraguay. During the rainy season (October through March) Rio Paraguay floods the entire savannah, transforming the area into a huge swamp. Pantanal means "swamp" in Portuguese. However, during dry season the swamps disappear and the land becomes a savannah dotted with lakes and ponds. The canals formed by the river are destinations in themselves.

The water birds seen in this reserve are countless, but there are also raptors, songbirds and dry land birds. Wild animals, such as howler and capuccine monkeys, capybaras, peccaries, tapirs, spectacled caiman, otters, marshland deer and giant anteaters are numerous and an excursion away from camp will always result in wildlife being spotted. Occasionally, jaguar are seen. Herons, storks, kingfishers, parakeets and orioles are numerous. Over 700 bird species have been recorded here and millions of migratory birds make the Pantanal their in-transit hotel during migration. Some butterflies, too, make this a migratory route. New species of fish are still being found and added to the 260 recorded species. The palms alone include the white, black, totai and the motacu.

The World Wildlife Federation is heavily involved in preserving the Pantanal and they work in Bolivia with the National Service for Protected Areas.

This area can be explored with Hombre y Naturaleza on an exciting six-day trip that requires travel by jeep, horse and boat through Bolivia and into Paraguay and Brazil. The tour stops at the most important places in the Pantanal. The excursion starts by boat from Puerto Suarez. Once at Rio Bahia Negra you will travel for two days, crossing the immense *pampas* of the Pantanal. There will also be one day dedicated to hiking up the tupuy Sombrerito. After this you will have a restful trip back to Puerto Suarez. There is a minimum requirement of six people for this tour and the cost is $30 per person, per day. During the rainy season it is not possible to do the entire trip. I would like to thank Manuel Español for all the information he gave me about the Pantanal.

Contact Humanos y Naturalesas, in Puerto Suarez at ☎ 710-67712 or 716-28699, eltumbador@hotmail.com or eltumbador@yahoo.com; or in Santa Cruz at ☎ 923-2239, hynb@bibosi.sca.entelnet.bo or prowames@cotas.com.bo.

To reach the Pantanal you can join a tour from Santa Cruz or La Paz if you want everything taken care of for you. Otherwise, take the train to

Puerto Suarez or to Quijarro and visit the preserve from there. Both villages have hotels and can offer river trips into the preserve.

For those going on to Brazil who want a travel and tour trip, Hombre y Naturaleza offers a relaxing but exciting three-day river trip down to Carumba in Brazil through the lush wetlands of the Pantanal. Along the way you will see all the wildlife the Pantanal has to offer. One of the things I found amazing in Bolivia is that when the tour operators say you will see something, you are pretty much guaranteed to see it because the areas are still so wild.

For those interested, there is a book of collected papers (mostly scientific) about the area called *The Pantanal of Brazil, Bolivia and Paraguay*, edited by Frederick A. Swarts and published by Hudson Macarthur Publishers in 2002. There are 14 color photos and 46 black and whites in the book.

❖ ROBORE

Robore is situated between San Jose de Chiquitos, on the missions circuit (see page 256), and the border town of Puerto Suarez. This is a hiker's/photographer's/birder's paradise. Besides the village, there is the mission of Santiago in the Tucavaca Valley and the hot springs at Aguas Calientes farther along the rail line. The valley has sandstone rocks dotted with caves and clear rivers. It offers an endless number of hiking possibilities. One can visit the area either on foot or by horse. There are caves with rock paintings and some spelunking can be done. Guides can be hired in the village of Robore.

Puerto Suarez

Puerto Suarez has one main street, called Bolivia, with hotels and places to eat and drink beer. Any activities like horse riding or boating up or down the Paraguay River can be arranged by the conservation group that operates El Tumbador or by the owners of Hotel Sucre.

◆ Adventures on Foot

Go on a three-hour forest walk near the **Laguna Caceres**, 3.7 miles/six km from the center of town. On this route, scientists have identified four species of monkeys, numerous reptiles and amphibians, tarantulas (of which there are numerous varieties) and birds (of which there are hundreds – there are 40 to 60 species of parrots alone). Along this walk you will pass the Santa Tecla waterfalls, a refreshing stop in the steaming jungle that you share with monkeys. A hat, bottle of water and mosquito repellent are essential. This hike should be done a few times to see all the wildlife, but your first hike should be done with a guide, available at El Tumbador (see below).

◆ Adventures on Water

The **Paraguay River** can be visited by either going upstream to the La Gaiba Lake, the Mandiore and the Uberaba Lakes where wildlife is the main (only?) attraction. You can also go downstream, visiting villages such as Morrinho, Puerto Esperanza and Fuerte Coimbra. The canals formed by the rising and falling water levels create a constantly changing terrain. All this is part of the **Pantanal Reserve**. Those staying at El Tumbador in Puerto Suarez can take one of the tours along the river or join a river trip into Brazil. Most day trips on the river take four to six hours.

Laguna Mandiore is 122 miles/200 km upriver from Puerto Suarez and is a two-day trip. Along the way there is an area of unique sandstone rock formations that surround the lake. The wildlife is exceptional simply because the entire area is unexplored. When things get a bit ho-hum, your boatman will tell you stories and anecdotes about the area. Once at camp, there is a hammock with mosquito netting for your bed and fresh fish for your meal. All you need then is a beer (not included) in your hand. The cost for this tour is about $80 with a minimum of two people.

Bahai Negra River is a primary contributor to the Paraguay River and a trip on this gem would take four days in all. Not only would you be in the Pantanal, but you would see parts of the Chaco too. Along the way is the archeological site of Fuerte Coimbra. The third day is spent on land, visiting local villages in Paraguay before returning to Puerto Suarez. This trip is an exceptional opportunity to experience cultural events and see wildlife. Should you not have four days to spend, the river can be explored for 1½ days on a tour that includes one night on the river, but this option excludes the villages in Paraguay. The cost of the tour for three days is about $80 per person with a minimum of three people.

Heading up **Rio Verde** from Bahai Negra is an exciting trip because the river is narrow and swift. One of the interesting stops is at a bunker used by the Paraguayan military during the Chaco War. It was also used as a prison because of its isolated location. This trip is not possible from February to May due to high water levels. This is a full-day excursion out of Puerto Suarez. The cost is $80 for one, or $55 each for two.

Rio Negro is well named. The water is black. On an overnight trip along this waterway, you will end at a camp on a group of islands that overlook the lights of Carumba, Brazil. From the camp you can go up a smaller river, one on which few people have traveled, and watch the abundant wildlife. This half-day trip costs $40 per person.

Coimbra Fort is a one-day tour that starts with a river trip down the Paraguay to the fort. Along the way you can expect to see toucans, many species of raptors, herons, storks, caimans, capybaras, turtles and iguanas. The fort, built by the Spanish, is on a hill overlooking the river. It was taken over by the Portuguese and then, in 1864, by the Paraguayans. Lunch will be served at the fort before the trip back upriver. This is a full-day excursion that costs $100 for one or two people. As the number of participants goes up, the per-person price comes down.

THE PANTANAL

◆ Adventures in Nature

Ten-kilometer Lagoon is reached in a 4x4 along the road to Filidefia on Rio Negro and is a trip specifically designed for birders. Although the plant life is lush and the animals during dry season come to the lagoon to drink, it is the immense number and variety of birds that one notices. Besides aquatic species, there are jabiru storks resting here, American mycteria, birds of prey, and herons, to name just a few. This is a half-day tour ($15) that could be made into a full-day excursion. Long-sleeved shirts, long pants and mosquito repellent are needed.

Kamba'aka is another 4x4 trip to an area deep in the Chaco jungles where plant life is the big draw. There is a jungle camp where you can sleep in a tent or in a covered hammock. The guides will be able to point out different plants and some of their uses. The cost of this two-day trip is $85 – that includes everything except beer.

Cueva de Motacusito is in the forest near the town of Motacusito. A guide will be required if you want to go inside the cave. Hombre y Naturaleza offers this trip (see *Tour Operators*, below). The cave goes in a third of a mile/half a km and is rich in stalagmites and stalactites. It also has insects, fish, amphibians and vampire bats. Being in good physical condition is essential as you must squeeze through one hall that is only 27 inches/70 cm wide. However, once through, the main room is over 99 ft/30 m high and is filled with rock formations.

To get to the cave you must travel nine miles/15 km from Puerto Suarez in a 4x4 and walk half an hour or so to the cave opening. Comfortable clothes (cotton is preferable) should be worn and good boots and mosquito repellent are necessary. This trip will take about four hours and costs $35 for one person or $11 per person if four people go.

◆ Places to Stay

Hotel Palace, ☎ 976-2098, $; **Hotel Robore**, ☎ 976-2190, $; and the **Executive Hotel**, ☎ 976-2270, $, are all fairly simple places that cost less than $5 per person for a room with a fan and communal baths. **Bamby**, ☎ 976-2015, charges $4 per person for simple rooms with private bath and fans in the bedrooms.

❖ HOTEL PRICING	
$	$10 to $20
$$	$21 to $50
$$$	$51 to $75
$$$$	$76 to $100
$$$$$	over $100

The **Beby Hotel**, ☎ 976-2290, $$, has tiny rooms with fans for $10 per person which is high for what you get.

El Tumbador, ☎ 716-28699, eltumbador@yahoo.com, $$, is on the shores of Laguna Caceres (often a destination in itself) just 3.7 miles/six km from Puerto Suarez on the road toward the border. This is the place to stay. The lake and property cover about 31 square miles/80 square km of reserve where the amount of wildlife is exceptional. The station charges $14 per person per night for a cabin that holds four people. There are six cabins in all and each has a modern bathroom complete with shower (hot is not needed). The place is clean and each room has mosquito netting over the bed. There are hammocks on the porch and lots of wildlife to be seen from the shore of the lagoon. The setting sun each day accents the beauty of the spot. The residence is operated by the NGO Hombre y Naturaleza of Bolivia and Amigos de Doñana of Spain. The volunteers working at El Tumbador can organize any tour you may want to take from a jaguar photo-hunt to a six-day trip upriver. There are numerous posters of the Pantanal for sale.

Hotel Sucre, *on the plaza,* ☎ 976-2069, *$$$,* has small rooms with air conditioning (almost a must) set around a tended garden.

Hotel El Pantanal, ☎ 978-2020, www.elpantanalhotel.com, *$$$$$,* is the luxury liner of the Pantanal. Resort rooms have tiled floors, matching décor, TV, fridge, air conditioning and room service. There are also tennis courts, palapa huts and a bar around the pool, volleyball court, soccer field, games room, karaoke bar, formal dining room, horses for rent and a tour office to help you get anything not included in the hotel services.

◆ Tour Operator

Hombre y Naturaleza, *at El Tumbador,* ☎ 716-28699, eltumbador@yahoo.com, offers superb tours. If you have time and want to see wildlife, I can't think of a better tour agency. Prices are all dependent on time, services and number of people.

Puerto Quijarro

Puerto Quijarro is nine miles/15 km past Suarez and just as hot (in winter) as Suarez. Both towns have small places in which to eat.

◆ Places to Stay

The Cascade, *Avenida Sucre,* ☎ 978-2099, *$,* has basic rooms with fans and communal baths. **The Border**, *Avenida Rolello Gomez,* ☎ 978-0210, *$,* is comparable to The Cascade.

Hotel Oasis, *Argentina #4,* ☎ 978-2159, *$$,* is a two-star hotel that has clean rooms with private bath and fans.

The **Santa Cruz**, *Avenida Brazil,* ☎ 2113-2044 *(cell),* *$$$,* has rooms with air conditioning and private baths. This hotel can also arrange tours on the Paraguay River.

THE PANTANAL

The Amazon Basin

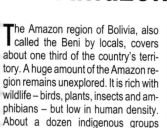

The Amazon region of Bolivia, also called the Beni by locals, covers about one third of the country's territory. A huge amount of the Amazon region remains unexplored. It is rich with wildlife – birds, plants, insects and amphibians – but low in human density. About a dozen indigenous groups inhabit the area.

The Amazon cannot be said to have a center. La Paz, really, is the trading center for the Beni and Madre de Dios drainage areas and Santa Cruz is the hub for the Mamore area. Trinidad is by far the largest city.

The Amazon has mysteries that reveal themselves in different ways. One example is the Llanos de Moxos, or earth mounds. It was an astute archeologist, who, while flying over the jungle, knew from experience that the lines of hillocks and canals that he could see from the plane were not natural. The area is now a major destination for researchers and tourists who are curious about the lives of the people who built these mounds of dry land in an ocean of swamp. An accessible, if not original, mound is on the outskirts of Trinidad, attached to a museum.

❖ "AMAZON"

The word Amazon comes from Greek mythology and refers to a group of women who lived just beyond the known world. They fought on the Greek side in the Trojan War. Some stories claim that they removed their right breasts so that they could shoot a bow better. When the Spanish first came to the area and found bare-chested women (mostly with two breasts), they named the area after the mythological women.

The Amazon is isolated. The towns are small and I don't believe there is one, outside of Trinidad, that has a bank machine. In Riberalta and Guayaramirim, you can cash traveler's checks at some hotels, but only if you are a guest. Basically, you must carry cash. During rainy season, you must fly, or take a boat up and down the rivers. When flying, you will see below the people using canoes on flooded roads. You must learn to ride on the back of a moto-taxi and other small motorcycles. These are the most popular form of transportation.

But best of all, the beer tastes better in the Amazon than it does in any other part of Bolivia.

The Amazon is hot and humid, even during its coldest dry spell, and activities are often low key or delayed altogether until after dark. Pack loose cotton clothing, especially shorts and short-sleeved shirts. The dress code of the Altiplano, that wants people covered so no skin shows, doesn't apply in the Amazon. You must look after your feet. If there are cuts or sores on them, wear shoes or boots, rather than sandals, so that you don't get attacked by one of the ubiquitous parasites. Finding hotels with air conditioning or fans is a must or you will suffocate in your sleep.

Trinidad

Altitude: 513 ft/156 m
Population: 275,000

Trinidad is a frontier town on the Mamore River, which flows north until it is joined by the Beni and the Madre de Dios. These three rivers merge at Villa Bella, north of Guayaramerin by about 31 miles/50 km, and flow into Brazil where they become the Madeira River.

Trinidad, the capital of Amazonia district, has clay roads that are used as canoe routes during rainy season. The upside is that the roads are flat.

In dry season, motorbikes, mule-carts, long-distance transport trucks and buses stir up dust that leaves an even film on everything.

In Trinidad, as in all Amazon towns, the favorite activity is riding around the plaza on a motorbike and howling at the opposite sex.

The bird life is often the reason foreigners come to Trinidad. From the moment you arrive, the feathered ones are exotic enough to catch the attention of even untrained birders.

◆ Getting Here & Around

Buses take a full 12 hours to reach Trinidad from Santa Cruz during good conditions. In rainy season, the trip can take 18 hours and may not get there at all. The buses pass through steaming jungle that you can't see most of the time during your nighttime journey. The timing is by choice. Daytime heat is unbearable when you are in a tin box that moves at 18 miles/30 km an hour.

Planes to Trinidad from Santa Cruz cost about $55 per person and take 1½ hours. If it is a clear day, you will get to see the impressive Lomos de Moxos (mounds believed to have been made by a society living here before the Spaniards arrived) from the air. Airlines going to Trinidad are **AeroSur**, ☎ 231-3233 or 336-7400, www.aerosur.com; **LAB**, ☎ 800-337-0918 (US), 800-10-3001 (Bolivia), www.labairlines.com; **SAVE**, ☎ 212-1548; and **TAM**, ☎ 244-3487, www.tam.com.br, and one flies every day.

Taxis at the airport are expensive, around $5 per person to town. The walk takes about half an hour.

You can also take a moto-taxi that means you and your luggage must perch on the back of a Honda 250 (or smaller). It is hardly worth the effort.

The cost of one of these is $1 to town from the airport and 30¢ from place to place in town.

Boat travel around the Amazon Basin is by far the best way to go. Buy a hammock, and take lots of local currency and a thick book. Negotiate a ride on one of the barges collecting food or rubber from villages along the river. The Mamore flows down to the Brazilian border at Guayaramerin. This is a relaxing way to spend a week or so. The traveling time depends on how often the boat breaks down and how often the crew stops at a village to party. The cost is about $10 a day, including your meals of beans and rice or rice and beans.

The port in Trinidad is actually 36 miles/15 km from the center of town at Puerto Almacen. If negotiating a ride, I suggest you avoid the large ocean freight barges heading for the Amazon River laden with train cars. They travel faster, but they are uncomfortable and the food is usually horrid.

◆ History

Father Cipriano Barace landed on the shores of the Mamore River in 1686 and built the first hut that later became the village of Trinidad. But in 1769 smallpox and floods wiped out most of the city and the remaining people moved about nine miles/15 km downstream to the city's present location on the Arrayo de San Juan, a river that rather resembles a creek.

After converting numerous indigenous groups to Catholicism, Father Barace was murdered on Rio Baures by some people who didn't really want conversion. Besides Catholicism, Barace is credited with introducing cattle farming to the area. This proved to be lucrative in the 1700s, but after the Jesuits with their exceptional managerial skills were expelled from Bolivia, prosperity declined. This resulted in farms being controlled by Spanish settlers and the indigenous people being forced to work as slaves.

It was during the struggles for independence that Trinidad became an industrial town and all traces of Jesuit influence were destroyed. However, within a hundred years of independence, the rubber trade became big and Trinidad prospered as a transportation center. This prosperity was again dependent on the labor of indigenous peoples. When they rose against the ill treatment, they were killed or driven off, leaving the rubber trade and the town to the Spaniards.

Once rubber was no longer a moneymaker, the men of the area turned back to cattle ranching. They interbred the half-wild cows that were brought in and then left by Jesuits with a breed from Brazil to form a line that is tolerant of the heat and also good for meat.

◆ Services

The **Entel Office** is next door to the post office on Calle Antonio Vaca Diez.

The **post office** is on Calle Antonio Vaca Diez, between Cipriano Barace and Avenida Cochabamba.

There's a hidden **tourist office** on Calle Limpiaz. To get there, go into the parking lot next to Farmacia Beniana on Calle Limiaz and turn right at the back of the lot. Go through the door at the end of the walkway. I found the people in the office pleasant and helpful. They have a map of the city for no charge; the tourist agency charged $1.50 for the same map.

The **police station** is on Calle Limpiaz and Cochabamba.

Cibermania Café and Internet on Calle Sucre and 18 de Noviembre, ☎ 462-1230, has good machines and they charge 75¢ an hour.

◆ Sightseeing

The **cathedral** was built in 1931, replacing the old Jesuit mission that was previously there. Inside are some items of value like the embroidered linen, the statue of Jesus as a boy done by Guamaga, and some fine semi-precious stones. But the building itself is not very beautiful.

◆ Adventures in Culture

Kenneth Lee Museum, Avenida Ganadera, 2,300 ft/700 m past the traffic circle, holds artifacts found by its namesake, an American geologist and archeology buff, who believed the lomas, when he first saw them as he flew over the area, were not natural mounds. To get there, walk up the east side of the square and continue along the road to the museum. There is no charge to enter.

After Lee started to explore in earnest, he found that the mounds, built on alluvial deposits that are about 10,000 ft/3,000 m deep started as burial mounds. He presented the theory that the people who had lived here buried their dead in jugs and buried the jugs in the ground. These indigenous people then lived on top of the burial sites. Other professionals disagree with Lee.

Lee found middens (full of pottery shards) on the mounds. The piles went as deep as 30 ft/10 m. These areas provided evidence that the people grew beans, squash, potato and manioc. In the canals between the *lomas*, they had fish farms stocked with both fish and shell fish. Lee believed that the societies lived on these mounds anywhere from 2,000 to 5,000 years ago.

The causeways between the mounds are 10-16 ft (three to five m) wide and three ft/one m above the highest water level. There are hundreds of *lomas* out on the Amazon savannah near Trinidad, but only a few have been excavated. A second excavated site is at Ibibate, 31 miles/50 km east of Trinidad.

A few other archeologists have worked on the *lomos*. William Denevan, who did his PhD thesis on the topic, believed that the mounds were pyramids and the canals were a means of transportation. He also claimed that the raised ridges were actually agricultural fields. It is a general belief that the mounds were abandoned between 1400 and 1700.

The museum is a tall, round, modern structure containing artifacts like vases, pestles for pounding chocolate and weights that are amazingly accurate. One section contains clay masks from the Moxos culture and the music section has a flute about 1½ inches long.

The museum grounds have a mound surrounded on one side by a pool of water and on the other by a canal. This is a good example of the *lomos* found in the jungle just east of Trinidad.

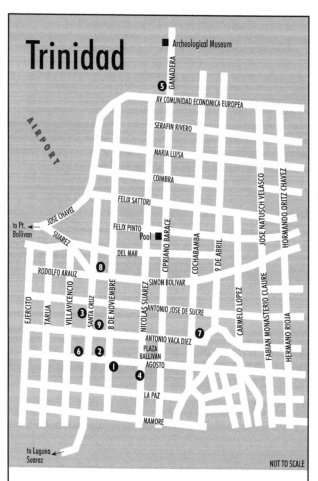

Trinidad

Archeological Museum

AIRPORT

GANADERA

AV COMUNIDAD ECONOMICA EUROPEA

SERAFIN RIVERO

MARIA LUISA

COIMBRA

FELIX SATTORI

JOSE CHAVEL

to Pt. Bollivan

SUAREZ

FELIX PINTO

Pool

DEL MAR

RODOLFO ARAUZ

EJERCITO

TARIJA

VILLAVICENCIO

SANTA CRUZ

8 DE NOVIEMBRE

NICOLAS SUAREZ

CIPRIANO BARACE

COCHABAMBA

9 DE ABRIL

JOSE NATUSCH VELASCO

HORMANDO ORITZ CHAVEZ

SIMON BOLIVAR

ANTONIO JOSE DE SUCRE

ANTONIO VACA DIEZ

PLAZA BALLIVAN

AGOSTO

LA PAZ

MAMORE

CARMELO LOPEZ

FABIAN MONASTERIO CLAURE

HERMANO RIOJA

to Laguna Suarez

NOT TO SCALE

PLACES TO STAY & EAT
1. Hostal 18 de Noviembre
2. Hotel Beni, Hotel Monte Verde
3. Hotel Sirari, Hotel Santa Cruz
4. Hotel Trinidad
5. Hotel La Hosteria
6. Hotel Gran Moxo
7. Mi Residencia
8. Hotel Jacaranda
9. Pollo Joel

N

HUNTER PUBLISHING

© 2005 HUNTER PUBLISHING, INC

Take insect repellent when you go to the museum as the mosquitoes are bad.

◆ Adventures on Water

The **swimming pool** on Avenida Cipriano between Calle Felix Pinto and Felix Sattori costs 50¢ for the afternoon. It's large and clean, and surrounded with shaded tables. There is no loud music and there is a place to purchase drinks and snacks.

Laguna Suarez, formerly known as Socoreno, which means animal lagoon, is three miles/five km south of Trinidad. The artificial lake is dotted with palapa palms and picnic tables. There are places to eat and you can get everything from fried fish to grilled steak or roasted chicken. There is also lots of *chicha*, beer, fruit drinks and sodas. If you don't want to swim in the lake itself, head to the Laguna Suarez Hotel. It is along the road by the lake. There, you can pay to swim in relatively clean water.

Puerto Almacen is five miles/eight km southwest of the city. This is where the Ibare River forms an estuary. It flows into a lake that, in turn, empties into the Mamore River. Just beyond Almacen is Puerto Barador. Tour operators in Trinidad offer one- and two-day trips from Puerto Almacen up the Ibare River in search of wildlife. You have a good chance of seeing the rare blue-throated macaw, of which there are only about 120 living in the wild. They nest in palm trees and eat palm nuts. This is one of the few places on the planet where the bird can be spotted. Other wildlife you could see are capybaras, caimans, pink dolphins, monkeys, turtles and snakes. If not doing a river trip anywhere else in the jungle, then do this one.

The *Reina de Enin* boat trip down the Mamore River is a first-class, five-day event starting and ending in Trinidad. The cost ($80 per person, per day) includes accommodations, transportation, meals and side tours with a guide. It goes through some primary forest growth to isolated villages before returning on the same river. You will ride in the jungle on a horse, swim in the river with the pink dolphins, hike through virgin forests, paddle a dugout canoe on a tributary river and do a night safari looking for nocturnal feeders. The river itself is busy. There are barges and canoes, tripledecker boats and private Sea Doos. For the most part, those on the boats are working, carrying freight up and down the river.

The *Reina de Enin* has rooms for singles or doubles, all with private bathrooms, hot water, air conditioning and fans. You should have light cotton clothing, including a long-sleeved shirt and long pants. Mosquito repellent is essential. Binoculars are recommended. There are not many places on the planet as remote as this, and the chances of seeing different and rare species of wildlife are great. If you are interested in this tour, see Fremen Tours, below.

◆ Adventures in Nature

Suarez Hill is seven miles/12 km northeast of Trinidad on Rio Ibare. The hill is artificial and has had many titles before this one. It was previously called Monovi Hill, but after the Suarez brothers bought the land, they re-named it the Ayacucho Hill. However, the people in the nearby village pre-ferred the name Llamaron Suarez Hill, in honor of the owners. The river below the hill is good for watching wildlife. To get here, hire a motorbike (see below) or take a taxi. About 1.8 miles/three km before the hill along the river, is a spot where locals go to swim with the freshwater dolphins. This river flows into the Mamore. It is possible to fish or canoe if you have your own equipment (not likely for a traveler). Some of the birds spotted here are the blue-headed parrot and the chopi blackbird.

While near the river you will spot a mansion that belonged to the wealthy Suarez family. The property has a sugarcane plantation, a fruit orchard and an agricultural school. The family is no longer around.

◆ Tour Operators

Paraiso Travel, 6 de Agosto #138, ☎ 462-0692, paraiso@sauce.ben. entelnet.bo, offers tours to Laguna Suarez and Rio Mamore. They also of-fer one-night camping trips in the jungle and a four-day birding tour. Rates vary from $25 per day to $110, depending on where you go and how many go with you. They will also accommodate you for festivals. Do not pur-chase a city map from them as they charge $1.50 for the map that is avail-able free at the tourist office.

Freman Tours, Avenida Cipriano Barace #332, ☎ 462-2276, www.an-des-amazonia.com or www.amazoncharters.com, offers the five-day river trip on a typical three-decker Amazonian boat. The cost is about $80 per day, all-inclusive.

Parais Travel, Avenida 6 de Agosto #138, ☎ 462-0692, offers many convenient half- and full-day trips in the area. The cost for one person to go to Laguna Suarez is $25, but if 10 go, the price drops to $10. They have a one-day Rio Mamore trip and an overnight jungle camping trip. Longer trips are available; negotiate particulars with them.

Moto Rental, 6 de Agosto #101, has small Suzukis and Hondas for rent at $1.50 per hour, $10 a day and $12 for 24 hours. The price includes gas. You must leave your passport as security and you must have a driver's li-cense that allows you to drive a small motorbike. You can take these bikes to Laguna Suarez or Chuchini, but no farther, as you need special traveling papers to go beyond. These bikes will easily hold two people, and locals put as many as five on them. If you do rent one, you will see why motorcy-cles are so popular in the Amazon. They are the outdoor substitute for the fan in your room.

◆ Places to Stay

It may be that when I checked these places they saw a *gringo* and raised the prices, but most places in Trinidad are just not worth the asking prices. Com-pared with Coroico, Sorata, Samaipata or Copacabana, Trinidad is expensive.

❖ HOTEL PRICING	
$	$10 to $20
$$	$21 to $50
$$$	$51 to $75
$$$$	$76 to $100
$$$$$	over $100

Also remember, no fan, no deal. There should be a fan in every room, preferably on the ceiling. With the ceiling fan, check to see if the lights are below the fan, especially if you suffer from epilepsy or motion sickness, or if you like to read.

Hostal 18 de Noviembre, ☎ 462-1272 $, offers clean and basic rooms with or without private bath. The flowered courtyard is pleasant and dotted with hammocks.

Hotel Sirari, *Avenida Santa Cruz, #526*, ☎ 462-4472, $$, is a new place with a well-tended garden, clean rooms, tiled floors and bath, large windows and big rooms. All rooms have ceiling fans. This is the best deal in town. The lady who runs the hotel is pleasant, as are her staff.

Hotel Santa Cruz, *Avenida Santa Cruz*, ☎ 462-0711, $$, is next best to the Sirari. The clean rooms have a TV and air conditioning and come with or without private bath. There is a courtyard. The owners are friendly.

Beni Hotel, *6 de Agosto #68*, ☎ 462-2788 or 462-2522, $$, has large rooms with tile floors, private bath, TV and phone. Some have air conditioning. But the rooms are dark.

Hotel Monte Verde, *Avenida 6 de Agosto #76*, ☎ 462-2750 or 462-2738, $$$. All rooms have private bath, air conditioning, fridge, cable TV and a small sitting area.

Hotel Trinidad, *Calle Pedro de la Rocha #80*, ☎ 462-1380, $$$$, is just half a block from the central plaza, between the market and the square. Each room has private bath, cable TV, fridge and phone. It is a small hotel (10 rooms) with a small pool on premises. Although the owners were friendly, the hotel is quite drab.

Hotel La Hosteria, *Avenida Ganadera in front of Camp Ferial*, ☎ 462-2911, $$$$, is the most comfortable place in town. It has a nice yard with trees and a pool. Large rooms come with TV, bar, phone and air conditioning, and there's a restaurant on site. La Hosteria comes highly recommended.

Chuchini Lodge, *8.7 miles/14 km from Trinidad*, ☎ 462-4744, $$$$$, is privately owned by Eferim Hinojasa and is located by Lomo Chuchini. Accommodations are in cabins with private bathrooms and meals are included. There is a plethora of things you can do while here, including night walks and fishing. Eferim offers a three-day, all-inclusive package for $210 per person, per day.

Hotel Gran Moxo, *Calle 6 de Agosto and Avenida Santa Cruz #146*, ☎ 462-2240 or 462-2462, moxostdd@sauce.ben.entelnet.bo, $$$$$, has wide, tiled halls open to the outside, so there is a nice breeze. They have made an attempt at elegance, but have cut corners (for example, the floors in the rooms are linoleum, rather than ceramic). But the place is clean and the owners offer a 20% discount for stays of three days or longer. Rooms have a private bath with a separate shower stall, fridge, air conditioning and telephone. This hotel also has cabins two miles/3.4 km from town on the road to Santa Cruz. Each cabin holds one to four people. One has two floors, and they all have kitchens, safe deposits for valuables and private bathrooms. The rooms in town are large and have sitting areas with little eating tables.

Mi Residencia, *Manuel Limpias #76*, ☎ *292-2464, $$$$$, half a block from the plaza; and at Felix Pinto Saucedo #555*, ☎ *432-2535, www. hotelmiresidencia.com.bo, $$$$$.* They have clean, bright rooms with tiled floors and private bathrooms. There are wood ceilings and sitting areas and the air conditioning works very well. These hotels have been around for nine years. Again, the rates are far too high, even with the complimentary breakfast.

Hotel Jacaranda, *Calle Bolívar #229 between Nocals Suarez and Ciriano Barace*, ☎ *462-1659, $$$$$,* has rooms with private bathrooms, air conditioning and fans, phones, TVs and fridgobars. They also offer the use of their safe. There is a restaurant on site (breakfast is included in your room rate), private parking and laundry service.

◆ Places to Eat

Kivon Restaurant, *on the square,* is the local ice cream parlor. I sat there and watched as one couple came in after me, received a menu, placed an order and got the incorrect food. I still had not received a menu. If you look like a *gringo* and want what you order, I'd suggest trying elsewhere.

❖ RESTAURANT PRICING	
$	under $5
$$	$5 to $10
$$$	$11 to $25
$$$$	$26 to $50
$$$$$	over $50

Pollo Joel, *on Vaca Diez,* charges $1.75 for chicken and fries, not the 75¢ that is on the sign. Although very popular with locals, the working conditions for the kitchen staff are the worst I have seen in Bolivia. The crowded kitchen is hot and the floors earthen. The food isn't all that good either.

La Casona, *on the square,* serves an excellent *almuerzo.* I thought it was better than Carlitos on the opposite side. The service is good, friendly and the fans work.

Carlitos, *on the square,* is popular and the food is okay but certainly not exceptional. The cost for one lunch is $1.75.

◆ Nightlife

Bar el Camion, *Avenida Santa Cruz,* just around the corner from Gran Moxos, has live entertainment on Friday night that is a huge improvement on watching the men whistle at the girls driving around the square on their motorbikes.

Cibermania Café and Internet on Calle Sucre and 18 de Noviembre, ☎ 462-1230, has good machines and charges 75¢ an hour. Next door to them is the **video shop** that has some English-language movies. Those staying at the Sirari can use the video machines that come with the TVs. It is great to lie under the fan and watch something like *Ghandi* in English. You must leave a $3 deposit for each video and the cost of the rental is 50¢ per movie. There is no problem getting your deposit back.

Noel Kempff Mercado National Park

Although Noel Kempff is easiest reached from Santa Cruz, it is actually located in the Amazon Basin and the area is a wildlife viewers' paradise. Due to its isolation, the park is seething with animal and plant life.

◆ About Preservation

There are two major organizations in Bolivia trying to keep things in the backcountry under control. They are the elusive FAN and SERNAP. Another two that are less known but that offer a more scientific slant to the wildlife viewing, are Hombre y Naturaleza of Bolivia and Amigos de Doñana of Spain.

Fundacion de Amigos de Naturaleza's, or FAN, is in charge of Noel Kempff National Park. Their address at Calle Agreda #1100 and Bumberque in Santa Cruz is an abandoned building. We were also told by Tourism Bolivia that they might be found at the Museum of Natural History on Avenida Irala. That turned out to be untrue. The last address we found was on the highway going to Samaipata, Km 7, Casilla 2241, ☎ 352-4921, but we did not get there and their latest e-mail does not work. Good luck trying to reach them.

According to statistics, in the last five years 800 tourists have gone into the park. The cost is $1,000-2,000 whether you book through an agency or try to go in through FAN. This comes to a total of $1.6 million. I have no information on how much is being pumped back into the park. However, the park is accessible from the mission town of San Ignacio and the cost ends up being less than $200.

SERNAP (Natural Prot. Areas Systems) works with FAN looking after the parks of Bolivia; FAN seems to do most of the front line work. The two organizations are now involved with a climate-control/monitoring facility in Noel Kempff that, in turn, means more grant money for them.

Hombre y Naturaleza and Amigos de Doñana have biological stations in Puerto Suarez, Concepcion (east of Santa Cruz), San Matais (in the northern area of the Pantanal) and Charagua (close to Tarija and Villamontes). The stations offer tourists an ecological approach to the area and scientists a base from which to explore. They will also facilitate drivers and tour operators to take you into the backcountry. Their living quarters are simple but certainly adequate and the volunteers work hard to accommodate your needs. There is always a small reference library on site and some of the places have museums. Contact them in Santa Cruz at ☎ 923-2239, hynb@bibosi.sca.entelnet.bo or prowames@cotas.com.bo.

◆ Animals & Land

Noel Kempff Mercado was first declared a park in 1979 and is one of the highlights of Bolivia's backcountry. It has tropical rainforests and flooded savannas, thorn scrub and dry forests, a huge area of wetland and the Caparu Plateau, 850,000 acres/345,000 hectares of Precambrian sandstone that has been carved by wind and water to create a fantasyland. Off this plateau, three dramatic waterfalls tumble over ancient red/brown rock that has roots of jungle vegetation clinging to every open space. The steam off the water forms a mist that acts like a filter and softens the view.

About 700 species of resident and migratory birds have been spotted in the park and people on birding tours often see 400 in one 10-day visit. Park officials have also recorded 2,700 species of plants but biologists believe that there are about 4,000 all told. As for wild animals, there are believed to be about 300 species. The park seems to have an endless number of monkeys, jaguars, otters, caimans and, my favorite, capybaras.

◆ Getting Here & Around

To get into the park you can either join a tour ($600 to $2,000) or you can go to San Ignacio on the missions circuit (see page 256) by train and bus. From there, take a bus north to La Florida, at the edge of the park. The bus leaves San Ignacio at 10 am and, after passing through Piso Firme where the road branches, it arrives in La Florida at 4 pm. If you can, call FAN to arrange for a driver and a 4x4 to pick you up in Florida and take you into Campamento Los Fierros in the park. The most recent number I have for FAN is ☎ 591-3-355-6800 (in Santa Cruz) and the person to speak to is Zaira Duque. However, I see no reason why you can't arrive at La Florida and hire a local to take you in.

Once inside the park you must have a guide. I recommend Manuel, a La Florida resident. He charges $10 per day. There are basic places to stay in the village. If Flor de Oro is the destination of choice, you will have to fly in.

La Florida is a tiny community at the boundary of the park where there are roads going to Los Fierros. The village has three small hotels, all basic but clean enough. You can also, before entering the park, rent a dugout canoe and take a trip upriver to see freshwater dolphins, often referred to as pink dolphins.

◆ Los Fierros Camp

Los Fierros Camp is the lodge in the park that can be reached without flying. It is more rustic than Flor de Oro. It has a capacity to hold 16 people in double-occupancy huts or 25 people in a dorm. There is running water, a large kitchen/dining area and over 37 miles/60 km of developed and maintained trails that have interpretive signs posted at interesting spots. Some tour companies take in birding groups who are able to spot species common only to this area.

The **Caparu Plateau**, also called the Huanchaco Plateau, is a mesa or tupuy made of Precambrian sandstone that rises 2,000 ft/600 m straight up out of the ground. The plateau is 850,000 acres/344,000 hectares of rock, jungle and wildlife that has three very dramatic waterfalls tumbling down its sides. From Los Fierros the plateau is five miles/eight km through steaming jungle.

Accessible from Los Fierros is the **El Encanto** (The Charmer) waterfall. This is probably the most spectacular of the three. To get there you will go along a road to a second set of cabins and walk to the base of the plateau. But the waterfall is only the destination. The wildlife and plants you will see

THE AMAZON BASIN

on the way could delay your progress by a full day. You may be lucky and spot plants not yet recorded by scientists.

◆ Flor de Oro Camp

Flor de Oro Camp, one of the camps under the care of FAN, is a renovated ranch on the banks of the Itenez River in the northern section of the park. It has the capacity to hold 35 people in double occupancy rooms, each with private bath and solar-generated electricity. There is also a large kitchen/dining area, an observation deck and an interpretive center. Flor de Oro is accessible only by plane.

The waterfalls accessible from Flor de Oro are the **Ahlfeld** and **Arco Iris**. To get to the Ahlfeld Falls, you must travel by boat for five or six hours up the Paucerna River to a basic campsite and walk to the falls through the jungle. These falls drop about 100 ft/30 m and form a pool at the bottom in which you can (or should) swim. A trail that goes through the jungle to the top of the falls and the view of the water and surrounding jungle is just as impressive from the top as from the bottom. The hike up to the top of the falls takes about an hour.

The Arco Iris waterfall drops 80 ft/24 m and is the one seen in most of the advertising brochures about Noel Kempff Park. This waterfall is accessible by walking from the campsite for about five hours. The terrain is rough; often rocks and roots have to be navigated before you reach the view point. However, it is the jungle heat that is the most difficult obstruction.

Los Torres (The Towers) are two huge hunks of rock that jut up out of the landscape like towers. They can be climbed (no climbing equipment needed) and used as a vantage point for viewing birds and other wildlife. It is in this area that jaguars have been spotted – but they are nocturnal hunters so seeing one during the day would be an accident.

The towers are accessible by taking a boat trip up the Itenez River for about two hours. They will reward you with sightings of capybara, herons, storks, caimans and other river dwellers. From the river it is a half-hour walk to the rocks. Once you are on top, the views of the plateau make the climb worthwhile.

Caiman Bay and **Monkey Lookout** can be reached by walking along a jungle trail for four hours to an old scientific research station. From there it is an hour or two hike up the plateau to Monkey Lookout Point. From the edge of the escarpment, the chance of seeing monkeys is excellent, of course. Other wildlife is difficult to spot because most is nocturnal. Camping here would be both scary and exciting and would have to be negotiated with the tour leaders. A trail from Monkey Lookout Point leads across the plateau and ends at the Arco Iris waterfall. This is a long way and you would need a guide to take you across.

From Flor de Oro, you can take a boat to the Arco Iris waterfall and then walk to the top of the falls following the trail. If you are adventuresome, you can cross the plateau along an old jungle trail to the Monkey Lookout on the other side. From there it is another four-hour hike back to camp. You would have to leave Campamento Ahlfeld early in the morning, carry lots of water and be prepared to get into camp around dark. This hike is only for the experienced.

Rurrenabaque

Altitude: 986 ft/300 m
Population: 9,600

The most popular reason to visit Rurrenabaque, called Rurre by the locals, is to take a river trip down the Yacuma River or a jungle trip to Chalalan. The area is hot and humid and the town is a dusty Amazonian river town-cum-resort. New hotels are constantly being opened and the restaurant services are excellent. The business people make foreigners welcome and hanging out is fun. Beer tastes best in the Amazon.

◆ Getting Here & Around

To get to Rurre, you can take a jeep from La Paz for $35, a bus for $11 or a plane for $55. A bus takes 15 hours from La Paz, a plane takes 1½ hours and a jeep takes somewhere in between.

Amazonas Air (☎ 333-8263) has a small plane (holds 12) that flies from Rurre to La Paz for $50, Trinidad for $48 and Santa Cruz for $80. The schedules change depending on the season and weather. **TAM** (☎ 244-3487, www.tam.com.br) also flies into Rurre on Monday, Wednesday, Thursday, Friday and Saturday. Flying times change according to the weather. The planes cannot land in Rurre on a wet runway (it is a grass area). There are four flights to Rurre from San Borja and Trinidad every week. The cost is less than $50 for a return flight.

Transportation at the airport costs about $1 per person for a ride into town. Airport tax out of Rurre is $2 for foreigners and 30¢ for locals.

Buses travel between Rurre and other destinations during dry season at reasonable speeds of under 30 miles/50 km an hour but over 10. During wet season, a 12-hour bus trip between Riberalta and Rurre will take up to 24 hours, and in very wet times the buses don't go at all. On the other hand, in dry season, the trip to La Paz takes close to 18 hours, hardly worth the saving of $40 over taking the plane. Most buses travel at night due to the heat. The bus station is nine blocks from the central plaza. That is a fair walk in the heat.

Boats and rubber rafts come to Rurre from Guanay, down the Tuichi from the Apolobamba and a very few come up the Beni from Riberalta. During rainy season, travel along the rivers may be the only way to get in and out. The Guanay-to-Rurre trip can be arranged through Floating Bolivia Tours in Caravani (☎ 823-2396) and the Tuichi River trip can be booked through Explore Bolivia (☎ 303-545-5728; see *Outfitters Who Do All the Work*, page 45).

Moto-taxis (small motorcycles) are the norm in Rurre and they can be hired on the corner of Calle Comercio and Santa Cruz at 35¢ for a trip anywhere in town or $2 an hour.

❖ **!! WARNING !!**

There have been women raped while on river trips out of Rurre. Although one culprit has been caught and imprisoned, he has also been released. His family lives in Rurre. The story is a sad/scary one. Do not travel in the jungle at night alone. Never take pills or drugs from anyone. One girl who was raped was offered some pills. They were a tranquilizer that put her into a heavy sleep. She woke up with the guy on top. Always be aware. The tours usually take six people. Try to pick the six you will go with and watch out for each other.

◆ History

Rurrenabaque was first made popular among tourists by **Yossi Ghinsberg**, an Israeli who was looking for adventure. In 1982, while roaming around South America, he met some other adventurers in La Paz and took a raft down the Tuichi River. Unprepared for that kind of jungle travel and after many misadventures, two of Ghinsberg's companions lost their lives. As the remaining two traveled through the jungle, they tipped their raft, became lost, without a knife or rifle, and encountered creatures like jaguars and anacondas. Ghinsberg was eventually rescued by his friend, who made it out and returned with Lulo, a man who lived in Rurrenabaque and knew the jungle well.

Ghinsberg wrote a book, *Back from Tuichi*, about his adventures. As a result, Ghinsberg is now a cult-figure to young Israelis who come to Rurrenabaque specifically to follow in Ghinsberg's tracks. The first of these followers contacted Lulo, the man who rescued Ghinsberg, so that Lulo could take them into the jungle. Lulo saw the potential and opened Fluvial Tours. His success was copied by a plethora of entrepreneurs who now take visitors almost anywhere in the jungle around Rurre.

◆ Services

The **telephone office** is on Calle Comercio and Santa Cruz.

An **Internet Café** next door to Camilas on Santa Cruz has four machines that are run off telephone lines. The cost is $2 per hour. The café is hot, but the machines are okay even if they are slow.

Lavanderia Rurrenabaque, Calle Vaca Diez next to Hotel Rurrenabaque, ☎ 892-2481, charges by weight. The laundry is open 9 am to 8 pm. Two other laundromats have varied times and comparable prices.

◆ Adventures in Culture

The **Communities Tour** visits four Amazonian communities, each featuring a different aspect of their life. La Union is an Aymara village that uses local trees to mill lumber for construction. At Playa Ancha you will see a Quechua man work in reforestation, fish farming, bee keeping and cattle ranching. At Nuevos Horizontes you will view natural forest materials transformed into hats, bags and boxes. At El Cebu, women make fruit wine, marmalades and drinks, while the men show how palm hearts are harvested. This tour starts at 7:30 am and returns to Rurre around 6 pm. It costs $40 per person if only two go, but dips to $22 per person when there are six or more.

◆ Adventures on Foot

MACUTI TRAIL: People live at the bottom of Mount Macuti, the mountain behind the church, and there is a trail leading to the top. It will take around 30 to 45 minutes to reach the top. Take water.

ETSAYA: Etsaya is a tiny village out of Rurre that takes 15 minutes to reach by motorbike taxi. The car taxi, found on Calle Comercio, will cost $1.25. Walking, by far the most interesting way to go, will take less than an hour.

JUNGLE HIKE: This trip is similar to the river trip except you go to a camp in the jungle. It must be done using a tour agency. The first day of the hike is usually spent walking to a lookout. The trails show primary and secondary forests and one trek goes to a natural swimming pool. Treks in the jungle are mostly for those interested in plants since a lot of jungle animals are nocturnal feeders and are difficult to spot.

◆ Adventures on Water

JUNGLE RIVER TRIP: One of the main reasons people come to Rurre is to get on a boat and go up a river to see things like anacondas, caimans, exotic birds, freshwater dolphins and capybaras.

The most common tour consists of getting to the Yacuma River in Santa Rosa del Yacuma Nature Sanctuary. Each camp is a bit different but, in fact, they are of two classes. One class has wood beds covered with mosquito nets under a tarp and the other has the same beds inside a hut that has screening around it. They are all only a short walk from each other along the banks of the river. If the weather is very hot, you should choose a place that has the beds outside. Even a small breeze is a blessing. Sleeping under a net is hot. However, if there is lots of rain you may want to be inside. The companies will show photos of their camps.

There are lots of sand fleas here. Wear long-sleeved shirts and long pants in the evenings. The locals laugh at tourists who come as a ready meal for the bugs.

A three-day tour is just enough. It takes half a day to get there and half a day to get back, so you have two days on the river and for a walk on the *pampas* to see snakes and birds. Getting to and from camp you will see every animal your tour operator has promised.

The tour costs anywhere from $10 per day to $20, depending on the accommodations, time of year and extras like an anaconda hunter. Park fees are $6 for foreigners, $1.50 for locals. This is not included in the cost of the tour. See *Tour Operators*.

THE AMAZON BASIN

MOUNT BRUJO: When waters are low you can take a boat upriver to see some Tacana rock paintings on the far side of Mount Brujo, the second mountain in the village. Talk to the boat operators at the dock.

SWIMMING POOL: The pool just off Calle Piscina is a great place to cool off and is popular with foreigners. To get there, walk along Piscina two blocks past the TAM office. It's open 9 am to noon and then again in the late afternoon.

◆ Adventures in Nature

Chalalan Lodge in Madidi National Park, ☎ 3-892-2419, www.madidi. com/chalalan.html, chalalan_eco@yahoo.com, is an eco-lodge that was built after the Yossi Ghinsberg story came out. The people of the area realized that foreigners really wanted to experience life in the jungle, even if it was for just a couple of days. With technical assistance from Conservation International and money from the InterAmerican Development Bank, the lodge was built.

Owned by shareholders who are permanent residents of San Jose de Uchupiamonas, a Quechua-Tacana village nearby, the cabins are built in traditional Tacana fashion with copa palm walls and woven jatata leaves on the roofs. There is solar power and a wastewater treatment disposal unit.

Inside the cabins, each bed has a mosquito net. Outside is a porch with hammocks. Bathrooms and showers are in a separate unit. The main hall has an interpretive center and a small reference library. The kitchen has modern conveniences like refrigeration so that food can be safely cooked and kept.

To get here, travel from Rurre up the Beni and Tuichi rivers by wooden scow for six hours. You must then walk along the Wichi Trail for half an hour to the lodge. The property is situated just above Chalalan Lake, where there are 15 miles/25 km of trails for you to hike, looking for medicinal plants or exotic birds. The trails are named and each is specific for a particular subject. For example, the Sivador Trail is where you will find most of the medicinal plants, while the Chichilo Trail will take you to a lookout point where you can see the Chalalan Lake, Madidi Park and the Andes Mountains in the distance. Most trails take two to three hours to walk and you will likely see things like capuchin, howler and squirrel monkeys, tapirs, spiders, capybaras and, occasionally, a jaguar. There are also peccaries, agoutis, boa constrictors and numerous species of frogs. Over 340 species of birds have been spotted in the area, including the capped heron, wood stork, Orinoco goose, osprey, great-black hawk, pied lapwing and large-billed tern. Local guides are available to help you scout and to explain how the plants and animals play a part in everyday life. Some guides who specialize in birding can imitate a few of the calls. Some of the trails cut through others so that you can combine them to make your walk longer or shorter. Canoes are available for scouting around the lake.

A cultural evening revolves around Tacana Indian traditions and includes food, music, dancing and Tacana stories.

The book *Chalalan*, by Hennessey, Rios and Perry, describes some of the animals and has drawings of their prints. It provides information on

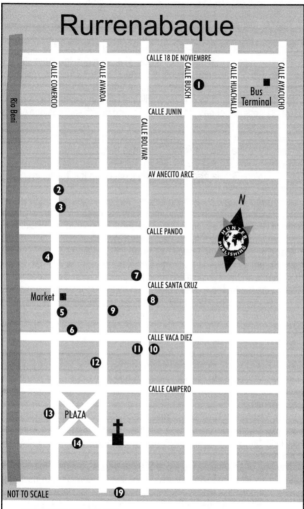

THE AMAZON BASIN

PLACES TO STAY & EAT
1. Hostal Paraiso Tropical
2. Hostal Beni
3. Hostal El Balsero
4. Club Social
5. Moskitto Bar, Pizzeria Italia
6. Hotel Porteño
7. Café Motaco
8. Hotel Rurrenabaque
9. Hostal Tuichi
10. Camila's Restaurant
11. La Perlade Rurre
12. Hostal Santa Ana
13. Hotel Bella Vista, La Cabaña
14. Hotel Oriental

© 2005 HUNTER PUBLISHING, INC

snakes and frogs and has sketches of the more common birds in the area. The price is $4.

This company hasn't figured out what a deal is or what cost-efficient trips would be. If you go for three nights, the cost is $280 and this includes transportation, guides and all meals. Four nights cost $380 and five nights run $480. This means that three nights cost $73 per night, four cost $97 and five cost $96. Considering the cost of travel, I suspect something has been miscalculated. However, if there are more than six people in your group, rates drop. You can also pay for additional days in Chalalan at a rate of $100 per person, per day. All profits go toward health services and education for the local people.

To make arrangements, you can either contact a tour office in La Paz or go directly to the office in Rurre. The ones handling tours in La Paz are American Tours, Crillon Tours, Magri Turismo, Transturin and Turismo Balsa. Explore Bolivia also takes rafting tours down the Tuichi, eventually landing at Chalalan.

If you want to do a custom trip farther into the jungles around Chalalan, contact biologist **Alan Perry**, who knows the area well. He is one of the authors of the book, *Chalalan*. For more information, go to www.madidi.com/chalalan.html or contact Alan direct at info@madidi.com.

Mapajo Indigenous Lodge, www.madidi.com/mapajo.html or www.mapajo.com, is similar in nature to Chalalan, except the river trip is only three hours and you go up the Beni to Rio Quiquibey, and then east to the Pilon Lajas Bio Reserve. This lodge is run by the Moseten and (Chimane) Tsimane groups. It has four cabins that sleep two people each and share a bathroom with other cabins. They feature tables, chairs, bedside tables, mosquito nets over the beds and balconies with hammocks. One of the cabins will hold six people and has a private bathroom.

The interpretive center is well stocked with a library, maps and a telescope. The group has published a large coffee table book called *Palabras Antigues y Nuevas del Rio Quiquibey*. It has numerous color photos depicting life in the Amazon in and near the river villages, plus it has stories and legends.

Over 12 miles/20 km of hiking trails surround the lodge and walking them can take anywhere from an hour to three hours. Guided night walks are also included, as is a cultural night where dancing, music, food and stories are shared.

The cost of an all-inclusive trip is $60 per person, per day. To reach the lodge costs less than $60 at present, but it could change with rising gas prices. Although this lodge is less expensive and a little less advertised, it does not mean that the standard is any lower. If you are interested, talk to the operators in Rurre: Mapajo Ecoturismo, Calle Comercio, ☎ 892-2317, www.mapajo.com.

◆ Tour Operators

As in La Paz, the tour agencies in Rurre will promise you anything just to get your business. There is no way of knowing if the company you are going with will provide you with what they promise. Although I recommend some companies here, the best approach is to talk to as many travelers as possible and see what they say.

Private guides can be hired if you do not want to join a tour group. **Obedio Valdez** is good for jungle trips. He has worked for some time at Chalalan as a guide and speaks working English. His price is $10 per day and he can be contacted at his office, ☎ 892-2419, or by cell phone at ☎ 10-2213 7391. For a more intense trip into the jungles around Chalalan, contact Alan Perry at info@madidi.com, PO Box 431, Hailey, ID 83333, ☎ 208-450-9010. Alan is a biologist who knows the area well and has written some books about the region, including the *Field Guide to Chalalan.*

Donato Tours, Avenida Comercio and Santa Cruz, ☎ 591-3892 or 591-2571, donato tours@hotmail.com. Donato takes groups of up to six people and his policy is to not traumatize the animals by touching. When I was there, workers kept the camp clean, carried out garbage, and located the toilet a long way from the river. Donato has a low-impact camp without cabins, only beds under a tarp with mosquito nets over the beds (this is cooler than a cabin). Donato can also arrange horse trips into the jungle.

Fluvial Tours, ☎ 892-2372, www.megalink.com/rurrenabaque, was first started when the owner, Lulo went out looking for the missing Yossi Ghinsberg. He now sells photocopied *Back from Tuichi* books to tourists for $10. Fluvial has five camps along the Yacuma River. Their tours are for groups of up to nine people and sometimes they join other groups on the river for evening activities. One of Fluvial's camps holds 20 people. The cost is $20 per person for three days and two nights. They also do the jungle tour for three days.

Mapajo Ecotourism Indegena, Calle Comercio, ☎ 892-2317, www. mapajo.com, offers a unique experience for the more adventuresome. See Mapajo Indigenous Lodge (above) for information.

Amazonico Travel, Calle Avaroa, is run and owned by the brothers who also run Fluvial. The cost, depending on the quality of the tour, is between $20 and $25 to go to the jungle and $25 to $30 to go to the pampas. Their camps have two buildings, one for eating and one for sleeping. Amazonico has five different camps in all, with varying prices. However, there are negligible differences between the camps themselves. Their maximum number is nine to a group.

Flecha Tours, Calle Avaroa, ☎ 7114-3529 (cell) or 284-0221 (contact Oscar Huanto in La Paz), flechatours@hotmail.com. This company offers both *pampas* and jungle tours. The jungle tours can last for up to 20 days. These people are good and I recommend you talk with them first. The guide at Flecha spoke fairly good English.

> ❖ **PALM BONUS**
>
> There are many types of palms in the jungle and the bark of the chuchu-wasa palm is used by locals as an aphrodisiac. Have your guide point one out, but don't chew on it.

Amazonia Adventures, Calle Avaroia, ☎ 892-2333, amazoniaadventures@latinmail.com, will take only six people in each group to the jungle or the *pampas*. They have a "no touch, no feed" policy. The cost is $25 per person, per day. This company does not put vegetable matter into the river and their trips don't include fishing. The jungle trips travel on the Beni River. The camp is isolated and takes four hours to reach by boat. For an extra $3, horse travel can be included.

Indigena Tours, Calle Avaroa, ☎ 892-2091, mercadofreddy@hotmail. com, offer two classes of trips, one for $25 and the other for $30. They take between three and six people per trip and will go for up to 12 days.

Inca Land Tours, Calle Aniceto Arce between Bolívar and Avaroa, www.incalandtours.com, has the usual selection of tours to the *pampas*, the jungle or the Chalalan. They do either touch or no touch tours, depending on the group. However, when I last spoke with them, they were pushing toward the no-touch tour as the only option. You can book with Inca in La Paz and have everything ready for you when you arrive in Rurre. Inca Land is the only company that will take you up to Ixiamas if you are interested in jungle logging or in fishing. I found Inca Land very busy, often going far out of their way to provide good service.

◆ Places to Stay

Hotel Rurrenebaque, *Calle Vaca Diez y Bolívar*, ☎ 892-2481 or (La Paz 279-5917), *$*, has 11 rooms in all. The rooms are large, with tiled floors, fans, clean bathrooms, mirrors and towels. There is a garden, parking a safe, laundry service, a money exchange and a baggage deposit. A coffee shop and bakery are attached to the hotel. This is a good deal.

❖ HOTEL PRICING	
$	$10 to $20
$$	$21 to $50
$$$	$51 to $75
$$$$	$76 to $100
$$$$$	over $100

Tuichi Hostal, *Calle Avaroa*, ☎ 892-2326, *$*, is next door to Fluvial Tours and is a hot spot in town, mostly because of Israelis following Yossi's path. It has dorms and private rooms as well as a small garden with hammocks that are constantly in use.

Hostal El Balsero, *Calle Comercio and Aniceto Arce*, ☎ 892-2042, *$*, is just up from the Beni and is run by a friendly and helpful lady. The 12 rooms are large and have fans, TVs and shared bathrooms. The showers are clean and have hot water. A second-floor balcony overlooks the front street.

Residencial Porteño, *Calle Comercio and Avenida Vaca Diez*, ☎ 892-2558 *$*, is a well-run place. All rooms are clean and well maintained. The bathrooms have hot water as well as towels, soap, and toilet paper. The rooms are large and tastefully furnished with dressers, mirrors, and built-in cupboards. The cost is $4 per person. She also has a dorm that costs $2.50 per person. There are many repeat customers here.

Hotel Santa Ana, *Calle Aboroa*, ☎ 892-2399, *$$*, has 18 rooms around the most beautiful garden in Rurre. There is also a patio with hammocks under a palm-thatched hut. Each room is tiled and spotless and has a fan. There is a sink to do laundry, a baggage deposit and a car park.

Hotel Oriental on *Plaza Principal*, ☎ 892-2401, *$$*, is an excellent hotel with rooms around a spacious garden that is shaded with large mango trees. Breakfast is served in the garden. The rooms all have private bathrooms, with hot water and daily maid service. This clean, quiet and relaxing place is run by a friendly and helpful family.

Bella Vista, *Calle Comercio on the plaza*, ☎ *892-2328, $$*, is under new ownership. At present the owner has 20 rooms available, but once renovations are complete, he will have 40. The rooms have high ceilings, fans and large tiled bathrooms. When the new rooms are complete, prices will be raised. There is no single rate.

Hostal Beni, *Calle Comercio y Aniceto Arce*, ☎ *892-2408, $$/$$$*. This well-run establishment has rooms with tiled floors, built-in dressers, table and chairs, TV (local channel only) and air conditioning. The shower is sectioned off from the toilet and soap, toilet paper and fresh towels are provided. The place is spotless. Parking is available, and there is a small patio with hammocks. The walkway between the rooms overlooks the river.

◆ Places to Eat

Restaurant La Perla de Rurre, *Calle Vaca Diez*, has a large, attractive courtyard decorated with flowering plants and linen-covered tables. The place is welcoming. The coffee is instant, but the papaya and milk are good. Breakfast costs $3.50. I did not try any other meals.

❖ RESTAURANT PRICING	
$	under $5
$$	$5 to $10
$$$	$11 to $25
$$$$	$26 to $50
$$$$$	over $50

Camila's Restaurant, *Avenida Santa Cruz*, is popular for a reason. The meal I had was large, excellent, and not expensive, only $2.50 per plate. I recommend the fish with garlic sauce.

> ### ❖ TASTY TUTUMA
>
> Tutuma is a large round fruit, green in color, that resembles a melon. It hangs by a stem from a tree that grows more than 23 ft/seven m high. The pulp resembles cocoa in flavor and texture and is scraped out and cooked with wheat or rice.

Café Motacu, *Avenida Santa Cruz*, is an excellent coffee shop that also serves good food. There is always someone sitting in the café scribbling in a journal or pouring over a novel. The café is open from 8:30 am till noon and 6:30 to 9:30 pm every day except Tuesday and Sunday. The restaurant will make a bag lunch for between $1 and $2.50.

Club Social, *Calle Comercio*, is a huge place that is popular with locals. The open-air restaurant overlooks the river. Although the service was good, my meat was tough and overcooked. I also found the room too big to be comfortable.

Restaurant Bella Vista, *Avenida Santa Cruz #1*, ☎ *790-6033*, is on the third floor overlooking the river. Part of the restaurant is under a thatch roof and part is open. Being high allows the place to catch a breeze and customers get a good sense of the landscape. The food is well prepared (the steak I had was tender) and the prices reasonable. A fish costs $2.50, a large beer was just over a dollar.

Restaurant La Cabaña, *below the Bella Vista*, is often patronized by upper-crust Bolivians. I thought the music was too loud, but the food is said to be good.

Restaurant Jatata, *Hotel Rurrenabaque on Calle Vaca Diez*, has a smorgasbord for under $5. Their à-la-carte dishes are good too. The restaurant is cosy and the service is excellent.

Pizzeria Italia, *Calle Comercio*, has a second location in Sorata. The pizza is thin-crusted and the toppings are thick. Excellent food. It is next door to Moskkito Jungle Bar and, if you are at the bar and do not want to abandon your beer, they will deliver. They also do not close during siesta as most places do, indicating that they are accustomed to *gringo* patterns.

◆ Nightlife

Moskkito Jungle Bar, *Calle Comercio*, ☎ *892-2267, moskkito@terra. com*, is the rockingest place in Rurre. The Pizzeria Italia, under the same thatch hut but on the other side of the games room (pool and darts), will deliver to the bar. A happy hour runs from 7 pm to 9 pm when mixed drinks are half-price. If you grow attached to the place, you can purchase a t-shirt as a reminder.

◆ Shopping

About 4,000 Tacana live in 20 communities just off the Beni River and its tributaries. They grow cotton and the fabric they design from this plant is like a language, rich in story. Numerous items made from this material – bags, skirts and blouses – are sold in shops throughout town. Café Motacu carries a good selection.

◆ Around Rurre

Buena Ventura

Buena Ventura is a little outpost that sits across the Beni River from Rurre. A boat-ferry crosses about once every 15 minutes at the cost of 30¢ per person. In the village, toward the back and away from the river, is the **Centro Cultura de Tacana**. The museum costs $1.25 per person and has a few pieces of art like handmade baskets and natural seed necklaces.

There are three hotels in town, with **Residencial Madidi** being the best. The seven rooms are basic but the floors are tiled and there is a fan, beds, and a chair. The cost is $1.25 per person. The second option is the **Florida**, on Calle Sucre and Palacio. The Florida is even more basic, with cement floors and no fans. It is the same price as the Madidi. The beds at the Florida were Inca, but the hotel is clean enough.

The Madidi National Park office is just up the street from Residencial La Paz. Don't waste your energy climbing the stairs to visit because information about the park is not available. A pamphlet cannot be handed out without the approval of the director, who is often in La Paz.

Reyes

Reyes is a small village nine miles/15 km in from the Beni River. It has the Hotel 6 de Enero where you can stay. There are also places to eat, and even more places to drink. The church on the plaza is fairly nice, but not spectacular.

The airport here is where TAM planes land if Rurre is wet. Should you land here, TAM will provide transportation to Rurre. If you happen to be staying in Reyes, you can take a local bus to Rurre, or catch a bus to Riberalta. The bus station, a basic and barely functional building, is on the road toward Santa Ana. There is a bus leaving for Riberalta every day. Time is dependent on road conditions, which depend in turn on the amount of rainfall.

Ixiamas

This small logging community of about 2,000 people was first occupied by Franciscan missionaries. There is one bus/truck leaving from La Paz every Saturday that can be caught in Rurre and that goes on to Ixiamas. The bus returns on Sunday. The village is close to Rio Madidi, where pacu and pintado fishing is the big draw. Madidi Park, a few miles away, has forests where jungle treks are exceptional. There is also a small airfield in Ixiamas. The hotel in the village is new. It's next to the airport and on Avenida La Paz. For reservations, call the Beni Hotel in Rurre, ☎ 892-2408.

Riberalta

Altitude: 557 ft/175 m
Population: 52,000

Riberalta is fairly large as compared to most cities in the Bolivian Amazon. It was created in 1894 as a center for moving rubber.

The city has a few things to do, great birding for example, and some good restaurants and coffee shops around the plaza. However, changing travelers' checks is not possible in this town. And remember, bank machines have not yet been introduced to the Amazon.

◆ Getting Here & Around

Flights from Santa Cruz, La Paz and Trinidad are offered by **SAVE**, ☎ 212-1548; **TAM**, ☎ 244-3487, www.tam.com.br; **Amaszonas Air**, ☎ 333-8263; and **LAB**, ☎ 800-337-0918 (US), 800-10-3001 (Bolivia), www.labairlines.com. The cost is about $115 from La Paz for a one-way ticket. There are also flights between Cobija, Cochabamba and Guayaramarin. The airport is a short walk from the center of town. If walking in the heat isn't to your liking, take a moto-taxi for 30¢.

Buses come from Guayaramarin each day during dry season, heading to Rurre. There is also transportation to the cities in the south via Trinidad. All trips are dependent on road conditions. I flew from Riberalta to

Cochabamba and watched out the window with fascination as canoes pad-
dled along the roads.

◆ Adventures in Nature

Birding is one of the big things around Riberalta. Because of the thick rub-
ber-tree forests in the area, the bird population is high. But actually *seeing*
the birds is a different matter.

The best places to see birds are in forest and scrub between the town
and the Beni River. It is a half-hour walk or 10 minutes by moto-taxi to the
banks of the river, where you can find birds like the chestnut jacamar, the
spotted tody-tyrants and the tyrannulets. There's also good birding along
the road to Guayaramerin and its tributary roads.

Parque Costanera in Riberalta overlooks the Beni River and has the
last steamer ever to come up the Amazon into Bolivia, the *Tahuamanu,* sitting on cement. Built in 1899, this boat was used to haul rubber until the
1930s. You can tour the boat.

◆ Places to Stay

Hotel Los Reyes, *a block from the Riberalta airport,* ☎ *346-8018, $.* They
charge $4 per person for a large room without private bathroom and $6 for
a room with.

Hotel Colonial, *Avenida Baptista,* ☎ *346-8212, $$,* is a colonial man-
sion that once belonged to a Bolivian rubber baron. The rooms have pri-
vate bathrooms and are set around a central courtyard that is lush in
vegetation. Rates include breakfast. The hotel's restaurant overlooks the
courtyard.

Hostal Tahuamanu, *a block from the plaza,* ☎ *346-8006, $$$,* has
rooms with private bathrooms and air conditioning. Breakfast is compli-
mentary. This is a pretty upscale choice for this area.

Guayaramerin

Elevation: 400 ft/125 m
Population: 40,000

This little border town is a great introduction to Bolivia for those just entering from Brazil. The river between Brazil and Bolivia is crossed on a ferry
that runs 18 hours a day and costs about 50¢ per person.

There are money changers on both sides of the border. They will change
American cash or Brazilian reales.

The town itself is spread across many blocks of dusty dry streets in the
hot season and slippery muck in wet season. The main activity, as in many
Amazonian towns, is to sit on the square, drink beer and howl at (or be
howled at by) the opposite sex as they rod around the plaza on their motorbikes.

◆ Getting Here & Around

Four airlines have small planes that will connect travelers from here to Riberalta, where you can catch a flight to other parts of Bolivia. The community is serviced by **TAM**, ☎ 244-3487, www.tam.com.br; **Amaszonas Air**, ☎ 855-3731; **LAB**, ☎ 800-337-0918 (US), 800-10-3001 (Bolivia), www.labairlines.com; and **SAVE**, ☎ 212-1548. At least one flight leaves daily from Guayaramerin, though it rarely runs on schedule. If a connecting flight is on your itinerary, be sure you have flex time because so much travel is weather-dependent in the Amazon area.

Buses will take you to Riberalta and from there you can go south to Trinidad or west to Rurrenabaque. Riberalta is only 60 miles/100 km away. During rainy season, the buses pass between Riberalta and Guayaramerin, but there are only a few that go beyond.

Boats take anywhere from four to six days to reach Trinidad and charge $30 per person. You must have a hammock, but food will be provided. To find a boat, go upriver from the border crossing.

Moto-taxis can be rented for the day at a cost of about $10. Be aware that passing the checkpoints at the edge of the city is a problem if you do not have your papers in order. Even if you do, there could be problems. You must have permission from the police to take the vehicle anywhere out of city limits.

◆ Places to Stay

Hotel Plaza Anexo, *on the plaza*, ☎ 346-2086, *$*, is a popular place for travelers. It is basic but clean. Rooms have fans and private bathrooms.

Hotel Central, *Avenida Santa Cruz and 6 de Agosto*, ☎ 346-2042, *$*, is just down from the San Carlos. They have basic rooms with fans for $5 per person.

Hotel San Carlos, *Avenida Santa Cruz and 6 de Agosto*, ☎ 346-2419, *$$$*, charges just a bit more than the Esperanza (not recommended) for a room with private bath, TV and air conditioning. This is the only hotel in town that will exchange travelers' checks, but only for paying guests.

THE AMAZON BASIN

Appendix

Recommended Reading

A Traveler's Guide to El Dorado and the Inca Empire, Lynn Meisch, Headlands Press, Penguin Books, 1977. This is a repository of cultural information rather than a travel guide.

Trekking in Bolivia, Yossi Brain, Andrew North, Isobel Stoddart, Mountaineers Books, Seattle, 1997.

Adventuring in the Andes, Charles Frasier with Donald Secreast, Sierra Club Books, San Francisco, 1985.

An Insider's Guide to Bolivia, Peter McFarren, Cultural Foundation of Quipus, La Paz, 2003. This fourth edition is full of cultural tidbits that give the traveler inside information on some of the activities one sees but does not understand while in Bolivia.

Bolivia: A Climbing Guide, Yossi Brain, Mountaineers Books, Seattle, 1999.

Bolivia: A Country Study, edited by RA Hudson, DM Hanratty, Library of Congress, 1991.

Ernesto, A Memoir of Che Guevara, Hilda Gadea, Doubleday, New York, 1972.

The Fat Man from La Paz, edited by Rosario Santos, Seven Stories Press, New York, NY, 2000. A collection of short stories written by contemporary writers. It is excellent.

Fire from the Andes, edited and translated by Susan E Benner and Kathy S Leonard, University of New Mexico Press, New Mexico, 1998. This is a collection of short stories written by women from Bolivia, Peru, and Ecuador.

Six Years in Bolivia, Anselm Verener Lee Guise, NotaBell Books, an imprint of Purdue University Press, West Lafayette, Indiana, 1998. A travel story written by a mining engineer.

Americas Before Columbus, EC Baity, Viking Press, New York, 1961.

Bolivian History, Charles Arnade, Los Amigos del Libro, La Paz, 1984.

Discovering Bolivia, Hugo Boero Rojo, Los Amigos del Libro, La Paz, 1994.

One River, Wade Davis, Simon & Schuster, New York, 1996. An ethnobotanist's story of exploring the Amazon.

The Mint of Potosi, 1997, published by the Cultural Foundation of Bolivia with the assistance of the Central Bank of Bolivia.

Baron de Estaño, is a hard-to-find, long biography of Patiño.

Memory of Fire – Genesis, Eduardo Galeano, Pantheon Books, New York, 1985. This is one book of a trilogy of collected folk tales from throughout the Spanish world.

Field Guide to Chalalan, A Bennett Hennessey, Boris Rios and Alan Perry, 1996. Available through the bookstore at www.madidi.com.

Consulates & Embassies

◆ La Paz

AUSTRALIA. Av. Arce & Montevideo, Edif. Montevideo Mezannine, ☎ 244-0459, 8:30 am-1:30 pm.

CANADA. Pl. España, Calle Victor Sanjinez #2678, Edif. Barcelona, ☎ 241-5021, 8:30 am-5 pm.

GERMANY. Av. Arce #2395, ☎ 244-0606, 9-noon.

GREAT BRITAIN. Av. Arce #2732 on Cordero & Campos, ☎ 243-3424, 9 am-noon and 2-4 pm.

MEXICO. Sanchez Bustamante # 509 on 11 & 12 Calacoto, ☎ 277-1824, 8-11:30 am.

UNITED STATES. Av. Arce #2780 & Cordero, ☎ 243-0251, 8 am-5 pm.

◆ Cochabamba

GERMANY. Edif. La Promotora, Piso 6, Of. 602, ☎ 425-4024, 10 am-noon.

MEXICO. 25 de Mayo, S-230, Piso 3, ☎ 425-671410, 10 am-12:30 pm.

UNITED STATES. Torres Sofer Bloque A, Off. 601, ☎ 425-6714, 9 am-noon.

◆ Santa Cruz

GERMANY. Calle Nuflo de Chavez # 241, ☎ 336-7585, 8:30 am-noon.

UNITED STATES. Calle Guemes # 6 & Equipetrol, ☎ 333-0725, 9 to 11:30 am.

Glossary

◆ The Calendar

dia	day
semana	week
mes	month
año	year
domingo	Sunday
lunes	Monday
martes	Tuesday
miercoles	Wednesday
jueves	Thursday
viernes	Friday

sabado . . . . Saturday
enero . . . . January
febrero . . . . February
marzo . . . . March
abril . . . . April
mayo . . . . May
junio . . . . June
julio . . . . July
agosto . . . . August
septiembre . . . . September
octubre . . . . October
noviembre . . . . November
diciembre . . . . December

◆ Numbers

uno . . . . one
dos . . . . two
tres . . . . three
cuatro . . . . four
cinco . . . . five
seis . . . . six
siete . . . . seven
ocho . . . . eight
nueve . . . . nine
diez . . . . ten
once . . . . eleven
doce . . . . twelve
trece . . . . thirteen
catorce . . . . fourteen
quince . . . . fifteen
dieciséis . . . . sixteen
diecisiete . . . . seventeen
dieciocho . . . . eighteen
diecinueve . . . . nineteen
veinte . . . . twenty
veintiuno . . . . twenty-one
veintidós . . . . twenty-two
treinta . . . . thirty
cuarenta . . . . forty
cincuenta . . . . fifty
sesenta . . . . sixty
setenta . . . . seventy
ochenta . . . . eighty
noventa . . . . ninety
cien . . . . hundred
ciento uno . . . . one hundred one
doscientos . . . . two hundred
quinientos . . . . five hundred
mil . . . . one thousand
mil uno . . . . one thousand one
dos mil . . . . two thousand

millón . . . . one million
primero . . . . first
segundo . . . . second
tercero . . . . third
último . . . . last

◆ Conversation

¿Como esta? . . . . How are you?
¿Bien, gracias, y usted? . . . . Well, thanks, and you?
¿Que pasa? . . . . What's happening?
Buenas dias. . . . . Good morning.
Buenas tardes. . . . . Good afternoon.
Buenas noches. Good evening/night.
Nos vemos. . . . . See you again.
¡Buena suerte! . . . . Good luck!
Adios. . . . . Goodbye.
Que la vaya bien . . . . Goodbye (used for someone special)
Mucho gusto. . . . . Glad to meet you.
Felicidades. . . . . Congratulations.
Feliz compleaños. Happy birthday.
Feliz Navidad. . . . . Merry Christmas.
Feliz Año Nuevo. Happy New Year.
Gracias. . . . . Thank you.
Por favor. . . . . Please.
De nada/con mucho gusto. . . . . You're welcome.
Perdoneme. . . . . Pardon me (when bumping into someone).
Permitame . . . . Pardon me (when passing in front of someone).
Desculpe . . . . Excuse me (when interrupting conversation).
¿Como se dice esto? . . . . What do you call this?
Lo siento. . . . . I'm sorry.
Quiero... . . . . I want/I like...
Adelante. . . . . Come in.
Permitame presentarle... . . . . May I introduce...
¿Como se nombre? . . . . What is your name?
Me nombre es... . . . . My name is...
No se. . . . . I don't know.
Tengo sed. . . . . I am thirsty.
Tengo hambre. . . . . I am hungry.
Soy gringa/gringo . . . . I am an American (female/male).
¿Donde hay...? . . . . Where is there/are there...?
Hay... . . . . There is/are
No hay. . . . . There is none
¿Que es esto? . . . . What is this?
¿Habla ingles? . . . . Do you speak English?
¿Hablan ingles? . . . . Is there anyone here who speaks English?
Hablo/entiendo un poco. . . . . I speak/understand a little Spanish.
  Español
Le entiendo. . . . . I understand you.
No entiendo. . . . . I don't understand.
Hable mas despacio por favor. . . . . Please speak more slowly.
Repita por favor. . . . . Please repeat.

¿Tiene...?	Do you have...?
Tengo...	I have...
Hecho...	I make/made
¿Puedo?	May I?
La cuenta por favor	The bill, please.
bolsa	bag
muchila	backpack

◆ Time

¿Que hora es?	What time is it?
Son las...	It is...
... cinco.	... five o'clock.
... ocho y diez.	... ten past eight.
... seis y cuarto.	... quarter past six.
... cinco y media.	... half past five.
... siete y menos cinco.	... five of seven.
antes de ayer.	the day before yesterday.
anoche..	yesterday evening.
esta mañana.	this morning.
a mediodia.	at noon.
en la noche.	in the evening.
de noche.	at night.
mañana en la mañana..	tomorrow morning.
mañana en la noche.	tomorrow evening.

APPENDIX

◆ Directions

Llevame alla ... por favor.	Take me there please.
¿Cual es el mejor camino para...?	Which is the best road to...?
Derecha..	Right.
Izquierda..	Left.
Derecho/directo.	Straight ahead.
¿A que distancia estamos de...?	How far is it to...?
¿Es este el camino a...?	Is this the road to...?
¿Es cerca?	Is it near?
¿Es largo?	Is it a long way?
¿Donde hay...?	Where is... ?
... el telefono.	... the telephone.
... el bano.	... the bathroom.
... el correos.	... the post office.
... el banco.	... the bank.
... el casa de cambio	the money exchange office.
... estacion del policia.	... the police station.

◆ Accommodations

¿Que quiere?	What do you want?
Quiero un hotel...	I want a hotel that's...
... buena.	... good.
... barato.	... cheap.
... limpio.	... clean.
¿Dónde hay un hotel buena?	Where is a good hotel?

¿Hay habitaciones libres? . . . . Do you have available rooms?
¿Dónde están los baños/servicios?. . . . . . . Where are the bathrooms?
Quiero un habitacion. . . . . I would like a room.
habitacion sencillo. . . . . single room.
habitacion con baño privado. . . . . room with a private bath.
habitacion doble. double room.
baño comun. . . . . without a private bath/with a shared bath
ducha. . . . . shower
¿Esta incluido? . . . . Is that included?
¿Puedo verlo? . . . . May I see it?
cama. . . . . bed
cama matrimonial. . . . . double bed
¿Algo mas? . . . . Anything more?
¿Cuanto cuesta? . . . . How much?
¡Es muy caro! . . . . It's too expensive!

◆ Food

comer . . . . to eat
pan . . . . bread
carne . . . . meat
papas. . . . . potatoes
leche . . . . milk
frutas . . . . fruit
jugo. . . . . juice
huevos . . . . eggs
mantequilla. . . . . butter
queso . . . . cheese
agua mineral. . . . . mineral water
cerveza . . . . beer
pescado . . . . fish
helado. . . . . ice cream
arroz. . . . . rice
ensalada. . . . . salad
jamon. . . . . ham
pollo . . . . chicken
toronja . . . . grapefruit
naranja . . . . orange (the fruit)
mariscos . . . . seafood
sopa. . . . . soup
vino tinto . . . . red wine
vino blanco. . . . . white wine

Index

NOTES

NOTES

NOTES

NOTES